ADVANCES IN APPRECIATIVE INQUIRY

Series Editors: David L. Cooperrider and Michel Avital

D1415189

CONSTRUCTIVE DISCOURSE
AND HUMAN ORGANIZATION

ADVANCES IN APPRECIATIVE INQUIRY   VOLUME 1

CONSTRUCTIVE DISCOURSE AND HUMAN ORGANIZATION

EDITED BY

DAVID L. COOPERRIDER

Weatherhead School of Management,
Case Western Reserve University, Ohio, USA

MICHEL AVITAL

Weatherhead School of Management,
Case Western Reserve University, Ohio, USA

2004

ELSEVIER
JAI

Amsterdam – Boston – Heidelberg – London – New York – Oxford – Paris
San Diego – San Francisco – Singapore – Sydney – Tokyo

ELSEVIER B.V.
Sara Burgerhartstraat 25
P.O. Box 211
1000 AE Amsterdam
The Netherlands

ELSEVIER Inc.
525 B Street, Suite 1900
San Diego
CA 92101-4495
USA

ELSEVIER Ltd
The Boulevard, Langford
Lane, Kidlington
Oxford OX5 1GB
UK

ELSEVIER Ltd
84 Theobalds Road
London
WC1X 8RR
UK

First edition 2004

Library of Congress Cataloging in Publication Data
A catalog record is available from the Library of Congress.

British Library Cataloguing in Publication Data
A catalogue record is available from the British Library.

ISBN: 0-7623-0892-3
ISSN: 1475-9152 (Series)

⊗ The paper used in this publication meets the requirements of ANSI/NISO Z39.48-1992 (Permanence of Paper). Printed in The Netherlands.

CONTENTS

PART III – NEW METAPHORS OF POSITIVE CHANGE

LIST OF CONTRIBUTORS

Michel Avital	Case Western Reserve University
Frank Barrett	Naval Postgraduate School
Jessica L. Carlo	Case Western Reserve University
David L. Cooperrider	Case Western Reserve University
Jennifer Dodge	New York University
Chris A. Geary	University of Nebraska
Mary M. Gergen	Penn State University
Kenneth J. Gergen	Swarthmore College
Bethany Godsoe	New York University
Marilee G. Adams	Institute for Inquiring Leadership
Michael R. Hoadley	Eastern Illinois University
Jessica Lipnack	NetAge, Inc.
James D. Ludema	Benedictine University
Rollin McCraty	Institute of HeartMath
Michael J. Mantel	Benedictine University
Nick Nissley	University of St. Thomas
Karen E. Norum	Gonzaga University
Dennis O'Connor	Le Moyne College
Sonia Ospina	New York University
Edward H. Powley	Case Western Reserve University
Judy Rodgers	Case Western Reserve University

Ellen Schall	New York University
Marjorie Schiller	Positive Change Corps
Leslie E. Sekerka	Naval Postgraduate School
Peter F. Sorensen, Jr.	Benedictine University
Jeffrey Stamps	NetAge, Inc.
Tojo Thatchenkery	George Mason University
Ray Thompson	University of South Dakota
Marcy Wells	University of South Dakota
Diana Whitney	Saybrook Graduate School & Research Center
Therese F. Yaeger	Benedictine University
Leodones Yballe	Nazareth College of Rochester

INTRODUCTION: ADVANCES IN APPRECIATIVE INQUIRY – CONSTRUCTIVE DISCOURSE AND HUMAN ORGANIZATION

The fields of organization development and human systems change are going through a theoretical metamorphosis in which change has become much less about detection of error, analysis of chronic problem, or exclusive treatment of the deficient, the broken, and the problematic. Like the exciting shift in medicine from anti-biotics to pro-biotics or the movement in psychology from analysis of dysfunctions to examination of human strengths, the field of organization and management theory finds itself in the midst of a positive revolution in change – something that now and for many years into the future promises to elevate and extend our images of what it means to organize, what it means to transform organizations, what it means to be an organizational citizen, and what it means to be-in-the-world. Kim Cameron, Jane Dutton, and Bob Quinn (2003) have recently announced it as an "exciting new field of study in the organizational sciences" – the field of "positive organizational scholarship."

Some of the most significant work that fuels and defines this positive wave has come from an area often simply referred to as "Ai." In the years since the original theory for *Appreciative Inquiry Into Organizational Life* was articulated by David Cooperrider and Suresh Srivastva from the Weatherhead School of Management at Case Western Reserve University (Cooperrider & Srivastva, 1987) there have been thousands of scholars, leaders, colleagues, and students involved in co-creating new concepts and practices for understanding Appreciative Inquiry, and for bringing its life-centric spirit of inquiry into organizations and communities all over the world. Major books, international conferences, journal special issues, dissertation projects, substantive web sites, and hundreds of articles have, in recent years, focused on Appreciative Inquiry (see for example, Avital, 2002; Barge & Oliver, 2003; Cooperrider & Srivastva, 1999; Fry et al., 2001; Watkins & Mohr, 2001; Whitney & Trosten-Bloom, 2003; http://ai.cwru.edu). As interest has mounted, Appreciative Inquiry has been singled out in arenas of scholarship as broad ranging as evolutionary thought (Hubbard, 1998), social constructionism and poststructuralist theory (Barge & Oliver, 2003; Gergen, 1990;

Gergen, 1994), organization management and leadership (Srivastva, Cooperrider et al., 1990), organization development and change (Pasmore & Woodman, 1987), action research (Reason & Bradbury, 2001) and again, most recently, positive organizational scholarship (Cameron, Dutton & Quinn, 2003). Commenting on this rapid and robust emergence, University of Michigan's Robert Quinn recently said: "Appreciative Inquiry is revolutionizing the field of organization development and change" (Quinn, 2000).

WHAT IS APPRECIATIVE INQUIRY?

Appreciative Inquiry is a constructive inquiry process that searches for everything that "gives life" to organizations, communities, and larger human systems when they are most alive, effective, creative and healthy in their interconnected ecology of relationships. To appreciate, quite simply, means to value and to recognize that which has value – it is a *way of knowing* and valuing the best in life. In the language of Positive Organizational Scholarship it means a research focus – a positive bias – seeking fresh understanding of dynamics described by words like *excellence, thriving, abundance, resilience, or exceptional and life-giving* (Cameron, Dutton & Quinn, 2003). In this context the word appreciate means to value those things of value – it is a mode of knowing often connected to the idea of esthetic appreciation in the arts. To appreciate also means to be grateful or thankful for – it is a *way of being* and maintaining a positive stance along the path of life's journey. And not incidentally, to appreciate is to *increase in value* too. Combining the three – appreciation as a way of knowing, as a way of being and as an increase in value- suggests that Appreciative Inquiry is simultaneously a life-centric form of study and a constructive mode of practice. As a form of study, Appreciative Inquiry focuses on searching systematically for those capacities and processes that give life and strength and possibility to a living system; and as a constructive mode of practice, it aims at designing and crafting human organizations through a process in which valuing *and* creating are viewed as one, and where inquiry and change are powerfully related and understood as a seamless and integral whole. But the key to really understanding Appreciative Inquiry is to put the emphasis on the second word in the inseparable pair. While many are intrigued with the Appreciative Inquiry positive bias – toward the good, the better, the exceptional, and the possible – it is the power of inquiry we must learn more about and underscore. Inquiry is all about openness, curiosity, creative questioning; its spirit involves what Whitehead once called "the adventure of ideas."

Inquiry can take us to the edge of the unknown and beyond – it is the prime engine of human development and boundary spanning; it involves systems of exploration by which people make sense of their experiences in, organize their knowledge about, and relate to the world. In this sense, even the smallest and briefest inquiry is powerful precisely because it shapes human life through modalities inherent in a culture's symbolic systems, for example, its language and discourse modes, the forms of logical and narrative explication, and the very patterns of meaning and value systems that are nurtured.

Whereas human systems move in the direction of what they most persistently, actively, and rigorously ask questions about, Appreciative Inquiry opts for a passionate and probing search into the life-generating essentials and potentials of human and social existence. It connects, quite deliberately, the means and ends of inquiry where methodology and phenomenon are increasingly made commensurate to one another. For example, if we were interested in learning about democracy we would not want to use undemocratic methods of inquiry, or, if we were interested expanding our visions for a future of joyful, inspired workplaces we would not want to limit our study to the subject of low morale; instead, Appreciative Inquiry would more expansively frame an exploration into exceptional moments of enthusiasm, passion, and excitement in organizational life, including systematic search for all the human and organizational factors serving to elevate and enable those moments.

The most anticipated in an inquiry is the unanticipated. It is not a controlled process with a preplanned outcome. Inquiry is always a journey off the beaten track, especially active inquiry that is embedded in the very medium of human systems, that is, in today's emergent and swirling worlds of permanent disequilibrium, novelty, surprise, and internet speed. The world, quite simply, seems to change as we talk. And because of inquiry's drive to discovery, the results of any given Appreciative Inquiry repeatedly challenge and disrupt, asking us to let go of our highest ideals and to create, in the company of others, even better ones when judged in relation to the calls and opportunities of our times. In this sense *inquiry* can be feisty. Secretly, the fundamentalist in all of us wants inquiry's openness eliminated. Co-inquiry in the presence of other human beings almost always discloses views not quite like our own and is capable, therefore, of dislodging treasured certainties. When we enter inquiry's theater we are often surprised with the ending. But then we are gifted, not with solid certainty but with something even better– the vertigo of new vision. And this is the special paradox of *Appreciative Inquiry*. Inquiry into the good or the life-generating is neither comfortable nor stable, even if positive. Abraham Maslow theorized about the agonizing difficulty of acknowledging our highest potentials because of the echoes of responsibility implied in such knowledge. Plato, too, could sense it. His words are memorable: "We can easily forgive a child who is afraid of the dark. The real tragedy of life is when men are afraid of the light."

So more than a method or technique, Appreciative Inquiry is perhaps best talked about as a way of living with, being with, and directly participating in the core of a human system in a way that compels each one of us to inquire into the deeper life-generating essentials and potentials of social existence. Our world, our future, and its pliant openness to new possibility is an astonishing mystery and that is why we naturally inquire. In many respects we are born to appreciate, value, and to co-create. To consciously and collaboratively inquire into the life-enhancing accounts of this mystery – searching for the true, the good, the better and the possible – this, in its most concise form, is what Appreciative Inquiry is all about.

Advances in Appreciative Inquiry is dedicated to bringing people and writings together to contribute to the enormous potential of positive organizational scholarship and new forms of affirmative inquiry – seeking first to give voice to all that is best in life, and then taking seriously the opportunities offered by the relational perspective of our world as an ever changing social construction. If, for example, the act of studying a human system actually changes it – via shifts in people's language, how they relate their feelings, their imaginations and meaning-making interpretations – then, we must seriously ask: what happens when people turn their inquiries toward the study of phenomenon like the human strengths of courage; optimism and wisdom; moments of exceptional achievement; sources of collective well-being; expressions of aesthetic sensibility; the cultivation of positive emotions of hope, inspiration and joy; expressions of civic virtues like compassion, love and being of benefit to others; the discovery of liberating institutions and thriving communities; or, at a larger level of scale, the emergence of generous, prosperous, and sustainable societies?

THE SPIRIT OF THIS VOLUME

In this first volume of *Advances in Appreciative Inquiry*, leading scholars from diverse fields of management, sociology, psychology, education, and philosophy pursue new directions in Appreciative Inquiry theory and research as well as new intervention practices and opportunities for action. While diverse in topic and discipline — for example, Appreciative Inquiry in corporations, classroom settings, communities, networks, national and global public conversations, and others – each of the following original chapters treats the reader to a view of the Appreciative Inquiry's revolutionary ways.

World constructions are formed in and through the ever-expanding relationships that occur from early family life to the most recent conversation. Indeed, it is through the tapestry of discourse, relationship, and meaning-making that what is taken as real and valuable for us emerges – and this, as each of this volume's chapters elaborate on, invites creative exploration of new and valued futures. Every chapter in this book explores the social construction of reality via the lens of discourse – where words create worlds (Cooperrider, Barrett & Srivastva, 1995). There is a tangible and distinctive message in each of the following chapters and it is a creative one: *that perhaps very soon in our new century, once the idea of the relationally constructed nature of reality finds its way into our shared public consciousness, there will be a vast liberation of human energy and transformational capacity, both as a sensibility that grounds Appreciative Inquiry theoretically and as a way of being that puts the continual creation of reality at the heart of every person's life.*

Change, especially change in human systems, is triggered by dialogic-relational modalities of learning and discovery. It occurs in those moments when, for example, discourse on hope connects with another's hope, when conversation into inspiration connects with another's inspiration, when the sharing of joy combines with another's sense of joy, and when inquiry into collective strengths allows people to unite with accounts of the "positive core" of their system's past, present and future capacities. *The big question is why and how would hope connected to hope, or, strength connected to strength, and consequently awaken change?* This question becomes particularly interesting in light of the so many conventional theories which argue the opposite, that is, that organizational, community, and societal change is best catalyzed through dissatisfaction with the status quo and analysis of the deficient or the problematic and their related causes. As the reader will soon see, we posit and bring evidence to support a 180-degree turn in our theory of the relationship between inquiry and change.

Assuming, that the appreciable world far exceeds our normal appreciative knowing capacity, and furthermore, assuming that through our relationships we have access, at least theoretically, to an almost infinite universe of emerging capacities (of course, given the right kind of relationships or interconnectivities), what emerges are two modalities or ways of talking about and igniting positive change (see Fig. 1): (1) the *elevation* of our appreciative capacities and inquiries (the horizontal dimension); and (2) the *extension* our forms of relatedness allowing for the free and super-fluid flow from the local to the universal of valued strengths, qualities, assets and all that valued as good (the vertical dimension). Like the warp and weft in a weaving, these thematic dimensions of Appreciative Inquiry are explored directly or implicitly in every chapter in this volume, and, as pictured, these thematic dimensions thread together and help us emerge a new pattern of change (Cooperrider & Sekerka, 2003).

Following Fig. 1, we would like to group and lift up the papers in several ways – either through an *advancement in our capacity to appreciate* the appreciable world, or through an *extension of our relationships and capacity of relatedness,*

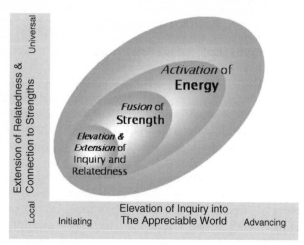

Fig. 1. Advances in Appreciative Inquiry Thematic Framework.

which, in turn, gives us a new collective connection to all that is best in the world, from the local to the universal. These two main themes thread throughout the chapters of this volume, and in the midst of their thematic interaction a third pattern appears. Pictured on the diagonal and best understood as interdependent thrusts, the initiation of appreciative knowing *and* the extension of relatedness, together, set in motion several possible developmental phases of non-deficit, positive change including: an initial burst of elevation-and-extension of inquiry, then the fusion of strengths, and finally, the activation of energy. This thematic interpenetration creates an emerging framework of what we might call a theory of non-deficit transformational change.

Not unlike William James' pioneering account of *conversion* – where often, in conjunction with a surprising connection to a "higher source," sudden shifts alter a person's life through an enormous influx of positive emotion and energy – the elevate-and-extend framework suggests that such alteration could be happening in everyday life. To clarify this point, we must ask what is it that happens when Appreciative Inquiry into collective life enables people, in collaborative conversation, to link with rich and elevated accounts of the "positive core" of their system's past, present and future capacities.

The relationship between Appreciative Inquiry and non-deficit positive change is evident, but far from being fully realized, let alone understood. We have barely scratched the surface of this territory (Cameron, Dutton & Quinn, 2003, p. 5). Likewise, William James commented on it much earlier when he notice that we have yet to create a vocabulary, or even a good label, for this kind of change. One term he tried out was "conversion" but he did not like the word for its religious connotations. Yet he liked the notion of positive change embedded in serious accounts of mystical experiences. Speaking in the most down-to-earth kind of way, James went on to say that what we truly need is better understanding about the kind of change that happens when things are *"hot and alive within us, and where everything has to re-crystallize about it"* (James, 1902, p. 162). In his view, deficit-based change (or changing only when the experience of the problematic becomes unbearable) is commonplace and relatively easy to understand, especially when charged with negative emotions. However, the domain that lags woefully behind in social scholarship is the area looking into those moments of extraordinary positive experience – and how these, too, can be cultivated to ignite "explosive" change. In James words:

> Emotional occasions, especially violent ones, are extremely potent in precipitating mental rearrangements. The sudden and explosive ways in which jealousy, guilt, fear, remorse, or anger can seize upon one are known to everybody. Hope, happiness, security, resolve, emotions characteristic of conversion, however, can be equally explosive. And emotions that come in this explosive way seldom leave things as they found them (James, 1902, pp. 163–164).

In the rest of this opening, we begin exploring advances in Appreciative Inquiry, the opportunities raised, and the implications for organizations, communities and societies engaged in Appreciative Inquiry. The writings to follow are expansive, vibrant, and thought provoking. Conceptually, they are grouped into three areas beginning, in part one, with primary emphasis on Appreciative Inquiry and the discursive construction of reality via the "extension of relatedness." Next, in part two, the chapters are linked to the theme of "elevation of inquiry," demonstrating for example how we live in worlds our questions create. Here the discourse explores the elevation of consciousness through inquiry and it is instrumental in revealing and developing our positive cores. Finally, part three, expands our vocabulary of positive change connecting the "elevate-and-extend" framework with a myriad of aesthetic, technical, and dialogical ways that transformational energy is activated, amplified and sustained. Let's now look briefly at the chapters as they unfold across each of these areas.

PART ONE: EXTENSION OF RELATEDNESS

Ken and Mary Gergen and *Frank Barrett* open part one with a provocative essay on Appreciative Inquiry as a generative and transformative dialogue that invites us to move into "the ever expanding domain of relatedness." Constructionism, as used here, is introduced as an approach to human science inquiry and practice that replaces the individual with the relationship as the locus of knowledge. Philosophically, constructionism involves a decisive shift in Western intellectual tradition from cogito ergo sum to communicamus ergo sum. It involves a concern with the dialogic processes by which human beings, their values, and their commonsense, scientific knowledge and communities are both produced and reproduced in conversation.

One of the prominent strengths of the constructionist perspective is that it seeks to open the door to a fuller interweaving of disparate communities of meaning – and hence, the chapter's thesis that *meaning is born in the act of appreciation*. No one's words or actions, write the authors, have meaning by themselves; meaning requires "supplementation" or another's assent, much like a handshake that requires both people to be meaningful. Appreciative interchange, therefore, is the basis of generativity in three senses: first, as a deep awareness of the complex potential for interpreting the nature and value of words or actions; second, as the affirming of meaning and value of words or actions; and, third, as adding to the meaning and value of words or actions. In appreciating others' words and actions, say the authors, so do we increase value within our relationships.

A viable pluralism in today's world depends on the power of appreciation, say the authors, because appreciation creates a language and a climate of interaction that embraces differences, affirms polarities, and helps creating new cultures where diverse values are heard and honored. Much needed, this chapter proposes, is a new kind of transformational dialogue capable of creating organizations in relational settings that are "polyphonic" where the different voices, like multiple melodies in polyphonic music, create a rich and complex musical totality.

Jeffery Stamps and Jessica Lipnack, two of the world's leading network theorists, extend further the theme of relatedness. For them, the grammar of interconnectivity is the essential discipline of our age. The idea of connecting the local to the whole is no longer a dream. Now, with the click of a button, we have the potential to link each strength, best practice, or a story of possibility and all forms of knowledge. We have passed, say the authors, the point of no return in the transition from the Industrial-Bureaucratic Age to the Information-Network Age. Unlike the relative stability and homogeneity of the organizations of the past, new configurations and relational modalities are part of everyday life and are manifested in the ubiquity of networks, alliances, cross-functional teams, partnerships, lattices, ensembles, cells, temporary project structures, virtual communities, and federated support networks – almost anything but monolithic pyramids go.

The chapter *Appreciative Inquiry in the Age of the Network* starts with a compelling premise that Appreciative Inquiry may be related to self-organizing networked forms as problem solving-based ways of knowing were related to command-and-control bureaucracies. Networks arise as the natural organizational outcomes of an ongoing Appreciative Inquiry process, and thus, whether explicitly recognized or not, Stamps and Lipnack argue, Appreciative Inquiry undergirds the development of successful distributed human organizations. The next leap forward in organizing depends upon a deep realization that networked organizations are webs of human relatedness, and that relationships come alive when there is an appreciative eye – where people are able to value and see the best in one another, where they can rapidly create alignments of strength, and when they are connected in liberating ways to realize valued hopes, dreams, and purposes.

Drawing on research with Royal Dutch-Shell and others, the authors give us a glimpse into the future of Appreciative Inquiry processes, methods, and opportunities in distributed networked forms. And while subtle, there is a fascinating nuance in this paper. Whereas most of the literature on Appreciative Inquiry writes about the power of appreciation in strengthening and generating relationships, there is a hint here that it may in fact be the other way around – where richer, vaster social complexity enlarges our capacity for appreciation. Indeed, in an everyday sense, we have all experienced it where extensions in emergent relationships, even if only by accident on the web, can create surprise, energizing interest, sense of awe and appreciation much like a first visit to a fascinating new culture. We "wake up" when we meet new people or groups, and such enthusiasm can be infectious. Oddly enough, the best way to cultivate our appreciative capacity – our ability to notice and connect to the appreciable world and the universe of infinite capacity all around us – may be simply to leap into and create new, extended relationships.

We are in the earliest stages of something quite large as people are consciously embedding themselves and their organizations in larger and richer webs of interdependence and mutual abundance. In this view, conclude Stamps and Lipnack, the emergence of Appreciative Inquiry is in the cards. One of the most promising areas of future research lies precisely at the intersection of Appreciative Inquiry and the new economy of partnerships, federated and networked organizations, digital communities, and the like.

In chapter three *Michel Avital* and *Jessica Carlo* take the previous chapter to another level exploring exactly why and how Appreciative Inquiry may be essential to inter-networked forms of extended relationships. The practical arena addressed in this chapter involves the rapidly growing domain of knowledge management. Whereas many have emphasized the information architectures, infrastructures and procedures that allow stakeholders in organizations to search multiple repositories of information this essay emphasizes the social and organizational dynamics that drive the organizational actors who create and use knowledge systems, such as, codified repositories, expert directories, and communities of practice. Although knowledge management systems were introduced over two decades ago, it is clear there are still many unsolved challenges concerning their implementation. For example, frequent resistance to sharing information, difficulties in identifying qualified core knowledge, actors' indifference towards organizational knowledge repositories, and continuous struggle of the systems' sponsors to sustain a viable knowledge community.

The key for any knowledge management system, argue Michel Avital and Jessica Carlo, is its dynamism and joint ownership and what they call "the generative co-creation and use of situated knowledge." It is all about relationships, argue the authors, and Appreciative Inquiry helps build and sustain them in part because of the positive "best practice" focus, but more importantly because of the *ownership creating power of inquiry* itself. Inquiry is the *"generative dance"* between knowledge and knowing; and Appreciative Inquiry emphasizes the relational aspect of *knowledge creation*. From the micro-social context of the appreciative interview to the scaled up electronic sharing across boundaries Appreciative Inquiry makes several high potential contributions: it systematically identifies and maintains a contextually relevant catalog of capabilities; it pays attention to the underlying questions that yield the knowledge, especially the "what if" and "what now becomes possible" questions that generate new developments; it helps create a reflexive capability of being sensitive to language and its effect on the way knowledge is produced and reproduced; and finally, it unleashes the power of stories.

But what connects each of these contributions is one overarching element – engagement. People that engage in Appreciative Inquiry – where they are searching for the good and the best in the system–generates ownership, relevance, dynamic updating, the replenishment of knowledge, and the spirit of generosity necessary for community. Much like a gift economy where each person's sharing of a gift generates reciprocal acts of gift giving, the process of Appreciative Inquiry offers a vehicle for such generous engagement. Where generous engagement is absent, there will be no community. While generosity, gift giving, and engagement are rarely talked about in the knowledge management literature, this is precisely what the new technologies are capable of nourishing. This paper, therefore, sets the stage and invites future research that will unleash the potential contribution of Appreciative Inquiry to the design and implementation of knowledge management systems.

Next, *Tojo Thatchenkery* builds on Hans Gadamer's hermeneutic theory of social existence whereby "Language is the fundamental mode of operation of our being-in-the-world and an all-embracing form of the constitution of the world." Not only does the interpretive scheme embedded in our language significantly influence our readiness to notice particular aspects of our situation, there is also a great difference between two pre-judicial modes of interpretation – the critical and appreciative. It makes a great difference, proposes the author, whether we see the world primarily as a problem that needs to be repaired, or fundamentally appreciating it as a mystery to be engaged in, especially in regards to the emergent, subtle, and paradoxical aspects of relational existence.

Key to a creative advance in human systems is this special capacity, that is, the capacity to embrace the life-generating energies of paradox of every kind. This paradox embracing capacity becomes increasingly important the more globalized and extended our relationships. As we move from local connection to global connectivity a new capacity is called for. Much needed, proposes the author, is better understanding of the process of *hermeneutic appreciation,* which serves to heighten our capacity as human beings to embrace today's paradox of unity in diversity, or the paradox of global networking vs. local networking, and the like. When there *is* a stance of hermeneutic appreciation, then the bipolar nature of the paradoxical construction generates the possibilities for a multitude of interpretations within those polarities. And this, perhaps, is the secret to understanding not only the survival, but also the expansive growth of some organizations and what we have called the extension of relatedness.

In a fascinating account of the Institute for Cultural Affairs – a global organization committed to building a sustainable world, the author concludes: Hermeneutic processes are present in all types of organizations; only their degree varies. A military set up in combat situation provides few hermeneutic possibilities because the nature of the contingency requires that all actors understand and interpret the task in a relatively homogenous way. On the other hand, the mission of the Institute for Cultural Affairs – creating a paradigm shift in the way people think about the human factor in development – was increasingly opened up for fulfillment in indeterminate ways, which in turn gave rise to intense hermeneutic appreciation in the organization as it extended its relationships, its mission, and its contributions from the local to the whole of humanity.

PART TWO: ACTIVATION AND ELEVATION OF INQUIRY

Inquiry is fundamental and ubiquitous in the human experience. We start most life journeys with a seed question, progress and find our way by answering guiding questions, and end up reflecting on our experience with retrospective questions. Excellence and innovation of both scholars and practitioners often stem from relentless pursuit of original questions that have challenged conventional forms, sparked the imagination, and spanned the boundaries of understanding.

By its very nature, the way we ask a question has an acute effect on the answers we get. In a recent landmark study Jonathan Haidt at the University of Virginia proposed a new positive emotion that has not been described thus far by social scientists: *elevation*. Elevation happens when people see *unexpected* acts of human goodness, strength, virtue, and compassion, which in turn, his research has shown, changes people's views about humanity, and in some cases to produce life-altering effects (Haidt, 2000). Upon close analysis of Haidt's work, we think that the trigger of change is not simply the emotion of elevation as it is the act of inquiry. The originating catalyst is inquiry or more precisely the *elevation of inquiry* – even if the inquiry into acts of goodness is unexpected – it precedes, and it is a necessary condition for the change in emotional elevation. Haidt's work is tremendously important here. Elevating questions lead to elevated observations, and elevated observations lead to elevated emotions.

The authors in part two are united in their conviction that the appreciable world is much larger that our normal appreciative capacity, and that one of our essential tasks as researchers, change-leaders, and educators, is to find ways to elevate our individual and collective capacity to value those things worth valuing. This, of course, is essential to the future development of a scholarship of the positive and, in practical terms, it can benefit any system interested in innovation and creativity. As Nietzsche once put it, "Valuing is creating: hear it ye creating ones! Valuation is itself the treasure and jewel of valued things" (in Rader, 1979).

The opening chapter in part two by *Marilee Goldberg Adams, Marjorie Schiller and David Cooperrider* says that elevation of inquiry, indeed our capacity to appreciate the appreciable world, vitally depends on our *questions* – and that we live in worlds our questions create. Like the treasure hidden in broad daylight, questions are at the heart and soul of good inquiry and change, whether one is involved in organization development, education, therapy, or societal change. If "Language is the house of Being," as Heidegger (1971, p. 135) wrote, and if language is made up of two parts – our statements and our questions – then we must understand question asking as primary and universal in any consideration about the ways that human beings perceive, feel, think, behave, create, change, and evolve.

However, despite the omnipresence of questions in our lives, few people appreciate their inherent power and potential. This chapter is about advancing this potential. For example, think about the meeting dynamics in a company where there are two supervisors. One begins the Monday morning staff meeting with the question – "Group, I want to know: why do we still have all these problems?" and the other begins her meeting with – "Well lets get started . . . what's the smallest change we could make that would have the biggest impact?" or "What is one possibility that we have never yet thought about?"

After examining the lives of geniuses like Albert Einstein, whose question "What would the universe look like if I were riding on the end of a light beam at the speed of light?" preceded the theory of relativity, the authors examine the relationship between questions asking and learning, and the ways in which the art of the question can elevate the capacity to appreciate. One of the most refreshing experiences in reading this chapter is the realization how suddenly we can become aware of how much we live in an answer-oriented, fix-it-quick world. And yet, in the clamor for answers, we overlook fresh possibilities, hidden strengths, and quiet distinctions all around us. After examining the mindsets that lead to "judger questions" and "learner questions," the authors provide insights and examples of ways to cultivate appreciative questions, expand the spirit of inquiry through simply doing more Appreciative Inquiry, and how to make "question thinking" a more active part of our research, our change practice, and everyday living. As the poet Rilke suggested: "Live the questions now. Perhaps you will then gradually without noticing it, live along some distant day into the answers."

The next chapter, "Appreciative Inquiry and the Elevation of Organizational Consciousness" by *Diana Whitney,* is perhaps the most daring of all the chapters. It is a beginning to a new conversation, the first that we know of, about Appreciative Inquiry and *organizational consciousness.* The chapter is an invitation to supplement years of successful Appreciative Inquiry practice with research into the tremendous power of Appreciative Inquiry to catalyze organizational and global transformation. The author submits that Appreciative Inquiry, through its attention to the positive core of a living human system, enriches and lifts up organizational consciousness, and thereby both transforms an organization's relationship to global consciousness and builds its capacity to contribute positively to global well-being and sustainability. The author suggests that each phase of the Appreciative Inquiry process – Affirmative Topic Choice, Discovery, Dream, Design and Destiny – creates a powerful elevation in organizational consciousness, and this higher consciousness has an almost inevitable world-benefiting, positive sum direction to it. Simply put, organizations like Nutrimental Foods and Green Mountain Coffee Roasters that are involved with Appreciative Inquiry tend to show a direction to their conscious activities – they become more socially responsible in relation to their local relations, the environment, and the global interconnected family of life. It is as if they sense not just responsibility *for* but feel an intimacy *with* the whole. And there is a big difference between these two.

After analysis of the literature related to two of organization theory's earlier key metaphors – *climate* and then later *culture* – Whitney makes the case for a third, namely, *consciousness.* Drawing on Nobel physicist David Bohm's theory of wholeness Whitney talks about organizations in a creative matrix relation to the world, each intimately co-creating the other and, in Bohm's words: "Thus we come to a germ of a new notion of unbroken wholeness, in which consciousness is no longer to be fundamentally separate from matter." While defining consciousness is admittedly very difficult, there are emerging numerous accounts of characteristics of consciousness and the author examines each one of them in relation to organizations. She proposes that in concept we can talk of organizations as having consciousness, as having a subjective presence, as having creative choice that impels or directs the body in its motions, and as a kind of knowing that manifests reality. Human organizations, be they business, education, government, service, profit or non-profit oriented in nature, are likewise part of a global consciousness. When we elevate inquiry beyond normal views of fragmentation and separateness to an emphasis on oneness and wholeness, then everything changes – accounting practices begin to take into account the actual costs of long-term polluting "externalities," competitors discover the mutual benefits of cooperation, doing good is not seen as something separate from profitability, and businesses are not viewed as machine-like structures fitting neatly into the boundaries of an organizational charts, but as adaptable organisms existing in and interacting with a larger whole.

Whitney's proposal is that elevation of inquiry – searching for the true, the good, the better, and the possible in any living system – widens our consciousness, and hence, our propensity to be of benefit. It may not be inevitable, she admits but inquiry into the good *does something*; it does not merely show something. Exactly what it does is fertile ground for next generation research, says the author, because "success in the future will go to those organizations that help humanity come into harmony and thrive as one global community."

Ellen Schall and her colleagues focus on Appreciative Inquiry as the cornerstone research method in their collaboration with the Ford Foundation program: "Leadership for a Changing World." The chapter explores methodological issues that are relevant to research endeavors in the rapidly emerging domain of positive organizational scholarship. For example, how should one approach a study of the good or positive in leadership research? What are appropriate methods for exploring the good or the positive? How can we increase the generative potential of theory building in the social sciences? And how can Appreciative Inquiry, as a research methodology, help create a new conversation about leadership in this country? With questions like these, the authors propose a creative synthesis of Appreciative Inquiry with narrative inquiry, ethnographic methods, and cooperative inquiry. The result is a relational form of research-action and action-research, where the distinction between subjects and researchers blurs as they both become simply "co-inquirers."

Beginning with assumptions of leadership as a collective relational phenomenon, the authors argue convincingly for the application of research methods that match the phenomenon, that is, methods that likewise extend and live the relational. In this case the authors went the whole way. The so called "subjects" of research became true co-researchers that were part of every phase of the inquiry: from creating the research questions, through helping with the narrative analysis, and up to being part of the actual write-up of the findings. At first, implementing the methodology was not easy due to role confusion and mixed expectations. But things changed. As the authors put it: "Once we were able to enact our appreciative stance, their role became much clearer to them." In the end, the authors give us a taste of their findings and a view of *leadership as re-framing*. Leadership as framing and re-framing was found to involve several things: passionate belief in the humanity of the marginalized populations with which the leaders worked; active engagement in reframing how the society values the people with whom they work; approaching the often-marginalized groups as unique people with dreams and aspirations; and finally, providing the moral ground for staff and community members as a way of fostering commitment over the long term.

Leodones Yballe and Dennis O'Conner say that the elevation of inquiry transforms the entire experience of learning, and hence, "the time is ripe for pedagogy of appreciation." This chapter is a fascinating cross pollination of the positive philosophies and visions of educators such as Dewey, Freire, Kolb, and Handy, with the vibrant and emerging organizational change ideas and processes of Appreciative Inquiry. It is a call to a pedagogical stance that is values driven, life-centric, embraces the relevance of personal experience, and is dialogical in the creation of knowledge. Building especially on Friere's *Pedagogy of Hope*, Yballe and O'Conner show how the classroom can be transformed in its energy and its positive spirit. Education too often is about inert knowledge transfer, say the authors, and what they propose instead is a kind of education that exists, in William James's contrast, not as a dull habit but an acute fever. What they propose is *education alive*, something that nurtures the romance and passion for learning through hands-on active inquiry, not just precision and wrote memorization.

"Obviously there have been ups and downs in your career" asks a student doing Appreciative Inquiry interview with an elder from the civil rights movement, "so I would like you to reflect across the years of your life work and tell me the story of a high point moment – a time that stands out when you felt most alive in your work, most engaged, or most successful in joining with others in creating change?" It is precisely through assignments like these, propose the authors, that the classroom is transformed. Its easy to imagine it: the students returning from their inquiries and sharing with one another exceptional moments of courage, hope, and change during the height of the civil rights movement; then, after sharing the narratives (real-life stories), creating their own dreams of the future society they want – and later, even further, "teaching" one another in the form of dramas and skits that lead to the creation of active experiments to enact their visions in their communities and homes. Through inquiry, the inexhaustible energies of the *best in life* enter into the classroom, and with important results: more energized and sustained interactions, increases in positive images of possibility, the nurturing of love of learning, more self-initiated exploration, and transformation in the educator role. Can you remember the first time you saw a child *enchanted*? Hold on to that image. This, we believe, is exactly the message of this chapter.

Karen Norum and colleagues are also about the elevation of inquiry, in this case, asking evaluation researchers to essentially drop the "e" – whereby evaluation becomes *valuation*. More that just a simple play on words, there is a developmentalist argument here that asks questions about the purposes of evaluation research. Isn't the ultimate aim of evaluation, in the final analysis, to help evolve, develop, and strengthen program performance? And if this is the case, then how might one design an evaluation inquiry to maximize its creative and developmental potential?

Changing the way we measure things changes everything, and with this assumption in place, what Norum and her associates came up with a dynamic program evaluation process they label "Ap-PRAISE-al." The essence of the approach is the formation of collaborative inquiry teams. The chapter describes an account of students and program faculty that join together to do a collective interpretation of the positive core of a program, including catalyzing dialogue on everyone's images of the program's next stages of development – hence the emphasis on PRAISE. In every program, write the authors, there slumber capacities for growth and development, and especially in new programs, where capacities are more visible.

Unfortunately, many evaluation programs simply miss out the generative patterns because of their correction-based inclination to disclose program failings. The result is a contribution to the bad name and defensive feeling many "evaluations" produce. The authors are quick to point out that their method does in fact deal with the "hard stuff," but this happens in an atmosphere of positive intent and whole system partnership through a deliberate analysis of deeper, more invisible assets, strengths, achievements, potentials, and the like. The authors propose that by transforming evaluation into a valuation, capacity grows and community expands. This chapter, like others in this section, offers a seed idea that is hopefully just the beginning in a new conversation.

PART THREE: NEW METAPHORS OF POSITIVE CHANGE

What if we really were all connected? And what if, through a super-fluid quality of relatedness, we could actually link with the unlimited capacities and life-energies of everyone and everything in our inter-connected worlds? Imagine, for example, Yellow/Roadway Express, one of the largest trucking companies in America: what would happen if they could instantly connect and have access to the universe of knowledge, technology, visionary thinking and elevated strengths from deep within their own system, as well as those valued capacities of Hewlett-Packard, Johnson and Johnson, Phillips, Sony, Southwest Airlines, and Merck? And what if this core of capacities could be potentized, that is, made even more relevant and powerful, through contextualization, conversational concentration and creative action? In a word, it would be a *change*. Not the kind of change written about in books on organizational diagnosis, problem management or intervention theory, but more like the kind written about in physics, for example, in books on fusion energy.

Part three is about the changes that happen through the elevation-of-inquiry and extension-of-relatedness that together create a broaden-and-build dynamic and can activate large amounts of energy comparable to what fusion energy accomplishes, which not incidentally, involves the difficult process of fusing two positively charged elements. Fusion is believed to be the enormous energy source that created the sun and the stars – and its main resource, hydrogen, is infinitely abundant and ecologically clean. Activating this energy is just the opposite of fission (as in the splitting of the atom). It involves something akin to what Alfred North Whitehead termed a "concrescence," or literally *a growing together*. Stated in more practical organizational terms, all this is reminiscent of Peter Drucker's comment about the task of organizational leadership, that it is the *process of creating an alignment of strengths in ways that it make our individual weaknesses irrelevant*. Exploring the circumstances that generate and sustain such change is the common thread that connects the chapters in part three.

Leslie Sekerka and Rollin McCraty begin with a thesis on the heart of change that increases in positive emotions, like hope, inspiration, and joy, are more than indicators of well-being, but are themselves catalysts of increased well-being. Building from Maturana's towering work on the nature of living human systems, which provides a new synthesis between biology and culture, and also between emotion and language, Sekerka and McCraty draw together exciting new research across disciplines and levels of analysis to argue that the key to understanding Appreciative Inquiry's non-deficit mobilization of change is an understanding of how it reduces negative emotions, cultivates positive emotion, and has subsequent impact on generative language and self-organizing change. The authors argue that the way we translate and make meaning of our experience has the propensity to influence the various components of our emotional response triad, feelings, expression, and physiology.

With language serving as a cognitive interpreter and conduit for emotional experience, we create reality by a language-emotion interface. Holding the aforementioned assumption, the authors contend that the reality of our emotional experience can be favorably altered, depending upon the nature of the dialogue we choose to socially construct in concert with others. They share from their research at the Heart-Math Institute just how quickly various techniques can cultivate the catalytic power of positive heart states. Sekerka and McCraty conclude that if a dialogue within an organization shifts to one that focuses on its "positive core" through appreciation, this shared reality in the workplace can transform individual and organizational well-being, much like the broaden-and-build theory says happens with individuals. This chapter, too, adds to our general hypothesis of positive change: *elevate-and-extend* generates a fusion, or a collective *broadening-and-building* of capacity, which in turn, leads to the *activation of energy*.

In the next chapter, *Ned Powley* explores one of the most powerful Appreciative Inquiry applications for change called the "AI Organizational Summit" methodology, and he builds a fascinating analysis drawing on anthropological theories on rites, rituals, and ceremonies. In particular, the author weaves together Victor Turner's concepts of liminality to bring fresh understanding to a whole scale organizational change. This chapter argues that the Appreciative Inquiry Summit produces positive organizational change precisely because of its inherent ritual nature.

The Appreciative Inquiry Summit described at Roadway Express involved a whole system strategic planning meeting, not just with the top ten executives of the company, but also with over 300 truck drivers, dock workers, senior executives, teamsters, managers and customers coming together across all boundaries to co-create their business plan. The Appreciative Inquiry Summit is not difficult, argues the author. Yet, its success requires a great deal of belief in collective human capacity and a desire to challenge conventional patterns of planning that continue to fragment and isolate us from one another. As the author attests, the Appreciative Inquiry Summit – bringing 100s of people together interactively for three to four days – requires at least a little dose of courage. Yet it is powerful. It creates a liminal space. "Appreciative Inquiry is an organizational change process" submits the author, that is "grounded in ritual patterns and characteristics, which are linked through the ritual moments of liminality: reduction of culture to core factors, dramatization of myths and sacred stories through ritual performances, and recombination of futuristic aspirations." In particular, change happens in four underlying areas: the internal dialogue of the culture, the sense of communitas, the forging of commitment, and the tendency toward longitudinal repetition. Nonetheless, says the author, most important is the liminal experience, the moment of passage where people and cultures are "in-betwixt and between" and are neither here nor there; they are between states. The people at an Appreciative Inquiry Summit, observes the author, stay "in it," and they do not run away from this fertile ambiguity. This chapter helps one realizing that we, as a field, may have seriously underestimated the role of ritual space, public celebration, rites of passage, the role of collective emotion, and the like as it relates to positive change in human systems.

Peter Sorenson and Therese Yeager in the next chapter examine the roots of the field of organization development and acknowledge that the field's deficit-theory of change may have reached its limits – it "works" but we can do better, they argue, especially if there can be a new synergy and integration between organizational development's long tradition of "survey guided development" and the exciting directions offered by Appreciative Inquiry.

Both Appreciative Inquiry and the survey-guided development approaches have a common shared commitment to the Lewinian call to Action Research. They share a commitment to a democratic and data-driven form of inquiry, and feedback as a way to generate change in human systems. But then they part company and their theories of change appear at odds. Early Survey Feedback work is associated with the work of Rensis Likert and the Institute for Survey Research at the University of Michigan. Likert's work is probably best remembered for the four systems of management and the profile of organization characteristics. The profile of organization characteristics served as an important introduction to *discrepancy-based change* – the use of deficit-base differences between the actual and the ideal organization (as described by respondents) as a catalyst for change. The authors propose a new hybrid that takes the strengths of the previous methods but lets go of the deficit-change theory, thereby creating a new kind of *Appreciative Inquiry/Survey Feedback*, which in their words "is uniquely capable of productive outcomes."

The most fascinating part of this chapter has to do with an unexpected finding in the authors' cross-cultural assessment of organizations using the Organizational Culture Index (OCI) in a hybrid AI/Survey Feedback format. In essence, they discovered that when using the OCI diagnostically (to identify and analyze the gaps between current and ideal practices) they find a great deal of variation between respondents. In contrast, when just focusing on the future and asking only for visions of the ideal states, as one might expect, less variation and more common ground appear – and this, the discovery of a common ground, is seen as an enabling factor in effective organizational change. Finally, the authors administered the OCI in a whole new way in which they first asked people to begin by reflecting historically on a "high point" moment in their organizational experience, and then with that experience in mind, to take the OCI survey in relation to *that* experience. Now, when inquiry into the high point experience was the anchor, the similarities in OCI patterns across respondents were astonishing.

To put it concisely, gap analysis does not produce much common ground, however when people are asked to share their visions of the ideal future more common ground emerges; and even more common ground is generated when people are asked to inquire into the best in their histories, their high point moments of being most effective, alive, engaged, and so on. The implications of this simple discovery are enormous. It challenges, with precision, fundamental practices of organizational development and what it conventionally teaches. It raises questions about the deliberate use of history in organization and community change; about the ordering of various types of questions; about the power of a people's relationship to their history and their relationship to their future; about how to bring forth resources from the past in order to bring a group together; and about the validity of various measurement instruments and popular benchmarks. The third way, as the authors put it, is to combine inquiry into organizational *history as positive possibility*, and to combine that with the best the field knows about *future visioning*.

Nick Nissely, in the following chapter, argues that the key to the future of Appreciative Inquiry is its "aesthetic" potential. In attempting to make sense of their challenges, organizations have become overly reliant on rational-analytical competencies, numeric criteria and formulae, compartmentalizing problems, and standard operating procedures. Rational-analytical competencies are obviously valuable, but, insufficient by themselves, without what the author labels *aesthetic competencies*. Not only do more aesthetic modes connect and carry forward the emotions for change, but the whole context of communications is in dramatic flux. The world is in the midst of an image revolution, argues the author. Pictures, stories, metaphors, and visual arts animate the language of the New Economy. The palette of communication options is expanding enormously, transforming the way people think. Thus, he submits for today's creative leadership a new kind of literacy is required: *a literacy of images*.

Among the proposals to advance Appreciative Inquiry the author suggests building artistic bridges for communication via "analogically mediated inquiry" including the use of drawing, sculpture, drama, visual art, music and poetry. The author draws on a fascinating set of literatures to describe a three-stage process, or model, that explains how mediated dialogue works: (a) it *surfaces* constructed meaning by attaching significance to an object; (b) it *displays* the object by placing it in a center of a public dialogue; and then (c) it deepens an *inquiry* into various meanings.

The author articulates two main benefits associated with the value of an organization's engaging with the process of artful creation. First, in the context of organizational learning, it appears we all limit our potential to inquire into organizational life if we only consider propositional knowing. Presentational forms of knowing, for example, artful creations, allow us to "see what we're thinking" and to inquire into that knowing. Simply put, artful creations (i.e. presentational knowing) and logic (i.e. propositional knowing) provide different ways of expressing ourselves. Thus, offering a richer way of knowing organizational life. Second, given the growing complexity of organizational life, we must seek ways that allow us to make sense of that growth and expansion. A work of art is a good way to condense, or even to visually model, the underlying complex reality. Moreover, aesthetic representation of past, present and future capacities of a human system can potentize the positive core as an energizing source of transformation. In all, this chapter speaks to our core and makes one feel the excitement. The language is different. The literatures are creative. The possibilities are enormous. And the code of change *is* changing.

While much research and literature on Appreciative Inquiry has focused either on Appreciative Inquiry as a way of developing generative theory or as an intervention, none has explored the *sustainability of change* that is initiated by an appreciative intervention. Throughout the literature about organizational change, one continues to find the question: "How is a change sustained?" This topic is the focus of the chapter by *Mike Mantel and James Ludema* that have studied the Appreciative Inquiry process at World Vision, one of the largest and most respected relief and development organizations world.

They developed a fusion-related theory about how "conversational convergence" leads to sustainable positive change over time. Their theory was built based on a massive data set from four sources collected over a nine-year period from 1992 to 2001, as follows: (1) semi-structured interviews with 197 people connected to the World Vision initiatives; (2) over 10,000 pages of historical documents such as memos, letters, faxes, emails, concept papers, strategy documents, meeting minutes, magazine and newspaper articles, and promotional brochures; (3) notes from a series of large-group Appreciative Inquiry summit meetings held with World Vision over the period of the study; and (4) participant observation and field notes. Data analysis using communication mapping techniques suggested that the "corporate conversation" went through a series of phases over time, and that these conversational phases served as harbingers of decisions and actions to come.

While developing the conversational maps, the authors began to see the organization as streams of conversations that rise and fall, grow together and diminish. The authors discovered that *once awareness of the conversational streams was developed, appreciative change could be maintained by intentionally and positively influencing those streams*. Sustaining change at World Vision required an unrelenting commitment to: (1) shaping the conversation; (2) engaging in appreciative leadership; and (3) applying appreciative principles to organization design.

These mutually reinforcing elements are used by the authors to generate a theory of sustainability. This paper goes far beyond the demonstration of Appreciative Inquiry's sustainability. While this study reminds us that organizations are made and imagined in our conversations, it also illustrates the agony and the ecstasy of it all. The chapter enriches our vocabulary of constructionist change. It provides a series of penetrating questions for future research. And for the practitioner it provides what could become an indispensable checklist for the conversational activation of the energy for change.

Judy Rodgers applies Appreciative Inquiry as the modality for public conversations at the national and global levels. The idea of using public forums to create understanding, consider new possibilities, and arrive at consensus is as old as civilization itself. However, the recent explosion in the use of public dialogue has created renewed interest in the possibilities it poses for creating real social innovation. The World Bank and the Archbishop of Canterbury have turned to public dialogue in an unlikely partnership to bring the international development community and the faith community together to share learning. Barnet Pearce and Kim Pearce have documented their use of dialogue in the civic affairs of Cupertino, California. The Public Conversation Project in Boston, Massachusetts, convened leaders on both sides of the abortion debate for six years. The list of public dialogue initiatives is a long one ranging from the Arts and Civic Dialogue project of Anna Devere Smith to the world-wide Appreciative Inquiry into Business as an Agent of World Benefit convened by the Weatherhead School of Management at Case Western Reserve University. The dialogue modality is exciting from an Appreciative Inquiry perspective, says the author. The public dialogue presents an opportunity to convene those with a stake in a particular issue in a process of mutual co-construction of a genuinely new way of looking at the subject. But when public dialogues start by looking at the history of problems and challenges, they miss this opportunity – and they become unsustainable.

To vivify the potentials and challenges of an Appreciative Inquiry approach to public dialogue, the author describes a worldwide conversation with a system whose approaches to world issues are notoriously deficit focused and increasingly formulaic, *the media*. "Images and Voices of Hope: A Question of Choice" has become a rapidly expanding public dialogue among media professionals, journalists and artists that considers the question, "What does it mean for media to be agents of world benefit?" By 2003 Images and Voices of Hope dialogues have opened in over 20 cities around the world from New Delhi to New York City. Simply telling this story would be exciting enough, but the author goes beyond narration to share an emerging theory of Appreciative Inquiry and public dialogue. The author submits that a public dialogue at its best is an attempt to intervene in the drift of public discourse towards fractiousness and stalemate, and to turn it in an entirely new direction.

The key to creating this shift is to light the fire of generativity, to engage the public imagination, the spirit of community, and a feeling of generosity. There are five conditions, Rodgers proposes, for such dialogue: (a) intention; (b) questions that guide a search for the positive; (c) whole system; (d) relational space; and (e) reflection. Though many of these elements are becoming familiar, we still need to develop better understanding of the practice of reflection, in this case, literally sitting periodically in silence with one another, as a whole community. Apparently, in view of the current scholarship, it just doesn't seem to be so relevant in a world that is focused on speed, on activity, and on the power of words.

But the intensity of dialogue in public conversation – times where the momentum of entrenched positions takes over, where people seem more puzzled and frustrated than ever before about the failure of conferences and programs to address the problems of the world, when the rush of conversations and lack of listening sows the seeds of the increasingly critical – it is precisely at those times that a space of silence can transform everything. While there is an impression that during silence nothing is happening, the author's experience demonstrates just the opposite; times of collective silence are enormously creative and magical. They interrupt our automatic patterns of thought and action; they bring our runaway conversations, especially the wasteful ones, into new perspective and priority; people come back to the dialogues more capable of listening and often with fresh questions and a renewed spirit of inquiry; words that emerge afterward seem more comfortable and able to communicate a mutual respect and shared understanding; people have the space for reflecting on what their individual contribution might be, what they have in common, and what is possible – indeed so much *is* happening that one questions why this simple concept is not built into every one of our public conversations. It is an area ripe for research.

Silence is, says the author, the pre-*language* we have always turned to as human beings in special moments of reflection and respect; and it provides access to deeper wells of resources when we need them the most. Silence elevates-and-extends. It broadens-and-builds. It connects. It sustains. The author is convinced that silence is essential to good inquiry, that slowing the tempo enlarges our sensitivities to one another and our capacity to appreciate and prize, and that silence will prove vital to the larger issues that lay ahead for the world.

It is also a great way to close this introduction to volume one of *Advances in Appreciative Inquiry*.

David L. Cooperrider and Michel Avital
Editors
February 23, 2004

REFERENCES

Barge, K. J., & Oliver, C. (2003). Working with appreciation in managerial practice. *Academy of Management Review*, *28*(1), 124–142.

Cameron, K., Dutton, J., & Quinn, R. (2003). *Positive organizational scholarship*. San Francisco: Berrett-Kohler.

Cooperrider, D. L., Barrett, F., & Srivastva, S. (1995). Social construction and appreciative inquiry: A journey in organizational theory. In: D. Hosking, P. Dachler & K. Gergen (Eds), *Management and Organization: Relational Alternatives to Individualism* (pp. 157–200). Aldershot, UK: Avebury Press.

Cooperrider, D. L., & Sekerka, L. E. (2003). Toward a theory of positive change. In: K. Cameron, J. Dutton & R. Quinn (Eds), *Positive Organizational Scholarship* (Chap. 15). San Francisco: Berrett-Kohler.

Cooperrider, D. L., & Srivastva, S. (1987). Appreciative inquiry in organizational life. In: W. Pasmore & R. Woodman (Eds), *Research in Organization Change and Development* (Vol. 1, pp. 129–169). Greenwich, CT: JAI Press.

Cooperrider, D. L., & Srivastva, S. (1999). Appreciative inquiry in organizational life. In: S. Srivastva & D. L. Cooperrider (Eds), *Appreciative Management and Leadership: The Power of Positive Thought and Action in Organization* (Rev. ed., pp. 401–441). Cleveland, OH: Lakeshore Communications.

Fry, R., Barrett, F., Seiling, J., & Whitney, D. (2001). *Appreciative inquiry and organizational transformation: Reports from the field*. Westport, CT: Quorum Books.

Gergen, K. J. (1990). Affect and organization in postmodern society. In: S. Srivastva, D. L. Cooperrider & Associates (Eds), *Appreciative Management and Leadership: The Power of Positive Thought and Action in Organizations* (1st ed.). San Francisco, CA: Jossey-Bass.

Gergen, K. J. (1994). *Realities and relationships: Soundings in social construction*. Harvard University Press.

Haidt, J. (2000). The positive emotion of elevation. *Prevention & Treatment*, *3*, np.

Hubbard, B. M. (1998). *Conscious evolution: Awakening the power of our social potential* (see Chap. 11 on AI). Novato, CA: New World Library.

James, W. (1902) *Varieties of religious experience* (pp. 162–163). New York: New American Library.

Pasmore, & Woodman (1987). *Research In Organization Change and Development* (Vol. 1). Greenwich, CT: JAI Press.

Quinn, R. E. (2000). *Change the world: How ordinary people can achieve extraordinary results*. San Francisco, CA: Jossey-Bass.

Rader, M. (1979). *A modern book of esthetics*. New York: Holt, Rinehart & Winston.

Reason, & Bradbury, H. (2001). *Handbook of Action Research: Participative Inquiry and Practice*. London: Sage.

Srivastva, S., Cooperrider, D. L., & Associates (Eds) (1990). *Appreciative management and leadership: The power of positive thought and action in organizations* (1st ed.). San Francisco, CA: Jossey-Bass.

Watkins, J. M., & Mohr, B. J. (2001). *Appreciative inquiry: Change at the speed of imagination*. Jossey-Bass/Pfeiffer.

Whitney, D., & Trosten-Bloom, A. (2003). *The power of appreciative inquiry: A practical guide to positive change*. San Francisco, CA: Berrett-Koehler.

PART I:
EXTENSION OF RELATEDNESS

APPRECIATIVE INQUIRY AS DIALOGUE: GENERATIVE AND TRANSFORMATIVE

Mary M. Gergen, Kenneth J. Gergen and Frank Barrett

ABSTRACT

In this chapter we are exploring Appreciative Inquiry within organizations through the dialogic process in its relational aspect. The present discussion is composed of four parts: An exploration of the myriad meanings of dialogue and a description of a useful orienting platform, dialogue as "discursive coordination." We then turn to the pivotal function of dialogue in the organizing process and the development of a vocabulary of discursive action with practical consequences for effective organizing. We next turn to the problematic potentials of dialogue. A contrast between generative and degenerative dialogue enables us to explore how certain forms of coordination ultimately lead to organizational growth or demise. Among our conclusions we propose that dialogue originates in public, is a form of joint-action, is embodied and contextually embedded, as well as historically and culturally situated. Dialogue may serve both positive and negative ends. Described are four aspects of dialogue – an emphasis on affirmation, productive difference, coherence, and temporal integration. Appreciative inquiry adds an enormously important element to the transformative potentials of dialogue. Other transformative practices and potentials are also described.

Constructive Discourse and Human Organization
Advances in Appreciative Inquiry, Volume 1, 3–27
ISSN: 1475-9152/doi:10.1016/S1475-9152(04)01001-4

INTRODUCTION

Underlying the process of Appreciative Inquiry (AI) is the assumption that dialogue is inherent in change practices. In general, the AI process depends upon people relating to each other through various dialogic forms of inquiry. People interview each other, tell each other stories, meet in groups to share ideas, create joint visions of the future, and prepare through conversations to activate and review them. Almost always the focus of an inquiry is on the questions asked at the instigation of the inquiry, but rarely, if ever, are the questions related to the nature of the inquiry process itself. In this chapter we are exploring the key ingredient of the dialogic process, which is its relational aspect. It is from the relational matrix that the very possibility of sense making comes into being, and without the existence of ongoing relationships communicative acts lose their status as such. Organizational worlds, in particular, are created and sustained through discourse, and it is through relational processes that discourse acquires its significance. More broadly stated, it is by virtue of relational processes within dialogue that Appreciative Inquiry works.[1]

THE CENTRALITY OF DIALOGUE: HISTORICAL PRECEDENTS

Although dialogue as a topic of study is rarely mentioned in traditional handbooks of organizational study and has remained generally unexplored in the Appreciative Inquiry literature, its importance to organizational functioning has been subtly apparent since the earliest scientific studies in the field. For example Kurt Lewin (1951), in his groundbreaking research on attitude change, attempted to convince housewives to serve undesirable meat products (e.g. beef hearts, kidneys) as a contribution to the war effort. Comparisons were made between groups exposed to persuasive information and groups that received the information and then discussed its implications. The results revealed that members of the discussion groups were far more likely to subsequently purchase and serve the meats. In effect, "involved participation" in decision making was critical to change. Yet, while this study is often credited with spawning the field of action research, we actually know very little about the essential process of the discussion itself. What aspects of the conversational activities influenced women to change deeply held food preparation habits?

Later studies continued in much the same vein. Classic research at Detroit Edison in 1948 aimed at improving work processes (Baumgartel, 1959). Again the researchers contrasted traditional training methods with group discussions.

They conclude that "Intensive, group discussion can be an effective tool for introducing positive change in a business organization" (p. 6). In their oft cited experiment, Coch and French (1953) experimented with organizational change in a clothing factory. In one group, managers informed machine operators about changes in their job. In this group "resistance developed almost immediately after the change," resulting in grievances, quitting, and lowered productivity. In the experimental condition, groups discussed how working methods could be improved and how to eliminate unnecessary operations. In this case there were no signs of resistance. These early studies have stimulated a robust line of inquiry (see Porras & Robertson, 1991). And yet, because of the exclusive focus on outcome rather than process, we have learned little about the actual process of dialogue, which seemed to produce the changes.

ORGANIZATION OF OUR INQUIRY

The present discussion is composed of four parts. As an introduction, we explore the myriad meanings of dialogue and develop what we view as a useful orienting platform: dialogue as "discursive coordination." This orientation will enable us to consider the practical consequences of various forms of dialogic action, including Appreciative Inquiry. We then turn to the pivotal function of dialogue in the organizing process. We are especially concerned with developing a vocabulary of discursive action with practical consequences for effective organizing. After considering the uses of dialogue in creating organization, we turn to the problematic potentials of dialogue. A contrast between generative and degenerative dialogue enables us to explore how certain forms of coordination ultimately lead to organizational demise. Indeed, the very forms of dialogue required for organizational well-being may also establish the grounds for deterioration. In the final section we turn to dialogic practices that may restore vitality to the organization. Here we focus on transformational dialogue, that is, dialogic practices designed to break through frequently encountered barriers to communication. Throughout this analysis we focus on the components of AI from which its power in organizational change is derived.

DIALOGUE AS DISCURSIVE COORDINATION

In recent years scholars and practitioners have become increasingly excited about the potentials of dialogue for creating and transforming social worlds (Palshaugen, 2001). However, such excitement is accompanied by a certain vagueness as to what is meant by dialogue. Choruses now sing praises to dialogue, but seldom stop to consider that their tributes may be directed toward entirely different practices. *The American Heritage Dictionary*, for example, offers the culturally shared definition of dialogue as "conversation between two or more people." However, virtually no academic treatises on dialogue shares this definition; scholars of dialogue are not interested in *mere* conversation. However, such scholars typically do not share definitions with each other. In our view, the focal definitional criterion of most contemporary analyses of dialogue is derived from a vision of an *ideal* form of dialogue. For most contemporary analysts, merely having a conversation does not constitute *true* dialogue.

It is primarily the particular vision of the ideal that sets various dialogic scholars apart. David Bohm's (1996) popular book, *On Dialogue*, defines dialogue as a form of communication from which something new emerges. In this sense, it is highly congenial with Appreciative Inquiry in that every inquiry process is designed to lead to unexpected and generative outcomes. Participants, according to Bohm, develop a "relaxed, non-judgmental curiosity," with the aim of seeing "things as freshly and clearly as possible" (p. ix). Robert Grudin's (1996) definition as presented in *On Dialogue* is not so much interested in relationships that create newness as he is in a "reciprocal exchange of meaning . . . across a physical or mental space" (p. 11). This form of dialogue recognizes difference as always present in a dialogic situation. The dialogue exists as the bridge. Many appreciative inquiry projects begin in a climate of difference, often emanating from hostile or critical camps that must be connected to one another. In this sense it captures the essence of Grudin's view. In contrast, Putnam and Fairhurst (2000) are not centrally concerned with either generating novelty or bridging differences, but rather with the creation of convergence in views; they define dialogue as "a mode of communication that builds mutuality through the awareness of others" (p. 116), and it does so through the "use of genuine or authentic discourse, and reliance on the unfolding interaction" (p. 116). Somewhat similarly, L. C. Hawes (1999), considers the central ingredient of dialogue to be conflict reduction; for him dialogue is "praxis for mediating competing and contradictory discourses" (p. 229).

While many of these scholars assume that dialogue takes place among equals, Eisenberg and Goodall (1993) are chiefly concerned with enhancing the voices of minorities. They see dialogue as allowing various groups of people a voice to challenge traditional authorities. This definition is a helpful reminder that all voices are not equally valuable in many organizations, although the appreciative inquiry process, by virtue of its design is a highly democratic change process. In terms of process, Isaacs (1993) stresses that dialogue is "a sustained collective inquiry into the processes, assumptions, and certainties that compose everyday experience" (p. 25). In this respect his emphasis on group inquiry is similar to that of Appreciative Inquiry. Finally, for Maranhao (1990), it is not everyday life that dialogue should throw into question, but all certainty of knowledge. For him dialogue is a logic of "stating and questioning," with the aim of generating the kind of skepticism that invites continuous inquiry. For Maranhao, dialogue is a form of "anti-epistemology." This approach is congenial with the undermining of any particular version of the real, in concert with A. I.

With such differing views of dialogue, each saturated as it is with values and visions, any general characterization of dialogue becomes perilous. In order to establish a more comprehensive analytic frame, while not sacrificing valuable distinctions embedded in these various accounts, it is useful to separate the normative from the descriptive. Rather than equating the term "dialogue" with any particular vision of ideal interchange, we offer an elemental descriptive definition. Variations in the specific patterning of interchange may thus reflect the various ideal forms sought by differing scholars. In this way we leave room for broad expansion in specific forms and functions. We do not propose a return to the view of "dialogue as conversation," as it does not serve our analytic ends here. The term "conversation" is both ambiguous and conceptually thin. Rather, for present purposes we propose to define *dialogue as discursive coordination in the service of social ends*. In this particular case, we might envision the social ends as the outcomes of appreciative inquiries. To amplify this view and its implications, we propose the following:

(1) *Dialogue originates in the public sphere*. In understanding dialogue many theorists have drawn from the individualist tradition in which language is a reflection or expression of the individual mind. On this account, dialogue is a form of inter-subjective connection or synchrony. The public actions are derivative of private meanings. In the present account we bracket the realm of subjectivity and focus on the public coordination of discourse. This enables us to avoid a number of intractable philosophical problems (e.g. the relation of mind to body, the problem of "other minds," and the hermeneutic problem of accurate interpretation) and to focus on the relational function of various utterances within ongoing conversation. We are informed here, in part, by J. L. Austin's *How to do things with words* (1962), in which the performatory character of speech is illuminated. Utterances are essentially actions performed with social consequences.

This orientation does not exclude psychological inquiry. However, it is to say that significant analyses of dialogue can ensue without recourse to psychological explanation. Effective analysis of dialogue need not refer to states of individual understanding, subjective biases or inattention, personality traits, and so on. This possibility was initially demonstrated in Garfinkel's (1965) groundbreaking work on ethnomethodology, and now more copiously in various forms of discourse and conversation analysis (Wetherell, Taylor & Yates, 2001a, b). If psychological inquiry is to proceed, our orientation here is most congenial with Vygotsky's (1986) view that higher order psychological processes are reflections of social process. This is to say that the process of thought is essentially public discourse carried out on a private site. This is essentially the view adopted by Bruner (1990) in *Acts of Meaning*, and by Harré and Gillette (1994) in *The Discursive Mind*. In our view, however, it is most useful to focus on the forms of public coordination that originate, sustain, transform, and potentially terminate what participants take to be meaning (Shaw, 2002). This perspective is especially congenial with A. I. as what is structured within the process is public conversations among interlocutors.

(2) *Dialogue is a form of joint-action.* In foregrounding the concept of collaboration we mean to call attention to the relational foundation of dialogue. That is, meaning within dialogue is an outcome not of individual action and reaction, but of what Shotter (1984) and others have called joint-action, or the patterning of juxtaposed actions by the participants. In this sense, the meaning of an individual's expression within a dialogue depends importantly on the response of his or her interlocutor – what has elsewhere been called "a supplement" (Gergen, 1994). No individual expression harbors meaning in itself. For example, what we might conventionally index as a "hostile remark" can be turned into "a joke" through a response of laughter; the "vision statement" of a superior can be refigured as "just more BS" through the smirks of the employees. In A. I. Projects, a shared assumption among participants is that they will supplement each other's comments with replies that are respectful of the other's statements. A. I. is not congenial with sarcasm, skeptical rejoinders, or other forms of gratuitous negation. This is not to say that there is no room for differences of expressed viewpoints among participants in A. I., but the form is unsuited to negative dialogic engagement.

In this context, Wittgenstein's (1963) metaphor of the language game is also useful. The metaphor calls attention specifically to the coordinated or rule-governed activities of the participants in generating meaning. The rules of the game are such that some phrases belong in the manner of speaking, and others do not. The words, "bottom line" and "quarterly report" acquire their meaning by virtue of the participation of the interlocutors in the rule constrained talk of corpo-rations. "The Power of Prayer" usually does not. Privately held words, invented by a single individual, would not constitute meaningful entries into dialogue. They do not belong to any language game. In this sense, the traditional binary separating monologue and dialogue is misleading. The term monologue cannot refer to the language of one person alone, for such a language would fail to communicate. The meaning of any utterance depends on its functioning within a relational matrix. Thus monologue is better understood as an extended (or dominating) entry of a single voice into a dialogue; in this sense monologue is an unevenly distributed dialogue.

(3) *Dialogic efficacy is bodily and contextually embedded.* While our orientation to dialogue emphasizes discourse, we do not embrace linguistic reductionism. Spoken (or written) language may be focal in our analyses, but other than for analytic purposes, we do not wish to separate out such language from the remainder of the life sphere entering into the production of meaning. Clearly the efficacy of spoken words within dialogue is fastened to the simultaneous movements of the speakers' bodies, tone of voice, and physical proximity. Further, dialogic efficacy cannot ultimately be separated from the world of objects and spaces – the material context. The efficacy of one's words may importantly depend, for example, on whether one is clutching a gavel, a dagger, or a bouquet of flowers. In the same way, the meaning of words within the dialogue may depend on whether they are expressed in an executive suite, in a bar room, or over the internet. Again to draw from Wittgenstein (1963) the language games in which we engage are embedded within broader *forms of life*. Thus, the meaning of "bottom line" and "quarterly report" do not only depend on the rules of organization talk, but on their function within a form of life that includes departments, managers, CEO's, Boards of Directors, headquarters, computer networks, benefit packages, downsizing, golden parachutes, promotions, and so on.

(4) *Dialogic efficacy is historically and culturally situated.* The contribution of any particular act of speech to dialogic coordination is contingent on its placement within a cultural context. In part this emphasis acknowledges Saussure's (1974) distinction between the *synchronic* and *diachronic* study of language. While we may effectively focus on contemporary forms of dialogue and their accomplishments (synchronic study), we must also be prepared for temporal transformations in what and how various ends are accomplished. For example, "the boss's orders" were once very effective within Western organizations, but they are slowly losing their power to direct activity. As concerns with workplace democracy, diversity, and organizational flattening become popular, an authoritative "top-down" voice becomes more and more dysfunctional (Yankelovich, 1999). The rise of A. I. as a dialogic change methodology is a stellar example of this process of increasing democratization in the workplace. Its major mode of transformation depends upon the inclusivity of its dialogic processes and the equality of diverse voices.

Bakhtin (1981) also draws our attention to the heterogeneous cultural traditions that typically contribute to the shared language of a nation. This analysis prepares us for the possibility that partners in a dialogue may be *polyvocal*, capable of shifting from one mode or form of dialogue to another across the course of conversation (Hazen, 1993). At the same time, the focus on cultural heterogeneity alerts us to the difficulties that may be encountered when participants do not share discursive traditions. As the mounting literature on cross-cultural (mis)understanding makes clear (see for example, Jandt, 2001; Pearce, 1989; Rahim, 1994; Ting-Toomey & Oetzel, 2001) such dialogues may be frustrating and ineffectual. The dialogic moves effective for achieving goals within one tradition may be counterproductive in conversations with those outside the tradition. Similarly, even within the same culture the dialogic forms effective in one condition may not carry over to another. (See for example, Well's, 1999, discussion of optimal forms of classroom dialogue.) Whatever is said about dialogic efficacy within organizations must thus be tempered by consciousness of contingency. Within the A. I. tradition, for example, successful consultants have counseled that A. I. is most effective when stakeholders at all levels of the organization have supported the process. A. I. is an inclusive approach, not a piecemeal fix within a limited "problem-focused" sphere.

(5) *Dialogue may serve many different purposes, both positive and negative.* Finally, by viewing dialogue as discursive coordination we attempt to avoid conflating normative and descriptive commitments. Coordination in itself is multifaceted. From our definitional framework, a highly coherent, lively and passionate argument is as much a dialogue as an attempt to gain an appreciative understanding of another's "point of view." This is not to abandon concern with the kinds of ideals central to most A. I. practitioners. Rather, it is to invite differentiation among forms of dialogue in terms of the ends they serve. Thus, while certain forms of dialogue may indeed succeed in reducing conflict, other moves in language may enable authority to be challenged, multiple opinions to be expressed, or taken-for-granted realities to be deliberated. As Robin Wagner-Pacifici (2000) describes it, a pragmatic approach to drawing two opponents into a jointly desired outcome requires multifaceted skills of improvisation. Drawing again from Wittgenstein (1963), "Think of the tools in a tool-box: there is a hammer, pliers, a saw, a screw-driver, a rule, a glue-pot, glue, nails, and screws – the function of words are as diverse as the functions of these objects" (6e). From this perspective, inquiry is invited into the specific forms of dialogue required to achieve particular goals of value.

It is important to note here that the value placed on dialogic outcomes may vary significantly from one standpoint to another. For example, a vigorous argument, from an outsider's perspective, may seem aggressive and hostile. For the participants, however, such skirmishes can be enlivening fun, much like a game of chess, as well as generative of new insights (Billig, 1987). The outcomes of any particular dialogue may be simultaneously both positive and negative (see also Thatchenkery & Upadhyaya, 1996). One may be pleased that a given dialogue succeeds in establishing new policies that facilitate relations with an external supplier, but simultaneously realize that certain critical capacities are simultaneously suspended. And too, what is accomplished in a dialogue may be judged differently in terms of what ensues at a later point in time. Many organizations have been disappointed by training exercises that generate immediate joy and communal good-will during the weekend, only to find that Monday morning life returns to dull normal. One of the distinct advantages of A. I. is that the conversations are grounded in shared past practices and historical events. While there may be distinctly different evaluations placed on any event, the relationship of the dialogues to organizational histories is strong. Many other organizational training programs are divorced from the fields on which the challenges of the organization are played out.

GENERATIVE DIALOGUE AND THE ORGANIZING PROCESS

If we understand dialogue as the process of relational coordination, it is immediately clear that certain forms of dialogue are essential to the process of building organizations. As people's words and actions become coordinated so do forms of life come into being – friendships, marriages, families, and organizations large and small (see also Taylor, 2000; Weick, 1995; Yankelovich, 1999). In this sense, there is no inherent difference in the process by which two children create a sand castle, a family eats Sunday dinner together, a strike is planned, or the Ford motor company produces automobiles. Processes of dialogic coordination are at work in every instance. Yet, while we acknowledge the significant implications of understanding dialogue as relational coordination, we are still left without the kind of detailing essential for creating and sustaining an effective organization. Invited, in particular, is an account of those dialogic moves that facilitate the process of organizing. What moves contribute to what might be called *generative dialogue*, dialogue that brings into being a mutually satisfying and effective organization? A full treatment of generative dialogue would require an examination not only of bodily movements, gestures, and gaze, but of the environment and the objects available to people in relationships. A focus on historical conditions contributing to various forms of generative dialogue would be helpful, as well as an account of cultural variations in effective dialogue. However, given limited space and the emphasis of the present volume on discourse, let us focus in particular on spoken and written language in the contemporary Western organization. This is no insignificant matter, as language is the chief means by which such organizations come into being and are sustained. It is the way in which A. I. supports life-giving activities in organizations. However, it is important to be sensitive to the limitations of such an analysis.

Further, what we offer here may be viewed as a "work-in-progress." That is, we act here without the benefit of a well grounded literature specific to the topic. We must piece together significant ideas from a number of disparate areas to offer a preliminary scaffolding. At the same time, we hope that this unfinished structure will enable more detailed elaboration as future study moves in this direction.

It should be noted that we are guided in our present treatment by a social constructionist orientation (Gergen, 1994, 1999). In effect we place a strong emphasis on the way in which discourse functions to structure both a sense of the real and the valuable within relationships. From the relational matrix, then, both ontology and ethics – agreement on what is, and what ought to be – can grow. And, as these agreements are cemented to action, local traditions (sub-cultures) emerge. In terms of generative dialogue, as offered by Appreciative Inquiry, then, the central focus is on those kinds of dialogic moves that may bring realities and ethics into being and bind them to particular patterns of action. With above provisos notwithstanding, we propose the following as central components in generative dialogue.

The Act of Affirmation

As proposed above, because meaning is born in relationship, an individual's lone utterance contains no meaning in itself, but only the potential to mean. This potential can only be realized through another's supplement. The supplement of affirmation may stand as the key building block to creating conjoint realities, in this case an affirmative one. To affirm is to ratify the significance of an utterance as a meaningful act (Cottle, 2002). It is to locate something within an expression that is valuable, to which one can agree, or render support. Merely responding to the question, "How are you?" with "Fine, thank you," is to render the question meaningful as a ritual of greeting. To respond with a blank stare would be to negate its significance as communication. In the act of affirmation elements of the initial utterance are also sanctioned as "real" and are given rudimentary value. The response of "Fine, thank you," simultaneously grants "personal well-being" an existence in the world and places value upon it.

Affirmation is important for other reasons as well, partly deriving from the individualist tradition and the presumption that thoughts and feelings are individual possessions. As we say, "It is my experience that . . .," or "These are *my* beliefs." To affirm such utterances is to grant worth to or to honor the validity of the other's subjectivity; failure to affirm places the identity of the other in question. Finally, in affirming an utterance one also sanctions the relationships from which it derives. If one dismisses a speaker's opinions, it is often to disparage the range of relations in which this opinion is embedded. To embrace an idea is to embrace new relationships, and possibly to threaten old ones.

Affirmation may take many forms depending on conversation and context. At the simplest level, careful or sympathetic attention provides a beginning. Curiosity or question asking also may serve as simple forms of affirmation, as they grant to the speaker's preceding utterance meaningful significance. In her volume, *Conversation, Language, and Possibilities*, Harlene Anderson (1997) speaks for many change agents when she proposes that therapy becomes effective when, "the therapist enters the therapy domain with a genuine posture and manner characterized by an openness to another person's ideological base – his or her reality, beliefs, and experiences. This listening posture and manner involve showing respect for, having humility toward, and believing that what a client has to say is worth hearing" (p. 12). More broadly, affirmation may be roughly equated with what many researchers call "mutuality" in dialogue (Markova, Graumann & Foppa, 1995). It is important to note, however, that we are not proposing that generative dialogue requires full agreement among interlocutors. Affirmation is not assent, in itself.

Productive Difference

While affirmation is of critical significance in serving the goals of inquiry and building an organization, it is important to draw a distinction between affirmation and duplication. At the most rudimentary level affirmation ratifies the reality and value of a preceding utterance. However, it functions in this way primarily against the backdrop of a contrasting possibilities or domains that are not affirmed. If agreement is simply a parroting of the original remark, there is no value as a meaning making supplement. The distinction is important in virtue of a more general theoretical point: The conjoint creation of meaning depends on the generation of *difference*. Any utterance in a dialogue acquire its meaning from its difference from other utterances. Thus, in a more general sense, generative dialogue depends on the continuous generation of differences. The meaning making process is rendered robust by virtue of distinctive voices (see also Hazen, 1993).

In gathering the stories that people contribute to an appreciative inquiry, the presence of difference provides a powerful scaffolding on which to build new visions of the future. If one person's story of intense satisfaction in working in an organization comes from leading a team through tough times, while another's comes from providing extra enthusiasm in a highly successful bond offering, so much the better. The resultant proposals for future activities are more diverse, comprehensive and practical as a result of the diversity of stories from which they came.

Not all difference is to be valued however. A further distinction is essential between *productive* as opposed to *destructive difference*. Dialogic entries that sustain or extend the potentials of a preceding utterance may be viewed as productive; utterances that curtail or negate what has preceded tend to be destructive. They essentially impede the process of constructing a mutually viable reality. Adding new voices to the conversation may also make a robust contribution to productive difference. A shift in perspective places previous entries in a new light, one that may significantly change the nature of the offerings. See also Barbules (1994) on "building statements." In contrast, to announce that another's utterance is "just plain wrong," unintelligible, or outrageous will typically bring dialogue to a halt. Because of the diverse nature of supplementary statements, and the many ways in which they can be interpreted, however, it is impossible to judge the exact contributions of any response. A well-disciplined debate, for example, may illustrate important advantages or fatal flaws in a formulation, ones that may have been invisible to those set to affirm the positive potential in a dangerous proposition. A critical question may bring a shift in the dialogue that allows for different slants on a conversational topic.

The Creation of Coherence

The combination of affirmation and difference contribute to the success of an appreciative inquiry process. However, in the same way that the meaning derived from a paragraph in a novel is highly dependent on its relationship to preceding paragraphs, so does meaning in dialogue depend on what precedes any particular turn-taking segment. To create a sustainable world thus requires dialogic acts that engender what is commonly termed conversational coherence (Craig & Tracy, 1983; Duck, 2002). Such acts enable preceding expressions to create a singular, ordered world about which to organize. Among the common dialogic inputs contributing to coherence are repeating conversational topics (topoi), offering comments relevant to a recognized issue, remaining in the same metaphoric space, and providing answers to preceding questions (Barbules, 1994; Wells, 1999). On a more subtle level, we wish to call attention to *metonymic reflection* as a means of generating coherence. Metonymy refers to the use of a fragment to stand for a whole to which it is related. In terms of dialogue, metonymic reflection occurs when one's actions contain some fragment of the other's actions, a piece that represents the whole. If an interlocutor asks a question about a given policy, and her colleague responds, "What's the weather report for tomorrow?"

the topic of interest to the first speaker fails to be represented in the reply. The reply fails to include some element of the initial utterance. If a response includes a metonymic fragment of what has just been said, then the interlocutor finds the message carried in the other. Collaborative coherence is achieved. Within most A. I. practices, metonymic reflections are created through the repetitions of stories and story fragments, through the use of general phrases that reappear at each level of analysis, and continue through various stages of development.

Narrative and Temporal Integration

As dialogue develops it leaves in its wake a repository of discourse and associated action. This repository may serve as both a resource for sustaining generativity and a potential threat to continuation. Its major contribution to the process of organizing stems from its integrative properties. That is, as interlocutors set about constructing a world of the real and the good, materials are required for solidification. This world must become compelling, reliable and significant. One major means of solidifying this world is through integrating materials from the past – accounts of events that can fortify the present, fill out its contours, add to its dimension, and/or ratify its value. Although all past events can be used in this way, the most important resources for such solidification come from events common to the interlocutors themselves and in the vein of an Appreciative Inquiry. By inserting accounts of the past into ongoing dialogues, the interlocutors also create a reality with historical depth (Thatchenkery & Upadhyaya, 1996). They cease to speak in terms of "what we are presently creating," but see the present as rooted in the past, an element of particular emphasis in A. I. The shaky quality of "here and now" is replaced by the concept of "tradition." For additional insights into the ways in which narratives serve as organizing devices (see Boje, 1991, 2001; Czarniawska, 1997; Gabriel, 1995).

EXPANDING THE ARENA OF GENERATIVE DIALOGUE

These four insertions into dialogue – emphasizing affirmation, productive difference, coherence, and temporal integration – may be viewed as central to creating the forms of reality and value necessary for effective organization. At the same time, these are only entry markers in a scholarly effort of extended duration and scope. For purposes of inviting collaborative expansion, we share here several additional contributions of significance:

Repetitive Sequences. Generative dialogue may be compared to the fluid and synchronized movements of dancers. A key to the success of the dance is a history of practice. Yet, this is not the practice of isolated individuals, but of the collaborative unit. Their practice together readies each of them for the movements of the other. The slight pressure of the male's hand may send his partner into a swirl, at the end of which his open arms are prepared to receive her return. And so it is in the case of generative dialogue. If effective organization is to be achieved so must there be repetitive scenarios of relationship, sequences of action that form a reliable core. This is not to propose that all relational sequences should move in the repetitive direction. The result would be a stagnation of meaning and the loss of flexibility. However, without major contributions to repetition, organizational efficacy will be lost. A significant degree of dialogic ritual is essential. In A. I. the power of interviews is largely locatable in the repetitious qualities of the responses. Through multiple voices each speaking independently, a common refrain is almost always found. The strength of numbers lends power to the next steps of the A. I. process.

Reflexive Punctuation. As dialogues unfold and repetition becomes more frequent, agreements will emerge as to what is real and good. However, because the meaning of what has been achieved is inherently ambiguous – subject to alteration as the conversation moves on – effective organization may require periodic reflection on what has been accomplished. Such punctuating insinuations into dialogue serve to collect and organize the sedimented realities and aspirations of the participants. Comments concerning "what we have agreed to" "our objectives," or "our visions of the future," may all have this solidifying effect. Metaphors may play an especially important role in this case, as they have the capacity to tie together many disparate facets of conversation and action into a coherent whole. The development of summary statements or provocative propositions in A. I. processes form the opportunity for this to take place. See also Weick (1995) on significance of "retrospective sensemaking."

Constructing Bonds and Boundaries. Participants in an A. I. process are involved in processes that move from the singular, "what gives me joy," "how I have been productive" to the social. Favored by A. I. are generative dialogues, then, that shift from a discourse of individual entities to a collective "we." In speaking of "our goals," "what we envision" and "our hopes," the "imagined community" becomes a reality (Anderson, 1997). The result is a bonding among the participants, the creation of a sense of unity in the organization, and an increased focus on future relations among participants.

In closing this discussion it is important to note that none of the discursive moves outlined here achieves its function until affirmed by one's interlocutors. While linguistic tradition forces us to single out specific "moves," "utterances," or "speech acts," this tradition simultaneously obscures the conjoint creation of their meaning. Thus, for example, a narrative is not a narrative until another ratifies it as such. One may tell what conventionally counts as "a story of a past success," but its reality as such depends on the affirmation of the listener. If the listener indexes the offering as a "manipulative ploy," or "a misleading distortion" the "story of past success" is destroyed. In this sense, the analysis of dialogue is not congenial with strategic views of communication competence. The success of a given move does not depend on the rational calculus of the actor, but on its relationship to what that which has preceded and follows. It might be germaine to note that the A. I. rests upon the assumption that actors who are involved participate in good faith, with an open mind and a spirit of cooperation. To the extent that actors are strategic – playing games or going through the motions only in order to gain some subalternate goal – the process itself is harmed.

DIALOGUE AND ORGANIZATIONAL DYSFUNCTION

While dialogic process is critical to the achievement of A. I., it is also clear that not all forms of dialogue function in this way. The preceding discussion has attempted to pinpoint dialogic contributions that seem pivotal to creating a shared reality. Here we turn to the problem of organizational dysfunction. First, we inquire in a more general manner into what forms of dialogue undermine or destroy organizations. Then we turn to the more subtle and ironic ways in which organizing processes themselves lay the groundwork for disorganization.

We shall not belabor the topic of dialogic dysfunction. In part this is because failure is implied by the absence or inverse of the various dialogic moves just outlined. The failure to affirm, for example, can lead to disharmony within a relationship; failing to create coherence can undermine concerted action. Further, most of us well understand the destructive forms of dialogue by virtue of our participation in the rituals of everyday life. Common experience is perhaps our best teacher. However, two contributions to dysfunctional dialogue may be singled out for their ubiquitous deployment:

Negation. Echoing our discussion of destructive difference, the negative move within a dialogue is one that essentially destroys the meaning making potential of a preceding utterance. This is not simply a failure to affirm, but the active obliteration of the utterance as a candidate for meaning. On a subtle level, active inattention also serves as negation. Turning away from an interlocutor, reading a document, starting another conversation, or interrupting without acknowledging what has been said all serve as forms of negation. More blatantly, hostile critique or volatile arguments against the interlocutor's utterances can function as negation. Again, this is not to imply that critique and argument are always dysfunctional. As indicated above, much depends on the form (including tone of voice and bodily posture). However, it is to say that the latter forms of discourse must be employed with care and sensitivity. As suggested earlier, in the Western tradition one's words are virtually expressions of personal essence. To attack another's views is not, then, a mere linguistic exercise; it is to invalidate the originary essence of the self.

Monologic discourse may also function as negation. As previously proposed, we view monologue as an unevenly distributed form of dialogue. If extended indefinitely it eliminates the space for the other's supplementation. In effect, the speaker preempts the affirmation process, placing the affirmation into the mouth of the otherwise mute listener. In this way, monologue subtly denies the listener participation in the creation of meaning. Here we are sensitized as well to the relationship between dialogic forms and organizational structure. Monologic communication is traditionally a prerogative of rank. Indeed the presumption remains in Western culture that the more senior the individual in the organization the more knowledge he or she should possess, and therefore, the more right to make an input into a dialogue. In this sense, the failure to display monologic prowess may be viewed as a sign of weakness in upper management. In the wave of recent support for workplace democracy and diversity initiatives, a presumption that the leaders must do monologues becomes questionable. Further, as organizations grow more complex and confront an increasingly chaotic world of meaning, monologic discourse seems increasingly counterproductive (Anderson et al., 2001). One salutary feature of A. I. is its design of processes that are inclusive of all the voices relevant to an organization. A. I. processes support direct democracy at the basic level of inquiry. This effort helps to subvert tendencies for monologues and the silencing of the less powerful, lower status people in an organization.

Individual Blame. From the Western ideology of "the individual self," also sprouts the concept of individual responsibility. If individual minds are originary sources of action, then we may sensibly hold the individual responsible for his or her deeds – both good and bad. Such assumptions make their way into our institutions of law, into the application of rule systems within organizations, and into the rituals of daily life. In all cases, there is longstanding legitimation for blaming the individual for his or her untoward actions. Yet, in significant respects acts of individual blame function much like negations. They symbolically assault what is taken to be the center core of self. Resistance is thus invited, a resistance that is further exacerbated by the typical sense of righteousness. From the present standpoint individuals function within shared visions of the real and the good; there is no place in such worlds for "choosing evil." Such actions would be incomprehensible. From the personal standpoint, then, all actions are justified – "right at the time." Acts of blame, then, often seem unjustified, gratuitous, and alien to those who are accused.. In terms of dialogue, the challenge is to locate alternative conversational entries that may serve sanctioning purposes without resorting to acts of blame (see McNamee & Gergen, 1998).

Organization as Disorganization

Negating and blaming may seriously impede the process of generative dialogue. However, there is a more subtle and ironic narrative of disorganization that requires special attention. To be succinct, if paradoxical, we propose that successful organizing establishes the grounds for disorganization. To elaborate, consider Bakhtin's (1981) important distinction between dialogue that functions *centripetally* (bringing language into a centralized form of organization), as opposed to *centrifugally* (disrupting or disorganizing centralized forms of understanding). In this sense what we have characterized as generative dialogue essentially functions centripetally to create effective organization. However, dialogue that brings organizational participants together into a shared space of understanding also functions in such a way that the dialogic traditions in which they are otherwise engaged are disrupted, suppressed, or in a word, disordered. Essentially the participants may come to embrace a particular reality, set of values, and practices that cut them away from other forms of life. The tendency is to become a "company man," "a bureaucrat," "a true believer," or "one dimensional." The result is a subtle negation of that which lies outside the sphere of organization. The centripital process simultaneously functions centrifugally. (Also see Baxter & Montgomery, 1998, on dialectic change as inherent in dialogue.)

This problem is exacerbated by a small group pattern long familiar to the social sciences, namely that of "in-group/out-group" formation. From the early work of Sherif (1966) to more recent accounts of group identity (Tajfel, 1981; Turner, 1991), researchers have noted a strong tendency for organized groups to become alienated from or hostile to those outside the group. In-group members come to celebrate their way of doing things, their ideals, and their members; other groups form a devalued exterior. They are discredited and suspicious. In more contemporary terms, Foucault's (1980) views of power/knowledge are apposite. As groups develop a shared vision of the real and the good, they tend to incorporate or suppress alien discourses. The hegemonic thrust of discursive communities tends to marginalize or alienate those who fall outside. Or, in more practical terms, as organizations become larger, more complex, and more geographically extended, so will multiple discursive communities emerge, each with a particular construction of the world, each with a potential distrust or animosity toward the others. Pockets of local organization – effective for carrying out the daily duties as understood within – carry with them potential resistances to other enclaves of meaning within the organization. The marketing division fails to appreciate the problems of Sales, Sales does not believe R&D is functioning effectively, the French subsidiary believes the home office in the U.S. is irrational, and so on. In sum, wherever dialogue is successful in organizing, there is a subtle undoing of organization, and an unleashing of potentials for intergroup negation. Within A. I. this danger should also be recognized.

Transformative Dialogue and the Reduction of Difference

In preceding sections we have focused on specific moves in dialogue that may contribute to both organization and disorganization. We turn finally to dialogic practices that may bridge the gap between alienated realities. Required here are moves in conversation that may sometimes differ substantially from those congenial to creating and sustaining a given reality, morality, or way of life. The challenge is that of bringing into productive synchrony groups that share solidified visions of the real and the good. We may speak, then, of *transformative dialogue*, a relational accomplishment that creates new spaces of meaning and enables the organization to restore its generative potentials (Gergen, McNamee & Barrett, 2001). In what follows we will consider a form of organized practice specifically focused on crossing boundaries (Gudykunst, 1998). Here we shall attempt to isolate those particular dialogic moves central to bringing about restorative change. At the same time we shall find the particular practice in question lacking in one major respect. Here we shall center on a key contribution of A. I. practices.

THE PUBLIC CONVERSATIONS PROJECT

The Public Conversation Project (PCP), founded in 1989, seeks to create an alternative to polarized debate by creating constructive dialogues between parties (see Chasin & Herzig, 1994; Chasin, Herzig, Roth, Chasin, Becker & Stains, 1996). Typically the PCP members work with groups that have a history of conflict and even violence. In some of their most important work, activists on both sides of the abortion debate were brought together in small groups for a meeting. The meeting began with a dinner in which participants were free to talk to one another about any issue except that of abortion. The dinner gave way to guided conversations in which participants specifically addressed the following questions:

(1) How did you get involved with this issue? What is your personal relationship or personal history with it?
(2) We would like to hear a little more about your particular beliefs and perspectives about the issues surrounding abortion. What is at the heart of the matter for you?

(3) Many people we've talked to have told us that within their approach to this issue they find some gray areas, some dilemmas about their own beliefs or even some conflicts. Do you experience any pockets of uncertainty or lesser certainty, any concerns, value conflicts, or mixed feelings that you may have and wish to share?

The first question enabled the participants to tell personal stories about events that shaped their views. Often they shared experiences from their own lives or the experience of a family member at a crisis moment. The second question gave participants an opportunity to express their personal, core beliefs about the abortion issue. Finally, participants were able to speak of their uncertainties or ambivalence. Participants in this and other projects have been almost univocal in their praises. Interestingly, in January 2001, six Boston women – public leaders from both sides of the abortion debate – revealed that they had been meeting in secret for six years after their participation in the project (see *Boston Globe*, Jan 28, 2001). Among other things the participants felt they learned to abandon polemical language; continued meeting enabled them to see "the dignity and goodness" of those they opposed. While not eschewing their original positions, they reported that they "learned to avoid being over reactive and disparaging the other side and to focus instead on affirming (our) respective causes."

What are the discursive moves that enabled the boundaries of animosity to be traversed? At the outset we find that the practice included certain generative moves in dialogue and avoided two more destructive possibilities. In the generative case, both the conversation at dinner and the session in which participants spoke of the "heart of the matter" for them, their "opponents" were cast in the role of respectful listening. The act of listening without responding with contentious questions subtly served an *affirming* function. At the same time, by steering the conversation away from uncompromising theoretical issues, few *destructive differences* entered the conversation. Finally, the dialogue was arranged in such a way that *acts of blame* were not permitted. However, the public conversations format also points to the importance of:

Narrative Revelation. Listening to the first person narratives of those to whom one is otherwise opposed seems to have a powerful ameliorating effect. The reasons are several. First, such narratives are *easily comprehensible*; from our earliest years we are exposed to the narrative form common in personal storytelling, and we are more fully prepared to understand this form as opposed to abstract arguments. Further, stories can invite *fuller audience engagement* than does the explication of abstract ideas. In hearing stories we generate images, thrive on the drama, suffer and celebrate with the speaker. Finally, the personal story tends to *generate acceptance* as opposed to resistance. If it is "your story, your experience," then the audience can scarcely say "you are wrong." Narratives do not invite opposition but indulgence.

Self-Reflexivity. One unfortunate aspect of traditional conversation is that we are positioned as *unified egos*. That is, we are constructed as singular, coherent selves, not fragmented and multiple. To be incoherent is subject to ridicule; moral inconsistency is grounds for scorn. Thus, as we encounter people whose positions differ from ours, we tend to represent ourselves one-dimensionally, ensuring that all our statements form a unified, seamless web. As a result, when we enter a relationship defined by our differences, commitment to unity is likely to maintain our distance. And if the integrity or validity of one's coherent front is threatened by the other, we may move toward polarizing combat. In this respect the invitation to explore one's "gray areas" or doubts releases the demand for coherence. In Baxter and Montgomery's (1998) terms, we demonstrate one of the most important dialogic skills, namely the "ability to recognize multiple, simultaneously salient systems." More broadly, self-reflexivity may be only one member of a family of moves that will inject polyvocality into the dialogue. For example, in their conflict work, Pearce and Littlejohn (1997) often employ "third person listening," in which one member of an antagonistic group may be asked to step out of the conversation and to observe the interchange. By moving from the first person position, in which one is representing a position, to a third person stance, one can observe the conflict with other criteria at hand (e.g. "Is this a productive form of interaction?" "What improvements might be made?").

APPRECIATIVE INQUIRY AND CO-CREATION

Appreciative Inquiry stands out from traditional participatory action and collaborative inquiry modes (e.g. Denzin & Lincoln, 1995, 2002; Reason & Bradbury, 2002), which are constrained by problem-solving orientations in which participants are encouraged to notice and talk about breakdowns in systems or relationships and plan action around solutions that address these problems. Deficit discourses, as for example that used in all editions of the *Diagnostic & Statistical Manual of Mental Diseases* (DSM) function to create a disphoric world of deficiency and decline. (See Gergen, 1994, for a more detailed critique of how deficit discourse expands problem talk and negativity.) As is clear from all of the descriptions in this volume, A. I. claims that organizations are not problems to be solved but are "centers of infinite relational capacity, alive with infinite imagination, open, indeterminate, and ultimately – in terms of the future – a mystery" (Cooperrider & Barrett, 2002, p. 236). A. I. practitioners begin with the belief that topic choice and question formation are the most important moves in shaping dialogue. Much effort is made toward creating questions around positive topics that guide attention toward peak experiences and strengths. The challenge is to ask questions that deliberately focus on those factors that contribute to the system's operating at its very best. Participants are encouraged to develop an appreciative eye, to explore the possibility that every human system, no matter how dysfunctional or conflictual, has elements of beauty, goodness, and value.

Appreciative inquiry facilitates transformational dialogue in many ways. As we have seen, there is a premium placed on mutual affirmation; productive differences are encouraged; individual blame is avoided; and, personal narratives create a strong sense of mutuality. However, A. I. adds an enormously important element to the transformative processes.

The Co-Creation of New Worlds. Appreciative inquiry facilitates transformational dialogue in many ways. As we have seen, there is a premium placed on mutual affirmation; productive differences are encouraged; individual blame is avoided; and, personal narratives create a strong sense of mutuality. However, A. I. adds an enormously important element to the transformative processes; specifically participants become engaged in the co-creation of new worlds. As stated earlier, transformative dialogue is essentially aimed at facilitating the collaborative construction of new realities. Required are transformations that spring from what might be called *imaginary moments*, in which participants join in developing visions of a desired future. These imaginary moments not only sow the seeds for constructing a common reality and vision of the good, but they also shift the position of the participants from combative to collaborative. As participants move toward common purpose, so do they redefine the "Other," and lay the groundwork for a conception of "us." Once the vision of the future is jointly established, the planners become co-authors and colleagues. This is precisely what is achieved as A. I. participants engage in designing new futures. In effect, the Design phase within A. I. practices represents a significant contribution to the process of transformative dialogue.

To be sure, the work of the Public Conversations Project and appreciative inquiry practitioners does not exhaust the possibilities for transformative dialogue. The interested reader is directed as well to the important work of the Public Dialogue Consortium (see Pearce & Pearce, 2001; Spano, 2001) on community change. The emphasis on a pragmatic approach that is oriented to an aesthetic appreciation of possibilities to conflict negotiation through hybridization and improvisation as brought forth by Wagner-Pacifici (2000) is highly recommended. In addition, a fascinating project involving the development of a leaderless group – a symphony orchestra – as described by Richard Hackman (2002) can be found at www.Arts.endow.gov/pub/lessons/casestudies/Colorado.html.

Further resources on dialogue may be located through several websites, including: www.uia.org/dialogue, www.thataway.org/dialogue, www.studycircles.org, and www.un.org/Dialogue.

LOOKING INTO THE FUTURE

A. I. has been a remarkably successful grassroots change process. Its reliance on democratic participatory methods and its contribution to a just society also are among its major dialogic strengths. *As* we have attempted to demonstrate, dialogue is essential to the vitality of an organization, and neglect of dialogic practices can create internal schisms and ultimately the collapse of an organization (Gergen, Gergen & Barrett, in press; Hudson, 2001; Zuniga, Nagda & Sevig, 2002). In this chapter we have developed a view of dialogue as discursive coordination, and within this framework moved on to consider dialogic practices that bring organization into being, that destroy organization, and that enable conflicting domains of meaning to be re-coordinated.

Yet, these are only beginnings. We have already noted the lack of attention in this analysis to non-verbal forms of discursive action, to material context, and to cultural and historical variations. A full treatment of dialogue should also be attentive to issues of power and voice. Deetz (1992) warns us that the institutions of the ordinary – and particularly the relations of power – may preclude the kind of dialogue from which organizational change may ensue. In the same vein, we have not discussed the many possible relational configurations in which dialogue may take place. Various configurations of gender, age, kinship, friendship, and social class might well reveal differing forms of effective dialogue (Duck, 2002; Friere, 1970). Further, Myerson (1994) draws our attention to "double arguability," essentially a distinction between the interactions of the interlocutors in a dialogue and the specific issue at stake. Ultimately we must consider the relationship between what is said, the way in which it is said, and the form of relationship (Taylor, 1999). The present analysis has focused exclusively on the former domain, while neglecting potentially significant issues of dialogic content. Finally, our analysis has failed to make contact with issues of dialogic ethics. Should there be ethical imperatives for effective dialogue (see for example, Baxter & Montgomery, 1998; Habermas, 1993; Krippendorff, 1989); are there ethical assumptions already implicit, or is it possible that ethical imperatives may interfere with the contextual necessities and generative potentials of dialogue? Perhaps we can look forward to an infinite unfolding of the dialogue on dialogue, and a continuing enrichment of practices.

NOTE

1. Developed by Suresh Srivastva, David Cooperrider and their colleagues in the 1980s. (See Cooperrider, Sorensen, Whitney & Yaeger, 2000; Cooperrider & Srivastva, 1987; Fry, Barrett, Seiling & Whitney, 2002; Ludema, Cooperrider & Barrett, 2000.)

REFERENCES

Anderson, H. (1997). *Conversation, language, and possibilities: A postmodern approach to therapy.* New York: Harper Collins.

Anderson, H., Cooperrider, D., Gergen, K. J., Gergen, M., McNamee, S., & Whitney, D. (2001). *The appreciative organization.* Swarthmore, PA: Taos Institute.

Austin, J. L. (1962). *How to do things with words.* New York: Oxford University Press.

Bakhtin, M. M. (1981). *The dialogic imagination: Four essays by M. M. Bakhtin.* In: C. Emerson & M. Holquist (Eds). Austin: University of Texas Press.

Barbules, N. C. (1994). *Dialogue in teaching.* New York: Teachers College Press.

Baumgartel, H. (1959, December). Using employee questionnaire results for improving organizations: The survey 'feedback' experiment. *Kansas Business Review*, 2–6.

Baxter, L., & Montgomery, B. (1998). *Dialectical approaches to studying personal relationships.* Hillsdale, NJ: Lawrence Erlbaum.

Billig, M. (1987). *Arguing and thinking.* Cambridge: Cambridge University Press.

Bohm, D. (1996). *On dialogue.* In: L. Nichol (Ed.). New York: Routledge.

Boje, D. M. (2001). *Narrative methods for organizational and communication research.* London: Sage.

Bruner, J. (1990). *Acts of meaning.* Cambridge: Harvard University Press.

Cooperrider, D. L., Sorensen, P. F., Whitney, D., & Yaeger, T. F. (2000). *Appreciative inquiry: Rethinking human organization toward a positive theory of change.* Champagne, IL: Stipes.

Cooperrider, D. L., & Srivastva, S. (1987). Appreciative inquiry in organizational life. In: W. A. Pasmore & R. W. Woodman (Eds), *Research in Organization Change and Development* (Vol. 1, pp. 129–169). Greenwich, CT: JAI Press.

Cottle, T. J. (2002). On narratives and the sense of self. *Qualitative Inquiry, 8*, 535–549.

Craig, R. T., & Tracy, K. (Eds) (1983). *Conversational coherence.* Beverly Hills, CA: Sage.

Czarniawska, B. (1997). *Narrating the organization.* Chicago: University of Chicago Press.

Deetz, S. (1992). *Democracy in an age of corporate colonization.* Albany: State University of New York Press.

Duck, S. (2002). Hypertext in the key of G: Three types of "history:" As influences on conversational structure and flow. *Communication Theory, 12*, 41–62.

Eisenberg, E. M., & Goodall, H. L., Jr. (1993). *Organizational communication: Balancing creativity and constraint.* New York: St. Martin's Press.

Foucault, M. (1980). *Power/knowledge.* New York: Pantheon.

Friere, P. (1970). *Pedogogy of the oppressed.* New York: Seabury Press.

Fry, R., Barrett, F., Seiling, J., & Whitney, D. (2002). *Appreciative inquiry and organizational transformation: Reports from the field.* Westport, CT: Quorum Books.

Garfinkel, H. (1965). *Studies in ethnomethodology.* Englewood Cliffs, NJ: Prentice-Hall.

Gergen, K. J. (1994). *Realities and relationships.* Cambridge: Harvard University Press.

Gergen, K. J. (1999). *An invitation to social construction.* London: Sage.

Gergen, K. J., Gergen, M., & Barrett, F. (in press). Dialogue: Life and death of the organization. In: D. Grant, C. Hardy, C. Oswick, N. Phillips & L. Putnam (Eds), *Handbook of Organizational Discourse.* Thousand Oaks, CA: Sage.

Gergen, K. J., McNamee, S., & Barrett, F. (2001). Toward transformative dialogue. *International Journal of Public Administration, 24,* 697–707.

Grudin, R. (1996). *On dialogue: An essay in free thought.* Boston, NY: Houghton Mifflin.

Gudykunst, W. B. (1998). *Bridging differences: Effective intergroup communication.* Thousand Oaks, CA: Sage.

Habermas, J. (1993). *Justification and application: Remarks on discourse ethics.* Cambridge, MA: MIT Press.

Harré, R., & Gillette, G. (1994). *The discursive mind.* London: Sage.

Hawes, L. C. (1999). The dialogics of conversation: Power, control, and vulnerability. *Communication Theory, 9,* 229–264.

Hazen, M. A. (1993). Toward polyphonic organization. *Journal of Organizational Change Management, 6,* 15–26.

Hudson, J. (2001). A directory of intergroup dialogue programs and organizations. In: D. Schoem & S. Hurtado (Eds), *Intergroup Dialogue: Deliberative Democracy in School, College, Community and Workplace* (pp. 345–352). Ann Arbor, MI: University of Michigan.

Isaacs, W. N. (1993). Taking flight: Dialogue, collective thinking, and organizational learning. *Organizational Dynamics, 22,* 24–39.

Jandt, F. E. (2001). *Intercultural communication.* Thousand Oaks, CA: Sage.

Krippendorff, K. (1989). On the ethics of constructing communication. In: B. Dervin, L. Grossberg, B. O'Keefe & E. Wartella (Eds), *Rethinking Communication. Paradigm Issues* (Vol. 1, pp. 23–45). Newbury Park, CA: Sage.

Lewin, K. (1951). *Field theory in social science.* New York: Harper.

Ludema, J. D., Cooperrider, D. L., & Barrett, F. J. (2000). Appreciative inquiry: The power of the unconditional positive question. In: P. Reason & H. Bradbury (Eds), *Handbook of Action Research* (pp. 189–199). Thousand Oaks, CA: Sage.

Maranhao, T. (Ed.) (1990). *The interpretation of dialogue.* Chicago: University of Chicago Press.

Markova, I., Graumann, C. F., & Foppa, K. (Eds) (1995). *Mutualities in dialogue.* Cambridge: Cambridge University Press.

McNamee, S., & Gergen, K. J. (1998). *Relational responsibility.* Thousand Oaks, CA: Sage.

Myerson, G. (1994). *Rhetoric, reason and society.* London: Sage.

Palshaugen, O. (2001). The use of words: Improving enterprises by improving their conversations. In: P. Reason & H. Bradbury (Eds), *Handbook of Action Research* (pp. 209–218). Thousand Oaks, CA: Sage.

Pearce, W. B. (1989). *Communication and the human condition.* Carbondale, IL: Southern Illinois University Press.

Pearce, W. B., & Pearce, K. (2001). Extending the theory of the coordinated management of meaning (CMM) through a Community Dialogue Process. *Communication Theory, 10,* 405–423.

Putnam, L. L., & Fairhurst, G. T. (2000). Discourse analysis in organizations. In: F. M. Jablin & L. Putnam (Eds), *The New Handbook of Organizational Communication: Advances in Theory, Research, and Methods* (pp. 78–136). Thousand Oaks, CA: Sage.

Rahim, S. A. (1994). Participatory development communication as a dialogical process. In: S. White, K. Sadanandan Nair & J. Ashcroft (Eds), *Participatory Communication, Working for Change and Development* (pp. 112–134). New Delhi: Sage.

de Saussure, F. (1974). *Course in general linguistics*. London: Fontana.

Shaw, P. (2002). *Changing conversations in organizations: A complexity approach to change*. London, New York: Routledge.

Sherif, M. (1966). *In common predicament: Social psychology of intergroup conflict and cooperation*. Boston: Houghton Mifflin.

Shotter, J. (1984). *Social accountability and selfhood*. Oxford: Blackwell.

Spano, S. (2001). *Public dialogue and participatory democracy*. Cresskill, NJ: Hampton Press.

Tajfel, H. (1981). *Human groups and social categories: Studies in social psychology*. London: Cambridge University Press.

Taylor, J. R. (1999). What is 'organizational communication'?: Communication as a dialogic of text and conversation. *Communication Review*, *3*, 21–63.

Thatchenkery, T. J., & Upadhyaya, P. (1996). Organizations as a play of multiple and dynamic discourses: An example from a global social change organization. In: D. J. Boje, R. P. Gephart & T. J. Thatchenkery (Eds), *Postmodern Management and Organization Theory* (pp. 308–330). Thousand Oaks, CA: Sage.

Ting-Toomey, S., & Oetzel, J. G. (2001). *Managing intercultural conflict effectively*. Thousand Oaks, CA: Sage.

Turner, J. C. (1991). *Social influence*. Milton Keynes, England: Open University Press.

Vygotsky, L. S. (1986). *Thought and language*. Alex Kozulin (Translator). Cambridge, MA: MIT Press.

Wagner-Pacifici, R. (2000). *Theorizing the standoff: Contingency in action*. New York: Cambridge University Press.

Weick, K. E. (1995). *Sensemaking in organizations*. Thousand Oaks, CA: Sage.

Wells, G. (1999). *Dialogic inquiry, towards a sociocultural practice and theory of education*. Cambridge: Cambridge University Press.

Wetherell, M., Taylor, S., & Yates, S. J. (2001a). *Discourse as data: A guide for analysis*. London: Sage & Open University Press.

Wetherell, M., Taylor, S., & Yates, S. J. (2001b). *Discourse theory and practice*. London: Sage & Open University Press.

Wittgenstein, L. (1963). *Philosophical investigations* (Translated by G. E. M. Anscombe). London: Blackwell.

Yankelovich, D. (1999). *The magic of dialogue: Transforming conflict into cooperation*. New York: Simon & Schuster.

Zuniga, X., Nagda, B. A., & Sevig, T. D. (2002). Intergroup dialogues: An educational model for cultivating engagement across differences. *Equity and Excellence*, *35*, 7–17.

APPRECIATIVE INQUIRY IN THE AGE OF THE NETWORK

Jeffrey Stamps and Jessica Lipnack

ABSTRACT

This chapter is about the relationship between Networked Organizations and Appreciative Inquiry. To set a context, Theory about networks is related to the expressed needs of Appreciative Inquiry. Stories follow, from both appreciative and network perspectives. Ideas are put to work through practice as expressed by method – consisting of principles, practices, and processes. Further, method is embedded in technology to support functioning networks. In research, we look at learning about human systems and suggest that online digital places form natural laboratories to collect, analyze, and synthesize data. Concluding with Search, we revisit the question of consciousness in human systems.

INTRODUCTION

In the early years of the 21st century we have passed the "point of no return" in the transition from the Industrial-Bureaucratic Age to the Information-Network Age. This century-long change process was tipped by the sudden coalescence of the World-Wide Web in the early 1990s, a combination of sufficient computer-communications infrastructure with the invention of the browser and the deceptively simple "link." With the Internet, the myriad islands of digital technology become irrevocably connected as a globally-networked computer, and

Constructive Discourse and Human Organization
Advances in Appreciative Inquiry, Volume 1, 29–55
Copyright © 2004 by Elsevier Ltd.
All rights of reproduction in any form reserved
ISSN: 1475-9152/doi:10.1016/S1475-9152(04)01002-6

with the Web, people connect with people and information anytime-anywhere in a seamless if chaotic global community.

Decades before the net snapped into place, networks were recognized as the emergent signature form of organization in the Information Age, just as bureaucracy was for the Industrial era, hierarchy was for the Agricultural, and small groups were for the original Nomadic era (Hine, 1976; Stamps & Lipnack, 1982, 1994). As the Information Age has matured, networks have appeared at all levels of organization, from small group virtual teams (Stamps & Lipnack, 1997, 2000), to enterprise-spanning teamnets (Stamps & Lipnack, 1993), to inter-enterprise and cross-country distributed global organizations.

Appreciative Inquiry arose in the late 1980s in reaction to the problem-oriented logical-positivist science that provided the intellectual foundation for the Industrial Era. Cooperrider and Srivastva (1987) generated the idea as an extension of the trend to action-research initiated by Kurt Lewin in mid-century, embracing the "sociorationalist" approach to science propounded by Gergen (1982). The sociorationalist views human reality as a constructed social reality immersed in a symbolic universe. Our ways of living and working together are not immutable givens, but rather inventions we create together drawing on shared images and languages. Human social science lives everyday with the effects of Heisenbergian indeterminacy as our "instruments" of investigation and assessment directly influence and help shape the very systems being studied. Thus, in the human domain, theory *becomes* practice. Appreciative Inquiry asserts that the moral choice is to discover and follow positive processes and projected images for the created human future.

As awareness has grown that *how* we conduct our search for human knowledge invariably becomes part of the created human reality, it is imperative to examine our method of study and the changes it induces in practice with an eye to *what* direction the social construction can and, most heretically for a science, *should* take. At the same time, as the consequences of our actions synergistically add up to new whole ways of being together, we are obliged to feed back our experience into research and theory to improve our understanding and subsequently enable better and more healthy practice.

Appreciative Inquiry and Networked Organizations are more than just coincidently linked in the epochal transition from one seminal human age to the next. They are mutually entwined in both theory and practice. Cooperrider and Srivastva suggest that action research, in the form of Appreciative Inquiry, supports "the emergence of a more egalitarian 'post-bureaucratic' form of organization," which to us is already evident as the network. Conversely, our experience with networks and virtual teams suggest that the mental models people have and the way they collectively develop and frame their purposes have everything to do with their ability to generate and sustain distributed organizations that are successful in achieving their goals.

The ideas we explore in this chapter suggest complementary premises:

- Networks arise as the natural organizational outcomes of an ongoing Appreciative Inquiry process; and
- Appreciative Inquiry, recognized or not, undergirds the development of successful distributed human organizations.

Stories illustrating these premises are told in a later section, one recounting the appreciative voyage of the Mountain Forum and its birth of a network, another telling of Shell's use of positive questions to flesh out its aspirations as a Networked Community.

There is practical power in bringing these two conceptual frameworks together. By anticipating the formation of networks, providing appropriate leadership, and supplying environmental nutrients for their development, the remarkable possibilities unleashed by Appreciative Inquiry processes acquire a robust internal organizational infrastructure that sustains the long-term promise of a collectively envisioned future. Where the focus is on people creating purposeful and relationship-rich virtual teams and networks, the action-research methodology of Appreciative Inquiry provides a strong and continuously improving developmental process that scales from very small associations to very large interventions.

What projects the impact of the application of these frameworks far beyond academic interest is the awesome magnifying effect of digital technology and the burgeoning electronic communications infrastructure. The roots of Appreciative Inquiry in face-to-face interactions, ranging from the gathering of appreciative stories to the remarkably effective Appreciative Summits that literally bring a representation of the whole system into a room for a multi-day launch process, become supplemented and enormously extended as ways are found to do Appreciative Inquiry virtually, particularly in the post-summit period. Indeed, a comprehensive approach to Appreciative Inquiry would combine face-to-face with virtual methods to create a process that includes both synchronous (same time, whether face-to-face or virtual) and asynchronous (different time) interactions. And the ability to create new "places" for human organizations to form, grow, and perform online vastly expands the territory that an appreciative engagement can cover. Indeed, with virtual methods, Appreciative Inquiry becomes available to connect and engage the immensely vaster worlds of non-geographically defined groups of people.

While we will be co-relating networks and Appreciative Inquiry, our expertise lies in network theory and practice, so our emphasis is on exposing networks to the appreciative community. Our underlying hope is that by knowing more about networks, practitioners will be more successful in helping people create structures and processes that persist and grow long after the initiating activities, stories, dreams, and designs fade.

THEORY

One of the primary motivators for the rise of Appreciative Inquiry was the perceived need for theory to inform and guide action research. Cooperrider and Srivastva (1987) call for a "generative theory" that serves as "a means for both understanding *and* improving social practice." "Good theory," they contend, "is one of the most powerful means we have for helping social systems evolve, adapt, and creatively alter their patterns over time." We concur with this engaged assessment of the role of theory in the life of growing social systems, and have integrated theory with our network research and practice.

As action-researchers, we have engaged as 1st-order participant-practitioners, both in our early experience as part of social-change movements, and later as part of leading-edge business organizations. As 2nd-order action-researchers, we have used the concepts and methods of networking to investigate and understand networks, thus giving rise to theory that could in turn be practiced and tested in the real world. Finally, we started with 3rd-order meta-theory, that there are emergent patterns of organizations that can be understood systemically, to guide our original research. We have continued to refine the meta-theory into a general language of networks that serves in the expression of methods that help people understand and act in networked organizations, large and small.

Network Theory and Appreciative Inquiry

To emphasize their assertion of the importance and power of theory to aid in helping people co-evolve more effective and healthy human systems and societies, Cooperrider and Srivastva (1987) offer five ways theory functions in this role. In each way, network theory not only fulfills its promise in its target domain, but also provides a potential framework for Appreciative Inquiry in its formulation of a theory of "intentional collective action . . . to help evolve the normative vision and will of a group, organization, or society as a whole."

(1) *Establishing a conceptual and contextual frame.* The network model, both in its shorthand (People, Purpose, Links, and Time) and its more elaborated taxonomic form, provides a lens for seeing the essential elements of organization, even types that are very difficult to grasp because of their distributed form.

(2) *Providing presumptions of logic.* Structured on a very common input-output systems model, network theory offers not only the (components + linear process + feedback) logic of systemic construction, but also a checklist of interrelated elements to examine in the context of an already defined whole.

(3) *Transmitting a system of values.* As a whole, the network model by nature embraces a participatory, engaged, values-oriented approach to organization, as well as providing active elements of purpose and relationship that both define and distribute shared values. Moreover, basic values like trust and integrity are essential for the vitality of the network itself.

(4) *Creating a group-building language.* Network theory's potency as a shared language for co-construction is illustrated by how well it translates into practice. More personally, in workshops and consulting engagements, we have frequently been told that an important contribution of the model is in providing people a common language for discussing and creating new organizational forms to meet their felt needs.

(5) *Extending visions of possibility.* In networks, people seem to understand that the means is an essential part of the envisioned end, that how they organize and undertake the journey greatly impacts the quality and viability of the end result. Since the theory embodies a participatory and relatively open-ended process approach, not infrequently people find new possibilities beyond those initially conceived, with sometimes unexpectedly positive consequences.

At the end of their seminal article, Cooperrider and Srivastva suggest four principles for guiding Appreciative Inquiry research "into the social potential of organizational life." They contend that such research should be:

- *Appreciative,*
- *Applicable,*
- *Provocative,* and
- *Collaborative.*

To cohere and exist at all, social systems must necessarily have characteristics of order and life greater than the complementary entropic forces of problems and disintegration. Successful networks must find *appreciative,* positive images of the future in order to create the impetus for formation and the will to sustain and grow. Appreciative Inquiry offers concepts, methods, and experience to help people find the positive core that enables them to form healthy networks.

Networks existed in action long before their "discovery" by writers and theoreticians. The theory we have propounded here has been engaged in the real world of *application* since its inception more than two decades ago. It has been tested by thousands of people with whom we have worked directly, and applied by many more thousands who have read our books. As a final assertion of applicability, we have recently embedded our network theory-infused methodology into a web-based technology that serves to help people create and operate in distributed networks and virtual teams.

As the emergent organizational form of a new era of human existence, networks are frequently perceived as *provocative* challenges to the traditional way of doing things, which inevitably in the modern world means the status quo hierarchy-bureaucracy so familiar to us all. Networks are by nature provocative now in this turbulent transitional time between eras, but in the long run they will become the new norm.

Finally, human networks are in their essence *collaborative*. Indeed, in this time of expansive communications options and increasing recognition of the reality of relationships, collaborative processes like Appreciative Inquiry that lead to co-created social structures will most likely adopt network forms at whatever scale is applicable to the system undergoing change.

General Systems Theory

To understand networks, we have stood on the shoulders of systems.

The first breach in the dominant scientific worldview of the Industrial Age occurred with the transformation within Physics from the presumption of immutable Newtonian Laws to the complexities of Relativity and Quantum Mechanics. Even as the most precise branch of science was throwing off the shackles of the classical logical-positivist analytic-only view, the data-impoverished and law-jealous social sciences were building a siloed, bureaucratic, measurement-centric model of theory and practice, most notably in the organizational fields by Fredrick Winslow Taylor. What became interesting in social sciences became what could be quantified, much like the Greek myth that tells of searching for a lost object under a street lamp because "that is where the light is." Unfortunately, most of what's important to human beings and their associations is not measurable in the classic sense – in the human domain, the qualitative nature of reality overwhelms the quantitative.

But measurement is not everything. Even as action-research was arising to counter the "objective," un-engaged, data-driven paradigm for organizational research and development, a new approach to the disparate, disconnected sciences arose. In 1949, Ludwig von Bertalanffy proposed an integrative approach to knowledge called General Systems Theory (Von Bertalanffy, 1968). Von Bertalanffy's premise was that common laws could be discerned in the realms of the separate sciences, physical, biological, and social. One example is the logistic growth curve (popularly known as the "S" curve), whose mathematic expression could be seen in phenomenon as different as the formation of galaxies, the growth of bacteria in a petrie dish, and the spread of new ideas in societies. Indeed, this cross-discipline principle underlies the "life cycle," which is both an explanatory vehicle for the development of human organizations, and the basis of processes and practices intended to help such organizations develop in an effective and healthy manner. And, not incidentally, the Appreciative Inquiry 4-D Cycle of Discover-Dream-Design-Destiny is a variant of the general life cycle pattern of change and development.

By the mid-1950s, this idea had given birth to a movement, best exemplified in the formation of the Society for General Systems Research by von Bertalanffy (a biologist), Kenneth Boulding (an economist), Anatol Rapoport (a mathematician), and Ralph Gerard (another biologist). Over the next few decades many of the systems ideas were gradually absorbed into mainstream sciences, such as synergy (the "whole is more than the sum of the parts") and the organization of complex systems in levels (whole-part hierarchies). But the overarching intention of systems to become the dominant scientific paradigm never caught on in the "hard" sciences that felt that they had all the robust theory they needed, thank you very much. The systems perspective flourished, however, in the softer sciences, which grew up without a firm foundation for theory. While it is far from a universally accepted paradigm, almost every human science discipline has a major school of thought based in systems theory.

As the early systems theorists were looking for mathematically expressible lawfulness across disciplines, there soon emerged a wide spread recognition that many of the most important phenomena, particularly in the human domain, could not be rendered in numbers and formulas. Hence, verbal models, common patterns, and "fruitful taxonomies" became legitimate expressions of systems theory. Rapoport's (1970) soft definition encompasses the very broad range of systems that includes people and their complexities, and it recognizes the role of the human knower in the apprehension of a system: "A system is a portion of the world that is perceived as a unit and that is able to maintain its 'identity' in spite of changes going on in it."

As the systems idea has evolved, it has moved from merely recognizing the reality of relationships against the dominant materialist worldview that sees only things, to asserting the ontological primacy of relationships. A half-century after the systems idea was first formulated, a group tasked by the International Society for the Systems Sciences (the successor group to the Society for General Systems Research) to prepare a primer on systems asserted: "Systems thinking's fundamental concept is the connecting relationship – what things are doing to each other." They defined systems this way: "A System is a Family of Meaningful Relationships (between the members acting as one whole)" (Mandel, 2000).

Things are as they are related. The world is interconnected and interdependent. This is the context in which we have understood networks. And this relational context is also the primal ground of Appreciative Inquiry.

Network Theory

Networks are social systems where relational reality is preeminent in the language used to express the organizational construct. People naturally form a clear model of a networked organization as a system of nodes and links based on common metaphors such as a spider's web or a fisherman's net. Our general model of networks, honed over 20 years iterating through cycles of theory-practice, consists of four dimensions: People, Purpose, Links, and Time. In brief, networks are people (individuals and/or groups) interacting interdependently for a purpose over time.

- *People*, recognized both in the singular as individuals and in the plural as groups, are the nodes in an organizational network and give the model scalability from very small groups (of individuals) to humanity-wide associations of countries.
- *Purpose* expresses the motivation and intent of human groups – what makes a human system meaningful – and is the articulated resultant of the quest for a shared vision as people co-create their organizations.
- *Links* embrace the essential nature of relationships, reaching from very ephemeral connections like trust and love to very concrete linkages such as those provided by communications technologies.
- *Time*, the fourth fundamental dimension, reminds us that human systems are living systems and not machines, so they arise and persist in time, experiencing events as marked on a calendar as well as organic processes of birth, growth, maturity, and death.

The next level of detail in the network model reflects a construction that is both faithful to the needs of theoretical rigor and mindful of the practice consequences of theory formulation in social systems. Elements of the network model are arranged in a taxonomy that is structured by the most basic systems framework: inputs, processes, outputs, and a feedback loop. Because of the common character of the elements in the columns and rows of the taxonomy, we label this assemblage a "periodic table."

We have discussed this model in detail elsewhere (see especially Lipnack & Stamps, 2000), but will elaborate it somewhat by looking briefly at the elements of one dimension, Purpose.

- *Goals* are the major components of an overall Purpose, which might be characterized as a mission or charter. They are most often generated in conversation, and represent aspiration and intention, the motivation for "flinging ourselves forward" into an uncertain but desired future.
- *Tasks* are the activities and processes themselves, the transformations inside the "black box" of the system that connect motivating goals with specific outcomes.
- *Results* are the concrete outputs of intentional activity, and are often contained within goal statements as targets we aspire to hit. They are relatively thing-like, reifications of ephemeral goals achieved.

While the model is framed to grasp the essential characteristics of networks, it functions more broadly as an explanatory vehicle for all forms of human organizations. Since, in our view, human organizational capabilities are cumulative, meaning that as each new age of human civilization provoked new forms, older forms were subsumed in the new. So characteristics of small groups are included in hierarchy, which is reflected in bureaucracy, and networks encompass all prior organizational forms. This is easily seen in networks where the comprising organizations are themselves dominantly earlier forms, such as military alliances, global associations of countries, or grassroots networks made up of small local groups. So it is essential that a model of networks be comprehensive enough to include earlier organizational forms.

STORIES

The telling of stories is basic to Appreciative Inquiry. Collecting stories that communicate positive possibilities is the essential first step in a transformation process. It is the foundation for (1) Discovery, the first stage of the 4-D Cycle of (2) Dream, (3) Design, and (4) Destiny (e.g. Cooperrider & Diana Whitney, 1999). For networks, too, stories play essential generative roles in conveying the underlying purpose and promise to the players in a forming organization, in providing the elements of socialization for new members, and reinforcing relationships through the repetition of common values.

In the context of organization, stories historically have been used to support the status quo, archetypically in tribal cultures. Where stories are used for generative or transformative processes, they are often deliberately initiated through questions. With the sociorationalist recognition that the question and its form (if not its medium, as in McLuhan's "the medium is the message") impacts what is said and how it is said, means that the responsible practitioner-researcher must carefully choose the general direction where the story-teller is to be led in the process of discovery. Using story-telling in action, particularly in an intentional context such as starting a network or an Appreciative Inquiry, suggests that the discovery process is driven by theory, whether consciously or, as is the usual case, unconsciously.

In our six books on networks, we have always combined stories, theory, and practice – and led with stories. Presented early to an audience of readers or listeners, stories help us to believe that there is a "there" there, something worth paying attention to, a reason to follow the discourse into more challenging theory and practice. Two examples illustrate the complementary premises that Appreciative Inquiry and networks are closely interrelated.

Mountain Forum: An Appreciative Inquiry Story About a Network

In the summer of 1998, one of the authors accompanied a UN mission to Asia to study the effectiveness of networks. Among the stops was Katmandu, Nepal, at ICIMOD, the International Centre for Integrated Mountain Development. This intergovernmental organization was founded in 1983 to support sustainable mountain development in the 2100-mile-long Hindu Kush-Himalaya mountain range, which passes through Afghanistan, Bangladesh, Bhutan, China, India, Myanmar, and Pakistan as well as Nepal. In telling this story (2000), we contrasted the vast historical span of communications capabilities represented in ICIMOD's operations: while it took a month to carry a message to northwestern Nepal, and a month to get a reply, since 1996 the Katmandu office has been connected by a very fast T1 line to the Internet and enmeshed in ongoing global conversations and activities about mountain regions.

ICIMOD, we learn from an extensive case study of a successful Appreciative Inquiry process published by Cooperrider and Kathryn Kaczmarski (in Cooperrider & Dutton, 1999), is only part of a larger story about mountain organizing worldwide and the establishment of a global electronic network to connect the many centers of activity. As regional mountain organizations formed, global mountain issues first became recognized at the Earth Summit in 1992, when a chapter on mountain ecosystems made it onto the world's agenda. This led to a series of meetings in 1994 convened by the UN's Food and Agriculture Organization to prepare a global conference on the Mountain Agenda, which took place in Lima, Peru, in February, 1995. Lima was highly successful and underscored the need for an ongoing effort. An Initial Organizing Committee was formed and held its seminal meeting in September of that same year.

In the early stages of the organizing meeting, people shared stories and made metaphors about the form of the organization they would like to see emerge. Most notable was the clear articulation of what people didn't want: "no one . . . articulated a vision of a conventional hierarchy: a secretariat with a secretary general, an organization with a large center and physical structure, and so on." However, one theme repeatedly expressed at this and prior meetings was the "need for an electronic information network," making concrete a key intention from the earliest meetings in Lima, which was "to create an ongoing network for information sharing and mutual learning, leading to innovative partnerships to implement actions."

When, on the last day of the committee meeting, the organizing form finally snapped into place, it was a network – a coalition of organizations, "nodes," that would bridge the local and global, acting together without a permanent center, where "any organization would be able to communicate directly with another through the network without traveling through any one node." And how would they connect? "The electronic information network would be a primary means of enacting mutual support across geographic and organizational boundaries, advancing the Mountain Agenda through information sharing and connecting all concerned parties." And so it happened. The next year, ICIMOD created its web site and connected to the net – and to all its sister mountain organizations as well as the worldwide community of related groups and individuals interested in mountain cultures and sustainability.

Reading the Mountain Forum Appreciative Inquiry story, we saw networking processes at work, the emergence of a network organization, and the symbiotic relationship of the technological support of an electronic network. This is a story about how some of the most marginalized peoples on the planet successfully organized as a network for mutual benefit. Hine (1976), perhaps the earliest observer of networks as the "future socio-cultural paradigm," wrote that this new form was emerging at the two extremes of society, among the poorest social movements and among the richest leading edge global companies. Which brings us to Shell.

Shell: A Network Story with AI

Royal Dutch/Shell is one of the largest and oldest businesses in the world, formed a century ago on a handshake between an English and Dutch company, a handshake that today still remains as the legal foundation of this enterprise. In 1991, Shell Oil Company, the U.S. and largest component of what is known as "The Group," reported its worst results ever. The reasons were the usual for an old-line company caught up in the rapid change environment of a surging global economy and the emergence of hundreds of niche competitors at every point on the value chain

... finding oil to delivering it to your gas tank. What was unusual was Shell Oil's response.

Phil Carroll took over as CEO in 1993, and shortly thereafter inaugurated a years-long process known as "The Transformation." The vision was nothing less than to go from the pits to "the premier company in the United States." Recognizing that it was a classic slow-moving, inflexible, not-very-smart hierarchy that was disconnected from the deep knowledge within the organization, the General Executive Office became the Leadership Council, business components reorganized with greater autonomy and more responsibility, and the top 200 senior leaders were convened as the Corporate Leadership Group. A revolution of relationships had begun.

Four years later, in October 1997, Shell's planners met with the Leadership Council at a retreat and presented this startling new picture of how the now-successful company had morphed: Shell had gone from owning 100% of the companies in which its assets were deployed, to 34%. It had moved from "control through ownership to influence through relationships." Who were we now, and what are we becoming, wondered the executives.

A month later 38 people, from across the company's businesses and diagonally through the ranks from senior management to boilermakers, joined the Leadership Council in a Strategic Initiative. Their mission was to answer four questions and make recommendations for action:

- How will we learn?
- What will it mean to be part of the Shell family?
- How will we develop our people?
- How will we govern?

These questions were very positive and approached in an appreciative way. They were focused not on solving problems but in choosing how to attain a desired future. So a process of discovery was inaugurated, and sub-teams were formed around each question. Interviews throughout the company were conducted and dialogues held. An additional group of 90 people were assembled to act as a sounding board for the Strategic Initiative Team, an assemblage that included members of Shell's larger community such as spouses, the local school superintendent, and suppliers.

When the group reconvened at its midpoint meeting, where we began our involvement as consultant-participants, there was wide agreement that Shell had become what they termed a "networked community." Stories were told of how networks and multi-party win-win partnerships had transformed operations and improved results. The conviction grew that Shell should embrace this new reality and become more conscious about its evolution towards the post-hierarchical-bureaucratic form. Information from the "discovery" phase was brought into the meeting with a process that proceeded from "dream" to "design" over three days. The question-based sub-teams reorganized to formulate integrated recommendations and to develop a "Network Community Fieldbook."

Two months later, a 7-point path to Shell's "destiny" was presented to the Leadership Council. Approval on the spot was a simple matter, since the Council had been part of the development process. Enactment started immediately, as each recommendation was assigned to one or more of the senior executives to sponsor. However, this was not a top-down-only change processes. The recommendations had been embedded in a practical action-oriented fieldbook that explained the "whys" and "hows" of the development of the networked community. The intention was to equip people throughout Shell with the information they needed to take action themselves to grow towards the enterprise vision. Team members knew that the work of transformation required thoughtful effort by people throughout the company, not just by people in the executive suite.

Shell did not call its process Appreciative Inquiry, but it was. It started with the use of questions, elicited stories, and followed a process that closely resembled the 4-D Cycle. Perhaps the most significant similarity is the fundamental assumption about the positive, essentially good, nature of people and the organizations they form. Shell believes in its people and knows it has a positive core.

Our Network Story

Our own appreciative inquiry story bridges narrative, theory, and practice. In the late-1970s, we decided to go looking for "networks." We were driven by a vision to discover a form of organization beyond hierarchy-bureaucracy. There had to be something better.

Our voyage of discovery was framed by a systems theory (Stamps, 1980) that posited that there were common patterns of organization in human systems, and that human systems evolved over time. Where to look for new forms, however, was directed from the heart.

The original field of discovery was populated by the wildly proliferating non-profit and grassroot organizations that arose during the turbulent 1960s and 1970s, groups and movements like those that we had helped form, sustain, and, in many cases, become disillusioned with over the course of two decades. As practitioners, we were immersed in the new form of organization, vaguely knew it (thus feeding our intuition), but needed to step up a level to truly grasp it.

For our first book, *Networking* (Lipnack & Stamps, 1982), we employed a networking strategy. We wrote to nine people whom we knew to be richly connected networkers, asking them about networking and requesting names of people and groups to contact. We started writing people and asking: "Are you a network or do you perform a significant networking function?" We asked for their stories and for artifacts, like missions, white papers, action plans, brochures, and other tangible reflections of their networking intentions and efforts. And we asked for more names.

The process snowballed. Over eighteen months we had received the names of 50,000 people. We wrote to 4000 of them and, using a "cold-call" letter, we had an astonishing response rate of 40%. *Networking*, which was sub-titled "The First Report and Directory: People Connecting with People, Linking Ideas and Resources," featured these 1600 groups not only as stories in the body of the text, but as entries in a directory that comprised half the book and gave description, keyword, and contact pointers to networks – what we hoped would be of service both to readers and to the organizations profiled in our book. These networks were grouped into seven interest areas, each reflecting a vision of a better, more life-affirming world:

• Health and the Life Cycle,
• Communities and Cooperatives,
• Ecology and Energy,
• Politics and Economics,
• Education and Communications,
• Personal and Spiritual Growth,
• Global and Futures Networks.

Our systems perspective, which led us to see the common network patterns, also led us to construe all of these groups as representing a much larger collection of networks and together comprising an encompassing inchoate meta-network, which we called "Another America" (Lipnack & Stamps, 1986).

Much to our surprise, we got a very strong reaction from a number of businesses, particularly global companies that were early adopters of computers and the then-new network technologies that were used to connect resources internally. For the next decade we worked as consultants with programs and teams spread around the world, trying to use the still clumsy, expensive, and limited connective technologies. As consultants, our mode of interaction was to become participant-facilitators, members of teams with the role to help support its leadership and life-cycle processes, particularly the formative stages. When we resumed writing in the early 1990s, our stories and examples came predominately from the for-profit sectors, especially those leading-edge global companies who had consciously undertaken change processes that moved them from traditional hierarchy-bureaucracy to flatter, relatively decentralized, more participative, more flexible, and faster-changing organizations.

PRACTICE

Since we met and began working together more than 30 years ago, we have chosen a path of action and thought, to be both researchers and practitioners. From the sociorationalist perspective, it would be impossible to be a researcher and not impact the systems being studied, whether desired or not. So, better to be aware of our co-created reality and consciously chose the direction we hope our engagement will lead, while also making our biases and intentions as clear as possible to others.

From Theory to Practice Via Method

Method provides the bridge from theory to practice. It includes *principles*, *practices*, and *processes*. While theory offers the lens to see social reality, method actually embodies the construction kit people use on an everyday basis.

Principles arise from the repeated application of theory in practice. What works survives and modifies the next use of the principle. What we have learned about what works in applying the elements of the model are reflected in the verbs we use to render the elements actionable. Hence, at the high-level of the four dimensions:

- Clarify *purpose*,
- Identify *members*,
- Establish *links*, and
- Live *time*.

At the next level of model detail (see Fig. 1), adjectives reflect qualifying characteristics that we associate with good (i.e. effective, efficient, and value-driven) networks. So, for the exemplary dimension of Purpose, we have found that successful networks clarify and articulate their purpose into:

- Cooperative *goals*,
- Interdependent *tasks*, and
- Concrete *results*.

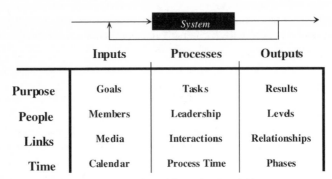

	Inputs	Processes	Outputs
Purpose	Goals	Tasks	Results
People	Members	Leadership	Levels
Links	Media	Interactions	Relationships
Time	Calendar	Process Time	Phases

Fig. 1. Periodic Table of Organizational Elements.

Practices are the accumulated wisdom of advice, warnings, tips, and techniques that experienced practitioners share with one another. Sharing of best practices is typically an informal process, but increasingly organizations are looking for formal ways of capturing and making available at least some of this largely tacit knowledge. People who have facilitated and/or led many Appreciative Inquiry processes, networks, virtual teams, or had repeated experience in any professional endeavor, know and apply many practices that help them in the next unique situation, only some of which are explicitly shareable.

Generative principles lead to practices, which express the trial-and-error hypothesis-testing activities that lead back to improved principles and, eventually, more robust theory. This social-scientific process only works if the practitioners are aware of their complementary roles of active participants and reflective thinkers. It is all too easy to adopt practices as "the way we do it" and not subject them to critical assessment as to their efficacy.

From an applied point of view, principles represent strategy, while practices represent tactics. For example, one network principle asserts that "cooperative goals" are key to a successful collaborative organization, so the strategy for group development would include helping a group formulate a set of goals that emphasize common areas of aspiration rather than competitive conflict. Conversations, activities, processes, and techniques used to elicit and make explicit cooperative goals are in the realm of practices. Where the admonition to seek cooperative (rather than neutral or competitive) goals is relatively general, the set of practices that will work in a particular circumstance are pulled from a larger set of possible approaches, and are often further adapted on the fly.

Processes reflect patterns of action over time. While different networks and virtual teams reflect the use of many different processes that flow from their type (e.g. community of practice, strategic alliance, product development program) and/or sector (e.g. manufacturing, financial, NGO), a process common to all organizations is the life cycle – human groups have beginnings, middles, and ends. In ongoing organizations (which from a long view are, of course, always embedded in a life cycle, even if we cannot recognize it), change and renewal processes follow the familiar "S" pattern of development.

Our experience in working with dozens of organizations that utilize formal life cycle processes (archetypically for new product development) is that everyone cuts the "S" curve into different stages and has a generally home-grown nomenclature that suggests a uniqueness in their process that is often unwarranted. Our practice in using the cross-systems life cycle pattern has resulted in a 5-phase process model with standard labels. In any particular application, we re-cut and re-name the phases to fit the circumstances.

For Appreciative Inquiry, the 4-D Cycle can be mapped onto the more general life cycle model. The 4-D stages are concentrated in the early and mid-portion of the life cycle. As with any real-world organizational application, the process model describes an approach both for the overall development of a group/network/organization and a design strategy for events within that overall development – such as a 4-day Appreciative Inquiry Summit (launch event), that uses the 4-D Cycle to structure the program schedule.

In our experience, the standard "S" curve is not necessarily a smooth one. Practice has taught us that there are predictable points of turbulence in this process, not surprisingly, given the theory, at the two inflection points of the logistic growth curve (Fig. 2).

Using our standard 5-phase rendition of the life cycle, we map the 4-D Cycle onto the generic logistic growth process, using descriptive terms associated with the development of teams.

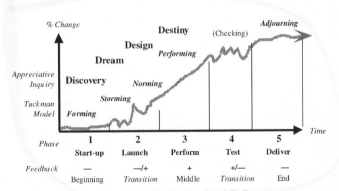

Fig. 2. Logistic Life Cycle with 4-D Stages.

(1) *Startup*. This initial phase can be very long as initial information is gathered, people recruited, purpose explored, and, above all, resistance encountered and overcome. In Appreciative Inquiry, this is the *Discovery* phase, including selling the idea, finding and training interviewers, and collecting the primary data, the stories.

(2) *Launch*. The second phase of development is usually much shorter but predictably turbulent as a critical mass of the organizing members gather to agree on the vision, hash out the initial purposes, settle some key roles, create an organizational framework, and, most importantly, generate the momentum to carry the group into the next phase. The stages of *Dream* and *Design* bracket this phase, with dreams of "what might be" leading into the launch, with the co-constructing design of "what should be" coming out of the launch event(s).

(3) *Perform*. This phase is often the bulk of the life cycle. With a successful launch and plan, this is where the "real work" gets done. The system dynamic is of accumulating positive feedback. Progress races up the long handle of the hockey stick. For 4-D, this is the *Destiny* stage, where the emphasis is on sustaining the evolving organization and "how to empower and adjust/improvise."

(4) *Test*. Unfortunately, progress is not forever. The growth curve begins to reach its maximum. The process runs into challenges from within and without, a second point of predictable turbulence ensues before results are delivered or a new level of stability is established. For the most part, Appreciative Inquiry does not, and most applied development processes do not, recognize this downstream stress point.

(5) *Deliver*. The concluding phase is the endgame, the conclusion for a temporary group, or a new plateau of stability for an ongoing organization. Results are delivered, information and learnings exchanged and archived, and successes celebrated. As a practice, the 4-D process does not focus much on endings. It is too busy with beginnings.

Embedding Methodology in Technology

Part of what defines us as human is our creation, use, and refinement of tools. Our tools have coevolved with our civilizations, economies, and organizations. For many who have looked at the grand sweep of human evolution and perceived major transitions in the human condition – which we have characterized as the nomadic, agricultural, industrial, and information eras – it is our tools and technologies that drive the change from one era to the next, as the very names of the eras suggest.

In the early stages of each new age, technologies lead, even force, epochal changes while organizational structures are slow to adapt. But change they do, engendering a momentum in the change process that enables the promise of the era to unfold on a large scale. Consequently, in the early stages of the next transformation, organizational patterns tend to persist and resist. In the current transformation, technological diffusion and cultural-economic globalization has pushed change to the point where a shift to new patterns of organization is likely and necessary. How and when emergent forms of organization become the dominant form will ultimately define how successful this new era of humanity will be.

Organizational networks have emerged with the development of network technologies. It is a happy coincidence (in our view) that the same word – network – is applied to the new technical systems of connectivity and to the new human systems of relationships. On the very big planetary scale, it is computer-based digital technologies, including digital communications media, that are transformative and driving the era-level change. The new given is the ability to connect anyone anywhere anytime, notwithstanding political and poverty barriers.

On a small scale, we are still very much learning how to converse, share interests, and work together using the new technologies. To date, most collaborative technology has been a collection of utilities supporting document management, online discussions, application sharing, chat, instant messaging, and the like. What has been missing is an understanding of and a methodology for organizing and working together virtually that is seamlessly integrated with the technology.

As a natural extension of our desire to help people develop effective networks and virtual teams, we have created an application on top of a major groupware platform that embeds our methodology in software (NetAge, 2002). This tool – which creates an online place for the formation, development, and sustaining of networked organizations – reflects all aspects of our method.

- The network model and *principles* underlie the interface architecture of the online "room" and the resulting navigation system. The six-sided room has "walls" with themes that include the four dimensions of the model. So, for example, you go to the People Wall to learn who is a member, their role, contact information, level of involvement, and other people-related material. Tools associated with the wall help a group develop and display key data about itself.
- *Practices* are embedded in the application through menu choices, help systems, and other content sources. For instance, the principle of making explicit operating agreements is supported by menu choices of suggested areas for

agreements, and a help system and other material that gives examples of specific agreements that have worked for other groups. And, of course, the online discussion and knowledge management features allow a community of practitioners to ask questions, engage in dialog, and catalog best practices.

- Life cycle *processes* are enabled through a set of tools designed to support teams in each phase of their development, as well as to function in a planned sequence of process steps, particularly in the startup and launch phases. Other processes that sustain virtual organizations, particularly meetings, are conducted in areas designed to enable good meeting practices while utilizing the power of both synchronous (e.g. con call, web conferencing, or even face-to-face) and asynchronous (e.g. threaded discussions, the persisting web room) media. Detailed transactional processes can be facilitated through a workflow capability that routes work objects (e.g. documents) through a network of people following a prescribed logic.

These methodology-infused technologies are at today's leading edge for supporting networks and virtual teams. But tomorrow, they will be widespread. We would expect to soon see the configuration of collaboration systems to specifically meet the needs and possibilities of Appreciative Inquiry.

RESEARCH

Being human systems scientists is tough in an intellectual environment still infused by the glow of Enlightenment scientific ideals. In a nutshell, this is the belief that in a "good" science, objective observers conduct value-free research leading to the discovery of immutable natural laws and absolute truth of a reality existing entirely separately from people and their humanness. To confirm the correctness of this set of assumptions and the connections between them, the "best" sciences create descriptions of the world from pure theory, then test the conclusions through repeatable experiments that by confirmation (or lack of it) enhance the theory and scientific progress is advanced.

From human systems and sociorationalist points of view, subjective scientist-participants engage in value-infused actions that lead to the discovery of relatively-true models and principles of a co-created, lived, and constantly changing human reality. While the meta-theoretical assumptions of these two scientific worldviews are sharply different, many aspects of the scientific program are common and continue to provide a powerful platform for seeking knowledge. Three such characteristics are: explicitness, openness, and community. To make scientific assertions, hypotheses, research protocols, and data must be made explicit, insofar as possible. Scientific research must be open to permit testing, critical evaluation, and repeatable outcomes. And, the final arbiter of the validity of specialized knowledge is the peer community of interrelating scientific experts recognized in the field.

We will look briefly at the potential Appreciative Inquiry-Network research program through lenses of people, data, and theory.

We are the System

One of the most fundamental challenges to Industrial era science came from Werner Heisenburg's demonstration of the "Principle of Indeterminacy." He showed that at subatomic levels, the observer's instruments of investigation (e.g. light) so influenced what was being observed, most particularly the impact of light "particles" (photons) on the subatomic particles being studied, that efforts to control one dimension (such as speed) increased the indeterminacy of measurement in another dimension (such as location). While this insight was an extremely important part of the scientific revolution in Physics, the subatomic micro-truth of uncertainty seems to have little impact in the human macro-world, where approximate Newtonian principles work well in practice, as in engineering.

But in the world of human systems, the human observer is of the same scale, within a few orders of magnitude, as the observed human system, particularly small ones. Thus the impact of scientists and instruments is very much at a macro-level. We live socially at a level where more control in one dimension leads to more indeterminacy in some complementary dimension. Moreover, it is relatively impossible to bring human systems into the classical laboratory insulated from external influences. As disappointing as it is to try to "bring" a small group into a lab to observe its "normal" behavior, the stretch quickly becomes impractical as larger human systems are considered. Finally, by its connected nature, a virtual, distributed group, large or small, cannot be located in a traditional laboratory.

However, the "problem" of indeterminacy only appears as such from a deficit-oriented perspective and against a background of antiquated assumptions of objective, analytically-parsed, values-free, absolute knowledge. What are the "possibilities" of indeterminacy and human involvement in a scientific approach to human systems? Some benefits to a positive approach are:

- Human theory would be more closely aligned with human reality;
- Recognizing and accepting that engagement leads to a built-in feedback loop between theory and practice and provides for the rapid diffusion and application of knowledge in the real world;

- Engagement denotes acceptance of the reality of values and thus implies a responsibility to consciously choose the value framework of the scientific enterprise;
- Indeterminacy leads to a respect for open systems and an irreducible element of awe and wonder in the mystery at the heart of sentient life; and
- Eventually, the prevailing scientific ethic moves from "knowledge for knowledge's sake" to "knowledge for human betterment."

Human Systems Data and Containers

Human social systems are "something more" than the sum of their human parts, people. The "more" lies in extra-individual characteristics like the system-level emergent properties generated through relationships among members and the motivating vitality of shared purpose and community. Data about collective reality lie in information objects – such as stories, dialogues, and documents – and in transaction records of activities that shine light on "invisible" relationships.

While we have a grasp, however imperfect, on how to understand ourselves as individuals, we have no generally agreed upon means for "grasping" ourselves as groups. Lacking a laboratory for collecting collective data and recording transactions, we have found no container, no systematic and categorically clean way of apprehending social reality scientifically.

Until now: With computers, the net, and the web, digital technology offers a newly-viable environment for doing action-oriented human systems science.

Consider virtual teams and networks that live some portion of their collective life online. In self-constructed web containers, which we have called "rooms," information objects of all sorts are collected and generated. Whenever interactions between people or between people and information happen through online media, that interaction is logged (or is capable of being recorded). For really-existing virtual organizations, the workplace is naturally the laboratory, a fully-wired container for group objects and interactions. Because of the digital nature of the place, there is no limit to size, nor is there a prejudice against distributed groups.

Such facilities are only now coming online for substantial numbers of people. The relative amount of meaningful group interaction or information exchange that happens online is small but growing. At some point, enough group reality will be expressed through the digital medium to constitute the basis for increasingly sound research. And, since these are living environments, the loop from research to practice can be immediate, particularly for localized tactical adjustments.

With larger communities of self-researching human systems, the path from theory-to-practice-to-data-to-theory may be rapidly iterated and the consequences for improvement fed quickly back into the participating systems.

Integrative Theorizing

Analysis is the modus operandi of the deficit-oriented, problem-centered Industrial approach to science. Synthesis, essential to the emerging systems-oriented sciences, is not the antithesis of analysis, but rather includes analysis and adds an integrative ingredient to interpretation and theorizing. Since the data collected through online containers can quickly become a flood of bits, methodological tools must be built into the digital place to enable people to make meaningful use of the information.

Fortunately, there are many social science approaches being developed that embrace analytic detail and provide useful integrative outcomes. Two examples:

- A Values Science of assessment and development (e.g. Brian Hall, 1994, 2000) that provides methods to measure individual and collective values within a human system through survey instruments. Hall has also developed complementary methods for digitally processing the content of a group's information objects to determine the pattern of values expressed through the shared record. Feeding values information back to people enables them to go from a base of "what is" to consider the constellation of values to which they aspire, to "what should be." Knowledge and method together provides ways for the values of human systems to shift and evolve.
- Social Network Analysis (e.g. Wellman, 1997) provides methods for doing surveys and analyzing transactional data to find "hidden" network patterns of, for example, influence within an organization. Such networks of influence can be compared and contrasted with the overt, formal networks of hierarchical power represented by the typical "tree" organizational diagram. Revealing patterns of influence to the system of course immediately influences those patterns, and may lead to changes in the overt structure.

Methods such as these would be immensely valuable to Appreciative Inquiry. A values analysis of appreciative story content, as well as other organizational expressions of its core self, offers a standardized view of this subjective data to supplement the active and engaged interpretation that arises through dialog about the stories. Using a normalized framework of cross-organizational, cross-cultural values as developed by Hall and others, allows comparison of discovery information across instances of Appreciative Inquiry.

Social Network Analysis would not only provide a map to guide the discovery phase, but also suggest the most fruitful places to ask questions with impact. Research that acknowledges and takes responsibility for the changes engendered by the scientific process needs to know how information and influence really flow in human systems.

SEARCH

To do research, you must have an idea of what you are searching for or looking at. It is a founding premise of the sociorationalist perspective that scientific worldviews act as primordial preconceptions that bound the search for truth. We "see" what we already think "is." Ontology (what is real) is interdependent with epistemology (how to know the real). Scientific revolutions are marked by new ways of seeing (Kuhn). New lenses and conceptual frameworks reveal previously "hidden" realities and open up large new territories for the exploration of knowledge.

Human Systems Are

Appreciative Inquiry assumes the entitivity of social systems, most specifically of organizations. If organizations were not really real, it would be meaningless to search for a "positive core." Without the assumption of systemic coherence, it would be pointless to engage in collective data gathering, convene groups to interpret the data, or take responsibility for influencing the co-creation of organizations by their members.

From the earliest conceptions of system science, there has been an acceptance that truly cross-system principles would include the social disciplines as well the established scientific fields of physical and biological sciences. This belief is shared by people from all the major sources of modern systems thought: General Systems Theory (e.g. especially Kenneth Boulding), Operations Research (e.g. Herbert Simon), and Systems Dynamics (e.g. Jay Forrester).

The given that social systems are ontologically real is only the first step in a useful foundation for knowledge. What kind of systems are social systems? To the Industrial mindset, the answer was obvious – organizations are machines, constructed artifacts built to last and fixed as needed. Even the most devout sociorationalist often uses the mechanistic language of construction to refer to the way people create their organizations (e.g. Gergen, *An Invitation to Social Construction*, 1999). When we are being especially careful, we treat our organizations as "living systems," taking advantage of all the organic language attendant to the use of biological metaphors.

There is a third view, one we have quietly inserted into this discussion – that social systems are *human* systems (see Stamps, 1980, for comparison of the Mechanistic-Organic-Human paradigms). The argument is simple: since the components of social systems are human, then the resultant system is human. That is, a system is at least as complex as any of its constituents, and it is an unacceptable simplification to comprehend social systems by evolutionarily less complex physical and biological models.

Are Human Systems Conscious?

Are human systems conscious? Is there a "group mind?" This issue has been the "third-rail" of social science theorizing for most of this century. Early in the formative decades of analytical social sciences, such speculation was routinely and loudly rejected as "anthropomorphic" and "metaphysical," redolent of the pre-Enlightenment scientific dark ages. As organizational development practitioners would say, consciousness has been the un-discussible "elephant in the room."

Social systems arise from interacting people. Regarding the intensely symbolic nature of groups, one might say, along with Cooperrider and Srivastva (1987), that organizations result from "interacting minds." For systems generally, emergent wholes inherit the characteristics of their parts, and generate "something more." Given the conscious nature of its parts, the leap to conscious human systems is short indeed.

Why is it important to recognize the conscious nature of our human systems? Some reasons:

- First and foremost is the integrity of the scientific search for truth. We can't know what we can't see, or be permitted to see. We must be willing to see things as they are in order to progress beyond convenient myths about our social condition together.
- By accepting the degree of complexity and mystery that accompanies the use of mental metaphors for understanding organizations and societies, we are better positioned to develop knowledge from a solid base than by obscuring simplifications.
- Awareness of group consciousness and using a Mind Metaphor points us to the fundamental importance of understanding the symbolic, informational, and communications-infused relational human universe.

- Alongside the Mind Metaphor would be renewed attention to the Brain Metaphor and the complementary role of concrete communications media in the evolution of human organizations (i.e. the analogy of connective technology infrastructures with the human nervous system), and the revolution inevitably unleashed with the development of new communications technologies – and in particular the current evolutionarily dramatic leap from analog to digital media and processing.
- Individual consciousness is by no means well understood, and we are far from an agreed upon way to conceive it, to say the least. Recognizing the probable existence of group consciousness and searching for systematic ways of representing and testing it may redound to the benefit of understanding consciousness generally and ourselves as individual mental beings.

The search is on for viable models of consciousness that include both individual and group domains. One example in the field of Appreciative Inquiry comes from Gervase Bush (1999). He uses the consciousness metaphor to contrast relatively conscious formal, "official" organizational meetings and artifacts from the relatively unconscious "inner dialogue" reflected in informal conversations and stories. We have suggested (2000) that the cross-cultural "category-image schema" approach to individual consciousness (e.g. Lakoff, 1987) can be fruitfully applied to understanding group consciousness. In both cases, such speculation informs the design of tools and processes to support and improve organizations.

The really big benefit, however, is improving our organizations for the betterment of humanity. By recognizing group intelligence, we can search for ways to improve that intelligence, to improve learning together, and to improve our collective outputs. Of course, smarter groups may not be better groups in the ethical sense; after all, networks are values-based organizational forms that can be used to support peace or terror, change or tradition. But while there may be conflict around "good" values, at least the debate is engaged in a framework that admits the reality and centrality of values.

Ultimately, the stance of optimist or pessimist on the eventual "goodness" of the human enterprise rests on a spiritual apprehension of people and the world we co-create as fundamentally good, bad, or randomly neutral.

REFERENCES

Cooperrider, D. L., & Dutton, J. E. (Eds) (1999). *Organizational dimensions of global change: No limits to cooperation*. Thousand Oaks, CA: Sage.
Cooperrider, D. L., & Srivastva, S. (1987). Appreciative inquiry in organizational life. In: W. Pasmore & R. Woodman (Eds), *Research in Organization Change and Development* (Vol. 1). Greenwich, CT: JAppreciative Inquiry Press.

Gergen, K. (1982). *Toward transformation in social knowledge*. New York: Springer-Verlag.

Gergen, K. (1999). *An invitation to social construction*. Thousand Oaks, CA: Sage.

Hall, B. P. (1994). *Values shift*. Rockport, MA: Twin Lights Publishers.

Hall, B. P. (2000). *The genesis effect*. Makati City: Don Bosco Press.

Lakoff, G. (1987). *Women, fire, and dangerous things*. Chicago: University of Chicago Press.

Lipnack, J. P., & Stamps, J. S. (1982). *Networking*. New York: Doubleday.

Lipnack, J. P., & Stamps, J. S. (1986). *The networking book*. London: Routledge & Kegan Paul.

Lipnack, J. P., & Stamps, J. S. (2000). *Virtual teams: second edition*. New York: Wiley.

NetAge, Inc. (2002). *Livelink virtualteams*. From Open Text, Inc. See www.virtualteams.com.

Mandel, T. (2000). Is there a general system? *Conference Proceedings*. International Society for the Systems Sciences.

Rapoport, A. (1970). Modern systems theory: An outlook for coping with change. *General Systems Yearbook, XV.*

Stamps, J. S. (1980). *Holonomy*. Systems Inquiry Series. Seaside: Intersystems Publications.

Von Bertalanffy, L. (1968). *General systems theory*. New York: Braziller.

WHAT KNOWLEDGE MANAGEMENT SYSTEMS DESIGNERS CAN LEARN FROM APPRECIATIVE INQUIRY

Michel Avital and Jessica L. Carlo

ABSTRACT

The underpinnings of knowledge management theories is that finding, keeping and leveraging an organization's information assets are critical to productivity, efficiency of operation and successful competition. Following a brief introduction of the knowledge management systems, this essay examines the corollary relationship between knowledge management and appreciative inquiry, and subsequently points to critical areas in which knowledge management practices can benefit from adopting the appreciative inquiry perspective. More particularly, we submit that appreciative inquiry can motivate organizational-wide adoption and it can provide language-based mechanisms that facilitate effective knowledge exchange. The development of an appreciative inquiry based mode of knowledge management as an alternative to the prevailing approaches opens new horizons and uncovers previously overlooked possibilities, which eventually can contribute to the overall organizational well-being.

The principles of appreciative inquiry provide a universal framework that can enhance and drive a multitude of facets of organizational life. As many practitioners of appreciative inquiry attest, appreciative inquiry is particularly effective if

Constructive Discourse and Human Organization
Advances in Appreciative Inquiry, Volume 1, 57–75
Copyright © 2004 by Elsevier Ltd.
All rights of reproduction in any form reserved
ISSN: 1475-9152/doi:10.1016/S1475-9152(04)01003-8

applied in organizational activities that build on grassroots knowledge, goodwill and action. One such organizational activity is the deployment of knowledge management systems, which cannot be sustained without an organizational-wide adoption and knowledge sharing among multiple stakeholders. This essay examines the potential contribution of appreciative inquiry to the design and application of knowledge management systems.

Finding, keeping and leveraging an organization's information assets are critical to productivity, efficiency of operation and successful competition. These are the underpinnings of the mainstream knowledge management theories, which focus on the technical and social aspects of knowledge creation, transmission, storage and retrieval. Whereas many have emphasized the information architectures, infrastructures and procedures that allow stakeholders in organizations to search multiple repositories of information (e.g. Markus, 2001; Zack, 1999), this essay emphasizes the social and organizational dynamics that drive the organizational actors who create and use these knowledge systems.

Although knowledge management systems were introduced more than two decades ago, we still experience many unsolved challenges concerning their implementation. For example, frequent resistance to sharing information (Ciborra & Patriotta, 1998), difficulties in identifying qualified core knowledge, actors' indifference towards organizational knowledge repositories (Dixon, 2000), and continuous struggle of the systems' sponsors to sustain a viable knowledge community (Rumizen, 2002). Our thesis is that appreciative inquiry principles can help designers and users of knowledge management systems meet the above challenges. Thus, we submit that appreciative inquiry can: (1) motivate organizational members to share and use information assets; (2) systematically identify and maintain a catalog of core knowledge; (3) synthesize situated taxonomies and ontologies of knowledge grounded in the organizational context; and (4) facilitate sustainable communities of knowing.

Following a brief introduction of the knowledge management systems domain and the appreciative inquiry principles, this essay examines the corollary relationship between knowledge management and appreciative inquiry, and subsequently points to critical areas in which knowledge management practices can benefit from adopting the appreciative inquiry perspective.

KNOWLEDGE MANAGEMENT

Knowledge management refers to the array of processes that deal with the creation, dissemination, and utilization of knowledge. Knowledge management, per se, is technology-independent. However, information technologies play an important role in an organization's knowledge management strategy, which, in turn, tends to rely on various knowledge management systems. A *knowledge management system* is a computer-based information system that is designed to facilitate effective and efficient creation, integration and sharing of knowledge. The design and operationalization of these systems stem largely from the complexity of the underlying knowledge and the designers' a priori ontological assumptions concerning the nature of knowledge.

The current landscape of knowledge management systems can be mapped onto three archetypes: codified knowledge repositories, expert directories, and communities of practice (Wasko & Faraj, 2000). The three-archetype typology is derived partly from the various degrees of complexity of the underlying knowledge. As illustrated in Fig. 1, knowledge complexity is characterized in this case as a two-dimensional space comprising of *knowledge depth* (specialization within a field of expertise) and *knowledge breadth* (diversity across fields of expertise). In addition, each of the archetypes, respectively, also represents a fundamentally different perspective concerning the nature of knowledge: knowledge as an objective and independent entity; knowledge as a tacit entity embedded in people; and knowledge as a socially constructed entity embedded in community-based relationships.

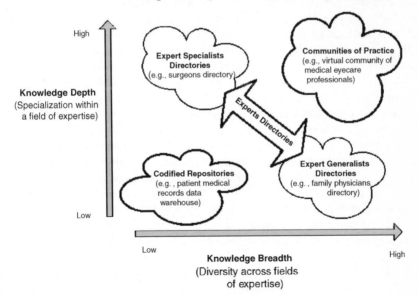

Fig. 1. The Knowledge Management Domain.

Codified Knowledge Repositories focus on relatively concrete and well-defined knowledge elements in a particular context that can be structured using an existing commonly acceptable classification scheme. An example of such a repository is the American Psychiatric Association's Diagnostic and Statistical Manual of Mental Disorders (DSM). The underlying assumption in this case is that knowledge about mental disorders is intrinsically objective and independent of any particular mental patient or the psychiatrist who made the diagnosis. It is believed that the knowledge exists outside a person's head and can be consumed by human beings and organizations that act as information processing systems (Galbraith, 1977). Consequently, the designers of such knowledge management systems aim to capture critical knowledge existing in people's minds and transform it into knowledge assets owned by the organization. Such knowledge repositories contain documents, routines specifications, historical data, inventories, and the like. Information technologies that support codified knowledge repositories include databases, data mining applications, file management systems, workflow systems and expert systems.

Expert Directories are concerned with keeping track of the various experts in a particular context. Expert directories list either specialists in a particular field of endeavor, such as brain surgeons, or generalists who can bridge across different bodies of knowledge, such as family physicians. By linking the right expert to the issue at hand, expert directories are geared to provide unstructured knowledge in the form of either specialized or cross-disciplinary knowledge. Expert directories are based on the underlying assumption that knowledge is embedded in people – it is personal and tacit. Knowledge and the person who created it are inseparable. Therefore, the designers of such knowledge management systems should aim to track and map the myriad expertise in the organization.

Another underlying assumption concerning expert directories is that organizational knowledge is the sum of all the knowledge of the individuals in the organization. Given that people gain tacit knowledge through personal involvement with the outside world and their interactions with others, expert directories allow people to connect to one another, thereby enhancing the organization's "transactive memory" (Moreland, 1999). In addition to information dissemination and continuous update, the designers of expert directories must create a climate in which the various experts are motivated to share knowledge and help each other. Information technologies that support expert directories include Internet applications, online knowledge directories, search engines, and electronic bulletin boards.

Communities of Practice are informal social networks that aim to facilitate an ongoing knowledge sharing, a discussion space, mutual support and other social exchanges among affiliates who share an affinity to a particular profession or area of interest (Wenger, 1998). A community of practice can be seen as a distributed knowledge system, in which knowledge transcends any one individual, and is embedded in the shared knowledge base and social practices of that community (Boland, Tenkasi & Te'eni, 1994; Tsoukas, 1996; Weick & Roberts, 1993).

The underlying assumption is that knowledge and knowing are situated, self-referential, and intrinsically entwined. Knowledgeable community members recreate, transform, legitimize, reinforce and disseminate the knowledge through their practice. Concurrently, the embedded knowledge also shapes, frames and anchors the practices carried out by these actors, thereby placing knowledge in a practice that can be seen as a collective act of agents who apply and appropriate it. Knowledge shared in a community of practice is considered a public good. Sharing and participation may stem from a sense of commitment, psychological ownership, self-identification – a need to be affiliated with the community and be recognized by its members.

Given its distributed nature, a community of practice is involved with unstructured, multidisciplinary knowledge that is both highly specialized and spanned across diverse fields. A community of practice resembles a "ba," a shared space for "emerging relationships" (Nonaka & Konno, 1998). For example, *EyeTownCenter*, an online virtual medical community for ophthalmologists, allows eyecare physicians in separate communities to network effectively with each other, very much the way they are able to do at clinical conferences. By visiting and interacting within the virtual community spaces, the physician members are able to share ideas and develop relationships with their fellow community members/physicians; access information applicable to their area of specialization; obtain assistance for both medical and professional issues relating to their practice from their peers; and pro-actively access, in a single location, a large number of vendors who offer services and products required in the operation of their medical practices (http://www.eyetowncenter.com).

Communities of practice, as an archetype, differ significantly from the other two archetypes of knowledge management systems. The most striking difference is in relation to the autonomy of individuals. Codified repositories provide a mechanism in which discrete, possibly anonymous, individuals can exchange knowledge objects, and expert directories provide a mechanism to match between experts and clients. In both of these archetypes the emphasis is on individual knowledge providers and knowledge seekers who operate as discrete autonomous actors. In contrast, a community of practice facilitates a public space where various individuals engage in shifting relationships in which they both seek and contribute advice in common, and thereby dynamically construct knowledge. The emphasis in this case is on individual actors who co-create and transfer knowledge via mutually dependent social exchange.

The communal facet of communities of practice also sets this archetype apart from the others in relation to the temporal nature of the knowledge exchange. Codified repositories imply a discrete exchange of knowledge objects, and expert directories imply a one-time, dyadic relationship between a knowledge provider and a knowledge seeker – in both archetypes, the emphasis is on a finite exchange. In contrast, communities of practice imply an ongoing dialogue and sharing among community members who act as both knowledge seekers and knowledge providers. The emphasis in this case is on open-ended, seemingly infinite exchange.

Often, communities of practice rely on groupware applications and other collaborative technologies, such as listservs, discussion boards, wikis, or electronic chatrooms to enhance human interaction and connectivity. System designers who prescribe and appropriate information technologies for communities of practice should aim to support creating a space conducive to continuous, multi-channel knowledge sharing. Furthermore, they need to account for the prevailing social norms, pay careful attention to the enrollment and initiation processes of new members, and provide archival facilities and other means that help in cultivating a sense of historicity.

The unique features of each archetype of knowledge management system are juxtaposed in Table 1. Although each archetype is fundamentally different, the three are not mutually exclusive: knowledge management systems of various archetypes may co-exist in one organization and reinforce one another. For example, specialist physicians may get patients through listings in expert directories, use extensively their hospital's proprietary codified knowledge repositories, and share some of this information as active participants in a national community of practice. Subsequently, based on feedback from peers elsewhere and their personal experience, they may make substantive contributions in their host organization, which, in turn, are codified in the local knowledge repositories.

Irrespective of their archetypical orientation, successful knowledge management systems must facilitate effective knowledge exchange, which is inherently dependent on a delicate balance between knowledge contributors and knowledge seekers. Maintaining and sustaining this balance is one of the major challenges of knowledge management initiatives. The voluntary nature of knowledge sharing, particularly if it involves an intersubjective or relational component, makes it dependent mainly on intrinsic motivations and social control, rather than on top-down managerial directives. The link between cultivating a culture of knowledge sharing and the successful implementation of knowledge management systems of all sorts has been already documented and discussed extensively in the literature (e.g. Davenport, De Long & Beers, 1998; Fulmer, 2001).

Further examination of the success factors of knowledge management systems reveals two top-level themes: (1) grassroots adoption by a critical mass of people

Table 1. Comparison of the Knowledge Management Systems Archetypes.

Feature	Knowledge Management Systems Archetype		
	Codified Repository	**Experts Directory**	**Community of Practice**
Nature of Knowledge	Objective and Explicit	Personal and tacit	Situated and socially constructed
Guiding Metaphor	Warehouse	Classified Directory	Membership Club
Provider-user Relationship	No direct relationships – knowledge is an isolated independent object transferred in asynchronous exchanges	Temporal dyadic, expert-client relationship narrowly focused on the concrete issue at hand	Continuous communal relationships based on solidarity, mutual support, a sense of historicity, and a shared vision
Knowledge Generation	Codify knowledge based on keywords and metastructures	List experts based on personal capabilities and reputation	Emerge through group interaction and dialogue
Knowledge Storage	Data repositories of saved knowledge objects	Expert's mind	Social fabric of the community membership or organizational memory
Knowledge Retrieval	Search based on keywords and metastructures	Identify and retain expert assistance	Solicit response from community membership
Knowledge Acquisition Directive	One should know where to look	One should know who knows	One should be engaged in the relevant socio-professional circles
Key Success Factors and Challenges	Identifying proper meta-structures or classification schemes to codify unstructured, complex, contextualized ephemeral, or dynamic knowledge	Mapping and maintaining current the myriad expertise, particularly the implicit capacities	Nurturing and sustaining ecology of knowledge sharing and mutual help

that use the systems regularly for knowledge exchange; and (2) careful attention to language-based mechanisms that facilitate effective knowledge exchange. These two considerations underlie any successful knowledge management system irrespective of its archetypical characteristics. While grassroots adoption and linguistics consideration seem to be a universal concern in knowledge management systems, their manifestation and the challenges they present in each archetype are quite different.

Codified knowledge repositories rely on continuous contribution and maintenance of proprietary knowledge by various professionals and the translation of this knowledge into reusable knowledge objects. Organizations that deploy these knowledge management systems face challenges in motivating ongoing knowledge contribution as well as knowledge reuse. The value proposition of these systems is subject to their metastructures or classification schemes, which affect the successful codification of relatively unstructured, complex, contextualized, ephemeral, or dynamic knowledge.

Expert directories rely on detailed mapping of the myriad expertise, particularly the implicit capacities of a certain group of professionals or affiliates. Motivating experts' availability and balancing between experts' supply and demand is particularly a challenge in instances of non-market driven systems, in which no concrete remuneration is dispensed to contributors. Expert directories have the potential to provide a direct link to leading-edge knowledge base, yet drawing and maintaining the map that facilitates matching between knowledge seekers and providers is still a challenge in highly contextualized, specialized, or cross-disciplinary instances.

Communities of practice allow a clear path to avoid many of the challenges to smooth knowledge exchange that may be caused in information environments governed by the other two archetypes. However, communities of practice also face a challenge in nurturing the ecology of knowledge sharing and mutual help, cultivating a stable core group that embraces new members, and sustaining a community based on long-term relationships. Furthermore, in spite of the emphasis on the relational facet, it is critical to develop shared institutions, repertoires, routines, narratives, symbols, or genres that the community members, especially the new ones, can draw upon. Another challenge in electronically enabled communities of practice is the need to create and balance between both private spaces that allow rich self-reflection and public spaces that facilitate dialogue and relationship building.

Next, we are going to look at how appreciative inquiry can bolster knowledge management initiatives in more detail. We assume here that the reader has a priori understanding of appreciative inquiry. If not, we suggest reading Cooperrider and Srivastva (1987).

THE COROLLARY RELATIONSHIP BETWEEN KNOWLEDGE MANAGEMENT AND APPRECIATIVE INQUIRY

First articulated by Cooperrider and Srivastva (1987) as an enhanced form of action research and later proliferated into organizational development and change circles as a methodology of choice (Braun, 2002; Bushe, 1995), appreciative inquiry is about the "co-evolutionary search for the best in people, their organizations and the relevant world around them" (Cooperrider & Whitney, 2000, p. 5). It is a philosophy of knowing that has been applied as a methodology for managing organizational change, community building, system design, and scientific research. We submit that it can also benefit the design and implementation of knowledge management systems.

In their root cause, both knowledge management systems and appreciative inquiry "involve systematic discovery of what gives *life* to a living system when it is most alive, most effective, and most constructively capable in economic, ecological, and human terms" (Cooperrider, 1998). Further insight into the entwined trajectories of the two is echoed in Stamps and Lipnack's (2004) discussion of the complementary relationship between appreciative inquiry and the networked organization that underlies any knowledge management system. This is not to say that knowledge management systems and appreciative inquiry are the same, but to argue that there is much overlap in the essence of their core processes and underlying objectives, which build on a generative co-creation and reproduction of situated knowledge through instances of dialogic acts.

Whereas knowledge management systems aims to help identifying the substantive organizational knowledge in its broadest sense and leveraging it to benefit the organization and its stakeholders (Alavi & Leidner, 2001; Dixon, 2000; Nonaka & Takeuchi, 1995; Von Krogh, Ichijo & Nonaka, 2000), appreciative inquiry is also about the search for the best in people, their organizations, and the relevant world around them (Cooperrider & Srivastva, 1987). Evidently, both knowledge management and appreciative inquiry attempt to amplify human and organizational capacities by leveraging on the best of each. On one hand, knowledge management implies an *appreciative stance*, holding that people are self-driven free agents having a curiosity to learn, a need for self growth, willingness to contribute, and a tendency to share (Senge, 1990). It also implies the appreciation of the core capacities and best practices already pervading the organization. On the other hand, appreciative inquiry implies a systematic search in an attempt to identify existing *core knowledge* and to leverage it in a system-wide co-creation of visionary futures. While some knowledge management theorists such as Cook

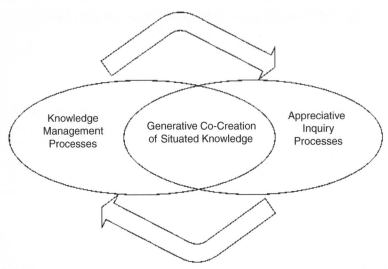

Fig. 2. Knowledge Management and Appreciative Inquiry Overlap and Reinforce One Another.

and Brown (1999) regard inquiry as the "generative dance" between knowledge and knowing, appreciative inquiry theorists emphasize the relational aspect of "generative knowledge." Therefore, we submit that knowledge management involves appreciative inquiry, and that appreciative inquiry involves knowledge management. They are intrinsic to one another, and thus we cannot discuss one without implying the other (Fig. 2).

In spite of the distance between their root disciplines and the different orientation of the intentions of their conveners, knowledge management and appreciative inquiry can reinforce each other. Building on their shared paradigmatic footprint, we can apply the strengths of each to enhance the capabilities of the other. This essay examines one side of this duality – the potential contribution of appreciative inquiry to knowledge management practices.

BOLSTERING UP KNOWLEDGE MANAGEMENT WITH APPRECIATIVE INQUIRY

A positive discourse can change our organizational life and add much value by emphasizing capabilities over deficiencies, possibilities over constraints, creativity over procedures, and esprit de corps over accountability barriers. While the current practices of managing the organizational knowledge often run the risk of being trapped in vicious cycles of self-inflicted shortcomings, a positive discourse allows for emerging virtuous cycles that build on homegrown insights. The development of an appreciative inquiry based mode of inquiry as an alternative to the ubiquitous problem-solving approach opens new horizons and uncovers previously overlooked possibilities, which eventually can contribute to the overall organizational well-being.

At this point, we would like to suggest that appreciative inquiry could help us refocus on the human factors of the development and management of knowledge systems. Appreciative inquiry can make a difference in the "way we know" by providing us with a fresh look at the organizational mélange that produces and is reproduced by knowledge management systems. More particularly, in the context of knowledge management systems, appreciative inquiry can motivate organizational-wide adoption and it can provide language-based mechanisms that facilitate effective knowledge exchange. These two elements are not only critical for the success of any knowledge management system, they are also the Achilles heels of most attempts to implement such systems.

Motivating Organization-Wide Participation

Knowledge management systems are effective only if they attract and sustain a wide base of contributors and users. One of the main challenges that knowledge management practitioners face is building up and sustaining a critical mass of vital knowledge. Knowledge management projects often fail simply because people are not willing to share with others what they know. Reluctance to share knowledge is attributed to various reasons, ranging from fear of losing power or leverage, highly competitive environment, a culture of confidentiality, to merely the perception that sharing is nothing more than a low-priority, time-consuming chore (Hansen, 1999). Many knowledge management initiatives that start very well often fade shortly after the launching phase (Rumizen, 2002).

As a remedy, the conveners of knowledge management projects usually attempt to motivate knowledge sharing using various incentives, from silver trophies to plush vacations in the Caribbean islands. While contributions to codified repositories tend to be recognized with concrete merit awards, contributions to communities of practice are more likely to be recognized with status symbols such as titles and privileges. Apparently, extrinsic incentives are not effective in the long run.

Appreciative inquiry is inclusive, affirmative, relational and self-driven. Given its inherent attributes, appreciative inquiry practices of managing the organizational knowledge systems may turn every stakeholder into a participating agent. A critical factor for the success of knowledge management systems is a wide and diverse user base. Many knowledge management systems aim to include all possible users, but often end up providing access and resources to a few privileged ones (Fulmer, 1999). By contrast, appreciative inquiry provides mechanisms for genuine, whole-system participation. It seeks common ground but also allows individual voices to be heard. It recognizes multiple ways of knowing, and regards social reality as being open to multiple interpretations, indefinite reconfigurations and changes.

Whereas the affirmative nature of appreciative inquiry provides a safe environment to share knowledge, the inherent inquiry process itself makes sharing a relevant and actionable priority. Sharing knowledge becomes a natural and integral part of the organizational experience and the professional practice. In spite of the a priori organizational sponsorship, appreciative inquiry is voluntary and builds on people's intrinsic motivation, which, in turn, lays the grounds for sustainable, long-term engagements embedded in situated social networks.

Appreciative inquiry also evokes many desirable side effects. It increases people's connective efficacy that positively influences people's motivation to contribute knowledge (Kalman, 1999). Moreover, appreciative inquiry allows people to take full control of their inquiry process, invest themselves into the process, and get to know their peers intimately. Studies show that this provides people with a higher sense of ownership (e.g. Pierce, Kostova & Dirks, 2001), and a greater inclination to contribute to the social network. Finally, this can lead to enhanced trust among people and a culture of activism and sharing.

Honing the Transformative Lingual Facet of Knowledge Exchange

The socio-rationalist underpinnings of appreciative inquiry, combined with its unique affirmative stance and the explicit emphasis on systematic inquiry makes it a natural counterpart in knowledge management systems projects. One of the key advantages that appreciative inquiry can bring to the prevailing knowledge management practices is its unique treatment of language through reflection, dialogue, and construction of the governing narratives, which, in turn, affect positive action, organizational culture, and everyone's well-being.

Identifying the vital knowledge. Knowledge acquisition often turns out to be a bottleneck in the construction of organization's knowledge base due to the difficulties in identifying, let alone keeping tabs on strengths, core capacities, capabilities, and best practices. The common practice prescribes the appointment of a handful of knowledge architects to be responsible for mining, soliciting, and capturing knowledge from key sources and translating it into a designated metastructure. This, of course, applies particularly to codified knowledge repositories and expert directories. In communities of practice, the schemas are informal, but still controlled by a small circle of gatekeepers and the in-situ culture.

Appreciative inquiry infused knowledge management practice moves the burden of identifying the vital knowledge to the community at large. Appreciative inquiry implies a system-wide discovery process in which everybody is engaged systematically in identifying and maintaining a catalog of capabilities. Instead of relying on a few knowledge architects, everyone in the organization is encouraged to be part of the discovery process through conducting interviews with several self-chosen relevant stakeholders. The interview process, in combination with summit meetings (Cooperrider & Whitney, 2000), provides a diverse view and overall better coverage of areas that otherwise might have been overlooked. Appreciative inquiry based discovery of the life-giving forces and organizational capacities is superior: it provides a fuller view of the knowledge resources, and it also enhances the sense of ownership and organizational vigor, which subsequently translates into action and desired outcome.

Asking the right questions. Questions are fundamental and ubiquitous in the human experience – they are the seeds of what we later discover. We start most life journeys with a seed question, we progress and find our way by answering guiding questions, and we end up reflecting on our experience with retrospective questions. Excellence and innovation often stem from original questions that have challenged conventional forms, sparked the imagination, and spanned the boundaries of understanding. Building, maintaining, and using knowledge management systems also involves asking numerous questions. By its very nature, the *way* we ask has an acute effect on the answers we get. In this respect, using knowledge management systems is similar to fishing – the catch-of-the-day is determined largely by where one looks and which tools one uses. As situated practitioners, organizational actors must engage in inquiry of their respective environments in order to do their work. The "next step" of their work process depends largely on where they look for information, who they ask, what, when, and, most importantly, in what way. Their actions emerge in response to this inquiry, which, as it turns out, determines both their process and product.

The design philosophy of current knowledge management systems tends to disregard the critical role of questions in shaping knowledge production and use. Overall, knowledge architects focus on a myopic description of past to present-perfect events, without much regard for how it may affect the future. For example, BP asks people to answer four questions: (1) What *was* supposed to happen? (2) What actually happened? (3) What worked well? (4) What *did* not work well (Rumizen, 2002). That they focused on the past without much concern for the future is evident. Of course, many knowledge management systems attempt to provide insight for the future. The terms "lesson learned" and "best practice" are among the words most commonly associated with knowledge management. However, best practices are contextual and a "core capacity" could quickly turn into a "core rigidity" (Leonard-Barton, 1995). Many companies that failed to challenge their own "best practices" found that past performance alone is not a good indication of the near future. For example, NCR, World Aluminum Corporation (Leonard-Barton, 1995) and Polaroid (Tripsas & Gavetti, 2000).

Paying attention to the underlying questions that yield the knowledge is a fundamental virtue of appreciative inquiry, which encourages people to challenge myths, the status quo, and other *sacred truths*. In appreciative inquiry, rather than aiming to emulate "best practices" as an end, we search for "best capacities" as the starting point of a journey into an envisioned desired future. The temporal perspective is equally distributed among past, present and future. Appreciative inquiry provides mechanisms to *practice* reflection, inquiry, and careful attention to the kind of questions asked. Questions are treated with the respect they deserve in the innovation value chain. They represent, sometimes naively, a sense of wonder and an urge to learn, rather than a post hoc rhetoric to introduce a known solution or an agenda to be promoted. Most importantly, a good question is one that raises more questions, provokes debate, encourages probing into deeper layers of a subject matter, challenges the guiding assumptions and status quos, and ultimately transforms social reality and conduct.

Understanding the power of language. Knowledge representation and language are inseparable. Knowledge architects seem to perceive the link between the two as trivial. They often fail to realize that the successful impact of the systems they design is not only subject to technology-related considerations but also to the kind of language used throughout the process. In codified repositories and expert directories, language is treated mainly in the context of formal classification schemes, knowledge metastructure, and search and retrieval. In communities of practice, language is treated as cultural glue that holds together the accumulated professional tradition and the prevailing social institutions. For example, Texas Instruments' *TI-Best* or *The Chevron Way* are held as a corporate value and add much to the sense of community and camaraderie (O'Dell, Grayson & Essaides, 1998); yet the emphasis is on commonality at the expense of those who do not share the dominant culture.

Building on the socio-rationalism perspective (Gergen, 1994), appreciative inquiry takes everyone's attitude to language to another level of consciousness – it places the notion of social construction in the forefront of any dialogue and makes language choice a bona fide consideration in both formal and informal engagements. Language choice has ramifications on every facet of knowledge management. Knowledge architects can apply appreciative inquiry to demonstrate and clarify the effect of language on organizational life and the way knowledge is produced and reproduced in the course of day-to-day action (Cooperrider, 1990).

By following the appreciative approach, we explicitly and intentionally focus our attention on seeking and building upon what we consider to be strengths, capacities, possibilities, goodwill, modalities of cooperation, and the grace of human spirit.

Unleashing the underlying narratives. Knowledge management literature has documented the power of stories. Practitioners usually resort to stories and case studies to transfer knowledge, especially tacit knowledge, within the workplace (Swap et al., 2001), communicate the importance of knowledge management (Rumizen, 2002), or to create an environment receptive to new organizational initiatives (Denning, 2001). Swap et al. (2001) argue that contextualized narratives are the preferred medium to communicate managerial systems, norms and values, because stories are vivid and grounded in direct or vicarious experience. For example, "war stories" was used by technicians at Xerox to diagnose the odd noises made by the machines (Orr, 1990); the legendary story about how Tom Fry invented the *PostIt* encourages 3M employees to think-out-of-box (Garud & Karnøe, 2001); and springboard storytelling has transformed the World Bank in to a knowledge-conscious organization (Denning, 2001). In spite of the important role of storytelling in supporting the organization's mission and value, current knowledge management systems rarely, if at all, deal with how exceptional stories are collected and told. Rather than leaving it to chance or ad hoc improvisation, appreciative inquiry provides mechanisms for the systematic collection and dissemination of high-point stories throughout the organization.

Most people tend to tell negative rather than positive stories about their organization (Neuhauser, 1993), and even positive images are often framed in negative terms. For instance, the World Bank's knowledge management initiative aimed at creating "a world free of poverty" (Fulmer, 2001), and best-practice stories were told to remind the audience of their own "problems" (Denning, 2001). Had they applied appreciative inquiry, they would have stayed away from such a deficit perspective, and reframed their mission as "a world of prosperity" or discussed best practices to remind people their "achievements." An inherent part of appreciative inquiry is its affirmative and positive stance with respect to the world. The appreciative inquiry approach generates positive images framed in positive terms, giving fuller wings to people's images of the future and enhancing the potential to turn these visions into thriving reality.

An Integrative View

Knowledge management systems have the potential to provide invaluable support in any organizational-wide initiative. The success of these systems is driven to a large degree by two critical factors: the adoption of the system by a critical mass of users and ability of the system to capture and disseminate knowledge effectively.

We have shown that appreciative inquiry can enhance both and make significant contributions to the current practices of knowledge management design.

Appreciative inquiry starts with sharing of personal stories that unleash the underlying narratives throughout the organization. The personal involvement, sense of purpose, and awakening of the spirit of camaraderie motivate further knowledge sharing and participation in the co-creation of the knowledge management system. In addition, the introduction of affirmative language combined

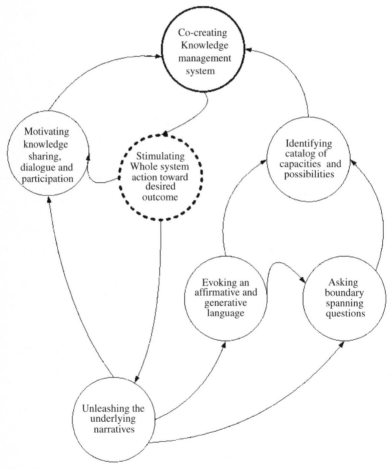

Fig. 3. The Potential Contributions of Appreciative Inquiry to Knowledge Management Systems.

with the underlying situated narrative stimulates further boundary-spanning inquiry, which, in turn, helps to identify the vital knowledge to be included in the system. Of course, the desired outcome produces new organizational narratives that translate into enhanced user participation and the production of new knowledge. The virtuous cycle of an appreciative-inquiry, infused-knowledge management system is illustrated in Fig. 3, which shows how appreciative inquiry can supplement and enhance the prevailing knowledge management practices.

CONCLUDING NOTE

The generic approach to managing organizational knowledge strengthens our ability to analyze processes that can be fine-tuned to fit with best practices and to exercise tight control over resources through efficiency-oriented, detailed procedures. The alternative approach in this essay offers an appreciative-inquiry based discourse that reveals core capacities, opens dialogue, and encourages co-creation of desired futures. Appreciative inquiry, as a methodology, can provide knowledge management with an additional new perspective – a collaborative, optimistic, inspiring, and thought-provoking new standpoint.

Beyond this rudimentary framework, future research can examine issues such as the effect of positive reframing of knowledge, the framework for nurturing knowledge-sharing cultures, the social process and work practice in knowledge management, and the development of cross-boundaries, knowledge-sharing networks. Considering the corollary relationship between knowledge management and appreciative inquiry, we also need to examine what appreciative inquiry practitioners can learn form knowledge management theory and practice.

The development of an appreciative-inquiry based mode of knowledge management as an alternative to the prevailing approaches opens new horizons and uncovers previously overlooked possibilities, which eventually can contribute to the overall organizational well-being. The appreciative inquiry approach is suggested here as one additional tool for the arsenal of knowledge designers and managers. We do not argue that the appreciative-inquiry approach should replace any other approach. We suggest that it provides a new vocabulary and new perspectives on looking at knowledge management, which may allow new possibilities to emerge. After all, words create worlds.

REFERENCES

Alavi, M., & Leidner, D. E. (2001). Review: Knowledge management and knowledge management systems: Conceptual foundations and research issues. *MIS Quarterly, 25*(1), 107–136.

Boland, R. J., Tenkasi, R. V., & Te eni, D. (1994). Designing information technology to support distributed cognition. *Organization Science, 5*(3), 456–475.

Braun, A. (2002). *Beyond the problem-solving approach to sustainable rural development.* Unpublished manuscript.

Bushe, G. R. (1995). Advances in appreciative inquiry as an organization development intervention. *Organization Development Journal, 13,* 14–22.

Ciborra, C. U., & Patriotta, G. (1998). Groupware and teamwork in R&D: Limits to learning and innovation. *R&D Management, 28*(1), 43–52.

Cooperrider, D. L. (1990). Positive image, positive action: The affirmative basis of organizing. In: S. Srivastva & D. L. Cooperrider (Eds), *Appreciative Management and Leadership: The Power of Positive Thought and Action in Organizations* (1st ed., pp. 91–124). San Francisco: Jossey-Bass.

Cooperrider, D. L. (1998). *Capturing what matters most in the practice of appreciative inquiry: A positive revolution change.* Unpublished manuscript, San Diego.

Cooperrider, D. L., & Srivastva, S. (1987). Appreciative inquiry in organizational life. In: W. Pasmore & R. Woodman (Eds), *Research in Organization Change and Development* (Vol. 1). Greenwich, CT: JAI Press.

Cooperrider, D. L., & Whitney, D. (2000). A positive revolution in change: Appreciative inquiry. In: D. L. Cooperrider, P. F. Sorensen, T. F. Yaeger & D. Whitney (Eds), *Appreciative Inquiry: Rethinking Human Organization Toward a Positive Theory of Change* (pp. 3–29). Champaign, IL: Stipes Publishing.

Davenport, T. H., De Long, D. W., & Beers, M. C. (1998). Successful knowledge management projects. *Sloan Management Review, 39*(2), 43–57.

Denning, S. (2001). *The springboard: How storytelling ignites action in knowledge-era organizations.* Boston: Butterworth-Heinemann.

Dixon, N. M. (2000). *Common knowledge: how companies thrive by sharing what they know.* Boston: Harvard Business School Press.

Fulmer, W. E. (1999). *Buckman Laboratories (A)(B).* Case Field: Harvard Business School.

Fulmer, W. E. (2001). *The world bank and knowledge management: The case of the urban services thematic group.* Case Field: Harvard Business School.

Galbraith, J. R. (1977). *Organizational design.* Reading, MA: Addison-Wesley.

Garud, R., & Karnøe, P. (2001). Path creation as a process of mindful deviation. In: R. Garud & P. Karnøe (Eds), *Path Dependence and Creation* (pp. 1–40). Mahwah, NJ: Lawrence Erlbaum.

Gergen, K. J. (1994). *Toward transformation in social knowledge* (2nd ed.). London: Sage.

Hansen, M. T. (1999). The search-transfer problem: The role of weak ties in sharing knowledge across organization subunits. *Administrative Science Quarterly, 44*(1), 82–111.

Kalman, M. E. (1999). *The effects of organizational commitment and expected outcomes on the motivation to share discretionary information in a collaborative database: Communication dilemmas and other serious games.* University of Southern California.

Leonard-Barton, D. (1995). *Wellsprings of knowledge: Building and sustaining the sources of innovation.* Boston: Harvard Business School Press.

Markus, M. L. (2001). Toward a theory of knowledge reuse: Types of knowledge reuse situations and factors in reuse success. *Journal of Management Information Systems, 18*(1), 57–93.

Moreland, R. L. (1999). Transactive memory: Learning who knows what in work groups and organizations. In: L. L. Thompson, J. M. Levine & D. M. Messick (Eds), *Shared Cognition in Organizations: The Management of Knowledge* (pp. 3–32). Mahwah, NJ: Lawrence Erlbaum.

Neuhauser, P. (1993). *Corporate legends and lore: The power of storytelling as a management tool.* New York: McGraw-Hill.

Nonaka, I., & Konno, N. (1998). The concept of "ba": Building a foundation for knowledge creation. *California Management Review, 40*(3), 40–54.

Nonaka, I., & Takeuchi, H. (1995). *The knowledge-creating company.* New York: Oxford University Press.

O'Dell, C. C., Grayson, J. J., & Essaides, N. (1998). *If only we knew what we know: The transfer of internal knowledge and best practice.* New York: Free Press.

Orr, J. E. (1990). Sharing knowledge, celebrating identity: War stories and community memory in a service culture. In: D. Middleton & D. Edwards (Eds), *Collective Remembering: Memory in Society.* London: Sage.

Pierce, J. L., Kostova, T., & Dirks, K. T. (2001). Toward a theory of psychological ownership in organizations. *Academy of Management Review, 26*(2), 298–310.

Rumizen, M. C. (2002). *The complete idiot's guide to knowledge management.* Indianapolis, IN: Alpha.

Senge, P. M. (1990). The leader's new work: Building learning organizations. *Sloan Management Review, 32*(1), 7–23.

Stamps, J., & Lipnack, J. (2004). Appreciative inquiry in the age of the network. In: D. J. Cooperrider & M. Avital (Eds), *Constructive Discourse and Human Organization: Advances in Appreciative Inquiry* (Vol. 1, pp. 29–56). Oxford, UK: Elsevier.

Swap, W., Leonard, D., Shields, M., & Abrams, L. (2001). Using mentoring and storytelling to transfer knowledge in the workplace. *Journal of Management Information Systems, 18*(1), 95–114.

Tripsas, M., & Gavetti, G. (2000). Capabilities, cognition, and inertia: Evidence from digital imaging. *Strategic Management Journal, 21*(10/11), 1147–1161.

Tsoukas, H. (1996). The firm as a distributed knowledge system: A constructionist approach. *Strategic Management Journal, 17*, 11–25.

Von Krogh, G., Ichijo, K., & Nonaka, I. (2000). *Enabling knowledge creation: How to unlock the mystery of tacit knowledge and release the power of innovation.* New York: Oxford University Press.

Wasko, M. M., & Faraj, S. (2000). It is what one does: Why people participate and help others in electronic communities of practice. *Journal of Strategic Information Systems, 9*(2–3), 155–173.

Weick, K. E., & Roberts, K. H. (1993). Collective mind in organizations: Heedful interrelating on flight decks. *Administrative Science Quarterly, 38*(3), 357–381.

Wenger, E. (1998). *Communities of practice: Learning, meaning, and identity.* Cambridge, UK: Cambridge University Press.

Zack, M. H. (1999). Managing codified knowledge. *Sloan Management Review, 40*(4), 45–58.

PARADOX AND ORGANIZATIONAL CHANGE: THE TRANSFORMATIVE POWER OF HERMENEUTIC APPRECIATION

Tojo Thatchenkery

ABSTRACT

Though paradoxes constitute a basic ontological condition of organizational processes, the modernist approach has always been to find ways to resolve them. In this chapter, an alternative approach called hermeneutic appreciation *is proposed. By accepting and affirming paradoxes through the process of hermeneutic appreciation, the generative potential inherent in them can be recognized and unfolded. This chapter presents a case study of an organization that demonstrated such a sophisticated understanding of hermeneutic appreciation. By not dismissing the paradoxes but by affirming and reframing them, members of this organization were able to reverse a visible organizational decline and instead infuse it with new energy and vitality leading to an eventual organizational renewal. Lessons learned from this appreciative inquiry project suggest that a hermeneutic appreciation of paradoxes may act as a change intervention and is likely to enable innovation and organizational transformation.*

Constructive Discourse and Human Organization
Advances in Appreciative Inquiry, Volume 1, 77–101
Copyright © 2004 by Elsevier Ltd.
All rights of reproduction in any form reserved
ISSN: 1475-9152/doi:10.1016/S1475-9152(04)01004-X

INTRODUCTION

F. Scott Fitzgerald (1963) once said that the test of a first-class mind is the ability
to hold two opposing ideas in the head at the same time and still retain the ability
to function. In *the Age of Paradox*, Charles Handy (1994) argues that the ability to
deal with paradoxes will be a core competence for organizations of the 21st century.
"Paradox I now see to be inevitable, endemic, and perpetual. The more turbulent
the times, the more complex the world, the more paradoxes there are . . . (they)
are "like the weather, something to be lived with, not solved . . . Paradox has to be
accepted, coped with, and made sense of, in life, in work, in the community, and
among the nations" (1994, pp. 12–13).

International nonprofit organizations are no exception. This chapter analyses
the type of paradoxes experienced by a large global social change organization
and demonstrates how its unusual ability to appreciate paradoxes as a basic
organizational condition helped it reverse what appeared to an organizational
decline.

OUTLINE

The chapter begins with a definition and description of paradoxes and a brief
sharing of the limited research that shows the value of it in understanding
organizational dynamics. An argument is presented to show that the most
appropriate way to leverage a paradox is to develop an ability for appreciating it.
It is shown that appreciation is mostly a hermeneutic and intentional act. When we
reframe appreciatively, the plurivocal (multiple meaning) properties of language,
discourse, and dialogue become apparent. This process is defined as *hermeneutic
appreciation*. The outcome is generative possibilities and expanding boundaries
as opposed to constraining choices and learned helplessness. Though the reader is
not provided with a "ten-steps" approach to appreciating paradoxes, the narrative
here is meant to allow for a contextual understanding of what one would need to
do when faced with paradoxes.

WHAT ARE PARADOXES?

Paradox comes out of the Latin root, which denotes apparent contradiction. In
philosophy it refers to contradictory, mutually exclusive elements that are present
and operate equally at the same time. Paradox is different from concepts such
as dilemma, irony, inconsistency, dialectic, ambivalence, or conflict (Quinn &

Cameron, 1988, p. 2). A dilemma is an either-or situation where one alternative must be selected over other attractive alternatives. An irony exists when an unexpected or contradictory outcome arises from a single alternative. An inconsistency is merely an aberration or discontinuity from past patterns. A dialectic is a pattern that always begins with a thesis followed by an antithesis and resolved by a synthesis. Ambivalence is uncertainty over which two or more attractive (or unattractive) alternatives should be chosen. And a conflict is the perpetuation of one alternative at the expense of others. Paradox differs from each of these concepts in that no choice need be made between two or more contradictions. Both of the contradictory elements in a paradox are accepted and present. Both operate simultaneously.

Paradoxical thinking is associated with creative insights and scientific breakthroughs, which involve the transformation of old ways of thinking about a problem to new ways (Quinn & Cameron, 1988). "Janusian thinking" is a term introduced by Rothenburg (1979) while investigating the achievements over fifty highly creative artists and scientists. Janusian thinking happens when two contradictory thoughts are held to be true simultaneously. The explanation of the apparent contradiction is what often leads to major breakthroughs.

Groups and organizations face inherent, unresolvable paradoxes that they must accept, confront, and manage (Smith & Berg, 1987). Yet, organizational theorists are not very sophisticated in understanding the nature of paradox (Quinn & Cameron, 1988). Maruyama, Sawada, and Caley (1994) pointed out that the traditional ways in which researchers think are inappropriate for analyzing the complex organizational phenomena of paradox. On the contrary, they are based on assumptions of linearity and consistency. The simultaneous presence of contradictory patterns is rarely discussed. Most theories also overlook the fact that organizations are pervaded by a range of emotions, thoughts, and actions that their members experience as contradictory (Frost, 2003).

There are a few exceptions. Csikszentmihalyi (1997) used paradoxes to examine everyday tensions. He explored how self-reflecting on the often conflicting yet interwoven facets of professional life might help individuals find the flow between work and family, and theory and practice. This was done by using paradoxes as much more than a label but as a thought-provoking tool or perspective. Murnighan and Conlon (1991) studied the relationships between the internal dynamics and success of a population of *intense work groups* called professional string *quartets* in Great Britain. Their research determined that the string quartets faced three important paradoxes: the leadership vs. democracy paradox, the paradox of the second fiddle, and the paradox of confrontation vs. compromise. Their findings indicated that the more successful quartets recognized but did not try to resolve the paradoxes. Pearlson and Saunders (2001) discussed what they called "telecommuting paradoxes" which were increased flexibility vs. increased structure, greater individuality vs. more teamwork and more responsibility vs. greater control. Lee and O'Neill (2003) considered the paradoxical impact of ownership structure on R&D investments in the United States and Japan. Finally, Lewis (2000), after a comprehensive review came up with three paradoxes known as paradoxes of learning, paradoxes of organizing, and paradoxes of belonging.

THE NOTION OF HERMENEUTIC APPRECIATION

So far we have shown that paradoxes constitute a basic organizational condition and that, based on limited research, learning to deal with them constructively is better than trying to resolve them. In the examples cited above, the participants accepted the paradox instead of defensively reacting to it. In subsequent sections, a more sophisticated understanding of this notion of acceptance is presented by expanding it to the concept of *hermeneutic appreciation*. A case study is presented to show how stakeholders of an organization can develop an intentional ability to reframe paradoxes in a generative manner. This process of reframing is called *hermeneutic appreciation*.

WHAT IS HERMENEUTIC APPRECIATION?

Ap-pre-ci-ate – (a prē' shē āt') *verb*, to grasp the nature, worth, quality, and or significance of something, to judge with heightened perception of understanding, or to increase the value of something.

Merriam Webster's Collegiate Dictionary, Tenth edition, 1993.

In appreciation, there is a process of selectivity and judgment. For example, consider the following scenario. You are browsing through an art exhibit at the museum while your friend happens to see something similar at the local flea market. Assuming neither of you is an art critique, you are more likely to have a better appreciation of the painting than your friend is at the flea market. Because you are in the art museum, you have an appreciative mind-set. You are intentionally looking for beauty in the painting. You are looking to see what might have made the experts pick the painting as worthy of being put in this famous museum. As you look intently, you see aspects of the painting you might have missed had you looked with a casual eye. You are interpreting or reframing the details of the painting as "beautiful" and "exquisite" because of the self-referentiality[1] of the appreciative context that has been created.

The concept of appreciation has its roots in the German word *Weltanschauung* and the philosophical tradition of *hermeneutics*. The word Weltanschauung has no exact parallel in English since it combines two concepts in one: a way of perceiving (anschauen) reality (Welt), and experience (anschauung) of the world (Welt). In the word, these concepts are unbreakable creating an *inseparability of interpretation from experience*. For example, Dilthey (1910) pointed out that in interpreting one's relationship to life events, some people develop down-to-earth explanations while others pursue greater purposes.

The term "hermeneutics" comes from the classical Greek verb *hermeneuein*, *to interpret*. During the 17th century, hermeneutic study emerged as a discipline devoted to establishing guidelines for the proper interpretation of Biblical scripture. Since then, hermeneutics has evolved into a form of inquiry primarily concerned with the processes by which human beings interpret or discover the meaning of human action. According to hermeneutical philosophy, language is the medium of all human experience. "Language allows humans to dwell in the house of being. . . . Language is the fundamental mode of operation of our being-in-the-world and an all-embracing form of the constitution of the world" (Gadamer, 1977, p. 3). The human world is linguistically preconstituted. We inherit language in the "social uterus." In other words, language precedes us in the world. Human understanding takes place within an emerging linguistic framework evolved over time in terms of historically conditioned concerns and practices.

The centrality of language in creating reality as highlighted in the hermeneutic philosophy is also at the core of the more influential postmodern discourse which followed (Anderson, 1997; Baudrillard, 1988; Derrida, 1980; Gergen, 2001, 1999, 1994; Gergen & McNamee, 1998; Lyotard, 1984; Ricoeur, 1981; Rorty, 1989) (see Note 1). Within organization theory, the postmodern view (Boje, Gephart & Thatchenkery, 1996; Gergen & Thatchenkery, 1996; Linstead, 1994; Wallace, 1998) has also been profiled under such areas as narrative analysis (Barry & Elmes, 1997; Czarniawska, 1997) conversation analysis (Ford & Ford, 1995), discourse analysis (Boje, 1995; Oswick, 2002), textual analysis (Golden-Biddle & Locke, 1993; Thachankary, 1992, 2001), language games (Mauws & Phillips, 1995), rhetoric (Watson, 1995), and anomaly, paradox, and irony (Oswick, Keenoy & Grant, 2002) just to name a few!

Gadamer (1977) maintained that to have a method is to already have an interpretation. Nowhere is this truer than in appreciation. Psychology, the discipline created to enhance our understanding of human behavior, has historically had a focus on deficits. Noted Psychologist Kenneth Gergen (1994) listed hundreds of concepts in Psychology that are deficit oriented and pointed out that only a few existed that were positive. Similarly, Martin Seligman (1998) pointed out that psychology journals have published 45,000 articles in the last 30 years on depression, but only 400 on joy. According to him, when psychology began developing as a profession, it had three goals: to identify genius, to heal the sick, and to help people live better, happier lives. Over the last century, however, it has focused almost entirely on pathology and deficits, following the science of medicine, itself structured around disease, as its model. Seligman felt that Psychology has been negative for 100 years. Theories have generally focused on damage, as have techniques for intervention. Over a period of time, human behavior got defined in deficit terms creating a powerful "historicity" in hermeneutical terms (Snyder & Lopez, 2002).

The tenets of hermeneutics have immediate application to the concept of appreciation. The interpretive scheme we bring to the situation significantly influences what we will find. Seeing the world is always an act of judgment. We can take an appreciative judgment or a critical or deficit oriented judgment.

Gregory Vickers, an English practitioner-turned social scientist was the first to talk about appreciation in a systemic way. In 1963, in an article titled *Appreciative Behavior* Vickers introduced the concept to the social sciences. This was followed by several including the notable *Science and Appreciative Systems* in 1968. Vickers' main contribution is that of conceptualizing "appreciation" and the "appreciative process" as elements of a system. An appreciative system may be that of an individual, group, or an organization. To quote Vickers,

> To account for the appreciated world . . . I postulate that experience, especially the experience of human communication, develops in each of us a readiness to notice particular aspects of our situation, to discriminate them in particular ways and to measure them against particular standards of comparison . . . These readiness in turn helps to organize our further experience, which, as it develops, becomes less susceptible to radical change. Circular relations of this kind are the commonest facts of life, though we are handicapped in accepting them by our long conditioning to the idea of causal chains, linearly linked in time. Since there are no facts, apart from some screen of 'values' which discriminates, selects and relates them, just as there are no values except in relation to some configuration of fact, I use the word appreciation to describe the joint activity which we call knowing and which we sometimes suppose, I think mistakenly, to be a separable, cognitive activity which is 'value-free'. Since these readiness are organized into a more or less coherent system, I speak of them as an appreciative system. I sometimes refer to their state at any point of time as their appreciative setting and to any act which expresses them as an appreciative judgment. The appreciative world is what our appreciative system enables us to know (1972, p. 102).

In explaining appreciation, Vickers used systems thinking which provided basic concepts with which to describe the circular processes of perceiving, judging and acting. Vickers saw the experience of day-to-day life as a flux of interacting events and ideas. To deal with them, humans use two kinds of judgments, *reality judgments* and *value judgments*. The former is about what "is" whereas the latter is about what is good or bad. Arising out of this duality are action judgments.

Vickers believed that the cycle of judgments and actions are organized as an appreciative system with continuous feedback loops.

For Vickers, appreciation is the process of identifying (perceiving) parts of reality, and choosing some part that supports the actions to be changed. It is both a descriptive and a constructive process. It *describes* what is required to change/improve an action. At the same time, it *constructs* what can be required to change/improve an action. Appreciation thus mediates "systematically" between the past, the present, and the future. An appreciative system is recurrently closing the loop between the world of events and those perceiving and judging them by "appreciating" it. For example, in the art museum instance cited earlier, the observer is trying to close the loop between the act of visiting the museum, looking at a piece of art that is supposed to be world-class, and trying to judge it as superior by intentionally appreciating it. It is the intentionality of perceiving and judging that is critical here. The more intentional or purposeful the perceiver is, the more efficient the closing of the loop.

OTHER WORKS ON APPRECIATION

There have been others works on appreciation as well. For example, Gabriel Marcel (1962) introduced into philosophy a distinction between problem and mystery. Mystery produces a diffused experience where the distinction between subject and object disappears. "A mystery is something in which I am myself involved, and it can therefore only be thought of as a sphere where the distinction between what is in me and what is before me loses its meaning and its initial validity" (Marcel, 1962). On the contrary, a problem is something to be fixed. There is very little to appreciate in a problem other than getting rid of it or solving it. As Wittgenstein said, "It is not how things are in he world that is mystical, but that it exists." Taking this metaphor a step further, Keen (1969) felt: "However odd it may be linguistically or logically, there are states of mind in which the very existence of the world seems strange and miraculous, as if its being were a triumph over nothingness" (p. 22).

This distinction between mystery and problems is the foundation of *appreciative inquiry*, an alternative to the traditional action research model. In what has now become a classic article, Cooperrider and Srivastva (1987) reasoned that once everyday life-experiences are seen in terms of efficiency, logic, precision, and something to be fixed, organizational experiences become a microcosm of that very mindset, creating two contrasting images of organizations, organizations as problems to be solved or as mysteries to be appreciated. In a later writing on the affirmative basis of organizing Cooperrider (1990) proposed that social systems have a natural tendency to evolve toward the most positive images held by their members. According to him, the greatest obstacle to the well being of an ailing group or organization is the dis-affirmative projection that currently guides it. When organizations find that attempts to fix problems create more problems, or the same problems never go away (Senge, 1990), it is a clear signal of the inadequacy of the organization's current images or projections of who it is. In that context, appreciative inquiry is an attempt to co-create a shared consensus of a new future by exploring the core competencies that are resident in an organization.

Appreciative inquiry seeks to locate and heighten the "life-giving-forces" (Cooperrider & Srivastva, 1987) or core values of organizations. An affirmation of the organization calls for an in-depth understanding of its core values. The focus on core values becomes persuasive when we see organizations as systems of shared meaning and beliefs where the critical activity is the continued construction and maintenance of the meaning and belief systems (Pfeffer, 1982).

Pfeiffer's definition amplifies the life-giving nature of values, beliefs and ideology around which people organize for collective action. An affirmation of the uniqueness of organizational values is most likely to help a researcher or consultant realize what makes such organizing possible and understand the possibilities of newer and more effective forms of organizing. Appreciative inquiry thus seeks the best of "what is" in order to provide an impetus for imagining "what might be." According to Karl Weick (1982), intense affirmation might also show faults and inadequacies more readily than do intense criticisms. In an interesting article titled "affirmation as inquiry," he argues that if we have only weak images of organizations to work with we are likely to end up with weak theories of their organizing. Another writer in this area, Peter Elbow (1973), reminds us that we could also make an intentional choice to play the "believing game" as opposed to the "doubting game." In the doubting game, the researcher has a suspicious eye whereas in the believing game the efforts are to understand the organizational dynamics from the participants' point of view. In this context, explanations and interpretations are affirmations that assert what organizations are more than what they are not. As Weick (1982, p. 445) says, "We first have to affirm that it is there, in order, second, to discover that it is there."

Affirmation makes inquiry more honest. As Weick (1982) points out, most social sciences research is a demonstration of things we already know to be true, but about which we feel hesitant to make propositions given our academic socialization and norms about the nature of truth. For the sake of peer and professional acceptability we picture the inquiry process as if it were a detached scientific observation and as if the goals were disconfirmation of the hypotheses. Ultimately we are moving toward affirmations rather than disproof, in which case, as in appreciative inquiry, we may do that more explicitly and directly.

What is common among all the above approaches is the framing, interpretive, or hermeneutic element in reality construction. Just as Vickers does, all these writers show that there is an element of interpretation in human perception and the resulting appreciation, hence the term hermeneutic appreciation. In other words, the interpreter makes a choice to view the situation one way over another, deliberately attempting to see what is present as opposed to what is absent. In the rest of this chapter, with the help of the case study, we will see how members of an international nonprofit organization engaged in hermeneutic appreciation in their effort to deal with the various paradoxes they faced. This organization showed a remarkable ability to reframe the paradoxes appreciatively. We will learn from this case study that when we reframe the paradoxes appreciatively, they become liberating constructs as opposed to constraining. With hermeneutic appreciation, the paradoxes reveal possibilities that would not have been visible otherwise.

THE CASE STUDY

As part of an appreciative inquiry project, the author worked with an organization called The *Institute of Cultural Affairs*, or in short, the ICA. The ICA is an international nonprofit organization engaged in community empowerment around the world for the last fifty years. At its peak they operated in 35 nations with over 100 field offices. Since the early 1970s, the ICA has been quietly in the forefront of social inventions, demonstrating the organization's innovative approaches to thinking, organizing, and action (See Cooperrider & Thatchenkery, 1990 to learn more about their social change activities). This chapter focuses on how the ICA dealt with paradoxes and how that helped them reverse an organizational decline process. When members of a research team (for which this author was the project leader) started working with them, the ICA was undergoing some fundamental organizational change issues. After having grown rapidly, the ICA had reached a plateau and subsequently what appeared to be "symptoms" of organizational decline. It is at this stage of transition and ambiguity that the university research team headed by this author initiated an appreciative inquiry project with the ICA. The result was a process of renewal whereby member of the organization got in touch with their core values and began to appreciate the significant impact they have always had on society in general. Until then, out of a deficit mode, the ICA was looking more on what they had not done as opposed to what they had accomplished. The project helped them see that they had indeed made a positive impact in the lives of communities in many parts of the world and that the process that they call organizational decline may indeed be a sign of maturity.

This reframing was accomplished by significant hermeneutic appreciation of the various paradoxes they had faced.

THE ICA AND PARADOXES

Historically, the ICA has always had a very sophisticated understanding of paradoxes. For example, in 1971, when the organization was very young, an annual gathering of all ICA members from all over the world produced a one-hundred-page document titled *Matrices of Contradiction* that exclusively dealt with paradoxes. The document identified several forms of paradoxes (which they called contradictions), such as "paramount contradiction, primary contradictions, secondary contradictions, and tertiary contradictions." The document begins with the following:

> The twentieth-century Cultural Revolution is giving form to a new vision of a globally inter-related society; the revolutionary man consciously struggles to illuminate the contradictions impeding the actualization of the New Earth. Illuminating contradictions gives the possibility of discerning what needs to be done to create the global society. Exploring contradictions provides the basis for the formation of practical proposals.

The focus on "exploring the contradiction" for "practical action" is a form of hermeneutic appreciation. The ICA believed in thinking in new paradigms in order to generate a new understanding of paradoxes that would lead to action as opposed to inaction. This is again evident in the introduction section of the *Matrices of Contradictions*:

> Until man holds the vision of society as dynamic rather than static, he cannot deal with contradictions relative to trends manifest in his time. It is important, then, to identify contradictions carefully in order to deal with the depth of social malfunctions. The method of identifying and ordering contradictions is the articulation of each succeeding intensity level, constituting the matrices of contradiction. This approach to organizing the discussion of contradictions has been used to construct an overlay on the current collapse of tension among the foundational, communal, and rational dimensions of human sociality.

The one hundred-page document, the source of the above paragraph, was a sophisticated narrative on the nature of paradoxes both from a philosophical and pragmatic point of view. The analysis of the historical documents of the ICA clearly revealed their ability to engage in hermeneutic appreciation towards the paradoxes of their organizational life.

These paradoxes continue to be part of the ICA today. The thematic analysis of over 140 interviews conducted by the research team in various locations of the ICA in the United States and overseas helped surface their core paradoxes. Statements such as "the great truths of life are paradoxical" and "we want creative

Table 1. Core Paradoxes of the ICA.

Grand Narratives	< < < > > >	Local Narratives
Global networking	< < < > > >	Local networking
Unity in diversity	< < < > > >	Diversity in unity
Theory driven action	< < < > > >	Method driven action
Holistic and comprehensive development orientation	< < < > > >	Specific and tangible development orientation

approaches to societal contradictions" were common from the interviewees. One of the communications that went to participants for an important global gathering in 1989 that this author participated anticipated this paradox:

> History is created in the dialectic. The dialectic between the Platonic and the Aristotelian. The dialectic between the Yin and Yang. The dialectic between the Scattered and the Gathered; and the No Longer and the Not Yet. To create history is to embrace the paradox of the mystery of life.... The question has been asked as to whether some new form needs to take its (the absence of assigned leadership) place soon or do we allow this loss to give permission to further openness and experimentation ... the answer is Yes and No.... We are going through a period of scatteredness and autonomy ... it needs to be balanced by a centering, gathering dynamic. (ICA Communication, 1989).

Table 1 depicts the five core paradoxes of ICA's organizational life that were identified based on the analysis of 140 interviews and secondary sources.

These paradoxes are explained below.

The Paradox of Grand Narrative vs. Local Narratives

"In the past, one village had people from five countries doing a project. Now it is moving toward each location taking care of its own needs," said one interviewee. In the beginning, the ICA emphasized a strong international presence in each location (mostly staff from North America). However, as the ICA had more practical experiences in a larger variety of global settings and trained more people in their participative methodology, the new recruits did not necessarily have the same socialization or transformational experience as the earlier members, nor did they share a similar history or culture. Meanwhile, the ICA members were profoundly impacted by what they were learning from the local people in the new cultural settings. As more and more local members got trained in the ICA methods and became part of the organization, a gradual pressure to indigenize arose.

We may call this a paradox between the Western perspectives and local understanding, or simply the paradox between *grand narratives* and *local narratives* (Lyotard, 1984). Grand narratives or grand theories are models that are generalizable to all situations. To that extent they are also called global theories. In the case of the ICA, the models that were developed using their success stories from early projects were thought to have direct transferability and applicability to other parts of the world. As a result, ICA members from North America traveled to other continents to set up various rural capacity building projects. Though well intended, such efforts were essentially replications of what worked well in one cultural setting to the new one and did not work well in several instances because they could not fully make use of the local knowledge. However, over a period of time, as more and more ICA members were exposed to the relevance and value of the local wisdom and understanding, they recognized this as a paradox and learned to balance the local-global knowledge dynamics. As we would see later, they developed a hermeneutic appreciation for responding to this paradox by learning to see the good part of each polarity instead of choosing one over another.

The Paradox of Global Networking vs. Local Networking

As a global social change organization, historically, the ICA had always emphasized global networking. The focus was on creating structures that would connect the ICA in different parts of the world into a single corporate entity. However, as a result of the phenomenal growth during the 1970s, several ICA units that were dispersed in distant locations from the United States began networking locally. This local focus was very much encouraged by the ICA when they recognized this as a paradox. "You cannot be global unless you are local," said one ICA interviewee who witnessed this transition.

At the same time, this did not mean that each ICA would merely engage in local networking only. As a "planetary association" the ICA members wanted to stay connected, make policies together, and have an impact in the world based on their mission. In their view, the need of the moment was to be local and global at the same time. As one interviewee pointed out, "we appreciated this paradox by recognizing and valuing the interdependence that was required of all of us in order to keep in balance the global-local tension."

The Paradox of Unity in Diversity vs. Diversity in Unity

Another paradox that the ICA dealt with centered on themes of diversity and unity. In the beginning, "corporateness" (the feeling of oneness) and spirituality, two core values of the ICA, helped the members focus on maintaining unity while respecting differences. It was relatively easy to tolerate differences out of a basic faith that everyone belonged to one single community. There was a strong attribution to the commonality of the human experience irrespective of race, gender, and class. However, the scenario changed with transnational growth. Members who did not necessarily share a common heritage of the ICA had different understanding of development, but their dedication to the ICA's mission did not suffer despite this difference. Nonetheless, the paradox was evident and the focus gradually shifted to diversity in unity or "how to acknowledge and celebrate our differences and yet be one."

The Paradox of Theory-Driven Action vs. Method-Driven Action

A tension between theory-driven actions and action-oriented pragmatism has always been part of the ICA. Historically, the ICA operated from a strong theory base in which member commitments to ideas and postulates determined the power of their actions. The most striking instances were the *Religious Studies-1* and the *Academy* curriculum, two required academic courses for anyone who wanted to become a member of the ICA. They were both highly theory driven. As a reflective community, the ICA would start with the theory, initiate actions, study their impact, and then revise the theory if necessary, based on the outcomes of the actions. Such a reflective focus kept the theory-driven nature of action alive. The process was very similar to the action research process popularized by Kurt Lewin (1951), often credited as the founder of organizational development. Like Lewin, the ICA developed their theories based on observation, and once developed, were applied in field settings. However, over a period of time, in many other parts of the world where the ICA operated, a pressing call of pragmatism influenced the actions to assume a method-driven character. This was also the time corporate America was becoming more bottom line oriented, the impact of which was felt for all types of organizations. Outcomes and tools rather than theories or principles became important at this time. That was the beginning of a phase popularizing the "methods of the ICA." One of ICA's publications, "*Winning Through Participation*" (Spencer, 1989), is a striking example of the action/method orientation. So is the emergence of ICA-related organizational forms such as the *Training Inc.*, *ICA Associates*, and *LENS International*. Looking at the documents published by the ICA at that time, one could clearly see a better appreciation of this side of the polarity.

Yet, the ICA did not merely embrace the method or tool focus and de-center the theory orientation. In a refined act of hermeneutic appreciation, along side this "tool" focus, the ICA began a serious effort to introduce a new theory-driven program called the *Earthwise Curriculum*. This initiative dealt with global issues from a holistic perspective, incorporating the strengths of various previous ICA programs and the learning from their field experiences of several decades. The hermeneutic appreciation for the ICA here consisted of knowing that a theory is kept alive by being method driven. When the method works, the theory is proved to be right. At the same time, the success of the method may stifle new theory development. This was the fine line they were comfortable walking. Their appreciation of this paradox also consisted in recognizing the cyclical nature of the theory-tool dynamic.

The Paradox of Holistic and Comprehensive Development Orientation vs. Specific and Tangible Development Orientation

The 1960s were a time when holistic and comprehensive mission statement such as the one the ICA used ("concerned with the human factor in global development") could arouse a powerful passion in young people committing them to such causes. The 1980s and 1990s, however, demonstrated a different volunteer commitment to specific and tangible goals where the impact could be seen quickly. A young volunteer working for a social change cause may want to see the impact s/he can create in the shortest possible time in the most concrete and visible way. Thus, when a Greenpeace volunteer dares to stop a whale hunting expedition, s/he is able to see the impact s/he has created in almost real time. The ICA has recognized this as a paradox and has started paying attention to specific development projects as well such as those focused on specific environment issues, low cost housing, etc. Thus, instead of only engaging in total, comprehensive development, most ICA units now focus on specific targets. However, here too, there is no "either this or that" mentality. They have developed a reframing outlook for valuing both types of commitment.

The sophistication with which the ICA has been able to affirm the polarities of the paradoxes and their recognition of the hermeneutic possibilities therein was remarkable. The above polarities are indicative of a paradoxical dynamics that is consciously sustained and nurtured in the ICA culture to maintain a continual interchange of ideas from each polarity. For the ICA, it is not one or the other, but both. Further, as shown in the previous examples, the ICA uses paradox as an opportunity for interpretation. As has become evident from the previous examples, the ICA members were able to look the polarities in the paradox and try to see the possibilities that might exist there as opposed to constraints. Again, this a very good instance of hermeneutic appreciation.

HERMENEUTIC APPRECIATION AND THE TRANSFORMATIONAL POTENTIAL OF PARADOXES

What might be the reasons for the transformational properties of paradoxes that the ICA faced? Again, the model of hermeneutic appreciation may provide a plausible explanation. The notion of "plurivocity" outlined by Packer (1985) is also helpful here. Plurivocity is a central concept in hermeneutic philosophy which, by its reference to the *"perspectival"* nature of action and *polysemic* nature of linguistic construction, implies "openness to several interpretations" (Packer, 1985, p. 1086). The bipolar nature of the paradoxical construction generates the possibility for a multitude of interpretations within those polarities. The ICA did not want to get stuck in any of the polarities in a "one vs. the other" mode but instead learned to appreciate and make use of the tremendous potential for creative constructions that exists within the polarities.

Two interpretive possibilities are inherent in the plurivocity of constructs. One is *epistemic relativism*, whereby the potential for an indeterminate number of interpretations may give rise to a "crisis in interpretations" (Marcus & Fisher, 1986), resulting in confusion and lack of focus. The second is the notion of hermeneutic appreciation whereby plurivocity harbors creative possibilities for generative meaning making. It allows organizational participants to look at experiences with openness, flexibility, and reflection, so that constructive reframing becomes possible. In the case of the ICA, the latter happened at each stage in its transition.

The following is a description of how the hermeneutic appreciation towards paradoxical constructions around mission, spatiality, value, power, and temporality generated possibilities for generative interpretations in the ICA.

Mission Plurivocity

The ICA's espoused missions evoke a universal, trans-cultural agreement as being just and compassionate. From justice and compassion arise the espoused missions of the ICA, such as enhancing human potential, alleviating human misery, seeking peace, and valuing basic human dignity. Yet, there is a plurivocity here between the espoused and enacted organizational missions. Espoused missions are stated missions of an organization; enacted missions are the ones that are in actual use. Argyris (1999) would call this the paradox between *espoused theories* and *theories in use*. For many business organizations, the difference between the two is minimal; there is little tension between the espoused value of making profits and the operating value of generating more revenue than expenses. However, this does not hold true for the ICA, because the espoused mission of promoting the "human factor in development" means different things in different parts of the world. For that reason, the ICA needed to have the flexibility to interpret the missions in a way that would be useful in each location. Because the mission construct was seen as a paradox existing between two polarities, a range of interpretations became available to the ICA to deal with the diversity in its expression. In each of these instances, the ICA had to be intentional in engaging in hermeneutic appreciation, because without it there was the danger that the mission would be greatly misinterpreted.

The Spatial Plurivocity

The ICA mobilizes people all across the world from diverse geographical, economic, social and cultural backgrounds in large numbers, with minimum material resources. This calls for high managerial and leadership competencies such as resource optimization, managing trans-cultural differences, and drawing deep commitment from actors (Drucker, 2002). As a result, members of the ICA experience a tension between: (1) local knowledge (Geertz, 2000) vs. global knowledge; and (2) centralization vs. dispersion. As described earlier, when they became dispersed, the local knowledge or wisdom began to question the veracity of several of their prior generalizations (global knowledge). For example, during their work in Indian villages, ICA members were greatly influenced by the local people's notion of development and progress which were not always congruent with Western views.

Staying dispersed and centralized at the same time is another paradox. The ICA is dispersed, yet they need to have cohesion. The higher the dispersion, the greater the centrifugal forces on the actors to get immersed in local issues, and the lesser the centripetal forces to stay connected to the symbolic center (Louis & Sieber, 1979). Dealing with such paradoxes is an integral part of the strategies of the ICA. Again, as in the missions, the potential to construct a multitude of interpretations tolerated a wide range of behaviors and policies in ICA locations across the world. This became evident as participants at the ICA International gathering at Brussels were interviewed by this author. It appeared that each ICA was developing its own locally based strategies for defining itself as a global organization. By hermeneutic reframing, the ICA was able to appreciate the global implications of the local actions that came out of the spatial plurivocity inherent in centralization vs. decentralization and local vs. grand narratives paradoxical constructions.

The Value Plurivocity

In Weberian terms, the rationale for organizing in the ICA is based on the notion of value rationality rather than on purposive/instrumental rationality (e.g. Weber, 1964). Purposive rationality involves an orientation to a set of distinct, but not absolute ends. It differs from value rationality in that means and ends are both open to change if the secondary consequences of either are unacceptable to the actor (Weber, 1964). Value rationality is oriented towards the realization of an absolute goal (Weber, 1964). The actor has a conscious belief in an absolute value or a faith in the absolute value of a rationalized set of norms (Satow, 1975).

As mentioned earlier, organizations usually exist on a purposive, instrumental, or economic rationality basis (Etzioni, 1988; Gilbert & Etzioni, 2002) which, in turn, is based on a neoclassical paradigm of society. Alternatively, it is possible to conceive of organizations where utility maximizing is balanced by values, emotions, morality, and notions of ethics and integrity (Etzioni, 1988, 1998). In contrast to the neoclassical assumption that people seek to maximize one utility, e.g. pleasure or profit, they may pursue at least two utilities: pleasure and morality (Etzioni, 1998). The latter is a value-rational (Weber, 1964), normative, ideological attribute and has important implications for understanding organizational governance (Monks & Minow, 2001).

The ICA represents organizations where utility maximizing is balanced by values, emotions, morality, and notions of ethics and integrity. However, the moral, normative, and value bases of organizing may not always be congruent with the instrumental/purposive notion of having the resources to sustain an organization. Again, the bipolarity of the constructs allows the ICA to engage in hermeneutic appreciation by intentionally reframing the attributes of value and instrumental rationality. An example is the creation of parallel structures such as *Training Inc.*, *The ICA Associates*, and *LENS International*. These are essentially training and consultancy organizations that use the methods developed by the ICA over the years.

The Empowerment Plurivocity

Empowerment is truly a plurivocal term in management literature (Torbert, 1991). Empowering another (a person, group, community) presupposes that the target is without power to begin with. It also places the empowering person/agency higher in a hierarchy of power and authority. However, such assumptions do not imply that one should shy away from an empowering act, because it begins with power differences. This issue is particularly important for the ICA which has always had a distaste for bureaucratic, hierarchy-based authority structure and a predisposition for developing an egalitarian culture. For example, corporate leadership in the ICA actively encourages the process of eliciting participation and consensus building. As a result, authority in the ICA is diffused so that hierarchy and bureaucracy can be substituted with egalitarian structures. The ICA tries to create similar structures in organizations or communities with which they work. Yet the ICA realizes that some structures and formalizations are inevitable. Consensus building and participation are consciously encouraged, but some decisions may have to be taken without them for various reasons. Finally, even with the best efforts, sometimes the ICA realizes that the process of empowering may indeed be one of dis-empowering. This could happen when the target (group, organizations) becomes too dependent on the empowering agent. Thus, the ICA appreciates that a delicate balance should be kept between being too detached for fear of creating dependency and too much direction that may indeed create the dependency (O'Connor, 1995).

The Temporal Plurivocity

For organizations like the ICA, there are exigencies to continuously deal with which may adversely affect their ability for planning for the future. Often it a choice between what is urgent and what is important. For example, the *Amnesty International* is engaged in generating world opinion against human rights violations. At the same time, they would like to create a global awareness about the significance of human rights so that the incidences of violations will tend to reduce in the future. Another example of having to integrate the crisis and strategic management aspects is the environmental organization *Green peace*. Climbing smoke stacks to dramatize the effect of air pollution, facing a nuclear ship in life boats to stop it from underwater nuclear testing, and going out into the high seas to physically prevent whale hunting are instances of how Greenpeace has dealt with the current exigencies. On the other hand, Greenpeace is equally committed in educating and training people in environmentally safe living habits, lobbying for legislation to prevent dumping and pollution and creating a blue print for ecological harmony.

The ICA had to deal with the temporal paradox from the beginning. Going to a village to do capacity building work, the first impulse of the ICA was to do something to fix the immediate deprivation. Yet, it was aware that a quick fix would not solve anything in the long run unless the villagers themselves were empowered and trained to deal with the problems. Thus, while the ICA focused on goals such as improving education, healthcare, economic development, recreation, and job creation, it was also aware that the process should be participatory so that by the time a project was completed, the local population would have become capable of sustaining the progress. Accomplishing this required constructing appropriate interpretations of what were the right things to do. The paradoxical construction allowed enormous flexibility in making appreciative judgments about such specific situations.

HERMENEUTIC APPRECIATION, PARADOXES, AND ORGANIZATIONAL TRANSFORMATION

The above analysis looked at some core paradoxes that the ICA faced and how they responded to them by appreciative reframing. At a pragmatic level, the paradoxes function both as a facilitator and inhibitor of change. Due to the flexibility of inter-pretations possible across the range of the polarities of the paradoxes (thanks to the hermeneutic appreciation process), the ICA has been able to change as well as stay stable. As we have seen, the ICA has shown remarkable adaptability and resilience in creating social change while at the same time allowing it to be influenced by the changes it created. It was able to evolve into diverse organizational forms globally and yet remain a "single corporate body of globally interconnected people" (quote from an interviewee at Brussels). We have seen how such paradoxes had existed in the evolution of the ICA since its beginning. Each time, the organization dealt with them by creating values that helped it make "choice points." The following narrative is meant to show this process of appreciative reframing that the ICA had done as it evolved from various organizational forms. The objective is to show that as the ICA faced difficult paradoxes at critical transition stages, the way it reframed them helped it survive.

For example, in 1963, as the organization (it was called the Institute then) moved from Evanston to the Chicago inner city (the 5th City) and began working with the local residents to discern the community's problems and design practical, locally based solutions, they faced the paradox of maintaining a balance of dependence and counter-dependence between the residents and the organization. A variety of options based on different interpretations were available at this point. The resolution came in the creation of a new value called "participation." It meant that for communities to change, they must first feel an ownership of what is being changed. Within four years, the ghetto was completely transformed. The *5th city* had community gathering places, a health center, preschool, stores, churches, and parks, along with new businesses and industries.

By 1968, the Institute wanted to expand from the Chicago base to rest of the world. They created a program called the "Global Odyssey" in which members traveled to a dozen countries in Africa, Latin America, Middle East, and Asia to do research on the core theme of "global development." This shift from local development to global development was also paradoxical. Their religious tenets taught them that the whole world is one place and its people are all of equal worth. This was in opposition to their commitment to work through local churches to deal with local issues. The paradox was resolved by the creation of a value of "planetary inter-connectedness." Inspired by this mission, its members dispersed all across the world in an effort to replicate their 5th city community participation model.

As the organization expanded and became international, its members got exposed to different cultures, religions (Buddhism and Hinduism), and customs creating another paradox: the need for the organization to adapt to more secular views. This resulted in the formation of a new organization called the *Institute of Cultural Affairs* in 1973. By the mid-1970s, the ICA had expanded from its base in Chicago to 100 offices in 30 countries.

The creation of the ICA marked yet another change in the interpretive scheme (Bartunek, 1984) as a result of responding to the plurivocity inherent in the paradox. The basic paradoxical stance of this organization had been an "in but not of the world" notion. The creation of the ICA represented the generation of a new paradox which the organization described as a "turn to the world." The change from a Christian faith to a secular one was understandably difficult. They had to continuously engage in hermeneutic appreciation and reinterpret their philosophical basis of existence so that it made sense to stay in the ICA and continue the work. However, the tension of the new paradox generated renewed energy, resulting in major expansion of the organization globally. This also supports the notion of Argyris and Schon (1978) and Sheldon (1980) that fundamental changes in interpretive schemes result in radical second order changes in which organizational paradigms are reframed. Similarly, Bartunek (1984) showed in her case study of a religious order that second order changes can be understood dialectically, with the original interpretive schemas as the thesis, other ways of understanding as the antithesis, and what will emerge from the interaction as a synthesis.

The next major organizational change for the ICA occurred in 1985, when the consensus of the international gathering decided to let every ICA become autonomous. The members had to let go of the centralization in Chicago that had existed since the organization's beginning. For several local ICA, it meant finding new ways of survival and dealing with autonomy and freedom. The organization continues to undergo structural changes. ICA in different places has developed different forms. The differences between ICA around the globe are striking, yet they are all ICA in the most fundamental sense. This is yet another instance of the generative capacity of multiple interpretations in the ICA.

Poole and Van de Van (1989) have discussed four ways of responding to paradoxes. The ICA seemed to have used the second one: *accept the paradox and use it constructively, and introduce new terms to deal with the paradoxes.* Hermeneutic appreciation is the underlying process that enabled them to do this. The above analysis also shows that structural changes in the ICA were more directly linked to action that results from changes in interpretive schemes than to the changing interpretive schemes themselves. Structural features are in a reciprocal relationship with individuals' actions and understanding (Giddens, 1979). Organizational structural properties both legitimize and constrain action. When interpretive schemes (cognitive schemata that map our experience of the world) and their expression in action change, then the structure will also undergo change, which in turn will legitimize and constrain later action and interpretive schemes. When second order change takes place, the original integrative schemas have to be unlearned so new ones can come into existence. Such changes involve substantial organizational uncertainty and chaos (Bartunek, 1984) and often are disorienting and paralyzing. In addition, they are likely to be experienced by organization members as a series of deaths and rebirths (Hedberg, 1981) which is inherently painful and threatening (Schein, 1980). In that context, shared interpretive schemes not only legitimize particular organizational structures, but also serve as a source of stability in the midst of change (Ranson, Hining & Greenwood, 1980).

What happens to an organization caught up in the plurivocity of a paradoxical dialogue? In the case of the ICA, it gave rise to peculiar organizational processes, the most prominent being the presence of *multiple interpretive schemes.* Several writers have analyzed such interpretive processes in organizations (Bartunek, 1984; Daft & Weick, 1984; De Vries & Miller, 1987; Heracleous & Barrett, 2001; Lee & O'Neill, 2003; Ranson, Hinings & Greenwood, 1980). For example, Ranson, Hining and Greenwood (1980) proposed that one of the factors that most affects an organization's structure is powerful organization members' interpretive schemes and the expression of these in "provinces of meaning," which in turn represent the organization's values (desired ends and preferences) and interests. They argued that "there will be a change in structuring if organizational members revise the provinces of meaning, the interpretive schemes, which underpin their constitutive structuring of organizations" (1980, p. 12). Others have suggested that organizations differ in their use of interpretive schemes; some are highly interpretive while in others narrowly define work and organizational roles. The notion of *hermeneutic organizations* aptly captures the qualities of those organizations where interpretive activities of a high intensity are prevalent in dealing with the plurivocity of the organizational constructs.

Constructs in the ICA like the mission, spatiality, temporality, value, and authority are subject to an indeterminate number of interpretations by different stakeholders. One consequence is that meaning is simultaneously constructed and deconstructed in the ICA (Gray et al., 1985; Lewicki, Gray & Elliot, 2002; Weick, 2000). This is so because organizational members continuously engage in sense-making activities of several key aspects, such as mission, environment, procedures, membership, and events. This process of meaning creation and recreation is essentially a hermeneutic process.

For example, the plurivocity inherent between the espoused and enacted missions is one of the most active sources of hermeneutic activities in the ICA. Similarly, hermeneutic processes are more likely to occur in the ICA, because they are dispersed. Dispersed organizations present themselves issues not typically dealt with in "concentrated" organizations (Louis & Sieger, 1979; Murphy & Louis, 1999). As the dispersed actors get intensely involved and influenced by the local situation, the centrifugal tendency to pull out increases against a centripetal tendency to be controlled by the central organization. Several break-away, small, local social-change organizations have been formed by activists who worked in remote areas far away from parent organizations. The dispersion also permits more hermeneutic possibilities regarding the meaning of organizational missions, tasks, and their fulfillment.

To give another example, the moral value rational stance of the ICA clearly provides immense opportunities for multiple interpretations. Moral and ethical values are highly subjective and convey different meanings to people, whereas instrumental or purposive rationality has relatively narrow definitions (e.g. profit). Lastly, considering the empowerment issues, participative practices claimed to be helping communities may be disputed as nothing more than a "pseudo participation" by some stakeholders.

CONCLUSION

The plurivocity of paradoxical constructions of reality in the organizational life of the ICA results in highly interpretive acts, making it highly hermeneutic in nature. Hermeneutic processes are present in all types of organizations; only their degree varies. A military set up in combat situation provides few hermeneutic possibilities because the nature of the contingency requires that all actors understand and interpret the task in a relatively homogenous way. On the other hand, the mission of the ICA – creating a paradigm shift in the way people think about the human factor in development – is open for fulfillment in indeterminate ways, which in turn gives rise to intense hermeneutic activities in the organization.

One of the learning out of analyzing the various paradoxes of the ICA may be that paradoxical constructions and the accompanying plurivocity will be functional for those organizations which have the capacity for reflection about their experiences. Secondly, as stakeholders recognize and reflect on these paradoxes, they tend to transform the organization to new possibilities by providing a new platform for conversation between the polarities of the paradoxes. Hermeneutic appreciation is the grammar of such conversations, allowing stakeholders see possibilities that they would not have otherwise.

NOTE

1. The doyen of postmodernism, Baudrillard (1988) has expanded the notion of self-referentiality. In simple terms, self-referentiality implies that all rules refer to other rules and have validity only in the context of such a network of inter-dependent relationships.

REFERENCES

Anderson, H. (1997). *Conversation, language, and possibilities: A postmodern approach to therapy.* New York: Basic Books.

Argyris, C. (1999). *On organizational learning.* Malden, MA: Blackwell.

Argyris, C., & Schon, D. A. (1978). *Organizational learning: A theory of action perspective.* Reading, MA: Addison-Wesley.

Barry, D., & Elmes, M. (1997). Strategy retold: Toward a narrative view of strategic discourse. *Academy of Management Review, 22,* 429–452.

Bartunek, J. M. (1984). Changing interpretive schemes and organizational restructuring: An example of a religious order. *Administrative Science Quarterly, 29,* 355–372.

Baudrillard, J. (1988). *Selected writings.* Palo Alto, CA: Stanford University Press.

Boje, D. (1995). Stories of the storytelling organization: A postmodern analysis of Disney as 'Tamara-Land'. *Academy of Management Journal, 38,* 997–1035.

Boje, D., Gephart, R., & Thatchenkery, T. (Eds) (1996). *Postmodern management and organization theory.* Newbury Park: Sage.

Cooperrider, D. L. (1990). Positive image, positive action: The affirmative basis of organizing. In: S. Srivastva et al. (Eds), *Appreciative Management and Leadership.* San Francisco: Jossey Bass.

Cooperrider, D., & Srivastva, S. (1987). Appreciative inquiry in organizational life. *Research in Organizational Change and Development, 1,* 129–169.

Csikszentmihalyi, M. (1997). *Good business: Leadership, flow and the making of meaning.* New York: Viking Press.

Czarniàwska-Joerges, B. (1997). *Narrating the organization: Dramas of institutional identity.* Chicago: University of Chicago Press.

Daft, R., & Weick, K. E. (1984). Toward a model of organizations as interpretation systems. *Academy of Management Review, 9,* 284–295.

de Vries, M. F. R., & Miller, D. (1987). Interpreting organizational texts. *Journal of Management Studies, 24,* 233–247.

Derrida, J. (1980). *Of grammatology* (tans. G. Spivak). Baltimore: Johns Hopkins University Press.

Dilthey, W. (1910/1991). *Selected works Vol. I: Introduction to the human sciences*. Princeton, NJ: Princeton University Press.

Drucker, P. (2002). *Managing in the next society*. New York: St. Martin's Press.

Elbow, P. (1973). *Writing without teachers*. London: Oxford University Press.

Etzioni, A. (1988). *The moral dimension: Toward a new economics*. New York: Free Press.

Etzioni, A. (1998). *The new golden rule: Community and morality in a democratic society*. New York: Basic Books.

Ford, J. D., & Ford, L. W. (1995). The role of conversations in producing intentional change in organizations. *The Academy of Management Review*, *20*, 541–570.

Frost, P. (2003). *Toxic emotions at work*. Boston, MA: HBS Press.

Gadamer, H. G. (1977). *Philosophical hermeneutics*. Berkeley, CA: University of California Press.

Geertz, C. (2000). *Local knowledge: Further essays in interpretive anthropology*. New York: Basic Books.

Gergen, K. (1994). *Toward transformation in social knowledge*. Thousand Oaks: Sage.

Gergen, K. (1999). *An invitation to social construction*. Thousand Oaks: Sage.

Gergen, K. (2001). *Social construction in context*. Thousand Oaks: Sage.

Gergen, K., & McNamee, S. (Eds) (1998). *Relational responsibility: Resources for sustainable dialogue*. Thousand Oaks: Sage.

Gergen, K., & Thatchenkery, T. (1996). Organization science as social construction: Postmodern potentials. *Journal of Applied Behavioral Science*, *32*(4), 356–377.

Giddens, A. (1979). *Central problems in social theory*. London: Macmillan.

Gilbert, N., & Etzioni, A. (2002). *Transformation of the welfare state: The silent surrender of public responsibility*. New York: Oxford University Press.

Golden-Biddle, K., & Locke, K. (1993). Appealing work: An investigation of how ethnographic texts convince. *Organization Science*, *4*, 595–616.

Gray, B., Bougon, M. G., & Donnellon, A. (1985). Organizations as constructions and destructions of meaning. *Journal of Management*, *11*, 83–98.

Handy, C. (1994). *The age of paradox*. Boston: HBS Press.

Hedberg, B. (1981). How organizations learn to unlearn. In: P. C. Nystrom & W. H. Starbuck (Eds), *Handbook of Organization Design* (Vol. 1, pp. 3–27). Oxford: Oxford University Press.

Heracleous, L., & Barrett, M. (2001). Organizational change a discourse: Communicative actions and deep structures in the context of information technology implementation. *Academy of Management Journal*, *44*(4), 755–780.

Keen, S. (1969). *Apology for wonder*. New York: Harper & Row.

Lee, P., & O'Neill, H. (2003). Ownership structures and R&D investments of U.S. and Japanes firms. *Academy of Management Journal*, *46*(2), 212–226.

Lewin, K. (1951). *Field theory in social sciences*. New York: Harper & Row.

Lewis, M. (2000). Exploring paradox: Toward a more comprehensive guide. *Academy of Management Review*, *25*(4), 760–777.

Linstead, S. (1994). Objectivity, reflexivity, and fiction: Humanity, inhumanity, and the science of the social. *Human Relations*, *47*(11), 1321–1345.

Louis, K. S., & Sieber, S. D. (1979). *Bureaucracy and the dispersed organization*. Norwood, NJ: Ablex.

Lyotard, J. F. (1984). *The postmodern condition: A report on knowledge*. B. Bennington, Massouri (Trans.). Minneapolis: University of Minnesota Press.

Marcel, G. (1962/2001). *The mystery of being*. Chicago, IL: St. Augustine Press.

Marcus, G. E., & Fisher, M. (1986). *Anthropology as cultural critique: An experimental moment in the human sciences*. Chicago: University of Chicago Press.

Maruyama, M., Sawada, D., & Caley, M. (1994). *Mindscapes: The epistemology of Magoroh Maruyama*. New York: Routledge.

Mauws, M., & Phillips, N. (1995). Understanding language games. *Organization Science, 6*, 322–344.

Monks, R., & Minow, N. (Eds) (2001). *Corporate governance*. New York: Blackwell.

Murnighan, K. J., & Conlon, D. E. (1991). The dynamics of intense work groups: A study of British quartets. *Administrative Science Quarterly, 36*, 165–186.

O'Connor, E. (1995). Paradoxes of participation: Textual analysis and organizational change. *Organization Studies, 16*, 769–803.

Oswick, C., Keenoy, T., & Grant, D. (2002). Metaphor and analogical reasoning in organization theory. *Academy of Management Review, 27*(2), 294–304.

Packer, M. J. (1985). Hermeneutic inquiry in the study of human conduct. *American Psychologist, 40*, 1081–1093.

Pearlson, K., & Saunders, C. (2001). There's no place like home: Managing telecommuting paradoxes. *Academy of Management Executive, 15*(2), 117–125.

Pfeffer, J. (1982). *Organizations and organization theory*. Boston: Pitman.

Poole, M. S., & Van de Ven, A. H. (1989). Using paradox to build management and organization theories. *Academy of Management Review, 14*, 562–578.

Quinn, R. E., & Cameron, K. S. (Eds) (1988). *Paradox and transformation: Toward a theory of change in organization and management*. Cambridge, MA: Ballinger.

Ranson, S., Hinings, B., & Greenwood, R. (1980). The structuring of organizational structures. *Administrative Science Quarterly, 25*, 1–14.

Ricoeur, P. (1981). *Hermeneutics and the human sciences*. J. B. Thompson (Trans.). Cambridge: Cambridge University Press.

Rorty, R. (1989). *Contingency, irony, and solidarity*. Cambridge: Cambridge University Press.

Rothenburg, A. (1979). *The emerging goddess*. Chicago: University of Chicago Press.

Satow, R. L. (1975). Value-rational authority and professional organizations: Weber's missing type. *Administrative Science Quarterly, 20*, 526–531.

Schein, E. H. (1980). *Organizational psychology*. Englewood Cliffs, NJ: Prentice-Hall.

Seligman, M. (1998). Building human strength: Psychology's forgotten mission. *APA Monitor, 29*(1).

Senge, P. (1990). *The fifth discipline*. New York: Doubleday.

Sheldon, A. (1980). Organizational paradigms: A theory of organizational change. *Organizational Dynamics, 8*(3), 61–79.

Smith, K. K., & Berg, D. N. (1987). *Paradoxes of group life: Understanding conflict, paralysis, and movement in group dynamics*. San Francisco: Jossey Bass.

Snyder, C. R., & Lopez, S. (2002). *Handbook of Positive Psychology*. New York: Oxford University Press.

Spencer, L. (1989). *Winning through participation*. Dubuque, Iowa: Kendall/Hunt.

Thachankary, T. (1992). Organizations as "texts": Hermeneutics as a model for understanding organizational change. *Research in Organization Development and Change, 6*, 197–233.

Thatchenkery, T. (2001). Mining for meaning: Reading organizations using hermeneutic philosophy. In: R. I. Westwood & S. A. Linstead (Eds), *The Language of Organization* (pp. 112–131). London: Sage.

The Letters of F. Scott Fitzgerald (1963). Andrew Turnbull (Ed.). New York: Scribners.

Torbert, W. R. (1991). *The power of balance: Transforming self, society, and scientific inquiry*. Thousand Oaks: Sage.

Weber, M. (1964). *The theory of social and economic organization*. New York: Free Press.

Weick, K. (1982). Affirmation as inquiry. *Small Group Behavior, 13*, 441–442.

PART II:
ACTIVATION AND ELEVATION
OF INQUIRY

WITH OUR QUESTIONS WE MAKE THE WORLD

Marilee G. Adams, Marjorie Schiller and David
L. Cooperrider

ABSTRACT

Appreciative inquiry is built upon recognition of the profound power of questions in shaping our worlds; a power invoked by the phrase, "questions are fateful." We wonder, "What kinds of questions can optimize our inquiry and contribute to catalyzing transformational change?" The goal of this chapter is to provide conceptual and practical answers to this question. We seek to enrich and contribute to the field of appreciative inquiry through expanded ways of thinking about inquiry and the generation of questions. We begin by considering how questions influence how we think, behave, and relate. How do questions affect outcomes? We examine the nature of thinking as intrinsically a question and answer process and highlight the vital role of "QuestionThinking™" for creating new possibilities. We present the Learner-Judger Mindset Model, which provides distinctions for strengthening the spirit of inquiry in constructing questions. Then we examine how appreciative inquiry practitioners can take advantage of the distinctions and practices of QuestionThinking using the Mindset Model. Finally, we provide practical question-centered practices that can lead to positive new futures for ourselves and the individuals and organizations we serve.

Constructive Discourse and Human Organization
Advances in Appreciative Inquiry, Volume 1, 105–124
© 2004 Published by Elsevier Ltd.
ISSN: 1475-9152/doi:10.1016/S1475-9152(04)01005-1

INTRODUCTION

Appreciative inquiry is built upon recognition of the profound power of questions in shaping our worlds; a power invoked by the phrase, "questions are fateful." In alignment with this realization, appreciative inquiry grows out of a deep-rooted commitment to using the forging power of questions to transform individuals, organizations, and the world. That commitment grows out of the realization that "...inquiry and change are a simultaneous moment" (Cooperrider, 2000). So we wonder, "*What* kinds *of questions can optimize our inquiry and contribute to catalyzing transformational change?*"

The goal of this chapter is to provide conceptual and practical answers to this question. We seek to enrich and contribute to the field of appreciative inquiry through expanded ways of thinking about inquiry and the generation of questions. We begin by considering how questions influence how we think, behave, and relate. How do questions affect outcomes? We examine the nature of thinking as intrinsically a question and answer process and highlight the vital role of "QuestionThinking[TM]" for creating new possibilities. We present the Learner-Judger Mindset Model, which provides distinctions for strengthening the spirit of inquiry in constructing questions. Then we examine how appreciative inquiry practitioners can take advantage of the distinctions and practices of Question-Thinking using the Mindset Model. Finally, we provide practical question-centered practices that can lead to positive new futures for ourselves and the individuals and organizations we serve.

This chapter grew out of the authors' recognition that the presuppositions, practices, and visions of Appreciative Inquiry and QuestionThinking are highly complementary. Coming from the distinct fields of organizational development and clinical psychology, we discovered a shared love for the world-shaping role of language and questions. We see appreciative questions as potent vehicles for world benefit. Therefore, we set out to explore how integrating our experiences, insights, and commitments might make a meaningful contribution to constructive discourse for building the kind of world we want to inhabit and leave as a legacy to our children.

To fulfill the twin goals of expanding our understanding about inquiry and providing question construction practices, we first offer a brief review of some challenges inherent in these two tasks. Questions are explicit yet ephemeral, ordinary yet mysterious. Questions offer tools to work with and simultaneously the material from which new construction occurs. Questions are intrinsically co-created since they require both asker and listener to construct meaning. Some questions are provocative and initiate introspection; these questions may push us into new territories.

For a variety of reasons, many people, to one degree or another, resist asking or answering questions. This resistance is further exacerbated by the fact that questioning skills are rarely taught and we assume we should already know how to be expert questioners. The end result is that most people develop few explicit questioning skills. Even so, it is important to note that there are numerous practices and mindsets available for developing such skills.

LANGUAGE, REALITY, AND THE POWER OF QUESTIONS

The subject of question asking is primary and universal; it is fundamental to any consideration about the ways we human beings perceive, think, feel, and make meaning. Questions are also at the core of how we listen, behave, and relate – as individuals and in organizations. Virtually everything we think and do is generated by questions. In this sense, questions exert a gravitational pull, compelling engagement, in a manner quite similar to the impulse of wanting to close a gestalt. We crave completion. To extract meaning from our lives, we continuously ask ourselves questions such as: *"What happened?" "Why is it happening?"* and *"What is going to happen?"*

Because questions are fundamentally related to action and reflection, they spark and direct attention, energy, and effort. They are at the heart of the evolving forms our lives assume. Author Neil Postman instructs us that, "... all the answers we ever get are responses to questions. The questions may not be evident to us, especially in everyday affairs, but they are there nonetheless, doing their work. *Their work, of course, is to design the form that our knowledge will take and therefore to determine the direction of our actions"* (Postman, 1976, p. 144; italics added). We might say then, that the shape of our lives at any moment represents the cumulative answers to all the foreground and background questions we've ever asked ourselves and others.

Philosopher Martin Heidegger noted that "Language [is] the house of Being ..." In this context, we consider questions as the primary means from which doing, accomplishing, and creating change are catalyzed to action. Moreover, if language informs the structures of reality, then questions inform the structure of language. Therefore, we think of questions as the fundamental linguistic tools with which we construct our worlds. Answers to questions such as, *"What's wrong?"* or *"Who's to blame?"* lead to a world quite distinct from that which emerges from questions such as, *"What's right?"* and *"How can we build on these strengths?"*

Questions arise from our relationships with ourselves, others, and the world around us. In fact, interpersonal questions are world-shaping precisely because they are, in essence, co-constructed. Externalized questions presuppose both a question *asker* and *receiver* (the listener). It is through listening and receiving that the interrogative sentence actually becomes a question. Professor Chris Argyris and Schon (1978) has defined communication as "a double loop of shared understanding." He highlights the role of the sender (asker) and receiver (listener) in all forms of meaning making.

Furthermore, we listen to ourselves, others, and the world around us through internal questions that are usually implicit. Depending on whether I listen to you through the question *"What is valuable about what she's saying?"* or *"Why is she wasting my time?"* I will hear very different messages. This perception about listening underscores the sense that questions are always co-constructed. Both the questions the listener forms in her mind, and the questions the speaker asks, are fateful. This imbedded, dynamic relationship can be likened to a linguistic dance in which we build our worlds together.

Recognizing the structure and components of this dance is fundamental to our ability to choreograph it. Just as no dance is separate from the dancer, there is no question separate from the asker or the mindset from which the question has emerged. The recognition that we might be listening, either to ourselves or others, through limiting questions, gives us the distinctions and the impetus to search for new and hopefully more effective questions to guide our listening. We would then design these new questions with underlying assumptions that are more life giving, generous, and expansive. Our goal would be to create an expanded repertoire of possible interactions and outcomes.

Every new product, process, service, and relationship was catalyzed by a new question. The theory of relativity stemmed from a question Albert Einstein asked himself as an adolescent when he wondered, *"What would the universe look like if I were riding on the end of a beam of light at the speed of light?"* An unanticipated future can only occur in response to new, unexpected questions. That future begins in our thinking, represented by the questions we ask ourselves. In asking himself a genuinely novel question, and being willing to receive surprising answers, Einstein expanded humanity's understanding of the universe, which allowed us to think in completely new ways.

Since we build our worlds through the questions we ask, opening new worlds requires asking new questions. We mean questions that are qualitatively and profoundly different, ones that leap over old boundaries of thinking and land us in new paradigms. Paradigm shifts are catalyzed *when questions asked inside* the *current paradigm can only be answered from outside of it* (Goldberg, 1998). A truly expansive, transformational, paradigm-altering question is one to which the answer is not yet known. The poet, Rumi, pointed to the possibility of landing in a new paradigm outside of polarized, oppositional right/wrong thinking when he wrote:

> Out beyond ideas of wrong doing and right doing, there is a field.
> I'll meet you there.

QUESTIONTHINKING: THINKING AS A QUESTION AND ANSWER PROCESS

It is natural to assume that question asking refers only to interpersonal questions, that is, the ones we ask each other. However, we assert this assumption masks the origin of interpersonal questions found in our internal queries, the ones we ask ourselves. Looking deeper, we find that our thoughts can take the form of *both* statements *and* questions. In this sense, we believe that while most people assume that thoughts are internal statements, those statements are, in actuality, answers to preceding implicit or explicit questions. This assumption is embedded in some of the seminal work of cognitive psychology (Beck, 1979).

By acknowledging the operation and ensuing results of internal questions and their relationship to internal statements, we discover important openings for new thinking, new action, and fundamentally new possibilities. We label this understanding of thinking as a question and answer process, "QuestionThinking," thus distinguishing it from the usual presumption that thoughts are only statements (Adams, 2004). We might view QuestionThinking as reframing Descartes' famous saying, "I think, therefore I am" into, "I question, therefore I am."

An assumption of QuestionThinking is that questions operate at the interface of thinking and behavior. In other words, we answer our internal questions with behavior as well as in language. Of the four speech acts (Flores, 1997), (requests, declarations, assertions, and promises), it is requests (or questions) that are constant catalysts for action. In this sense, external behaviors, as well as internal statements, can be understood as representing answers to background questions, i.e. those prior queries that are usually assumptive, implicit, and silent.

Here is an ordinary example demonstrating how behavior responds to internal questions. In making the everyday decision about getting dressed, we ask ourselves a series of questions such as: *"Where am I going today? What's the weather? What's appropriate?"* and even *"What's clean?"* Our answers represent our choices, they are *behavioral answers*. Someone got dressed. We might even say they are wearing their answers. If we ask so many questions about something as simple as getting dressed, imagine how many more questions we ask ourselves about major life events such as what career to pursue, where to live, or whom to marry!

Organizational culture and norms also represent behavioral answers to the tacit questions that shaped them. The same assertions we've made about the impact of questions in guiding individual behavior, we also believe to be descriptive of the ways that implicit and explicit questions lead to organizational behavior and outcomes. By articulating organizational behavior as driven by guiding questions (usually unconsciously), we gain a useful lens for seeing the norms that guide behavior. For example, asking, "How can we optimize our railroad business?" in contrast to, "How can we optimize our transportation business?" would yield quite different responses. In a larger frame, we might recognize that when nomadic societies roamed the earth, their behavior could be understood as answering the question, *"How can we get ourselves to water?"* Both their behavior and history shifted in response to a new implicit question, *"How can we get the water to come to us?"*

We conclude, therefore, that we first make the world we inhabit in the questions we ask ourselves, that is, in our QuestionThinking. This means that strategic thinking, problem solving, and decision-making can all be seen as internal question and answer processes. We consider these internal queries as being, by far, the most creative, generative, and world-altering aspect of both internal and interpersonal language. Because the operations and outcomes of questions and statements are profoundly distinct, this never-ending dance of questions and answers provides a widening lens on mental processes and on our perceptions of what is possible. It also deepens our appreciation for the Buddha who, in his boundless wisdom, is reputed to have said, "With our thoughts we make the world."

THE LEARNER-JUDGER MINDSET MODEL

Our mindsets frame the way we perceive, experience, and interact with the world. These frames of mind simultaneously "program" what we believe to be our personal limitations as well as possibilities. They define the parameters of our actions and interactions. As a consequence, our mindsets implicitly and explicitly affect what happens in our lives. Hundreds of studies on the placebo and Pygmalion effects demonstrate the impact of belief and attribution on self-image, behavior, and outcomes.

A practical way to think about mindsets is to imagine them as defined by particular kinds of internal questions. The questions we ask ourselves instruct us about where to put our attention, what to expect, how to behave, and how to relate. Our internal questions and the mindsets from which they are asked are intermingled. In this sense, the questions we ask ourselves and others are *literally* fateful; they lead to the texture and form of our experiences, possibilities, and results in life.

The distinctions elaborated by the Learner-Judger Mindset Model and Learner and Judger questions provide a practical way to observe, categorize, and understand thinking, feeling, and ensuing behavior. The model illustrates that each of us continuously operates from these distinct mindsets. At any given moment

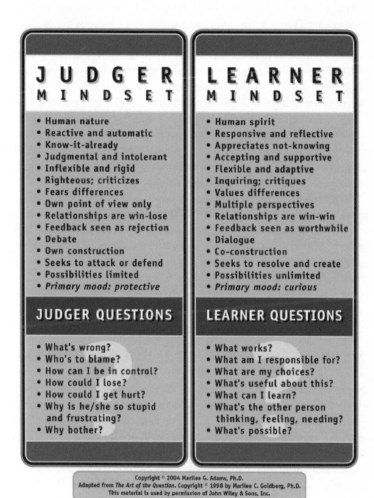

JUDGER MINDSET	**LEARNER MINDSET**
• Human nature	• Human spirit
• Reactive and automatic	• Responsive and reflective
• Know-it-already	• Appreciates not-knowing
• Judgmental and intolerant	• Accepting and supportive
• Inflexible and rigid	• Flexible and adaptive
• Righteous; criticizes	• Inquiring; critiques
• Fears differences	• Values differences
• Own point of view only	• Multiple perspectives
• Relationships are win-lose	• Relationships are win-win
• Feedback seen as rejection	• Feedback seen as worthwhile
• Debate	• Dialogue
• Own construction	• Co-construction
• Seeks to attack or defend	• Seeks to resolve and create
• Possibilities limited	• Possibilities unlimited
• *Primary mood: protective*	• *Primary mood: curious*
JUDGER QUESTIONS	**LEARNER QUESTIONS**
• What's wrong?	• What works?
• Who's to blame?	• What am I responsible for?
• How can I be in control?	• What are my choices?
• How could I lose?	• What's useful about this?
• How could I get hurt?	• What can I learn?
• Why is he/she so stupid and frustrating?	• What's the other person thinking, feeling, needing?
• Why bother?	• What's possible?

Copyright © 2004 Marilee G. Adams, Ph.D.
Adapted from *The Art of the Question*. Copyright © 1998 by Marilee C. Goldberg, Ph.D.
This material is used by permission of John Wiley & Sons, Inc.

Fig. 1. Learner-Judger Mindset Model.

one of these mindsets is activated in the foreground while the other waits in the background. In this respect, we are each a dynamic, interactive, and complex combination of two distinct ways of being that lead to very different ways of thinking, acting, and relating (Fig. 1).

We consider each of these mindsets as an archetype within which particular characteristics, ways of being, and verbal and non-verbal expressions are clustered. The characteristics of each column are (loosely) internally consistent and self-referring. The utility of the model requires that we recognize that these are just *mindsets*, not fixed roles or permanent attributions. Nobody is purely Judger or Learner.

The Mindset Model, with its focus on internal questions as the starting place for our behaviors, interactions, and outcomes holds vital implications for our life orientation, attitudes, skill sets, and behavior. Consciously choosing our frame of mind is a powerful act, as Albert Einstein implied when he said, "There are only two ways to live your life. One is as though nothing is a miracle. The other is as though everything is a miracle." In this sense, we can think of questions as leading to answers that are either contracting, expanding, or neutral. Inherently limiting internal questions lead to a limited repertoire of possible answers. Expansionist affirmative questions open the doors of potential.

The Learner-Judger Mindset Model is intended to help build our ability to observe our own thinking and behavior. The power of intentional observation lies in stimulating higher-level cognitive capacities, and strengthening our "emotional intelligence." We use this awareness and skill to continuously help bring about transformative shifts from the "Judger" position into the "Learner" one where new ways of being, thinking, behaving, and relating become possible. With observation and intention we are empowered to choose which mindset to inhabit and live from – in every moment.

EXPLORING LEARNER-JUDGER MINDSETS

The deeper our understanding of these two mindsets, the more empowered we become to observe ourselves, question our questions (both the internal and interpersonal ones), and make life-affirming question-based choices. When we operate from our Learner mindset, our mood is one of acceptance of self and others. We value "not knowing" and come from a place of genuine curiosity that opens us to be flexible and responsive to life's circumstances. We are positioned to think strategically, seeking opportunities and possibilities. Our Learner mindset allows us to be empathic. We can see the world from others' points of view. Our Learner mindset allows us to live at the core of our most elevated human spirit.

Learner relationships are win-win. From this place we focus on connecting, learning, resolving, and creating. Learner mindset questions are typically life giving, appreciative, and energizing. These questions are grounded in optimism, and presuppose new possibilities, sufficient resources, and a future shaped by hope. The title of Martin Buber's classic book, *I and Thou*, points to the empathy, oneness, and sense of connection exemplified in our Learner being.

While Learner mindset fosters connection and expansion, Judger mindset promotes separation and contraction. Judger mindset questions are reactive, automatic, and judgmental. They are based on certainty about "knowing" and being right about one's own opinions. They are generated from assumptions of limited options, scarcity, and potential failure. They focus primarily on past problems rather than on new options. When we allow our Judger mindsets to push to the foreground, we simultaneously and unintentionally impede the creativity and freedom required to move us towards fresh possibilities. Judger thinking cannot lead to genuinely positive new futures because its source lies in adherence to old consciousness. The future available from Judger presumptions and questions is limited to a recycled version of past questions and answers.

Central to understanding the effect of Judger mindset is the recognition that our judgmental attitudes can be focused either internally or externally. If we focus judgment on *ourselves*, the effects include pessimism, loss of energy, low self-confidence, and feelings of depression. That same judgmental attitude, focused on *others*, leads to blame, anger, hostility, and conflict. That's why Judger questions usually result in win-lose, or lose-lose outcomes, unleashing the fight or flight response. We get relegated to operating from an "attack or defend" paradigm since every utterance is framed as either an attack or a defense. Whether the cognitive, operational focus is on ourselves or others, the Judger orientation, to one degree or another, constrains learning, collaborating, resolving conflict, and creating new possibilities.

That said, it is important to hold the Judger mindset as being neither good nor bad, neither positive nor negative. It just is. What we've labeled as "Judger"[1] is simply human nature – for *all* of us. The reason is that the underlying moods of Judger rest in being fearful, protective, and oriented toward survival. It is far too simple to think of Judger mindset as "bad" and Learner mindset as "good." Such dichotomous thinking presupposes an either/or stance while our higher nature as human beings is both/and. We consider our Learner mindset to be the place from which we can construct the most generative, appreciative, life-giving questions.

In addition, it is essential to recognize that without awareness, understanding, and *acceptance* of the Judger aspects of ourselves and others, we lose the freedom to continuously choose to return to Learner thinking, being, relating, and behaving. Embracing the shadow allows us to come to wholeness. By recommending that we "embrace our core of rot," author and consultant Charles Seashore is suggesting that we make friends with our shadow self. When Joseph Campbell enjoins us to recognize that "Where you stumble, there your treasure is" he also implores us to view the consequences of our difficult experiences as potential doorways to liberation and learning. Our Judger self is necessary and valuable because it can become the doorway leading to acceptance of ourselves and empathy for others, thus providing us access to the full range of our humanity.

A MATTER OF CHOICE

The Choice Map is a learning tool that shows the divergent worlds that ensue from asking either Learner or Judger questions. It illustrates the assertion that we create and then inhabit different worlds depending on the kind of questions we ask. Employing the distinctions of the Learner-Judger Model empowers personal choice and therefore personal power. We make these choices individually as well as collectively. Teams, families and organizations may also be characterized as either primarily Learner or Judger at any moment depending on their attitudes, norms, and behaviors (Fig. 2).

There are three aspects of the Choice Map that make it a useful tool for learning and making transformational cognitive and behavioral choices. First, the Choice Map demonstrates that we *always* have choice, moment to moment, even when this is not immediately apparent – with our choices based on the questions we ask ourselves. This empowering recognition reinforces hopefulness. If there is a way to move beyond negative emotions and defeat, then there is always a way to a new, more preferable future. Our job is to move forward by utilizing Learner questions, fueled by Learner intentions. Thus, appreciative inquiry is a continuously available vehicle.

Second, the map shows the consequences of traveling the divergent paths of Learner mindset and Judger mindset; they take us to different worlds of relatedness and possibility. Third, the Switching Lane is the practical location of new choices. It is where we find hope, action, and change. In this sense, hope is always alive, always an available possibility because we can ask a "turnaround" question to rescue us from tumbling down the Judger path and landing in the Judger Pit.

Choosing to switch from Judger to Learner is a life-affirming decision. Switching questions help us reverse direction and move up to Learner territory. Such questions simultaneously shift moods, allowing us to see solutions and possibilities that would otherwise be invisible. Examples of questions that allow us to step onto the Switching Lane include: *"Am I in Judger? Do I want to go in*

Fig. 2. The Choice Map.

this direction? Will it make the difference I/we want? Where would I rather be?" and *"What positive possibilities are present?"*

APPRECIATIVE INQUIRY AND LEARNER MINDSET

The intentional Learner mindset is at the heart of appreciative inquiry just as the practices and values of appreciative inquiry rest securely and energetically within this way of being. With appreciative inquiry we choose the strategy of operating from appreciative curiosity. In striving to embody this stance, we begin with intentionally shifting from seeing the problems inherent in situations to recognizing expansive opportunities and challenges. The very words "problem" and "solution" convey built in limitations that the words "challenge" and "puzzle" do not. Problems call for solutions. Solutions suggest a permanent, fixed state. Challenges, on the other hand, invite us to meet them, replicating the dance of co-construction. The vehicle for this attitudinal and perceptual choice is a Learner question, i.e. a question that is unconditionally positive and filled with possibility.

In choosing appreciative ways of thinking, feeling, being, and behaving, we must also honor the Judger aspects of ourselves and others, simply because this is our shared human nature. At the same time, we choose a deep commitment to the possibilities inherent only from the Learner position. To resolve this seeming paradox, we advocate *accepting Judger while continuously practicing Learner.*

In the quest for transformational questions, the first focus should be on our mindset and intentions as question *askers*, rather than on the question itself. This is where the real action and traction first occur. This is the place from which expansive, paradigm-altering questions are born. This is also consistent with Gandhi's dictum that, "We must be the change we seek in the world." So as we get ourselves ready to ask a question, ". . . we should begin with the 'in' of inquiry" (Schiller, 1998). In the act of seeking these new appreciative, life-giving questions, the more we maintain, nourish, and operate from our Learner mindsets, the more successful we can be in guiding change, both organizationally and personally.

APPRECIATIVE INQUIRY, A
LIFE-CENTRIC PRACTICE

Every question has the potential to contract or expand life-centric possibilities. Every question has the potential to damage or enhance a relationship. Our challenge is to couple the wonder and mystery of question asking with the skill and mastery of question construction. The wedding of appreciative inquiry theory and practice to the idea and implementation of Learner mindset and methods become apparent in the life-centric questions that guide each of the 4 D phases. "What gives life?" guides Discovery. "What might be?" and "What is the world calling for?" lead us to Dream. "What can we innovate to create our preferred future?" allows us to Design. "How will we sustain ourselves and others in this transformative cycle?" guides us in the direction of Destiny.

Research in appreciative inquiry is intrinsically life-centric. Research is always about questions. "The Questions we ask, the things that we choose to focus on . . . determine what we find. What we find becomes the data and the story out of which we dialogue about and envision the future. And so, the seeds of change are implicit in the very first question we ask."

POSITIVE IMAGE; POSITIVE ACTION

The theory and practice of appreciative inquiry is relatively new. It is continuously exploring and investigating, which constantly provides us with new questions and new directions. Qualitative and quantitative research in organizations and at universities is opening new avenues for exploration. We know only a small percentage of what we will discover as practitioners experiment, document, and share their findings. Therefore we operate out of a Learner questioning mode. As we gain skill and learn to "live" as appreciative inquirers, our skill revolves around reframing almost all questions into Learner questions. And our roots in social constructionism invite us to take an open, "not knowing," and critical stance towards any taken for granted conclusion.

Great questions are often ones that invite us to tell a story. Appreciative inquiry is based in the stories we tell about ourselves and others, stories that spark the imagination and give us the essence of who we are and what our purpose is in the world. Appreciative questions call forth appreciative stories of wonder, transformation, and guidance. At best they are Learner stories. It is this spirit that Antoine de Saint-Exubery refers to when he said, "If you want to build a ship then don't drum up men to gather wood, give orders, and divide the work. Rather teach them to yearn for the far and endless sea."

In the quest for organizational transformation, we might first look to the questions the organization is already answering in its implicit and explicit behavior. Oftentimes, these questions can be discovered in the stories that abound in the organization. Consider what kind of organization might result from a guiding question such as, "*How can we produce long-term profitability while adhering to our positive core values?*" in contrast to one that answers this question, "*What must we do in order to make our predictions for the next quarter?*" What kind of organization might result from primary guiding questions such as, "*How can we best serve our customers?*" in contrast to one that primarily focuses on a question such as, "*How can we please stockholders?*"

Transformation in organizations will most predictably and efficiently follow a transformation in the questions that animate it. The field of appreciative inquiry is replete with such stories of "before and after" questions. Here are several eloquent examples of such success stories, each of which resulted in remarkable, positive change. In each of these situations, one can clearly see how the guiding question would direct thinking, behavior, and results, as well as the story the organization and others would tell about it.

Lead consultant Diana Whitney helped British Airways address a major concern by shifting their question from "How can we have less lost baggage?" to "How can we create an exceptional arrival experience?" Lead consultant Marjorie Schiller served Avon Mexico in ameliorating a diversity issue by switching their question from "How can we correct the current situation of too few woman corporate officers?" to "What will it take to have men and women involved at every level of organizational decision-making?" She also helped the West Springfield Public Schools in Massachusetts alter their question from "How can we have fewer students failing state mandated tests?" to "How can we be the school where everyone smiles?"

THE ART OF THE TRANSFORMATIONAL QUESTION

A question calls forth that which does not yet exist (Goldberg, 1998). Creating world-opening new queries is the central mandate for practitioners of appreciative inquiry. In our quest for discovering paradigm-shifting questions, a partnership of our creative and logical selves catalyzes the most imaginative and positive possibilities. Mozart is said to have asked, *"What would music sound like if the notes loved each other?"* This is not a question that one can construct in a logical, linear manner! You just can't get there from here. Such questions arrive in a flash and require that we be open to receiving them.

Constructing questions, on the other hand, requires a logical, conscious process. It is much like building a structure by following a blueprint that prescribes the steps along the way. It calls for linear thinking. But transformation does not occur from following a set of logical plans. Rather, it is evident in the inspiration and imagination that *preceded* the blueprint. Using an architectural metaphor, a transformed way of conceptualizing and configuring space would appear *first as an answer to a paradigm-shifting question of the architect.* Perhaps Frank Lloyd Wright asked himself a breakthrough question like, *"What's a unique way to conceptualize and configure a 'container' of light and space for human beings to inhabit?"*

We believe that the spirit of inquiry, along with specific guiding inquiry practices, generates the most positive, world-creating questions. Since the spirit of inquiry animates our creative selves, this is where we first turn attention in this section. Next we provide question construction practices that can be used, both individually and collaboratively. Finally, we propose an inquiry format for "questioning our questions" to help assess the transformational potential inherent in new queries.

Cultivating the Spirit of Inquiry

Everything that serves to infuse what OD has referred to as the "spirit of inquiry" emanates from experiences of awe, curiosity, veneration, surprise, delight, amazement, and child-like wonder. We believe that OD practitioners need to reclaim and aspire to openness, availability, epistemological humility, the ability to admire, to be surprised, to be inspired, and to inquire into our valued and possible worlds. We are naturally more effective when we maintain the spirit of inquiry of the everlasting beginner (*Cooperrider, child as agent of inquiry*). "Beginners mind" lives in a stance of innocent "not knowing." The President and CEO of the Fetzer Institute, Dr. Tom Inui, has a reputation for his "delight in the unknown" and the way he models "not knowing" as the leader of this national philanthropic organization (*Appreciative Leaders: In the Eye of the Beholder*, Schiller et al., 2001). The more we intentionally place ourselves in this position of open wondering, the more appreciative and spacious our questions can naturally be.

While we can't force this spirit, we can invite it. We can be an opening, a clearing, where such questions can presence themselves. Such world-altering questions rarely arrive in the rushing demands of everyday life. They may occur when we're in the shower, or on a walk, or meditating. When we "call for" transformational questions, we must be patient and still, allowing time for percolating, mulling, gestating, and reflecting. Here are some sample self-queries for inviting such queries.

- How can I cultivate curiosity, stillness, and spaciousness?
- Who must I be to attract beautiful new questions?
- What practices can I use to create a receptive space in myself?

Learner mindset is firmly anchored in valuing the openness of "not knowing," in being a clearing for possibility. Centering ourselves in Learner mindset helps us operate with the curiosity, flexibility, acceptance, and openness required for truly novel questions to show up. The following list of self-questions is meant to encourage the activity of Learner mindset. The list is not inclusive and we suggest you add other questions that inspire you.

- Am I in a calm, centered, open Learner place? How can I shift to there?
- Is there any Judger mischief going on that could inhibit curiosity or possibility?

- What assumptions might I be making?
- Am I being honest? Am I missing or avoiding anything?
- Can I move beyond self-interest to see the larger picture and serve others?
- Am I calling for questions with an open heart, an open mind, and positive commitment?

Practices for Constructing Questions

All communication begins with intention, regardless of whether the individual is aware of his or her goals. The three practices described below share a background question, "What do I want my question to accomplish?" This question is easy to overlook either because it appears obvious or because it feels like too much trouble. Perhaps it seems too time-consuming to articulate the answers. Here is our caution: to take question generation seriously, we must approach it as a *discipline*. This means taking the time to consider and examine each question, especially the ones we might want to avoid, either because they make us uncomfortable or because we might not welcome the answer.

The questions in each of these three practices are phrased in the first person singular (I/me). However, in the spirit of co-construction, we encourage you to also ask them in the plural (we/our). So, for example, we get, "What do *we* want *our* question(s) to accomplish?" We suggest you add queries that are particularly relevant to your particular goals. The answers to each of these questions will suggest follow-up questions and further responses to ponder and act upon.

(1) *Reframing*. In order to reframe something, one must first understand and articulate the original frame, including the presuppositions that hold it in place. In other words, when searching for powerful, positive, life-giving questions, we must first make explicit any implicit frame we wish to transcend. The process can go like this:
   (a) First, make explicit the original question, "frame," or limitation one wishes to transcend.
   (b) Next, make your goals for the new question explicit. What do you want the new question to accomplish? What new possibilities do you intend for the reframed question to open or point to?
   (c) Then, write down new questions as they occur to you (perhaps using Q-Storming, which is described below).
   (d) Finally, assess each new question (see below for some criteria questions).
(2) *Strawman Questions*. To illustrate question writing in workshops, we provide a good "strawman" question, one that we have already authored. Then we ask

participants to work together in teams to make the question even better. The original questions are always enhanced by the workshop participants' ability to more powerfully rewrite them. Just as fine old wood needs to be buffed and shined, so do questions need to be cared for and nurtured. Moreover, each time we alter our questions, we also alter the consciousness that allows us to see, design, and unleash even deeper and more transformative possible new ones. Appreciative Learner question development requires continual reconsideration (Schiller, 1997).

(3) *Q-Storming*. Q-Storming is a collaborative QuestionThinking exercise. It is like brainstorming, but with an important difference. It seeks new questions, *not* answers, suggestions, or ideas. Because this is a QuestionThinking exercise, the questions sought must be stated in the first person singular; these are questions for the individual to ask him or herself, not to ask others.

The premise is that "a question not asked is a door not opened" (Goldberg, 1998). New possibilities lie behind those doors, which can best be unlocked with the key of a new question. The goal, therefore, is to generate and collect as many novel questions as possible. The more new questions, the more new doors may be opened, with the promise of more imaginative and potentially transformative new possibilities laying in wait.

The exercise begins when an individual requests some collaborative Question-Thinking to help with a situation in which he or she feels stuck or frustrated. The facilitator asks for the volunteer to describe the situation along with his or her goals. Then the Q-Storming begins. Scribes capture each new question and give them to the volunteer at the end of the exercise. In a fifteen-minute period we often generate fifty or more questions, any one of which could be the key to open new possibilities. The exercise ends when the volunteer reports having been gifted with questions that open new possibillities. We know we've struck gold when he or she exclaims with wonder, "I've never thought of that before."

With this harvest of questions in hand, the individual is encouraged to later cluster, prioritize, and sequence the question list. Reworking and reconfiguring promotes the discipline of considering each question seriously. Q-Storming can be done with a group, with another individual, and even alone by "calling for" new questions and writing down what "arrives."

Questioning Our Questions

Regardless of how we generated our new questions, we still must assess which ones are more likely to lead to the direction and futures we seek to create. Some of the new questions will be obviously transformative – one experiences an "aha" merely upon hearing them. Other questions may be helpful, even though the "earth didn't move under our feet" in response to them. In either case, it is important to engage in a discipline of assessing the possibilities suggested by the questions.

What we thought was a wonderful question might seem unclear or repetitive for dialogue partners. The goal of question generating is not simply to write a *beautiful* question. Rather, it is to *write a great question that calls something new into existence*. It is as simple as that. Since questions are always contextual, one that may seem inadequate today may become the perfect opening tomorrow, or with a different group, or at a different stage in a group's development. Here are some criteria questions with which to consider the new question crop:

- Is this question expansive and bold?
- Does this question access heart, head, and hands?
- Am I uplifted, energized, inspired by this question?
- Is this question life affirming?
- Could this question lead to unforeseen answers?
- Am I surprised by this question? Does it provoke an "ah ha?"
- Does this question succeed in reaching a transcending view?

CONCLUSION: THE SPIRIT OF INQUIRY

The solution, like all solutions to apparent contradictions, lies in moving away from the opposition and changing the nature of the question, to embrace a broader context (Maturana & Varela, 1987).

The spirit of inquiry is animated by awe, wonder, and curiosity. When infused with its grace, we live "in the zone" or the "flow state" of creativity for its own sake (Csikszentmihalyi, 1990). In those moments, discovery and learning are all that exist. In the joy of exploration, we succeed in temporarily suspending attachments to old answers, particular outcomes, or thinking that we already know. This is the fertile void from which transformation becomes a vibrant possibility. It is from an Appreciative Learner stance that the most startling, innovative, and life-affirming new questions and possibilities can arise. This is the heart of appreciative inquiry.

Through our questions we can create the world we desire but this can happen only when we cultivate the spirit of inquiry and use it to enliven specific question construction practices. In this way, we become strategically and continuously more skillful in spontaneously generating Appreciative Learner questions. By becoming exemplars for the richness of not-knowing we embody the courage to transcend question reluctance in ourselves and others. Through questions we access our own innate wonder and creativity. We believe that this wonder-full Appreciative Learner mode of inquiry provides the context and skills for inspiring, mobilizing, and sustaining transformative human system change.

SIDEBAR: A TOOL FOR LEARNING

Experiencing Learner and Judger Mindsets

Look at the Mindset Model and slowly read all the questions in the Judger column. Notice how these questions affect your physical and emotional reactions. Now take a deep breath, release those feelings, and slowly read the questions from the Learner column. Notice whether you are affected differently after experiencing the Learner questions. Which set of questions makes you feel uplifted or depressed, energized or deflated, optimistic or pessimistic?

When this structured experience is introduced in workshops, we always begin with Judger mindset and nearly everyone reports some feeling of discomfort. Some people even unconsciously hold their breath when Judger questions are read. Participants report that Judger questions evoke feelings of depression and depletion. Some of their comments include feeling out of control, lost, pessimistic, fearful, despairing, helpless, and hopeless. In contrast, Learner questions usually access for them feelings of energy, optimism, hopefulness, openness, enthusiasm, control, and proactively looking for solutions and possibilities. One individual noted, "When I'm looking with Learner eyes, I can be hopeful about the future."

Workshop participants recognize that, in just a few moments, asking either Learner or Judger questions has the effect of putting them in distinctly different moods. Since questions can be asked from either stance, they realize that it was not the actual "question sentence" that impacted them so strongly. Rather, it was the presuppositions encoded in the questions. In other words, "coming from" either Learner or Judger has a programming effect on the world of experience and possibility made available.

NOTE

1. The term "Judger," as we use it here, is not related to how it is used in the Myers Briggs Type Indicator. There, the term points to a preference for closure; here the term references judgmental attitudes and behaviors.

REFERENCES

Adams, M. G. (2004). *Change your questions, change your life: Powerful tools for life and work.* San Francisco, CA: Berrett-Koehler Publishers.

Argyris, C., & Schon, D. A. (1978). *Organizational learning: A theory of action perspective.* Reading, MA: Addison-Wesley.

Beck, A. T. (1979). *Cognitive therapy and the emotional disorders.* New York: Penguin.

Cooperrider, D. L. (2000). The 'child' as agent of inquiry. In: *Appreciative Inquiry: Rethinking Human Organizations: Toward a Positive Theory of Change.* Champaign, IL: Stipes Publishing.

Cooperrider, D. L., Sorensen, Jr., P. F., Whitney, D., & Yaeger, T. F. (Eds) (2000). *Appreciative inquiry: Rethinking human organization: Toward a positive theory of change.* Champaign, IL: Stipes Publishing.

Csikszentmihalyi, M. (1990). *Flow: The psychology of optimal experience.* New York: Harper & Row.

Flores, F. (1997). The leaders of the future. In: P. J. Denning & R. M. Metcalfe (Eds), *Beyond Calculation: The Next Fifty Years of Computing.* New York: Springer-Verlag.

Goldberg, M. C. (1998). *The art of the question: A guide to short-term question-centered therapy.* New York: Wiley.

Maturana, H. R., & Varela, F. J. (1987). *The tree of knowledge: The biological roots of understanding.* Boston: Shambala.

Postman, N. (1976). *Crazy talk, stupid talk: How we defeat ourselves by the way we talk – and what to do about it.* New York: Delacorte Press.

Schiller, M., Holland, B. M., & Riley, D. (Eds) (2001). *Appreciative leaders: In the eye of the beholder.* A Taos Institute Publication.

APPRECIATIVE INQUIRY AND THE ELEVATION OF ORGANIZATIONAL CONSCIOUSNESS

Diana Whitney

ABSTRACT

This chapter creates a logic that links the transformation of organizational consciousness with the creation of a more life affirming global consciousness. In it the author examines the relationship between the practice of Appreciative Inquiry, the concept of organizational consciousness and the need for global transformation. She suggests that Appreciative Inquiry, with its life giving focus, is uniquely suited to simultaneously bring about change in organizations and society through the elevation and evolution of organizational consciousness. Recognizing the need for transformation on a global scale, she challenges the field of organization development to move beyond the metaphor of organization culture toward the metaphor of organizational consciousness. Cultures are defined and bounded by national and corporate borders. Consciousness is all pervasive. It knows not boundaries of organizations, countries nor continents. Appreciative Inquiry practices, that involve the whole system in valuing the best of what is, envisioning generative possibilities and creating life-sustaining organizations, hold great potential for the evolution of organizational consciousness.

Constructive Discourse and Human Organization
Advances in Appreciative Inquiry, Volume 1, 125–145
Copyright © 2004 by Elsevier Ltd.
All rights of reproduction in any form reserved
ISSN: 1475-9152/doi:10.1016/S1475-9152(04)01006-3

As webs come out of spiders, or breadth forms in frozen air, worlds come out of us.

(Thompson, 1989)

Until very recently in history, people have responded to global phenomena as if they were local; they have not effectively institutionalized their responses across sectors or societies, nor have they been able, in organizational terms, to respond by deliberately altering the course of global changes.

(Cooperrider & Dutton, 1999)

We are at a turning point in the history of organizing. There are few places on the planet untouched by the "progress of the industrial era" and the "dawning of the information age." Cars, computers and cell phones are apparent in cities and local markets from New York to Chang Mai to Santiago to Lahore. The planet is wrapped in a web of airplane routes, satellite orbits and telecommunication signals.

The transformation from the industrial era to the information age has brought with it the realization that we are one planet. The earth is one body of energy, matter and spirit, intimately connected on many levels from the air we breath to the water we drink to the energy that powers our life styles to the pain, hunger and sorrow in the eyes of our children around the world. With the help of technology we have discovered, as if for the first time, something that has always been and will always be: global connectivity and wholeness.

This time is not the result of some great mysterious force in which we humans have played a passive role. It is the emergent culmination, the punctuation of years, decades, and millenniums of conversations and exchange among people around the world. What we are experiencing today might be considered a kind of "global collective karma," the unfolding of social realities that have been imaged, hoped for, prayed for and worked toward for many years, supplemented by those that have been feared, avoided and worked against for as many years. We have given life to a global creatrix: the planet as a living, self-creating, socio-spiritual ecology.

The dye is cast and the fate of organizations around the world is clear: *success in the future will go to those organizations that help humanity come into harmony and thrive as one global community.* President of the World Business Academy, Rinaldo Brutoco expressed this call when he stated, "Now more than ever, the world business community must face the inescapable conclusion at the core of the Academy's very existence: business must be willing to become responsible for the whole of global society" (Brutoco, 2002).

The field of organization development (OD) must also respond to this call. It is time to rethink what we do and how we do it. It is time to organize globally as if all life matters. Human, organizational and global evolution will go hand in hand or not at all. As Catholic Visionary Teilhard de Chardin foreshadowed, the future destiny of humanity is tied to the future destiny of our planet. To meet this call the field of organization development will need to advance. We will need to create macro theories of organizing based on principles of wholeness and large-scale change. We can no longer generalize from the individual up to organizations in theory or in practice. We can no longer build theories of human organizing upon understanding of mechanistic or material scientific principles. The scope of what is needed requires that we envision organizations as sentient social organisms naturally and integrally interrelated with the whole of all life of the planet. With this new story of organizing we need a philosophy and methodology of change that links organizational practices to global practices, so that organizational change and global change go hand in hand.

The thesis of this chapter is that Appreciative Inquiry, through its attention to narrative wholeness, enriches and lifts up organizational consciousness and thereby transforms an organization's relationship to global consciousness and builds its capacity to contribute positively to global well-being and sustainability. Figure 1 shows these relationships.

This chapter is a starting point, a beginning of the conversation about Appreciative Inquiry and organizational consciousness. It shows the relationship between organizational climate, organization culture and organizational consciousness and how Appreciative Inquiry positively impacts each of these macro aspects of organizing. It offers a preliminary description of organizational consciousness and shows how it is impacted through an organization's engagement with Appreciative Inquiry. And in laying the foundation for an understanding of organizational consciousness, it is a call for further research in three key areas:

(1) How does Appreciative Inquiry through its relational, narrative, focus influence both the nature and the realization of organizational consciousness?

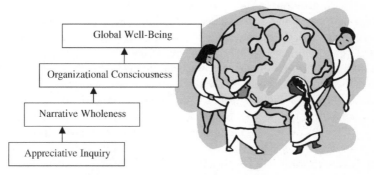

Fig. 1. Appreciative Inquiry: A Path to Global Well-Being.

(2) What is the nature of organizational consciousness that enables an organization to be "responsible for the whole of global society?"
(3) How does the affirmative focus of Appreciative Inquiry longitudinally support the evolution of organizational consciousness and the realization of organizational designs toward more globally life giving potentials?

This chapter is an invitation to supplement years of successful Appreciative Inquiry practice with research into the tremendous power of Appreciative Inquiry to catalyze organizational and global transformation. It suggests that each phase of the Appreciative Inquiry process: Affirmative Topic Choice, Discovery, Dream, Design and Destiny creates a powerful elevation in organizational consciousness; and this higher consciousness exerts an imperative for the organization to serve the global good, to be an agent of world benefit. Consider two of many examples of Appreciative Inquiry taking organizations to higher ground and helping them do good business by serving society at large. Through the use of Appreciative Inquiry, Nutrimental Foods, SA changed its mission from food processing and distribution to "Creating a Healthy Society through Food Products." The Cathedral Foundation in Jacksonville, Florida transformed its purpose from taking care of elderly people to "Lifting Up a Positive Image of Aging."

THE CALL FOR ORGANIZATIONAL CONSCIOUSNESS

In the past decade organizations using Appreciative Inquiry have benefited financially, socially and strategically. Companies such as Roadway, Hunter Douglas, McDonalds, John Deere and Green Mountain Coffee Roasters have improved financial performance through whole system Appreciative Inquiry processes. Organizations including British Airways NA, Lovelace Health Systems and GTE have seen significant increases in employee survey results as well as employee retention. There is no doubt that Appreciative Inquiry contributes to the well-being and sustainability of organizations. Experience in hundreds of for profit and non-profit organizations around the world attest to the viability of Appreciative Inquiry as a process for successful positive change.

That Appreciative Inquiry makes a difference is empirically substantiated. From a theoretical perspective, however, an interesting question is raised: What changes when an organization engages in Appreciative Inquiry? The intention of many organizations using Appreciative Inquiry is cultural transformation and yet I believe something else happens through the use of Appreciative Inquiry that changes both the culture of the organization and its relationship to the world at large. It is through the transformation of organizational consciousness that is its self a part of our global consciousness that Appreciative Inquiry makes a difference in organizations and in their ability and willingness to positively contribute to global well-being. I believe that Appreciative Inquiry transforms organizational consciousness, which in turn leads to the realization of very different kinds of organizations, those that in purpose, structure, culture and strategy, are better suited to serve the world.

THREE METAPHORS FOR ORGANIZING: CLIMATE, CULTURE AND CONSCIOUSNESS

Organization development practitioners and theorists have long used metaphors to make sense of the intangible yet powerfully binding aspects of organizational life.

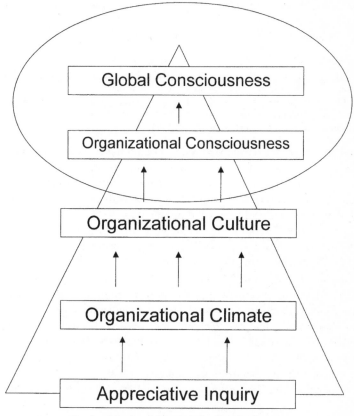

Fig. 2. Levels of Appreciative Inquiry Impact.

In this section I give a brief overview of three metaphors for organizational life: climate, culture and consciousness and make a case for the notion of organizational consciousness as a useful and globally significant aspect of human organizing. As Fig. 2 shows, Appreciative Inquiry positively impacts organization climate, culture and consciousness. It is however, its ability to impact organizational consciousness that enables its impact on global consciousness, well-being and sustainability.

ORGANIZATIONAL CLIMATE: WHAT IT FEELS LIKE AROUND HERE

In the late 1970s the field of organization development was occupied with ideas, tools and practices for understanding organizational climate. Attention to organizational climate – metaphorically, the weather within the organization – was thought to generate changes in both employee and organizational performance. Litwin, Humphrey and Wilson described it this way,

> When people refer to an organization as "a fun place to work," "tightly knit," or "a big bureaucracy," they are referring to and giving us clues about that organization's climate. Although organizational climate might appear to be an intangible quality, it does have a very real effect on the people who live and work in the organization. Research has demonstrated that climate dramatically affects not only the people but also the performance and growth of the organization (Litwin, Humphrey & Wilson, 1978).

Litwin, Humphrey and Wilson went on to say, "climate can be controlled" (Ibid., p. 189). They described doing so as so a holistic process, based on feedback to managers – on the six dimensions of climate: clarity, commitment, standards, responsibility, recognition and teamwork – along with guidance for improvement in achieving organizational health and productivity.

While not directed at controlling or changing organization climate, Appreciative Inquiry does have a positive effect on the feeling of an organization. Organizations engaged in Appreciative Inquiry move from; apathy to enthusiasm; from conflict to collaboration; and from hopelessness to hopefulness. Appreciative Inquiry has been shown to positively impact morale, employee survey results and employee engagement. In a study of Hunter Douglas two years after a whole system Appreciative Inquiry, Whitney and Trosten-Bloom (2003) found that Appreciative Inquiry had liberated the energy and enthusiasm of the organization and indeed, performance had improved. The outcomes of Appreciative Inquiry practices across many organizations, profit as well as not for profit, suggest that the more positive the affect in an organization, the healthier the relationships and the results.

ORGANIZATION CULTURE: THE WAY
WE DO THINGS AROUND HERE

By the early eighties the dominant metaphor used to understand and change organizations had become organizational culture, defined by Schein as, "the deeper level of basic assumptions and beliefs that are shared by members of an organization" (Schein, 1985, p. 6). Organization culture too was seen as integral to performance. Deal and Kennedy described the elements of culture as: business environment, values, heroes, rites and rituals and cultural network; and made the link between culture and human behavior,

> A strong culture is a system of informal rules that spells our how people are to behave most of the time. . . . A strong culture enables people to feel better about what they do so they are more likely to work harder (Deal & Kennedy, 1982).

The means to improving organization culture was to manage to it. In his book entitled, *Managing Corporate Culture*, Stanley Davis put forth a process for identifying and managing organization culture in relation to business strategy. It includes "capturing the guiding beliefs (in words), assessing cultural risks, and then creating strategy that is compatible with the culture" (Davis, 1984). High performance stemmed from the management of culture in alignment with strategy.

The metaphor of organization culture has been and continues to be a useful one. It provides a way of talking about organizations that is socially derived rather than mechanistic or material. It privileges relationships and human communication as vehicles for creating, transmitting, sustaining and transforming organizations.

Indeed Appreciative Inquiry has been used for a number of projects aimed at the transformation of organization culture from "enhancing a culture of service excellence" to "building a culture of partnership" to "celebrating a culture of inclusion" to "lifting up leadership at all levels." In each of these cases Appreciative Inquiry, through the 4-D Cycle, significantly impacted the way things were done and the business results attained.

For more on how Appreciative Inquiry positively impacts organization culture read Whitney and Trosten-Bloom, *The Power of Appreciative Inquiry* (Whitney & Trosten-Bloom, 2003) and Ludema, Whitney, Mohr and Griffin, *The Appreciative Inquiry Summit* (Ludema et al., 2003). In both books, the authors provide rich stories and research findings about the impact of Appreciative Inquiry on the businesses, governments, educational systems, non-profits and communities that have used it for culture change. These organizations include McDonalds, John Deere, Roadway Express, the U.S. Navy, Hunter Douglas Window Fashions Division and Nutrimental SA as well as numerous non-profit organizations such as World Vision and the United Religions Initiative.

ORGANIZATIONAL CONSCIOUSNESS: THE
KNOWING THAT MANIFESTS REALITY

There are two conversations prevalent today that are converging toward the notion of organizational consciousness. They are the conversations about spirituality at work and diversity. Each in a different way calls for a theoretical and practical understanding of organizational consciousness. And each positions Appreciative Inquiry as an action research methodology especially suited to the task of building – through discovery, dream, design and destiny – organizations that embody a globally life-affirming consciousness.

The first of these conversations is the growing dialogue about spirituality at work. The increasingly large number of articles, books and conferences focused on spirit in business clearly suggests that spiritual well being and development are now on the organizational agenda. It further suggests that the most vital and successful organizations attend to the spiritual needs of people, in and out of the organization. As the vocabulary and practices of spirituality saturate organizations questions of organizational consciousness come to the foreground.

Rabbi Michael Lerner in *Spirit Matters* makes a direct connection between spirit and consciousness when he states,

> Try thinking of Spirit as the ultimate consciousness of the universe, a consciousness that pervades, sustains and includes All Being and yet cannot be reduced to any part of it. We are part of this ultimate consciousness in the way a particular theory or orientation might be "part" of our minds. Each of us is a particular part of spiritual consciousness and a part of the process through which Spirit is becoming self-consciousness . . . The consciousness of the universe is not separate from other aspects of Being but is that through which All Being exists and becomes manifest to us and to itself (Lerner, 2000).

In this explanation of consciousness we see the link between organizational consciousness, global consciousness and Spirit or ultimate consciousness as Lerner names it. Each organization is a particular consciousness, a part of global consciousness and a part of the process through which Spirit is becoming self-consciousness. To attend to organizational consciousness is to attend to global consciousness.

The second conversation that is inviting us to consider organizational consciousness as a macro aspect of organizing is the ongoing conversation about diversity. What is often considered a politically correct code word for the inclusion of women and minorities in organizational life is an arena for organization innovation, sustainability and evolution.

Just as biodiversity is essential to maintain all of the relationships necessary for the health and sustainability of the rainforest, so too is social diversity essential to organizational life that fosters global sustainability. When life is understood as the intimately interconnected relationships among life forms, the life of the various forms: plants, animals and people is essential to the life of the other forms. In other words, relationships give life. For example, in the mountains of New Mexico the Aspen trees and the Pine trees grow in relation to one another. Aspens populate an area first. The soil and environment that is suitable for Aspen growth becomes fertile ground for Pine growth only through the presence of the Aspen. During the Aspens' short tree life, 25–30 years, they provide nutrients and cover for the growing Pines whose life in turn creates the potential for the life of dozens of other plant and animal forms.

In social terms this same relational necessity can be seen in the relationships of students and teachers, managers and subordinates, pitchers and catchers, and authors and readers. The identity of one depends upon and gives form to the identity of the other. Physicist David Bohm claims that a primary distinction between machines and living systems is that each part of a machine is formed independently of the others, while the parts of a living system grow interdependently,

> By contrast, in a living organism, for example, each part grows in the context of the whole, so that it does not exist independently, nor can it be said that it merely 'interacts' with the others, without itself being essentially affected in this relationship (Bohm, 1980, p. 173).

The Chinese philosophy of Taoism takes the notion of relational necessity beyond identity interdependence and into the question of organizing. According to the *I Ching* (Wilhem, 1950), the Chinese book of change, differences or diversity is a requirement for union. There can be no uniting without things that are different to unite. The ultimate organizing principle is harmony, the orderly union of diversity, or the alignment of strengths toward a purpose.

This suggests that successful organizing may be more about inquiry into diversity than about the reduction or control of diversity or variety. Organizing in situations of high diversity requires a consciousness of the whole. It rests upon an ability to maintain relationships and to keep dialogue open and flowing among people of diverse and at times opposing cultures, views, perspectives and positions. Organizing is possible when people and groups are in relationship and conversation with one another. It becomes impossible when conversations end and relationships are not acknowledged. Inquiry into the unique strengths, capabilities, resources, ideals and dreams of differing people, groups and organizations is more likely to lead to harmoniously interdependent actions on behalf of the whole than are command and control structures which are designed to control through the reduction of variety.

Through the practice of Appreciative Inquiry large groups of people- communities and organizations come to know themselves as whole. They come to

Table 1. A Comparison of Organizational Climate, Culture and Consciousness.

Organizational Metaphor	Correlate to Performance	OD Strategy	Focus of Analysis	Results
Climate	Feel of the Place	Control	Dimensions of Climate	When people feel good about work they work better.
Culture	Common Values and Beliefs	Manage	Elements of Culture	Alignment of personal values with organization values enhances personal commitment and productivity.
Consciousness	Positive Ideals and Images	Inquiry	Positive Core of the Organization	Appreciation of diverse strengths leads to greater contribution to the organization and to society.

know themselves as capable of mobilizing a unique core of strengths, assets, resources and competencies – the positive core of their organization. Appreciative Inquiry is a call to higher consciousness, to intentional collectivity and collective intentionality toward the well-being of all living beings. Table 1 provides a comparison of organizational climate, culture and consciousness.

Change of organization climate is internal to the organization. It is the feel of the organization and as such occurs within the boundaries of the organization. Change of culture is also internal. Relationships beyond the boundaries of the organization with stakeholders, customers, community members, etc. change to the extent that they are in the value chain of the organization and that it is in the organization's interest to change them. Change of organizational consciousness is global. As it changes so does the relationship of the organization to the whole of life on the planet. Organizational consciousness and global consciousness have a co-creative relationship. As one changes so does the other, for better or for worse. As a result, the life giving, affirmative orientation of Appreciative Inquiry holds great promise as a catalyst for positive organizational change and global transformation.

HOW TO TALK ABOUT ORGANIZATIONAL CONSCIOUSNESS?

I have wondered for quite some time now how one might reconcile the "mind centered" concept of consciousness with social constructionist theory and organizational practices such as Appreciative Inquiry. Thus far, I have asserted, without definition, that organizational consciousness is a macro aspect of organizing that links organizations to the global consciousness, or biosphere as Teilhard de Chardin called it. It is the bridge that connects the well-being of particular organizations with the well-being of the whole of the planet. What follows is a preliminary discussion to define organization consciousness. It is the case for organizational consciousness as a macro principle of organizing that:

- Places social constructionist practices such as inquiry, conversation, narrative and relational knowledge creation as central to successful human organizing.
- Recognizes that harmony of the whole emerges when inquiry and conversation among diversities are open and alive.
- Accepts consciousness as an integral and essential aspect of human organizing.
- Asserts that evolution is a process of mutual co-creation: consciousness animates the organization of life, while simultaneously; life in its multiple forms supplements and gives meaning to consciousness.

Consciousness as Mind

Historically, consciousness has been defined in relation to mind, interiority of being, and truth. A Zen Buddhist story illustrates:

> Two monks were arguing about a flag. One said, "The flag is moving." The other said, "The wind is moving." The sixth patriarch happened to be passing by. He told them, "Not the wind, not the flag; mind is moving."

Consciousness, as mind, has been distinguished from matter and talked about as separate and distinct from material being, as in the separation of mind and body, spirit and matter. Professor Allan Combs describes this view of consciousness:

> Centuries ago the Enlightenment legacy of Descartes, Newton, and other architects of modern mechanistic science, left us with a notion of reality that centered almost exclusively on material objects. In this view processes were reduced to by-products of motion. Consciousness had no place at all in such a cosmos, and was in fact evicted from it by Descartes' influential dualism (Combs, 1996, p. 25).

From this point of view, organizations that deal in the material, mechanistic realm would have no consciousness or at least no need of a concept of consciousness. An indeed, there has been little talk of organizational consciousness in the literature of organization theory and behavior.

More recently, however, the separation of mind and body, consciousness and matter has been called to question. Physicist, David Bohm in putting forth his theory of wholeness and the implicate order proposes, "Thus we come to a germ of a new notion of unbroken wholeness, in which consciousness is no longer to be fundamentally separate from matter" (Bohm, 1980). Philosophy Professor,

Table 2.   de Quincey's Characteristics of Consciousness.[a]

---

1. Sentience/feeling (capacity to experience)
2. Subjectivity (capacity for experienced interiority; for having a unique and privileged point of view)
3. Knowledge (capacity for knowing anything)
4. Intentionality (ability to refer to, or be about, something else)
5. Choice (capacity to create "first cause"; to move itself internally)
6. Self-agency (capacity to orient and/or move itself externally)
7. Purpose (capacity to aim at a goal)
8. Meaning (capacity to be intrinsically "for-itself")
9. Value (capacity for intrinsic worth)

---

[a] Adapted from de Quincey's (2002, p. 66).

Christian de Quincey concurs with Bohm and draws on indigenous beliefs, postmodern psychology and quantum physics for his claim that all matter is infused with consciousness. He suggests that consciousness be considered a verb rather than a noun, and describes it as, "the process of matter-energy informing itself . . . the ability that matter-energy has to feel, to know, and to direct itself."

Characteristics of Consciousness

Acknowledging the difficulty in defining consciousness de Quincey offers instead a set of nine "Characteristics of Consciousness." They are listed in Table 2. He suggests that to be an entity with consciousness is to possess any or all of these characteristics.

As I reflect upon de Quincey's characteristics I find myself saying yes, organizations, not just the people who populate them, have these capacities. I find this list of characteristics a potentially useful way of talking about organizational consciousness. Organizations as macro social entities are conscious by the measure of de Quincey's characteristics. While it may stretch the conventional understanding of consciousness to apply it to human organizations, I have taken the liberty in Table 3 to offer meanings and examples of the some of the ways organizations meet de Quincey's characteristics of consciousness.

Table 3 shows that in concept we can talk of organizations as having consciousness – as having a subjective presence, as having creative choice, that impels or directs the body in its motions (de Quincey, 2002), as a knowing that manifests reality. Human organizations, be they business, education, government or service oriented, profit or non-profit in nature are part of a global consciousness. Organizational consciousness exists among, around and because of the people and relationships among people who are members and stakeholders of the organization. It is the collective capacity of the organization to purposefully sense,

Table 3.   Characteristics of Consciousness Applied to Organizations.

Characteristics	Organizational Applications
1. Sentience: Capacity to Experience	Organizations as a whole do experience and feel. They do no feel in an emotional sense, rather they experience and feel changes, impacts and events such as: • Changes in Interest Rates • Changes in Population Demographics • Results of a Customer Survey • Impacts of Medical Epidemics • Impacts of Employee Union Strikes
2. Subjectivity: Capacity for a Unique and Privileged Point of View	Organizations as a whole often have unique and privileged points of view. In many cases they cultivate them as competitive advantages. Consider: • Business Strategy • Guiding Principles • Hiring Criteria • Proprietary Products • Patents and Trademarks
3. Knowledge: Capacity for knowing anything	Organizations as a whole do produce and utilize knowledge such as: • Strategic Plans • Budgets • Employee Surveys
4. Intentionality: Ability to refer to, or be about, something else	Many organizations as a whole have the ability to refer to or be about something else such as: • Societal Well Being • Global Good • Environmental Sustainability This characteristic may be central to differentiate the quality of consciousness of organizations' that are self-serving from those that succeed by serving society at large.
5. Choice: Capacity to create "first cause"; to move itself internally	Organizations as a whole have the capacity to move and change the relationships of which they are constituted. Consider for example internal changes such as: • Reorganizations • Promotions • Development of New Products
6. Self-agency: Capacity to orient and/or move itself externally	Organizations as a whole do move locations. More significantly they orient and move in external relationships. For example, they orient externally in relationships through: • Partnerships, Alliances and Mergers • Negotiations and Mediations • Customer Services and Pricing Strategies

Table 3. *(Continued)*

Characteristics	Organizational Applications
7. Purpose: Capacity to aim at a goal	At their best organizations as a whole are guided by clear and compelling images of the future such as • Mission • Purpose • Goals Organizations are purposeful in their creation and are sustainable to the extent that their purpose is relevant.
8. Meaning: Capacity to be intrinsically "for-itself"	Most organizations as a whole are intrinsically "for themselves" primarily in terms of financial considerations. This many would contend is the factor that prevents organizations from serving a larger good. For example: • Reinvestment Strategies • Profitability More enlightened organizations place continuous learning and social good as a life giving priority.
9. Value: Capacity for intrinsic worth	Organizations as a whole do produce intrinsic worth: benefit to employees and shareholders. The intrinsic worth of highly conscious organizations is the Triple Bottom Line: • Financial Viability of the Business • Human and Societal Well Being • Environmental Health

know, reflect and create itself and its environment. Organizational consciousness is an active phenomenon that is both a collective state of being and the source of that state of being. It is a vital aspect of organizing.

HOW DO WE KNOW ORGANIZATIONAL CONSCIOUSNESS

Answering the question "How do we know organizational consciousness?" may be more important and useful to social change agents, business leaders, and organizational development practitioners as the answer to the question "What is organizational consciousness?" Being conscious of organizational consciousness requires a vocabulary of consciousness and a way of talking about it. I suggest that the answer to the question – "How do we know organizational consciousness?" – comes from understanding organizations as centers of human communication.

Organizational consciousness can be recognized as the dialogic pattern of relationships within, around and about an organization. In other words, organizational consciousness can be operationally defined as "Who tal about what." It is not the mind of the organization, collective or an phized. It is the apparent pattern of conversation among people in and around the organization. Organizational consciousness is embodied, comes into being and is known in the collective conversations among organizational stakeholders. It is a relational reality.

LEVELS OF ORGANIZATIONAL CONSCIOUSNESS

Organizational consciousness can be seen as existing in different states, called levels. Michael Lerner offers the following explanation of levels of consciousness, which I believe have direct application to organizational consciousness.

> One of the greatest errors of human consciousness is to think of ourselves as fixed objects and to then seek to control ourselves and the world. In fact, our consciousness is part of the universal consciousness, a local manifestation of the Unity of All Being, and a stage in the development of the self-consciousness of the universe. When I am talking about stages in the development of Spirit, I am actually talking about increasing levels of consciousness in which we are able to gradually comprehend the oneness and unity of all (Lerner, 2000, p. 34).

To say then that one organization has a higher level of consciousness than another is to say that it demonstrates an understanding and care for the oneness and unity of all. The level of organizational consciousness is the degree to which the organization is aware of and acts in harmony with the whole of all life. Table 4 offers three levels of organizational consciousness as a progression toward contributing to the unity and well-being of all life.

Table 4. Three Levels of Organizational Consciousness.

1. Awake to Knowing: "Is he conscious?" Yes or No?
   - Does the organization know that it is an indivisible part of the larger global context of life?
   - Do conversations within the organization about products, process or strategies consider global dimensions of organizing?

2. Aware of Specific Context and Content: "Are you conscious of the police officer following you?"
   - Does the organization recognize its impact in the world?
   - Does the organization recognize its role as an active co-creative entity?

3. Intentional Choice: "It sounds like you made a conscious decision."
   - Does the organization intentionally choose to "do no harm," create no waste, or embrace concepts and practices such as "Natural Capitalism?"
   - Does the organization intentionally create designs that are life giving and embrace concepts such as "Cradle to Cradle" design?

WHO TALKS TO WHOM, ABOUT
WHAT, AND IN WHAT MANNER

There are three observable characteristics of interest pertaining to organizational consciousness: (1) who talks to whom; (2) about what; and (3) in what manner. In other words, organizational consciousness can be known by who's involved, what they talk about and the process they use.

The first defining characteristic of organizational consciousness has to do with who is included in the conversation. The diversity of people, roles, sides of an issue, stakeholders past, present and future is an apparent statement about an organization's consciousness. The greater the number and diversity of the people included the higher the organizational consciousness. Whole system inclusion in a process of planning or change is an indicator of elevated organizational consciousness.

The second defining characteristic related to organizational consciousness has to do with the scope of the agenda and the topics of conversation. The ability to focus on positive possibilities, to work in the energetically positive and to appreciate the best of what is contributes to and signals higher organizational consciousness. Those organizations whose inner dialogue is filled with conversations and stories of best practices, valuing and life giving potential can be said to have a higher consciousness than organizations locked in deficit discourse and problem analysis.

Third notable characteristic of organizational consciousness is the nature of conversation – the process of communication or the way knowledge is created, shared and used throughout the organization. High consciousness organizations are inquiry based. They are highly inclusion and collaborative learning organizations. They are recognized for equality of voice and honoring of multiple ways of knowing. Knowledge is socially constructed in multiple mediums including reports, memos, creative illustrations, poetry and even dramatic enactments.

APPRECIATIVE INQUIRY: ELEVATING
ORGANIZATION CONSCIOUSNESS

At each stage in an Appreciative Inquiry process there is the potential to transform organizational consciousness. Taken together the phases in the Appreciative Inquiry 4-D Cycle create an irrefutable invitation to higher consciousness.

This occurs first by who is included in the process. At its best Appreciative Inquiry is a whole system process through which all employees and stakeholders are engaged in co-creating the organization's future. Social Innovator, Paul

Hawken makes the point that who is included in the conversations is central to the question of global sustainability when he writes,

Trade is great. Trade is civilizing. Trade is not the issue. The question is who sets the rules and who enforces them. What will the shape of the relationships be among nations, regions, peoples, companies, markets and the commons which support all life on earth? . . . In short, do we want a world structured by rich, mostly white men, or a world that is an expression of the fabulous qualities of all human beings? (Hawken, 2003).

Including the whole system in an Appreciative Inquiry process ensures that the voices of all the fabulous human beings are included in envisioning and designing the future. As such, narrative wholeness is an invitation to higher organizational consciousness.

AFFIRMATIVE TOPIC CHOICE: SETTING THE AGENDA FOR HIGHER CONSCIOUSNESS

Organizations move from deficit discourse to affirmative discourse in the course of affirmative topic choice. They shift from problem analysis and "degenerate conversations" that create a sense of hopelessness and depression to positive core analysis and generate conversations that create energy, enthusiasm and the impetus for action on behalf of the whole.

In Appreciative Inquiry we understand that human systems move in the direction of what they study. In an intimately interrelated world, what one organization studies moves not only that organization but all of life in the direction of what is studied. The conversations within and about any one organization or community make a difference in the quality of all life on the planet. To help one organization shift focus from deficit discourse is to help the planet. Table 5 shows the shift in focus that occurs with the selection of affirmative topics using Appreciative Inquiry.

Perhaps the biggest shift organizations can make is from: "How do we use resources – social, economic and natural – to achieve our goals?" to "How do we

Table 5. From Deficit Topics to Affirmative Topics.

Deficit Topics	Affirmative Topics
Unequal Distribution of Wealth	Fair Trade
Employee Dissatisfaction and Turnover	Employee Enthusiasm and Retention
Reduction of Pollution	Safe, Healthy Environment
Less Toxic Products	Products with Positive Environmental Impact
Reduction of Waste in Manufacturing	Zero Waste

provide resources to build 'a world conducive to life' " (Benyus, 2003). In shifting their topic of conversation and inquiry organizations open the door to learning, collaboration and courage needed to create a sustainable future for them selves in service to the planet.

THE 4-D CYCLE

Each phase in the Appreciative Inquiry 4-D Cycle offers something different to the potential for elevating organizational consciousness.

Discovery: Uncovering the Ground of Higher Consciousness

In the process of inquiry and studying the best of what is and has been organizations discover instances of elevated human connection, compassion and consciousness. By sharing these stories the organization becomes full of human goodness, cooperation and hope for the future. As people connect through appreciative interviews they gain a sense of belonging and feel as if they are part of something larger than themselves and their organization. The sincere human contact that emerges through appreciative interviews generates a respect for differences among people and creates a capacity to accept differences as essential aspects of the whole. As people open to one another and share stories of cooperation organizational consciousness soars.

Dream: Imaging the Possibilities of Higher Consciousness

Consciousness researcher, John Lilly believed that it was sometimes possible to move to a new state of consciousness by imaging it and simply leaping there (Lilly & Lilly, 1976). This is what happens organizationally in the dream phase of Appreciative Inquiry. When members of an organization are given the opportunity to imagine and express dreams for a better world and organization they do so as the first step toward the realization of those dreams. As Professor David Cooperrider, originator of Appreciative Inquiry, articulated in his landmark article, *Positive Imagery, Positive Action: The Affirmative Basis of Organizing* (Cooperrider, 1990), the more positive the images held among members of the organization the more hopeful and positive their actions. An organization's capacity to imagine positive possibilities elevates its organizational consciousness.

Design: Giving Form to Higher Consciousness

Architects and Social Innovators, alike, from Frank Lloyd Wright to Buckminster Fuller to Aldo van Eyck to William McDonough have long advocated the significance of intention in design. And so it is with the design phase of Appreciative Inquiry. As members and stakeholders of an organization or community move from dream to design they are invited to an increased awareness of the power of intention and the relationship between intention and manifestation. For Architect and Author of *Cradle to Cradle: Remaking the Way We Make Things*, William McDonough design is one of the first signals of human intention – "its purpose can be either to support life or to destroy life" (Holland, 2003).

With its life affirming orientation, Appreciative Inquiry challenges people to design with life-centered intent, to design organizations that support and sustain life. As this happens the organizational consciousness rises and people, individually and collectively are liberated to realize their dreams.

Destiny: Manifesting the Realities of Higher Consciousness

As Appreciative Inquiry fosters the elevation of organizational consciousness it enables the realization of higher ground – realities that support and serve an increasingly larger scope of life, realities that recognize and value life in its multitude of forms and expressions. Organizational consciousness is both created by and creator of the communication, cultural habits and climate of an organization. As organizational consciousness increases so too does the quality of life within and around the organization. Intention and manifestation are intimately linked, as are image and action. In the process of lifting up generative images of the future and crafting life giving propositions of design Appreciative Inquiry opens the door for the manifestation of higher order, sustainable realities. As the opening quote to this chapter states, "worlds come out of us." As we elevate organizational consciousness through inquiry and open dialogue, through envisioning positive possibilities and through the articulation of organization design ideals, we open the way for globally sustainable worlds to emerge.

ELEVATING ORGANIZATIONAL CONSCIOUSNESS FOR A NEW WORLD ORDER

Lakota Sioux Holy Man, Howard Bad Hand told me upon first meeting that spiritually developed people live and work in the energetic positive, that they focus on what gives life to the people in any time and situation. When I met David Cooperrider and Appreciative Inquiry some ten years later I knew I had found an organizational philosophy and methodology that would enable me to put the "life giving spiritual principle" into practice. And now after years of consulting, writing and research with Appreciative Inquiry there is no doubt: Appreciative Inquiry positively impacts the narrative, relational and subtle levels of organizational life and beyond.

When engaged with Appreciative Inquiry, organizations change, people change, their relationships to one another change and more importantly, their way of being in the world changes. Without prescription or recommendation, people take Appreciative Inquiry beyond the boundaries of their organizations. They use it in their churches, little league coaching, with their children's schools, with their partners and in the most contentious community relations. And it works for them. It helps them achieve the goals they intend. It helps them create the world they want to live in and to leave for generations to come.

Whether or not Appreciative Inquiry will endure for generations to come, I cannot say. What I do know for certain, however, is that Appreciative Inquiry is needed now. It is a philosophy and methodology whose time has come. And with it comes a hope for the planet, a hope for elevating organizational consciousness to support and sustain life on earth.[1]

NOTE

1. In this chapter, I introduce "planet centric" organizing while wondering about the well-being of the larger universe in which we live.

REFERENCES

Benyus, J. (2003). Dreams of a livable future. In: P. Hawken (Ed.), *Utne*. May/June.
Bohm, D. (1980). *Wholeness and the implicate order*. London: Routledge Press.
Brutoco, R. S. (2002). President's report year 2002 in review. *Year in Perspective 2002: Responsibility for the Whole* (p. 9). Ojai, CA: World Business Academy.
Cooperrider, D. L. (1990). Positive imagery, positive action: The affirmative basis of organizing. In: S. S. Svrivastva & D. L. Cooperrider (Eds), *Appreciative Management and Leadership*. San Francisco, CA: Jossey-Bass.
Cooperrider, D. L., & Dutton, J. E. (1999). *Organizational dimensions of global change: No limits to cooperation*. Thousand Oaks, CA: Sage.
Davis, S. M. (1984). *Managing corporate culture*. Cambridge, MA: Ballinger Publishing Company.
de Quincey, C. (2002). *Radical nature*. Monpelier, VT: Invisible Cities Press.
Deal, T. E., & Kennedy, A. A. (1982). *Corporate cultures*. Reading, MA: Addison-Wesley.

Hawken, P. (2003). Dreams of a livable future. *Utne*, May/June.

Holland, G. B. (2003). Beyond sustainability. *Ions: Noetic Science Review*. June/August.

Lerner, M. (2000). *Spirit matters*. Charlottesville, VA: Hampton Roads Publishing.

Lilly, J., & Lilly, A. (1976). *The dyadic cyclone*. New York, NY: Simon & Schuster.

Litwin, G. H., Humphrey, J. W., & Wilson, T. B. (1978). Organizational climate: A proven tool for improving performance. In: W. Warner Burke (Ed.), *Current Theory and Practice in Organization Development* (p. 187). La Jolla, CA: University Associates Publishers & Consultants.

Ludema, J., Whitney, D., Mohr, B., & Griffin, T. (2003). *The appreciative inquiry summit*. San Francisco, CA: Berrett-Koehler.

Schein, E. H. (1985). *Organizational culture and leadership*. San Francisco, CA: Jossey-Bass.

Thompson, W. I. (1989). *Imaginary landscape*. New York, NY: St. Martin's Press.

Whitney, D., & Trosten-Bloom, A. (2003). The liberation of power. *The Power of Appreciative Inquiry*. San Fransciso, CA: Berrett-Koehler.

APPRECIATIVE NARRATIVES AS LEADERSHIP RESEARCH: MATCHING METHOD TO LENS

Ellen Schall, Sonia Ospina, Bethany Godsoe
and Jennifer Dodge

ABSTRACT

This chapter explores the potential of appreciative inquiry for doing empirical work on leadership. We use a framework that matches a constructionist theoretical lens, an appreciative and participative stance, a focus on the work of leadership (as opposed to leaders), and multiple methods of inquiry (narrative, ethnographic and cooperative). We elaborate on our experiences with narrative inquiry, while highlighting the value of doing narrative inquiry in an appreciative manner. Finally, we suggest that this particular framework is helping us see how social change leadership work reframes the value that the larger society attributes to members of vulnerable communities.

INTRODUCTION

Appreciative inquiry is best known as an intervention strategy, but it can also be thought of as a stance for inquiry, a way of joining with others to explore the world. Our contribution in this volume is to build on the research side of

Constructive Discourse and Human Organization
Advances in Appreciative Inquiry, Volume 1, 147–170
Copyright © 2004 by Elsevier Ltd.
All rights of reproduction in any form reserved
ISSN: 1475-9152/doi:10.1016/S1475-9152(04)01007-5

appreciative inquiry by exploring its potential for looking at leadership. We argue that, given the roots of appreciative inquiry in constructionism, and an emerging trend to see leadership as a social construct, appreciative inquiry emerges as one of the most appropriate methodological frameworks to pursue empirical work on leadership.

Most leadership research operates from a positivist frame on a set of implicit assumptions that does not explicitly address the logic of the relationship between theory and methods.[1] In this chapter, we reflect on our use of appreciative inquiry to develop what we believe is a sound and internally coherent approach to research on leadership. We offer a story about the emergence of a research design to study leadership that has lessons about the nature of leadership, the role of appreciative inquiry and the power of the match between methods and lens.

This story begins with the definition of our particular lens, the idea that leadership is a social construction. A constructionist lens implies that our understanding of leadership is socially constructed over time, as individuals interact with one another. This means that people carry mental models of leadership (Gardner, 1995) and that groups of individuals come to mean the same thing when they use the term "leader." (By invoking these models, it is possible for any of us to imagine or even picture a "leader.") A constructionist lens lets us see that leadership fulfills a social function. But more importantly, it suggests that leadership happens when people construct meaning in action. In other words, we can consider leadership to be a shared act of meaning making in the context of a group's work to accomplish a common purpose (Drath & Palus, 1994).

The choice of lens has clear implications for both focus (what to study) and stance (who defines what is important and does the research). In terms of focus, we argue that a social construction lens leads us to pay attention to the collective work of leadership in context, more than to the behaviors of people called leaders. If leadership is about meaning making, then it is inevitably relational and collective, and therefore, more about the experience people have as they try to make sense of their work and less about individual traits or behaviors. In terms of stance, once a researcher has decided to focus on the experiences associated with the work of leadership, not on the leader as an individual, we argue that it becomes compelling to invite the people engaged in the work to stand with the researcher and inquire together about its meaning, thus studying the work of leadership from the inside out. The stance then, becomes one of co-inquiry, a participative approach where we as co-researchers conduct research *with* leaders *on* leadership. It is in developing our stance that we have discovered appreciative inquiry as a powerful tool.

Having declared a preference for a lens, and elaborated the implications of our lens for focus and stance, we suggest that certain methodological choices follow naturally. A constructionist lens on leadership, a focus on the experience of leadership, and a co-inquiry stance demand ways of research engagement that can uncover the relational, shared and meaning-making aspects of the work of leadership. We have discovered that appreciative inquiry plays a critical role in enhancing our stance and therefore defining the way in which we implement our methodologies.

In this chapter, we work from our experience in a particular research project that is part of a broader program, *Leadership for a Changing World* (LCW).[2] Our task is to conduct research about leadership using the experience of program participants in order to contribute to creating a new conversation about leadership in this country, one where social change leadership is understood and valued. We created a multi-modal design that consists of three parallel streams of inquiry – ethnographic inquiry, co-operative inquiry, and narrative inquiry – that all focus on the work of leadership and take an appreciative co-inquiry stance in order to match our conceptual lens: leadership as a social construct.[3] These streams are anchored in our commitment to develop appreciative and participatory approaches to research and our belief in the value of conversational encounters with LCW participants as the core activity of the research process. The multi-modal design is aimed at generating practice-grounded research that answers our guiding question: *In what ways do communities trying to make social change engage in the work of leadership?*

Each research method has a tradition of its own, separate from appreciative inquiry, but we argue that each can be taken up in an appreciative manner so as to allow us to add even more coherence to our multi-modal approach and more power to the end result. We focus mostly on the narrative inquiry stream in this chapter and argue that when joined with a participative and appreciative approach, narrative inquiry offers a unique opportunity to join with leaders as co-researchers to reflect on and learn from their experiences with leadership, thus revealing how they make sense of that experience (Fig. 1).

The structure of this chapter is to first elaborate on lens, focus and stance, linking our perspective to the broader leadership field and highlighting the contribution of appreciative inquiry. We then describe in depth the logic behind our methodology. We suggest that the explicit match between methods and lens provides an important contribution to building the cumulative value of leadership research over time. We discuss the contributions of appreciative inquiry in the context of a specific piece of work, LCW, but argue the implications are broader. Finally, we share some reflections about the process of implementing our research design, and hint at what this kind of approach can reveal about leadership by reporting on some of our early insights.

Although we do not report systematic findings, some of our early "hunches" point to the importance of the ways in which our co-researchers and their

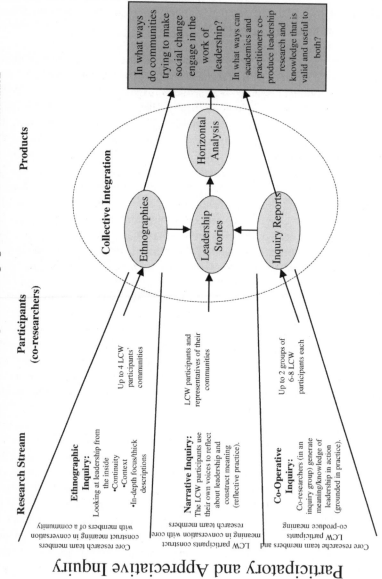

Fig. 1. A Multi-Modal Design: Ethnography, Narrative and Cooperative Inquiry.

colleagues reframe how the society values the groups with whom they work. Their reframing approaches often highlight the humanity of these groups and put into stark relief a context that systemically tends to devalue and de-humanize vulnerable populations. These framing processes can help to emphasize the injustice of an issue thereby giving direction to the work and deepening commitment to it among insiders and outsiders alike. We have also found some early hints of collective forms of leadership where the work is negotiated or shared among several different individuals or groups. While this chapter focuses on our process of doing leadership research, these early hunches are elaborated in more detail below. The formal reports of findings from the project will be co-authored with participants of LCW.

LENS: AN EMERGING TREND TO SEE LEADERSHIP AS A SOCIAL CONSTRUCTION

Instead of entering the leadership definition debate, we made a choice to explore leadership as a social construction.[4] Through this lens we view leadership as a social construct that is created through dialogue among groups of people in context, not as a fixed attribute of individuals. Our thinking builds on a foundation of contemporary work on leadership.

We begin with a body of work that explores the role of cognition in the emergence of leadership (Gardner, 1995), and its transformational and symbolic nature (Burns, 1978; Schein, 1990). These approaches frame leadership not as a single fixed entity but as something that allows people to agree on direction and action around their common concerns. Building on this beginning, several organizational scholars (Pfeffer, 1997; Smircich, 1983; Smircich & Morgan, 1982; Tierney, 1987; Tierney & Lincoln, 1997) have pursued the idea that leadership emerges from the constructions and actions of people in organizations. According to this perspective, leadership becomes a reality when one or more individuals in a social system succeed in framing and defining how the demands of the group will be taken up, and what roles, including "the role of leader," will be attributed to whom (Hunt, 1984; Meindl, 1995; Meindl et al., 1985). Pushing this idea to its limit, Pastor (1998) views leadership as "a collective social consciousness that emerges in the organization," and is not only cognitive, but also rooted in social interaction. Because we adopt this lens we are concerned with looking at how groups collectively make sense of their work. However, while breaking new ground theoretically, the agenda to test these constructionist ideas empirically is still in its early development.

Wilfred Drath and Charles Palus at the Center for Creative Leadership offer a particularly intriguing strand of constructionist thinking about leadership that can be used as a foundation upon which a powerful research agenda can be built. In their view, leadership is a type *of meaning and sense making* that can be understood as happening over time and in community. It is "a social process in which everyone in the community participates" (1994, p. 13). This process is shaped by what Drath calls the "knowledge principle," or dominant, underlying, and taken-for-granted set of assumptions a community holds about how best to approach the work of leadership.

The knowledge principle that frames a group's work is directly related to a group's context. The principle Drath calls personal dominance emerges when people agree to understand leadership as the personal quality of a type of person called leader, who acts toward and upon another type of person, a follower. In this view, a dominant figure is the source of leadership and takes a role as the leader. Under the interpersonal influence principle, leadership is seen as emerging from a process of negotiation among different actors with different perspectives until an individual or a group positions itself as the most influential actor and enacts a particular role of leader. The relational dialogue principle happens when people with differing world views use dialogue and collaborative learning to create spaces where a shared common purpose can be achieved while the diversity of perspectives is preserved and valued. Leadership, then, in this third principle, does not reside in a person or in a role, but in the social system.[5]

Drath observes that relational dialogue is the newest and least developed knowledge principle, both in the theory and practice of leadership. We would agree that it is the least developed in the theory of leadership, but that scholars have overlooked it in practice due to the lack of conceptual clarity between "leader," an individual with admirable qualities, and "leadership," the negotiated property of a social system. This challenge draws our attention to the importance of *focus*.

FOCUS: A SHIFT FROM STUDYING LEADERS TO STUDYING THE WORK OF LEADERSHIP

A constructionist lens helps us to understand that existing mental models of leadership – that tend to be individualistic and positional – emerged out of collective processes of meaning making developed in context, and have then taken on a life of their own. As we began to develop the focus of the research in a manner consistent with our lens, we noted three important shifts in the study of leadership: one that allows for attention to shared leadership and the collective meaning making processes that shape the experience of leadership; a second that encourages us to step back and look not at the behavior of individuals but at the tasks groups face as they try to take action; and a third that pushes us to look for leadership in new places.

A handful of researchers have begun to explore the shared quality of leadership (see Bennis & Biederman, 1997; Goldman & Kahnweiler, 2000; Gronn, 1999; Hesselbein, Goldsmith & Somerville, 1999; Huxham & Vangen, 2000; Lipman-Blumen, 1996; Yukl, 1999), and its practical value as a means to produce socially useful outcomes through adaptive work (see Heifetz, 1994). This work also takes the idea that leadership is fluid; its dimensions often distributed among several people in the group, rather than concentrated in a single individual (Yukl, 1999). Taking it a step further, Kaczmarski and Cooperrider view leadership as the "art of creating contexts of appreciative interchange", where "differences are embraced rather than being a source of dominance and conformity pressures" (1997, p. 251). This line of thinking sees leadership as a collective effort and a collective accomplishment.

Attention to ideas like shared leadership is critical, not just because it allows more people to get in the picture, but because the focus of the picture shifts – away from actions of two or three people, to the work the group undertakes together and the way the group authorizes individuals to act on its behalf. For example, by focusing on leadership as activities that stem from a collective challenge, Heifetz's groundbreaking work directs attention away from an exclusive focus on the "leader" to consider also the acts of leadership, leadership in process, and the public aspects of leadership work.

Drath articulates a similar process that shapes our focus on the work of leadership. He argues that leadership happens when people in a community create a shared understanding of their mutual and moral obligations so that their common cause is realized. Thus, any group of persons attempting to accomplish goals collectively face three crucial tasks: setting direction, creating and maintaining commitment, and adapting to the challenges that appear on the way (the latter refers to what Heifetz calls adaptive challenges). If a group does not respond to these challenges that call for leadership, it will not survive to serve its purpose. While these challenges are not meant to be an exhaustive list of all that happens when leadership is at work, they help to set the boundaries of our inquiry. Without such boundaries we could fall into the trap of imagining that everything that happens in the context of a social change effort is the work of leadership.

As we inquire into program participants' stories, we talk with them about the nature of their work, not about leadership directly. Because of our understanding of the socially constructed nature of leadership, we want to avoid invoking dominant mental models of leadership. Instead, we aim to elicit stories about our co-researchers' experience with their work and the meaning they make of that experience. Because of our appreciative frame, our questions focus on high points – stories of what our co-researchers identify as their work at its best. These stories should help us understand how they attend to the tasks of leadership, and what knowledge principles underlie the experience of leadership in each context as groups pursue their collective work.

Finally, even when research is focused on the collective work of leadership, it is frequently set in traditional contexts – corporations and government. The civic reform literature on leadership opens up new venues and reveals new models for understanding leadership. Several of these scholars (Bryson & Crosby, 1992; Chrislip & Larson, 1994; Crosby, 1999; Luke, 1998; Terry, 1993) suggest that the interconnectedness of contemporary society demands a different kind of leadership to address public problems, one that is more collective than individual. Similarly, the social movement literature (Couto, 1993; Morris & Staggenborg, 2004; Robnett, 1996) and the community and labor organizing literatures (Hinsdale, Lewis & Waller, 1995; Sacks, 1988) reinforce the attention to the relational nature of leadership.[6] These examples allows us to see how a focus on new contexts draws attention to the leadership that exists at multiple levels – not just in the individual who is publicly recognized as a leader.

In sum, a shift in focus directs our attention to new possibilities: shared leadership, leadership as a process of a group not a trait of an individual, and leadership more broadly attributed and understood as existing in many places and taking many forms. Combined with our lens, it follows that we pay attention to the experiences of leaders, their colleagues and members of their communities as they make sense of their collective work.

STANCE: THE CONTRIBUTION OF APPRECIATIVE INQUIRY

Shifting the focus away from leaders and toward the collective work of leadership in social change efforts is not meant to diminish the important role that individuals called leaders do play. Instead, it calls for a shift in the role they play in research and a shift in the scholar's stance as well. Given our focus on the experience of leadership in context, we believe that we can best understand how leadership happens "by entering into the community and inquiring into the shared meaning-making languages and processes of the community" (Drath, 2001, p. 49). Leaders then stand with scholars as co-researchers together inquiring into the work of leadership from the inside out.

This logic led us to take a participatory stance to the research process. In doing so, we join with those who stress the participatory nature of knowledge production and, in particular, the democratic and practice-grounded nature of action research.

As Peter Reason and Hilary Bradbury describe it, "action research is a participatory, democratic process concerned with developing practical knowing in the pursuit of worthwhile human purposes ..." (2001, p. 1). Further, participatory action research (PAR) has made huge strides to involve communities in learning about their own concerns and to find the tools to address them, aiming to alter the power relationship between researcher and subject (Fals-Borda & Rahman, 1991; Stringer, 1999; Wadsworth, 1997; Whyte, 1991).[7]

Our stance pushes us to go beyond trying to alter the power relationship between researcher and subject to entirely re-constructing that relationship into one between co-researchers. For this we turn to John Heron and Peter Reason's work on co-operative inquiry. Co-operative inquiry is a radically participatory approach to social research in which all participants are considered to be co-inquirers, serving as both co-subjects and co-researchers as they pursue an issue of common interest through cycles of action and reflection (Heron & Reason, 2001). While co-operative inquiry is just one of the three specific methods we use in our work with the LCW participants, we apply its definition of co-inquirers to our overall design.

In practice, the challenges of working as co-inquirers are enormous and much has been written about the difficulties involved in having the "subjects" be full participants in shaping the research agenda as well as its implementation (see for example, McGuire, 1987; Ospina et al., 2002; Whyte, 1991). So while we started with a participative stance, we came to understand that it was not enough. The traditions of action research, participatory action research, and co-operative inquiry are concerned with positive social change, but they do not guarantee an *appreciative* stance. Scholars have criticized action research because it has "largely failed as an instrument for advancing "second order" [i.e. structural] social-organizational transformation ... because of its romance with critique at the expense of appreciation" (Ludema et al., 2001).

We understood conceptually the complementary nature of using an appreciative and a participative stance to our inquiry process. As we entered the field and began working collaboratively with our co-researchers, we later came to realize that if we had used only a participatory approach, we would have been missing a powerful dynamic. Our appreciative approach has helped us overcome some of the challenges associated with participatory research by making the task of research less threatening to participants (we do not aim to uncover what is going "wrong" in their work) and thereby helping us to build trust. More importantly, our appreciative and participatory stance with our co-researchers has allowed us to witness and learn about the cutting edge of leadership work in such a way that is and feels qualitatively different from other research traditions we have used in the past, because it is built on valuing.

Even though it is challenging at times (Ospina et al., 2002), our inquiry space is enhanced by our collaboration with the social change leaders. At the time of this writing, our research team consisted of 20 award recipients, including individual leaders and leadership teams (32 people in all), the four authors of this paper, and several outside researchers with whom we have contracted to do specific pieces of the work (e.g. ethnographies), all serving as co-researchers.[8] As the research and documentation team for *Leadership for a Changing World*, we play no direct role in selecting the award recipients who ultimately become co-researchers.[9] Our partner institution, the Washington D.C.-based Advocacy Institute, manages this process. However, we were involved in defining the criteria used for both outreach and selection so that groups that practiced shared leadership and leaders who were committed to learning with others were included.[10]

As a group, these award winners bring a diversity of knowledge and experience of social change leadership to the research effort. For example, one is an AIDS policy advocate working to empower African-American communities to tackle the growing epidemic of HIV/AIDS among African-Americans. Another award winner organized a coalition of 17 immigrant and refugee groups in Chicago and helped them hold the INS accountable. There is a team of women fighting mountain top removal mining in rural West Virginia, an organizer of taco vendors in Phoenix, and a team of janitors in Los Angeles who have catalyzed a national campaign to organize their fellow building-service workers. Each co-researcher has a complex story to tell of their experience with leadership.

Once we decided to use a constructionist lens to study leadership, it became compelling to work with these participants to inquire collaboratively into their experience of leadership in their communities. Our stance of co-inquiry allows us to do research with leaders on leadership. In developing this stance, we have discovered that appreciative inquiry is a powerful complement to a participative stance, not only for the positive stories it generates about the work, but because of the way in which we are in relationship to our co-researchers. What follows is a discussion of how we are trying to build leadership theory by using an appreciative frame to match three specific methodologies to our constructionist lens.

METHOD: THE IMPERATIVE TO MATCH METHOD TO LENS

An internally coherent research design demands that methodological choices be made in accordance with the understanding of the topic being studied. If one sees leadership with a positivist lens, then positivist research methods are most appropriate. However, if leadership is viewed as a social construction, then methods based on social constructionist thinking will be most appropriate. This means creating a design that allows us to focus on the relational, shared and meaning making aspects of the work of leadership while engaging with the participants as co-researchers.

Because a constructionist approach to leadership research is relatively new, the methods associated with it are less developed. There has been work using qualitative research to look at sense making, but it has used traditional positivist paradigms (Meindl, 1995; Pastor, 1998). Our work attempts to design and test a variety of methods that we believe hold promise for understanding leadership. In assessing the appropriateness of these methods, our appreciative and participative stance, and our focus on the work of leadership in the context of social change have served as important guidelines.

We could have chosen to use appreciative inquiry as the single methodology in our work because, with its social constructionist roots, it offers a perfect match to lens. However, because the focus of the research is the experience of meaning making, many angles are more likely to generate a full picture of that experience than one. In addition, we knew that our co-researchers would be a diverse group of social change leaders who would respond to different methodologies in varying ways. Finally, a multi-modal design offers the additional benefit of enhancing the trustworthiness of our findings. Therefore, we chose three streams of inquiry: ethnography, co-operative inquiry, and narrative inquiry.

Ethnography – We are using a collaborative and community-based approach to ethnography that looks at the experience of leadership in three to four of the participant communities. Award recipients serve as co-researchers from the very beginning of these ethnographies by first requesting the ethnography, then proposing a focus for it, and ultimately helping with the selection of an ethnographer. By working with the award recipients to define an area of their work that could benefit from being studied, the ethnographers insure that their inquiry focuses on the work of leadership in context rather than on the individual leaders. The use of an appreciative stance within the ethnographic stream brings a generative element to the research and provides a point of entry into reflecting on the participants' experience with their work.

Co-operative Inquiry – Of the three methods we are using in the LCW program, co-operative inquiry has the most natural fit with our stance. In this stream, participants provide complete direction for the inquiry, defining the question and their action strategies, and reflecting on the sense they make of their experience while taking those actions. While co-operative inquiry is essentially about the participants and their own practice, it is clear that their inquiry focuses on the work of leadership. For example, one of the first LCW co-operative inquiry groups inquired into the question, "How can we create the space/opportunities for individuals to recognize themselves as leaders and develop their leadership?" The "how" of this question focuses on the work.

We have used an appreciative stance in this stream over the full course of the inquiry. In the beginning we used it to allow co-inquirers to share with one another what was most important about their work, so they could begin to hone in on an inquiry question. Throughout the ensuing reflection cycles, appreciative inquiry has been used to emphasize what has worked well as participants generate findings to answer their question. The appreciative stance has also been critical to build the confidence of the participants as "researchers," given that many of them come into the inquiry with some distrust toward the academy and the traditional research often associated with it.

ENRICHING NARRATIVE INQUIRY: AN APPRECIATIVE APPROACH

In conceiving and implementing the narrative stream of our research design, we have developed an integrated approach to the study of leadership that draws from appreciative, participative, and narrative traditions of inquiry. We chose narrative as our core method[11] for the LCW program because it is the means through which people make sense of and understand their experience, including their experience of leadership. Narrative inquiry, as a process, has much in common with the way in which we understand leadership. We view both leadership and narrative to be socially constructed and begin with the understanding that the narratives do not "objectively" mirror reality; "they are constructed, creatively authored, rhetorical, replete with assumptions, and interpretive" (Riessman, 1993, p. 5). We are interested precisely in seeing how participants interpret the work they do and how those interpretations tell us something about leadership.

We ground narrative in the participative tradition because we see the need to get inside peoples' experience, to make sense of leadership from the inside out. We could have simply taken a participative approach to narrative inquiry to generate new understanding of how leadership happens in these social change efforts. The argument we develop here, though, is that by enriching a participative narrative inquiry with an appreciative stance we can take the work further. The combination of these elements – narrative with a participative and appreciative stance – creates a synergy that helps us deepen our connection with the award recipients, add value to their work, and ultimately, we hope, create stories that generate new understanding about leadership.

More specifically, appreciative inquiry shares a constructionist epistemology with our approach to narrative inquiry that makes for an internally consistent and enhanced hybrid methodology. As Cooperrider and Srivastva describe it, appreciative inquiry assumes that the "social order at any given point is viewed as the product of broad social agreement, whether tacit or explicit" (1987, p. 137). An important implication of this assumption is that sense making is open to revision through interaction and dialogue with others, whether with colleagues, researchers, or anyone else. Appreciative inquiry capitalizes on this insight and uses processes of shared meaning making to generate positive images of the future. For our purposes in doing leadership research, meaning creation is relational, and that conversation, including interviewing, can be generative of "fresh alternatives" or new ways of understanding one's experience.

This constructionist and "life centric" focus of appreciative inquiry takes us away from a problem-solving stance to an appreciative one that "draws the researcher to go beyond superficial appearances to deeper levels of the life-generating essentials and potentials of social existence . . . to illuminate the factors and forces involved in organizing that serve to nourish the human spirit" (Cooperrider & Srivastva, 1987, p. 131). In other words, appreciative inquiry allows for deep reflection about the work of leadership, and searches out practices (factors & forces) that already nourish the human spirit in the hope of contributing to their development and enhancement.

Our narrative inquiry approach adopts this appreciative stance so that it becomes an inquiry not simply about (re)telling stories but "retelling of stories that allow for growth and change" (Clandinin & Connelly, 2000, p. 71). In other words, working collaboratively to enhance our understanding of leadership has the potential to be grounding for action, for our co-researchers, and, if we are able to generate sound theory, for others as well. Jim Ludema noted this generative connection between narrative inquiry and appreciative inquiry in his dissertation where he writes, "[e]liciting positive narrative responses from interviewees [is] most generative of collective hope, knowledge, and action in the organizational and communal contexts" (p. 115).

For these reasons, it is our belief that these appreciatively constructed stories, once shared, will inspire and give substance to new conversations about leadership in this country. What follows is the story of how we engaged our co-researchers in this particular approach to narrative inquiry and how appreciative inquiry enhanced both our co-researchers' experience and our collective learning.

DEVELOPING THE INQUIRY

We began this work by asking our co-researchers to identify the two or three dimensions of their work that they would like to focus on throughout the narrative inquiry and ultimately in the leadership story we committed to co-producing with them. By doing this we focused the inquiry from the outset on the work of leadership rather than on the leaders (following Drath, 2001). Our invitation served a second and perhaps even more important purpose. It allowed us to engage them as co-researchers early in the process, at least theoretically. At first our attempt to be participative was not an immediate success. Despite having information about the conversation ahead of time, many were still unclear about our intentions and did not immediately take up their role with ease. What did we mean by dimensions of the work, they wondered, and where was this process going?

Once we were able to enact our appreciative stance, their role became much clearer to them. When we posed questions like, "What dimensions of your work do you think most contribute to your organization's success? What elements of your work would help others learn the most from your experience?" then our co-researchers were more able to join the conversation. This first step helped us to establish trust and gave us some early insights about their leadership work. For one thing, the emphasis so many put on bridging and partnering affirmed our sense of leadership as a collective and relational process.

To honor the social nature of their leadership stories, we invited our co-researchers to include a diversity of colleagues and community members in the telling of their stories. We encouraged them to select people who knew their work well, brought a range of views, and represented the different "milieus" affected by the work. Our appreciative stance seemed to help our co-researchers feel safe about including multiple perspectives to enrich their stories, and some even took our suggestion to include a thoughtful critic. Further, we organized the interviews as group conversations to model leadership as it happens in their community. By conducting these conversations in groups, we could encourage the development of integrated and multi-faceted stories that contain some interpretation that might be missing in a one-on-one conversation.

We then developed an approach to eliciting stories about the dimensions of the work that our co-researchers identified. A straight narrative approach might have asked questions like, "How did you first begin establishing ties with non-traditional allies in your community?" Again, this approach may have helped us to develop an understanding of how they approach their work, but we wanted something more. We wanted to engage the co-researchers, their colleagues, and community members in deep reflection that would uncover their knowledge principle: the underlying and taken-for-granted set of assumptions their community holds about how best to approach the work of leadership (Drath, 2001), that are at work when leadership is happening at its best (Ludema, 1996).

To facilitate this kind of deeply reflective and generative conversation, we created appreciative protocols[12] for two two-hour conversations and customized them for each co-researcher based on the dimensions they defined. Our first conversation was with the awardees and their close colleagues. It was designed to elicit stories about the work, to set the context, to understand key issues, triumphs and conflicts, as well as their relationships to the wider community. We paid particular attention to the main practices (such as "building coalitions") that our co-researchers had identified. The main purpose of the second conversation with other members of the community was to enrich the leadership story, add multiple perspectives, and flesh out the social dimensions of the work.

For both conversations, the protocols had three sections. They opened with an invitation to participants to share either what they value about the organization or one of their earliest positive memories of it. We found that this question helped build trust with people we had never met before, largely because it began from a stance of valuing and appreciation. Then, the majority of the conversation was dedicated to exploring the dimensions of the work that our co-researchers had identified as central. Through this part of the conversation, our role was to intervene only to probe for details of a story, to keep the conversation moving, to reinforce our appreciative stance, or to keep focused on themes relevant to our research question and the co-researchers' interests. The final part of the protocols included an appreciative question about the future, something like, "What do you see happening in the organization right now that gives you hope for the future?" In this way, if it had not happened already, we were able to bring a generative element to the conversation.

To conduct these conversations, we visited each of our co-researchers. Our travels took us from Maine to Alaska and many places in between – the mountains of West Virginia, the immigrant communities of Nebraska and Arizona, and the inner city of San Francisco to name a few. While this was generally our first visit to our co-researchers' place of work, we were often welcomed as old colleagues, invited to dinner in their homes or to go out "into the field" to meet the people who are most affected by the issues on which they work. We had built trust with our co-researchers much more quickly than usually happens in a more traditional research project, and we believe this is due, in part, to our appreciative stance. The intimate atmosphere of many of our co-researchers' work places – some work out of their home, others work alone in casual offices – also facilitated trust building.

Similarly, once we entered the field through these visits – bringing colleagues and community members together to reflect collectively – other participants felt at ease with the process. The wheels of conversation were greased by questions like, "Can you tell me about a time when you were particularly proud of the way you handled conflict in your organization?" A potentially contentious issue like conflict, which had been defined as a central dimension by one of our co-researchers, was easily discussed by organizational insiders and outsiders alike because of the appreciative way in which it was framed. We have been gratified with the way in which our appreciative stance helps our co-researchers' colleagues jump into the conversation in such a natural and passionate way to tell us how they feel when things are at their best.

Since we view leadership as a relational process, narrative accounts of the work are not possessions of the participants telling the stories but are instead possessions of broader sets of relationships (Ludema, 1996, p. 167). In other words, stories are social products, much in the same way that leadership is a social product. Through these social products, we were able to see how these communities address the leadership challenges Drath defines: setting direction, creating and sustaining commitment, and adapting to change. We believe that both the stories and the way in which they were told provided an understanding of their experience of leadership that may allow us to begin to uncover the community's knowledge principle.

Of course we encountered challenges. Cultural differences still mattered and made mutual understanding difficult in some cases. Our intended design for the conversations did not always work. For example, the word "success" turned out to be loaded language for our co-researchers. Before answering questions like "Could you tell me about a time when you were particularly successful at establishing partnerships?" they would want us to explain what we meant by success. The power of appreciative inquiry, though, was in its ability to quickly ease anxiety. When re-framed as "Could you tell me about a partnership that has really helped you deliver on your mission in ways you didn't imagine before?" or "Tell me about a partnership that you are particularly proud of. How did it develop?" our co-researchers and the others jumped to share stories with us. In fact, we discovered that a sense of pride was a very helpful feeling to tap into, one that led them to collectively develop rich narratives of their experience with leadership.

At this point in the research, we have completed the first stage of the transcript analysis. This stage involved taking large amount of raw data and transforming them into analytical, or synthesis texts (Kelchtermans, 1999) that captured key themes, processes, and stories focusing primarily on the uniqueness of each award recipient's work. During the final part of this stage, the analytical texts were transformed into "leadership stories" that were shared with our co-researchers for reflection and feedback. The final stories will result from an iterative process of co-production. As we move forward with the work, we are beginning to link the data and stories from each co-researcher through a "horizontal analysis" (Kelchtermans, 1999) across sites to find patterns and similarities that go beyond the particulars of each context. As we begin the early stages of this work, we have great hope that our appreciative stance will yield important insights about leadership for social change.

REFLECTIONS ON OUR WORK

In reflecting on the visits to our co-researchers' community, we noted that the process of the group conversations felt very different than other interviewing techniques we have used in the past. These conversations not only introduced us to each co-researcher's work, and gave us insights about the contexts in which they are carrying it out, but they also gave us insights about the values that uphold the work, the factors and relationships that make it possible, and the commitments that nourish it.

Conceptualizing our interviews with award recipients and their colleagues as conversations to generate appreciative narratives allowed us, the award recipients and the community members with whom we spoke to reflect on multiple levels. The conversations offered people a chance to tell stories about the here and now of their experience as well as step back and reflect on the meaning of those stories. In Heron and Reason's terms, the conversations used experiential, presentational and propositional ways of knowing (2001). In Ronald Heifetz's terms, they were stories from the dance floor as well as from the balcony (1994). In most cases, the research space we created generated deeper, more reflective conversations than we could have hoped to have in such a short time.

We are not the only ones who have commented on the value appreciative inquiry added to this process. Some of our co-researchers have enjoyed the chance to take time out of their busy schedules to reflect on their work in ways that are not usually possible, and using a framework that moves them away from traditional problem solving. One award recipient was even inspired to write something on his own about the leadership that happens in his community. We are gratified that the process spurned more inquiry about his experience of leadership even though at the beginning he had expressed ambivalence about the value of the process for his own work.

In other cases, this work has provided the opportunity for different members of an organization to share their stories and learn something about the work from each other that they might not have known, something they have valued. We have also seen some evidence that these conversations have the potential to generate new images and vocabularies that participants can bring back to their communities to motivate the work.

With respect to early insights about social change leadership, we know that it is too early in our process to have anything more than "hunches" to help answer the question: in what ways do communities trying to make social change engage in the work of leadership? As expected, ideas and possible leads have started to emerge. These leads seem promising and we will pursue them more systematically as we continue to engage in the cross-site analysis.

For example, we have found that the work of most award recipients is supported by a passionate belief in the humanity of the marginalized populations with which they work. The relentless commitment to this premise has a direct impact on how the work is framed. At the same time, as this commitment gets to be "embedded" in the actions and products of the work, it also challenges the common perceptions that the larger society has of these populations.

The cognitive leadership literature (Gardner, 1995; Schon & Rein, 1994) and the contemporary social movement literature[13] have already brought attention to the power of reframing (Morris & Staggenborg, 2004; Snow & Benford, 1992). According to Alberto Melucci (1996), actors in social movements engage in redefining reality symbolically, rejecting dominant representations of issues (and, if we are right, the people who are affected by issues). Our preliminary work suggests that most of our co-researchers and their colleagues engage in reframing how the society *values* the people/groups with whom they work. For some, this means treating often-marginalized groups as unique people with dreams and aspirations. For others, it means holding people accountable – i.e. *capable* – for addressing the seemingly insurmountable obstacles they face. Both these approaches highlight their humanity, given a systemic context that tends to devalue and de-humanize vulnerable populations.

The lens, focus, stance and methods we use in our research have helped us see that, as recognized leaders of their organizations, our co-researchers seem to be giving voice to something that belongs to the community, not just to themselves. They seem to be holding for the group – and helping them enact – the core belief that as human beings they deserve better and that it is worth taking a stance for this belief. They are involved together in a process of reframing, a process that is taking place individually and collectively. Borrowing insights from the social movements' literature we can say that reframing the meaning of the community underscores and exaggerates the social injustice of an issue, or makes a formerly tolerable problem into an unjust issue thus setting direction to the work and catapulting people into action (Snow & Benford, 1992).

In the case of social change leadership, reframing may help mobilize the community or the members of a given population to take action for their own sake and encourages commitment to the work. The very process of engagement is empowering for people because they can see their own ideas taking shape and often creating real change. Furthermore, by working with marginalized groups, and having high expectations of what they can accomplish, our co-researchers and the colleagues in their organizations help to present an image of the population to the public that flies directly in the face of common perceptions.

As we see this reframing happening, we also see collective forms of leadership emerging. Indeed, the collective aspect of leadership seems very present among the award recipients' organizations despite the variations in structure. We see consistency here with the shared leadership literature (Bennis & Biederman, 1997; Goldman & Kahnweiler, 2000; Gronn, 1999; Hesselbein, Goldsmith & Somerville, 1999; Huxham & Vangen, 2000; Lipman-Blumen, 1996; Yukl, 1999) and most importantly, with the civic reform leadership literature (Bryson & Crosby, 1992; Chrislip & Larson, 1994; Crosby, 1999; Luke, 1998; Terry, 1993). Many of the stories we have heard suggest that, whatever the organizational form, leadership emerges from open and, and, at times harshly honest, feedback and negotiation among at least two or more people. While too early to make a formal claim, we venture here to say that there may be some evidence in the work of our co-researchers, of what Drath calls the "relational dialogue" knowledge principle of leadership.

In the more hierarchically structured organizations, the executive director may have a "right hand" person who either acts as a rudder to make the work stay on course, or acts as the visionary to push innovation in a well-managed organization. In some of the less bureaucratic organizations, formal leadership is assumed by a team and the structure is very flat and horizontal, with room for lots of exchange from other stakeholders that goes beyond simple consultation. One award recipient team, for example, is very intentional about creating a decentralized structure and checks and balances on power within the organization to ensure that the work is driven by the members and "leaders" (or members who take on greater responsibility for the work). In some cases the formal leader and staff work closely with a Board whose members are often actively involved in both the internal decision-making and external actions on behalf of the organization's primary population. In some cases, board members *are* members of that population.

In all these cases, we have heard stories that suggest that often the leadership functions are more diffused than what the traditional leadership literature has suggested; leadership seems to take the form of a group of complementary actors who share various functions, for example, organizing and connecting with constituents, lobbying and negotiating with high-level officials, and coordinating publicity. This idea may not seem new, especially in the light of community organizing and the social movements' literature, but we believe that the leadership applications of this insight have been missed before. For example, if successful leadership in these organizations includes a complementary group of individuals, similar to what Morris, Robnett and Sacks propose for the social movements they studied, then leadership transitions and succession efforts in organizations need to take this into account. Too frequently, an executive director will groom one individual as a replacement, when it might make more sense to nourish and recruit several individuals, perhaps one who officially leads the organization, and others who provide critical support.

These reflections are, of course, still very tentative, as it is too early in our work to have developed systematic findings. Our intention has been to illustrate the usefulness of our approach rather than to present formal claims about the nature of leadership for social change.

CONCLUSION

If our hunches prove to have some merit, reframing may represent a critical dimension that needs to be further explored to understand leadership as a process of meaning making in a community of practice. In insisting on humanizing a community that has been dehumanized by others, the work of most of our co-researchers challenges basic societal assumptions about how the world is and ought to be. We suspect that this challenge opens up a new range of possibilities to help frame the direction of the work, to provide the moral ground for staff and community members to commit to it, and to find ways to adapt to the challenges of achieving the social change goals that sustain their organizations. Pursuing this line of thinking further may provide evidence to support the emerging constructionist conception of leadership reviewed earlier in this chapter.

Given our argument – about the role of appreciative inquiry in helping us more effectively understand leadership – it is worth speculating whether attention to the reframing process would have emerged as it has, had we used a more traditional approach in our study. We cannot be sure, of course, but we suspect that, had we not emphasized the meaning-making nature of leadership (lens), or had we focused on the leaders rather than the work (focus), this idea would have gotten lost. Our lens makes us very attentive to how members of the community, including our co-researchers, understand their own experience, how and why they do their work, and in doing it, how they enact leadership. Therefore, we have noticed their commitment to humanize members of their communities as an important starting point to understand how they make collective sense of their work.

Similarly, had we only used a participative stance, without emphasizing the generative dimensions of the work that an appreciative stance proposes, the conversations and stories the participants would have told may have had a very different tone. By framing the questions appreciatively, it was only natural for participants to talk about the appreciative stance that they themselves have about their own communities, and to express how this vision drives their work. We have a long way to go before we can report the hunches we describe here as solid claims that provide insights about leadership. But we believe that what we are seeing will offer new vistas of the work of communities making social change that will enrich our present understanding of leadership.

It truly is the combination of narrative inquiry with a participative and appreciative stance that has allowed the research process to be of such value to all involved. Because this work was grounded in narrative, it uncovered people's understanding of their experiences in a rich way; because our conversations were participative (in their design and focus), they resulted in practice-grounded (and therefore "on the mark") interpretations of the work of leadership; and because we took an appreciative stance, we were able to engage with people in a trusting way. It is because the work has been at once appreciative, narrative, and participative that we have confidence that it will generate positive stories that are grounded in practice, that highlight how one can do social change work successfully, and that inspire others so they might work toward "worthwhile human purposes," and "imagine different ways of being together" (Reason & Bradbury, 2001). Appreciative inquiry, then, will fulfill its potential when its use as an inquiry tool flourishes as well as its application in interventions.

NOTES

1. A critical standard by which to judge the quality of research is called "indication," or the extent to which the methods one chooses matches one's theoretical framework (Bauer & Gaskell, 2000). For a discussion of indication in leadership research, see Ospina (2002).

2. Leadership for a Changing World is an awards and recognition program sponsored by the Ford Foundation in partnership with the Washington D.C.-based Advocacy Institute and the Robert F. Wagner Graduate School of Public Service.

3. See Fig. 1 for an illustration of how these streams fit together, the connections of these streams to the guiding research question, the expected products for each stream, and the degree of participation of co-researchers in each stream.

4. For a more in depth exploration of our constructionist approach to leadership, see Ospina and Schall (2001).

5. Drath (2001) argues that these knowledge principles have emerged progressively over time, as society has become more complex and the simpler tools of sense making hit the limit of usefulness. These principles can also be found contemporaneously or in combination, because the principle that helps solve more complex challenges incorporates elements of the principles used to address simpler challenges.

6. For example, in her study of an organizing effort among working-class African American women, Karen Sacks (1988) distinguishes two types of mutually reinforcing leadership roles necessary for success in a social change effort: spokespeople who take on a public presence and centerpeople who are less visible but no less critical to the work. In another example, Robnett (1996) identifies the critical role of women as "bridge leaders" in the civil rights movement. In this role, women were the connectors between the highly visible leaders and community members, doing much of the meaning making work.

7. Kelly's (1999) work with African American communities in Chicago represents an excellent example of participatory action research on leadership.

8. Currently, our research team has grown to include an additional 20 award recipients (10 teams, and 10 individuals, for a total of additional 36 people), and several additional outside researchers working with us in all three streams of inquiry.

9. For a discussion on the paradox of looking at the collective work of leadership in the context of an awards program for leaders, see Ospina et al. (2002).

10. Other criteria are that award recipients be leaders who are tackling tough social problems with effective, systemic solutions, that leaders be largely unrecognized outside their field or community but who, if recognized, would inspire many more people to believe they can make a difference. In addition, LCW seeks to recognize leadership that is strategic, brings different groups of people together, is sustainable beyond any individual effort, and gets results.

11. Narrative inquiry is the one stream in our research that engages all twenty award recipients.

12. Copies of this protocol can be obtained by writing to Amparo Hofmann, Associate Project Director, CHPSR, 726 Broadway, 5th Floor, New York, NY 10003.

13. We suspect that not all award recipients would claim a connection to a social movement, even though their work is clearly geared toward making social change. However, we would argue that concepts developed in social movement theory are relevant to their work. The difference does not seem to be qualitative, as much as a matter of scale.

REFERENCES

Bauer, M. W., & Gaskell, G. (2000). *Qualitative researching with text, image and sound*. London: Sage.

Bennis, W., & Biederman, P. (1997). *Organizing genius: The secrets of creative collaboration*. Reading, MA: Addison-Wesley.

Bryson, J., & Crosby, B. (1992). *Leadership for the common good: Tackling public problems in a shared-power world*. San Francisco, CA: Jossey-Bass.

Burns, J. (1978). *Leadership*. New York, NY: Harper & Row.

Chrislip, D. D., & Larson, C. E. (1994). *Collaborative leadership: How citizens and civic leaders can make a difference*. San Francisco, CA: Jossey-Bass.

Clandinin, D. J., & Connelly F. M. (2000). *Narrative inquiry: Experience and story in qualitative research*. San Francisco, CA: Jossey-Bass.

Cooperrider, D. L., & Srivastva, S. (1987). Appreciative inquiry in organizational life. *Research in Organizational Change and Development, 1*, 129–169.

Couto, R. (1993). Narrative, free space, and political leadership in social movements. *Journal of Politics, 55*(1), 57–79.

Crosby, B. (1999). *Leadership for global citizenship: Building transnational community*. Thousand Oaks, CA: Sage.

Drath, W. (2001). *The deep blue sea: Rethinking the source of leadership*. San Francisco, CA: Jossey-Bass.

Drath, W., & Palus, C. (1994). *Making common sense: Leadership as meaning making in a community of practice*. Greensboro, NC: Center for Creative Leadership.

Fals-Borda, O., & Rahman, M. A. (Eds) (1991). *Action and knowledge: Breaking the monopoly with participatory action research*. London: Intermediate Technology Publication.

Gardner, H. (1995). *Leading minds: An anatomy of leadership*. New York, NY: Basic Books.

Goldman, S., & Kahnweiler, W. M. (2000). A collaborator profile for executives of nonprofit organizations. *Nonprofit Management & Leadership, 10*(4), 435–450.

Gronn, P. (1999). Substituting for leadership: The neglected role of the leadership couple. *Leadership Quarterly, 10*(1).

Heifetz, R. (1994). *Leadership without easy answers.* Cambridge, MA: Harvard University Press.

Heron, J., & Reason, P. (2001). The practice of co-operative inquiry: Research 'with' rather than 'on' people. In: P. Reason & H. Bradbury (Eds), *Handbook of Action Research* (pp. 189–200). London: Sage.

Hesselbein, F., Goldsmith, M., & Somerville, I. (1999). *Leading beyond the walls.* San Francisco, CA: Jossey-Bass.

Hinsdale, M. A., Lewis, H. M., & Waller, M. (1995). *It comes from the people: Community development and local theology.* Philadelphia: Temple University Press.

Hunt, S. (1984). The role of leadership in the construction of reality. In: B. Kellerman (Ed.), *Leadership: Multidisciplinary Perspectives.* Englewood Cliffs, NJ: Prentice-Hall.

Huxham, C., & Vangen, S. (2000). Leadership in the shaping and implementation of collaboration agendas: How things happen in a (not quite) joined-up world. *Academy of Management Journal, 43*(6), 1159–1175.

Kaczmarski, K., & Cooperrider, D. (1997). Construction leadership in the global relational age. *Organization & Environment, 10*(3), 235–258.

Kelchtermans, G. (1999). Narrative-biographical research on teachers' professional development: Exemplifying a methodological research procedure. Presented at Annual Meeting of the American Educational Research Association, New York, NY.

Kelly, J. (1999). Contexts and community leadership: Inquiry as an ecological expedition. *American Psychologist, 54*(11), 953–961.

Lipman-Blumen, J. (1996). *The connective edge.* San Francisco, CA: Jossey-Bass.

Ludema, J., Cooperrider, D., & Barrett, F. (2001). Appreciative inquiry: The power of the unconditional positive question. In: P. Reason & H. Bradbury (Eds), *Handbook of Action Research* (pp. 189–200). London: Sage.

Ludema, J. (1996). *Narrative inquiry.* Unpublished Doctoral Dissertation. Cleveland, OH: Case Western Reserve University.

Luke, J. (1998). *Catalytic leadership: Strategies for an interconnected world.* San Francisco, CA: Jossey-Bass.

McGuire, P. (1987). *Doing participatory research: A feminist approach.* Amherst, MA: The Center for International Education.

Meindl, J. (1995). The romance of leadership as a follower-centric theory: A social constructionist approach. *Leadership Quarterly, 6*(3), 329–341.

Meindl, J. R., Ehrlich, S. B., & Dukerich, J. M. (1985). The romance of leadership. *Administrative Science Quarterly, 30*, 78–102.

Melucci, A. (1996). *Challenging codes: Collective action in the information age.* Cambridge: Cambridge University Press.

Morris, A., & Staggenborg, S. (2004). Leadership in social movements. In: D. A. Snow, S. A. Soule & H. Driesi (Eds), *The Blackwell Companion to Social Movements.* Malden, MA: Blackwell.

Ospina, S. (2002). Reconsidering leadership research: Insights from emerging perspectives. Paper Presented at AOM Research Conference, Denver, CO, August.

Ospina, S., & Schall, E. (2001). Leadership (re)constructed: How lens matters. Paper presented at APPAM Research Conference, Washington, DC, November.

Ospina, S., Schall, E., Dodge, J., & Godsoe, B. (2002). From consent to mutual inquiry: Balancing democracy and authority in action research. Paper presented at the Academy of Management's Conference on Action Research, Constructivism and Democracy, Stockholm, Sweden.

Pastor, J.-C. (1998). *The social construction of leadership: A semantic and social network analysis of social representations of leadership.* Ann Arbor, MI: UMI.

Pfeffer, J. (1997). The ambiguity of leadership. *Academy of Management Review*, 2, 104–112.

Reason, P., & Bradbury, H. (2001). Introduction: Inquiry and participation in search of a world worthy of human aspiration. In: P. Reason & H. Bradbury (Eds), *Handbook of Action Research*. London: Sage.

Riessman, C. K. (1993). *Narrative analysis*. Thousand Oaks, CA: Sage.

Robnett, B. (1996). African-American women in the civil rights movement, 1954–1965: Gender, leadership, and micro mobilization. *American Journal of Sociology*, *101*(6), 1661–1693.

Sacks, K. (1988). Gender and grassroots leadership. In: A. Bookman & S. Morgen (Eds), *Women and the Politics of Empowerment*. Philadelphia, PA: Temple University Press.

Schein, E. (1990). *Organizational culture and leadership*. San Francisco, CA: Jossey-Bass.

Schon, D. A., & Rein, M. (1994). *Frame reflection: Toward the resolution of intractable policy controversies*. New York: Basic Books.

Smircich, L. (1983). Leadership as shared meaning. In: L. Pundy, G. Morgan & T. Dandridge (Eds), *Organizational Symbolism*. Greenwich, CT: JAI Press.

Smircich, L., & Morgan, G. (1982). Leadership: The management of meaning. *Journal of Applied Behavioral Science*, *18*, 257–273.

Snow, D. A., & Benford, R. D. (1992). Master frames and cycles of protest. In: A. Morris & C. Mueller (Eds), *Frontiers in Social Movement Theory*. New Haven: Yale University Press.

Stringer, E. (1999). *Action research* (2nd ed.). Thousand Oaks, CA: Sage.

Terry, R. W. (1993). *Authentic leadership: Courage in action*. San Francisco, CA: Jossey-Bass.

Tierney, W. (1987). The semiotic aspects of leadership: An ethnographic perspective. *American Journal of Semiotics*, *5*, 223–250.

Tierney, W., & Lincoln, Y. (Eds) (1997). *Representation and the text: Reframing the narrative voice*. Albany, NY: State University of New York Press.

Wadsworth, Y. (1997). *Do it yourself social research* (2nd ed.). St. Leonards, Australia: Allen & Unwin.

Whyte, W. F. (1991). *Participatory action research*. Newbury Park: Sage.

Yukl, G. (1999). *An Evaluative Essay on Current Conceptions of Effective Leadership in the European Journal of Work and Organization Psychology*, *8*(1) 33–48.

TOWARD A PEDAGOGY OF APPRECIATION

Leodones Yballe and Dennis O'Connor

*The time is ripe for a pedagogy of appreciation. This chapter is a cross pol-
lination of the positive philosophies and visions of educators such as Dewey,
Freire, Kolb, and Handy with the vibrant and emerging organizational change
ideas and processes of Appreciative Inquiry. This pedagogical stance is values
driven and embraces the relevance of personal experience. There is a distinct
bias towards success and positive change through supportive relationships
and dialogue in the creation of knowledge. This chapter details step-by-step
classroom applications that follow the 4-D model (Discover, Dream, Design,
Destiny) and extend the experiential learning cycle. For the student, these
applications have led to more energized and sustained interactions, an
increase in positive attitudes towards other students and the professor, more
relevant and personally meaningful concepts, and a fuller and more hopeful
view of the future. For the professor, a deeper engagement with the students
and their stories leads to a stronger connection with the values, concepts and
models of the course. The chapter concludes by identifying some challenges in
applying and extending an appreciative approach to educational systems as
a whole.*

One of the tasks of the progressive educator . . . is to unveil opportunities for hope, no matter
what the obstacles may be.   – Paulo Freire

Constructive Discourse and Human Organization
Advances in Appreciative Inquiry, Volume 1, 171–192
Copyright © 2004 by Elsevier Ltd.
All rights of reproduction in any form reserved
ISSN: 1475-9152/doi:10.1016/S1475-9152(04)01008-7

INTRODUCTION

Educational institutions at all levels are hearing the urgent call to quality. Business organizations have had to fashion effective responses to deep and widespread changes brought on by technology and globalization. Many of the boundaries to travel, information, finance, and ideas have disappeared around the globe and a web of new connections proliferates (Friedman, 2000). Today's educational institutions are likewise under enormous pressure to streamline operations, improve quality, and respond to new global realities. Invariably, the classroom becomes the context for heeding the call to quality. How can excellence in the classroom be attained?

Einstein suggested employing a radically different way of thinking in order to create a new reality. In the organizational world, Appreciative Inquiry offers exactly that. We have been impressed by its transformative power and creative implementation in a wide range of industries and organizational types. As educators, we began to wonder if there was room for Appreciative Inquiry in education as well. This paper will describe just such pedagogy of appreciation. We will draw upon positive visions from educators around the world, delineate a set of guiding values for an Appreciative Pedagogy attuned to these philosophies, detail step by step classroom applications, consider some exciting consequences, and identify some challenges in applying and extending this approach to teaching. We hope to show that Einstein's advice can be enacted in the classroom as well.

A POSITIVE VISION OF EDUCATION
AND PEDAGOGY

John Dewey, a contemporary of Einstein, called for a radically different way of conceiving the nature and task of education. Dewey (1966) was deeply concerned with understanding the purpose of education in a democratic community. He reasoned that education is intricately connected to the flow of life itself. Living things, whether a single cell, a species, or a human culture, maintain themselves by renewal through interaction with an environment. Yet, no living being is equal to the task of endless renewal. All succumb. Every individual is born helpless and immature, and each individual who carries the life experience of the group, in time, passes away. Yet, the life of the group goes on. On a physical level, DNA is passed along; on a social level, beliefs, hopes, ideals, and practices are recreated and passed along. Education in the broadest sense is the means of this social continuity of life (Dewey, 1966).

Historically, we "learned at the elbow." Through joint activity, we developed common understandings and dispositions; and culture was "transmitted through the communication of habits of doing, thinking, and feeling from older to younger" (Dewey, 1966). By doing one's share in a common venture, "the individual appropriates the purposes which actuate it, becomes familiar with its methods and subject matter, acquires needed skills, and is saturated with its emotional spirit" (Dewey, 1966).

As societies grew in size and complexity, learning by direct sharing became problematic. All must acquire a wide store of knowledge from many sources. Eventually, fragmented knowledge was believed to exist in the published word, detached from direct experiences, and isolated from its social context. With limited time and much to cover, educators learned to narrowly define their work to favor a detached, efficient, symbolic mode of teaching. The short-term benefits of this approach seemed obvious and it became easy to mistake this form of pedagogy as the only form of real education. Yet, if we look closely at the nature of learning, this is extremely unfortunate. Dewey argues that any social engagement is educative to those that share in it, but activities cast in a mold and taught in a routine way lose this depth of educative power. As educators, we face the difficult problem of keeping a balance between the experience-based informal and the symbolic formal modes of education.

At their core, educational methods need to align with our nature and the nature of intelligence. Dewey argues for a pragmatic theory of knowing. Knowledge is an act that brings one's intellectual resources to consciousness with a view to straighten out a perplexity or to engage in an activity that purposely modifies the environment. Thus intelligence resides in shaping an aim and moving toward a future result by means of a set of actions and interactions with others. A real aim or curiosity activates the mind, and energizes initiative and exploration. This "inquiry mode" drives everything. Following through on one's aim in joint activity with others implies social direction and builds social intelligence, which we would now identify as emotional intelligence (Goleman, 1995). When aims and controls are imposed by those outside the learning process, we "lose the chance of enlisting a person's own participatory disposition" to develop intrinsic direction (Dewey, 1966). Such direction is as central to the learning venture as it is to successful organizational change strategies, including Appreciative Inquiry.

When we re-design educational inquiry into a cooperative process with intrinsic direction and dialogue with others, we not only learn better, but also pick up critical cultural "dispositions" towards work, learning, and relationships. Handy (1998) identifies such intangibles as the qualities that are essential for doing well in life, e.g. curiosity, relatedness, self control, the capacity for deferred gratification, and confidence. These must be practiced and inculcated at various levels of education.

As a protected place to practice for life, the school must, therefore, pay attention to "how" instead of just "what" people learn.

The "how" makes all the difference. Method and subject matter are intricately interwoven. It *is* possible to design learning activities that deepen knowledge of a subject, build broad dispositions, and result in emotional, interpersonal, and team skills. Knowledge is distributed across various structures of the brain. Rich complex activity activates more areas of the brain and results in more resilient, longer lasting learning, a knowledge that is integrated and connected. Verbal, symbolic knowledge, the main conduit for traditional education, is important, but is only one piece of the puzzle.

While Dewey's logic seems compelling, the pedagogical battle was already lost. In 1916, Dewey (1966) wrote, "That education is not an affair of telling and being told, but an active and constructive process, is a principle almost as generally violated in practice as conceded in theory." From the perspective of a much faster and more complex world today, it seems particularly ironic that educators were unable to slow down and do it right so long ago.

Eighty Seven years later, there still seems to be an Education Problematique. The constellation of deeply ingrained beliefs, practices, and the institutional structures that Dewey hoped to transform has gained even more momentum. "Education is suffering from narration sickness" observes Paulo Freire (1970). He decries education as dehumanizing, a mechanism for maintaining and embodying oppression. Ackoff (1974) warned of the emergence of schools as prisons. Charles Handy (1998) called his own education "positively disabling," where content seemed irrelevant, and the process "cultivated a set of attitudes and behaviors which were directly opposed to what seemed to be needed in real life" (p. 200).

One merely has to walk quietly down the hallways and corridors of academia and witness, with very rare exceptions, teachers making deposits of information to students who passively record them. In this banking model, "the contents, whether values or empirical dimensions of reality, tend in the process of being narrated to become lifeless and petrified," (Freire, 1970, p. 57). Education as preparation for a distant future diverts attention from the *only* point of leverage: the needs and possibilities of the immediate present (Dewey, 1966). Furthermore, the imposition of external controls generates dysfunctional responses as students learn to value their experience mainly for the grades and diplomas they acquire. The degree of dependence on reward, punishment, grades, and fear in the system might be best seen as a measure of the disconnection of students from more intrinsic motive forces of learning. The irrelevance of the classroom experience to today's students is captured very clearly in one student's e-mail to a colleague early this spring. He wrote the professor: "It is so beautiful outside I have decided to miss class today and enjoy the sun. I hope you are not disappointed about my decision." For this student, there was no sun in class.

At quick glance, the educational state of affairs seems hopeless. A May, 2002 Department of Education report indicates "truly abysmal scores" in U.S. history by soon-to-vote, high school seniors. Only 11% scored at grade level or above. 57% fell below the most minimal standard imaginable. Efforts to solve such problems can too often be characterized as either one of finger pointing, trivial incremental tweaking, or piling on even more of the same methods that Dewey and Freire would implicate as the cause. Many educational stakeholders feel helpless and hopeless.

Freire (1994), however, insists that there is hope, that hopelessness is not the final ontological reality. Humans cannot "be" without the impulse to hope. Hopelessness, in fact, is hope in masquerade. Generating a positive vision of education and pedagogy must therefore begin with the question of hope. "Hope as an ontological need demands an anchoring in practice" (p. 9).

APPRECIATIVE PEDAGOGY: TOWARD POSITIVE CHANGE IN EDUCATION

What are some of the characteristics of education where there is hope? Based on Appreciative Inquiry, we propose that Appreciative Pedagogy can be effective in bringing about an avalanche of positive change in education, rendering obsolete the Education Problematique. Appreciative Pedagogy seamlessly combines a mindset that is oriented towards appreciating and valuing the best in human experience, and a commitment to generative action that seeks to realize the fullness of human potential. Like Appreciative Inquiry, Appreciative Pedagogy involves a way of viewing the world that is at once realistic, positively transforming, and hopeful. It is realistic because the focus of inquiry and source of vision is the abundant experience of the learners. It is positively transforming because it radically changes experience from irrelevance and boredom to one of high energy, connectedness, and importance. It is hopeful because what is apprehended engenders positive images of the future that can guide action and transform current realities of the participants.

CORE VALUES: AN ORIENTATION TOWARD DISCOVERING SUCCESS

Value 1. Appreciative Pedagogy is Experience-Centered

If thought is to be aroused and not just words acquired, personal engagement is critical. We suggest that highly meaningful engagement results when the process of learning proceeds from the rich experiences of learners, about life, themselves, and the world. We have a clear bias for "inside out" learning. The learner's experience is an abundant and highly engaging source of knowledge that matters (Dewey, 1966). Kolb (1984) articulates a learning cycle where concrete experience occupies a central beginning role. Freire (1994) refers to a process of "unveiling" one's reality.

Appreciative Pedagogy begins with personal experience and expends vast energy to explore and unveil these experiences. In doing so, it places learners in their proper place – an elevated place of substantial relevance. The unspoken message is loud and clear: your experience is important. Students know that this education is about them and starts with them. Learners become relevant as potential sources and co-creators of knowledge.

Value 2. Appreciative Pedagogy Proposes a Bias in Favor of Success

A positive vision of education must focus on experiences of success. While a significant part of the human experience is littered with failures, mistakes, and dis-appointments, a more vital portion sparkles with success, peak and proud moments of growth, and with gloriously satisfying relationships.

Appreciative Pedagogy focuses attention on those moments of success when one experienced excellence, and when relationships were great. The kinds of questions we ask are critical in defining the quality and direction of conversations. We construct our worlds in the direction of what we persistently ask questions about (Cooperrider, 2002). We can consistently ask questions that guide conversations toward identifying life giving forces, sources of great energy, and experiences of personal success and growth. Fredrickson (2000) provides evidence that "positive emotions, when tapped effectively, can optimize health, subjective well being, and psychological resilience."

CORE VALUES: AN ORIENTATION TOWARD GENERATING POSITIVE CHANGE

Appreciative Pedagogy, aside from its spirit of discovery, rests on a fundamental belief in the capacity of positive vision to engender radically transforming action. This belief is captured in the following value statements.

Value 3. Appreciative Pedagogy has a Transformative Bias, as Opposed to Description and Knowledge Banking

The appreciative mindset cannot be understood nor defined apart from trans-formation and radical change. A full education "stimulates true reflection and action upon reality thereby responding to the vocation of men as beings who are authentic only when engaged in inquiry and creative transformation" (Freire, 1970, p. 71).

Appreciative Pedagogy seeks to build a sense of heightened possibility and abundance of potential where the unveiling of possibilities and the creation of actualizing processes and structures become central features of the learning adventure, rather than the filling of empty receptacles.

Value 4. Appreciative Pedagogy is Strongly Oriented Toward the Challenging Vision of a Life Worth Living

The task of enhancing value is one that Appreciative Pedagogy addresses very seriously. Not only is a positive vision of human existence essential to the learning adventure, education must be oriented towards the realization of the dream of a life that is worth living (Shepard, 1995). Because this dream is based on real experiences there is no question on the dream's feasibility.

Handy challenges education to be a safe place to practice for life. Our educational institutions must become a place where there is continuous articulation and striving towards becoming better, e.g. more responsible, more ethical, more appreciative of beauty, more active in community, and more fully human. Maslow referred to this as self actualization (Maslow, 1976). The educational endeavor cannot simply be about herding people through fences that go nowhere. It should be about guiding a living, not making a living.

Value 5. Appreciative Pedagogy is Biased in Favor of Supportive Partnerships Rather than Hierarchic Relationships in the Learning Experience

Life worth living is characterized by healthy and happy relationships that are contexts for respecting human dignity, for enacting productive interdependence and collaborations, for safely facing developmental challenges, and for actively supporting the growth of others (Shepard, 1995). Freire (1970) envisions an ideal relationship between teachers and students. While an oppressive educational system relegates students to being empty receptacles of knowledge, a humanizing and liberating system is one that connects both teachers and students as ". . . subjects, not only in the task of unveiling reality, and thereby coming to know it critically, but in the task of re-creating that knowledge" (p. 56). A spirit of partnership that characterizes the educational task generates "committed involvement" instead of "pseudo-participation" (p. 56).

To sharpen abilities that create and nurture healthy relationships, the pedagogical milieu must be one that models and encourages active experimentation with partnering, collaboration, and interdependence. Rigid hierarchical relationships and autocratic structures must be suspect and possibly deemed counterproductive, because these tend to project negative self-fulfilling prophecies of human nature. McGregor's (1995) Theory X is quite instructive in this sense.

Value 6. Appreciative Pedagogy Favors Dialogic Processes,
Where Students and Teachers are Constantly Engaged in the
Re-Creation of Knowledge – Knowledge that Matters

Knowledge that matters and is relevant to practice is the exciting result of discovery and creation (Dewey, 1966). It is not that we deny the existence of an "objective" knowledge. We realize more that relevance of such knowledge is best discovered and uncovered through the learner's active involvement including dialogue with others. It is also clear that when students have been engaged actively and fully, there is an abundance of insights that are deeply embedded in awareness and there is less susceptibility to memory loss.

This set of fundamental values lead to powerful possibilities for the: (1) discovery of the best, thereby allowing us to truly appreciate the grandeur and mystery of human existence in general, and one's experience in particular; and for (2) enacting and realizing the best in human nature, thereby engaging us in a radically transforming adventure that has for its ultimate mission the realization of human potential. We realize these values represent lofty aspirations. They are a vision to move towards, not a statement of fully accomplished reality. But, assuredly, this vision is achievable, because it springs from experiences of success.

APPRECIATIVE PEDAGOGY, EXPERIENTIAL LEARNING, AND THE 4-D MODEL

Over the years, we have witnessed the emergence of various approaches for improving the relevance and effectiveness of management education. A guiding philosophy and method that has gained almost universal acceptance among management faculty is experiential learning. Experience-centered pedagogical approaches espouse a common value. They regard students' experience as relevant and valuable. They acknowledge the usefulness of students' past and present experience as a well-spring of insight into organizational life, an interesting focus for reflection, and a credible source of guidance for action and experimentation (Kolb, 1984).

Appreciative Pedagogy complements and extends the power of experiential learning in education in two important ways. First, the appreciative mindset tunes our attention to moments of success. The potential range of experiences to allow into or create in the classroom can be overwhelming in quantity, variety, and richness. The professor with limited time must choose the experiences to make figural for the day. The appreciative tuning focus makes our choices more deliberate when drawing upon our collective reservoirs of memory or in debriefing a classroom experience such as a role-play or simulation. The concrete experience is still the foundation for learning, but the wheat has been separated from the chaff.

Secondly, the appreciative focus qualitatively extends the processing of the raw experience in the reflective and conceptual stages of Kolb's experiential learning cycle. In both approaches, we reflect on the experience and distill its key essences. We uncover concepts that seem to give us a better handle on the core elements of the experience and so provide potential leverage for future action. Detached rational understanding is not sufficient though. The appreciative process incites us to continue converging before moving to action. A positive image or a provocative proposition for the future is necessary as the end product of the reflective and conceptual steps. These images and propositions take us beyond mere explanation and exert a "pull" energy for change by literally bringing an exciting future into the present. In Lewin's terms, this further unfreezes the current equilibrium of forces by building a positive "felt" need for change, which is hope. Consequently, appreciative understanding inspires hope, builds momentum, and heightens commitment to action.

Appreciative Pedagogy facilitates the exploration and creation of positive realities in the classroom on a daily basis and we have found the 4-D model (discover, dream, design, and destiny) a useful frame to organize our thoughts and activities. In the following sections, we would like to offer some concrete examples of appreciative exercises that we have designed and to share our thoughts about some of the learning processes that occur in and between individuals during these activities. *The 4-D model in pedagogy is about connecting: to our own experience, to others and their stories, to theory, and to the future and wider environment through vision and action.* As the semester unfolds, Appreciative Pedagogy guides the professor to make conscious and positively oriented decisions as to what material to use, what aspects of student experiences to tap and highlight, and how to finish the converging stage in the experiential learning cycle with an inspired clarity of future possibilities.

Discover

We are guided by the belief that students come with a rich array of positive experiences in many, if not all, the topics we deal with in management. Appreciative Pedagogy trusts in, celebrates, and deliberately seeks out students' experiences of success and moments of high energy and great pride.

A concrete example might help to illustrate the discovery step and its secondary benefits. When students learn that they will work in teams all semester long, there is a detectable range of emotions from fear and anxiety to hopeful anticipation. Kim had a typical explanation to her reaction when she filled out the "Where You Stand With Teams" worksheet: "I normally do not like working in groups because of uneven distribution of work. I usually end up doing much of it while others have fun." We have experimented with the process of building learning teams by asking students to focus on groups that they remember with happiness, pride, and a sense of accomplishment. Since everyone has had experience in groups (try to imagine an individual who has never been in a group!), this is an excellent opportunity to spend some time in discovery of best team moments.

When Kim and her teammates participated in this process, they focused on re-connecting with experiences in their "best teams" – experiences of success, fun, closeness, and other positive characteristics of their own best teams. After her team reported out and turned in a very lengthy list of "Best Team Characteristics," a composite from all their experiences, Kim remarked: "I had a lot of fun listening to all these positive stories. I had forgotten I was part of a great team before ... I think we will do well."

A variety of methods are possible to surface positive experiences, but all start with students taking a few moments to quietly reflect and identify one or more experiences to explore further. Students could be asked to individually write a few notes to share later, or they could be paired up to conduct interviews with each other. As students begin to articulate their success stories, positive emotions are re-experienced and animate the expression of the story. This tends to pique the listeners' interest and curiosity. Animated conversations ensue, the energy in the room swells. Jason, a shy sophomore, noted on his reflection sheet,

> I felt so comfortable talking in my team today. I never felt this before and I hardly knew them! After the first question or two I was not afraid of their questions anymore 'cuz each one was more out of curiosity . . . chance for me to show them things that I did well. Ok, I had to be careful not to sound like I was making it up.

The professor provides guidance for this discovery task in several ways: (1) context, by giving an overview of Appreciative Inquiry, its values, and the 4-D model; (2) focus, by shaping a question that targets the inquiry; (3) energy, by inspiring and encouraging the search for the best; and (4) a quiet reflective mood for thoughtfulness and adequate time for dialogue. We encourage students to be curious and to ask probing questions of each other in order to clarify and obtain very specific descriptions of the events and the forces that made them occur. In Jason's team, this curiosity and questioning is exactly what happened.

Several benefits accrue from this initial storytelling. Putting one's experience into words for others pushes the individual to clarify aspects of an experience that have remained fuzzy and unexamined. Sometimes, as in Kim's story above, success is often forgotten and buried in a pile of negative experiences, and invariably this appreciative process leads to new insights and energy. Second, a well-told story provides listeners with new perspectives on topics that are naturally complex given the diversity of human experience. Third, by "loading our best experiences into memory," we create a set of "hooks" to connect with the stories of others and with the more abstract models and readings of the course. Finally, as with all Appreciative Inquiry, by focusing on the best of what was, we create an unspoken anticipation of what might be. Using our team example, students who are hesitant about groups reawaken memories that demonstrate that there is also fun and hope in joining with others. Kim was able to overcome her earlier fears. Here's how her story ended:

> My experience with my team was a very positive one for me . . . Everyone in my group was very responsible for their work, and wanted the group to succeed as a whole . . . I would describe my team as hardworking and flexible . . . Each member of the team had their own part organized, and the parts of others. For example, Ashley was responsible for editing . . . and then putting everyone's part in logical order.

When we connect first to our experience of success, a subtle and important shift of perspective takes place. The usual pedagogical goal of memorizing and banking some set of other people's abstract theories is no longer prominent. Rather, reading theories becomes a way to deepen one's understanding of the personal experiences brought to light during the discovery step. Good readings are then a helpful sharing by others who were also seeking to understand. This order of learning activity reinforces the value of inside-out learning over the more traditional outside in approach.

This does not minimize the value of other's thinking as conveyed through the written word. Great writings are resources to help us on our journey of learning and action, not burdens to be held accountable for. In fact, in finding and choosing worthy pieces to read, we might ask if a particular piece is rooted in the best of our nature and does it help inspire us to a new sense of possibility.

The discovery step occurs in two phases. The first phase of discovery is about extending out and exploring the range of a topic. In a class of 30, we might have

30–60 stories of great team moments. While experience (and stories or cases) unconsciously accumulate as expertise to draw upon, we also benefit greatly from an inductive process of distilling the essence of experience. This second phase is a converging process. The themes that we distill are easier to hold onto and provide usable elements for later vision and action. They are particularly useful because the student has experiential referents for what these themes or concepts mean and for what authors might mean when they use the same or similar ideas such as cohesion, shared leadership, consensus, integrity, etc.

During this converging phase, pairs or small groups work on themes followed by reports in a plenary session that allow the professor to help summarize, clarify, or connect various ideas. Here is one team's list of best team qualities derived from their 5 stories: passion for topic, goal oriented, time used wisely, respect for one another, strong work ethic, enthusiasm, quality focus, easy to talk with each other, and one person's weakness is another's strength. Students feel confirmed when they find that other groups have identified many of the same key elements to group success. They are also pleasantly surprised to hear additional ideas that they hadn't considered as they hear reports from other groups. "My classmates know something!"

In fact, students will often generate 90% or more of what expert readings will cover, although it is unorganized. In this team example, the professor might help bring order with the distinction of task or people-related behaviors as a simple way to begin organizing and discussing the rich data that come from students. In the plenary session, both the professor and students have the opportunity to connect to other ideas from the course, other appreciative inquiries, and to readings that could precede or follow the in-class discovery.

There are secondary benefits to taking the time necessary for the appreciative process. On many occasions, we observe student dependency, anxiety, and confusion. This is especially true when a major team project is first mentioned. However, the time spent exploring prior experiences of great projects provides hope and guidance. Drew noted in his reflection sheet, "Now I know my teammates and their motivations. Like me, they want to do really well." Alicia describes this experience in her Team Assessment paper.

> We talked about great projects we did before. This was so helpful. From our stories we identified important things, like each one pulling their weight, having fun, helping each other, listening, being open minded, considering everyone's interests.... At first, we had so many different interests...they were all sorts. (The professor) helped us realize we can be creative...we decided our project will be on effective communication, using dolphins as our focus.... I don't know why but I just felt like I wanted so much to study dolphins.

The topic of teamwork is only one of many. We have looked into moments of peak performance, extraordinary motivation, exemplary leadership, core values becoming clear, deep commitment, emotional intelligence, and more. Many, if not all, of these topics are intricately intertwined. As students inquire into any one of these, they begin to find significant connections to others. A story of personal peak performance can be a good case with multiple paths to follow in discussion. A peak performance could hint at the type of motivation in play and the nature of leadership imbuing the situation. The number of focuses that are possible in the discovery phase is almost equal to the possible number of topics in a management course.

We have also used variations of this process to explore and build competencies of various kinds. We can unpack the idea of leadership in teams by looking more closely at the skills behind the best team qualities. For example, we might ask students to think of a time when they really listened and understood what another was saying as a starting point for a session on active listening. We could explore moments of initiative or persistence, or we might guide students to explore moments when they have convincingly influenced others as one lead-in to the related topic of power. Asking students to examine their experience to help prepare criteria for presentations and written reports leads to a better understanding of what is required and serves as a review. With little extra effort, the appreciative focus can also be applied to many of the active learning materials that most teachers currently use. "What did we see being done well in the ____ (role play, case, simulation, etc.)? What made this possible? What positive images could we generate?"

Discovery can also extend beyond the boundaries of the class. A managerial interview is a very useful activity for most undergraduates. Many have never talked to a person in their major field of study. This simple exposure is beneficial. By adding several questions, however, we can turn this experience into an appreciative inquiry. For example, the student may ask the manager to remember a time of peak performance on the job and further inquire about the various factors that contributed to the performance (system, self, etc.). Motivation, quality, and creativity can all be explored as students and managers become co-inquirers and builders of knowledge.

Whatever the topic or activity, the guideline is to focus discussions on identifying peak experiences and life-giving forces. Students discover that they are comfortable asking affirmative questions about experiences of success, because these elicit positive reactions and responses. We argue that energy tends to be heightened and more productively invested when directed towards discovery of what works rather than what does not work. What works contains the seed that might transform. Appreciative Pedagogy puts into constructive practice what Bennis (1995) calls "management of attention." The conversation should not dwell on stories of failure. Meticulously, the professor would not even allow tales of "failure avoided." Statements like "does not look over your shoulders all the time" or "doesn't have favorites" can be reoriented by asking, "What does your manager do that makes her so great?" Probing questions like these can help to refocus the conversation on "the best of what is" rather than "what is not" there.

Dream

> The more subjected and less able to dream of freedom, the less able will concrete beings be to face their challenges (Freire, 1994).

Building on the profound connection between positive image and positive action (Cooperrider, 2000), the dream step connects the student to the future by drawing from the themes of best moments to help shape an exciting vision of self in action and in relationship to others. Education is ultimately about preparing its participants to join with others in achieving agreed upon outcomes (Dewey, 1966; Handy, 1998). While the discovery phase is beneficial in and of itself in relation to learning, it is dreaming that increases the likelihood of future action and thus contributes to the education of those involved. Topics become relevant and take on personal meaning when we connect them to our dreams. Roger put this especially well,

> This class was about me, my life. We look at many ideas and topics, and all of them became about me and my life, my work, even my relationships. He made me work hard, but he made it feel like play, but also seriously about life.

The themes and images of the discovery phase provide the source material for the dreaming step. While we may draw upon the writings and thoughts of experts and others outside the class, this step is not about getting or guessing the "right answer" that some expert already has. Personal experiences of success ground the ideal in what is subjectively real, fulfilling, and energizing, rather than on the objectively distant, often filtered narratives of "best practices" in some famous, but often quite unfamiliar corporate realities. Our own experience helps shape the details of the vision that is right for us and provides the light in the image that pulls us forward and "convinces" us of its rightness. Like a plant that grows in the direction of the light source, the person strives to grow towards the positive image, steadily transforming from "what is" into "what can be."

A sharp image has more motivational pull, so it is necessary to spend adequate time working with the discovery material to create guiding images and propositions. In the team example, after hearing all the various stories and ideas associated with highly successful teams, each group is asked to distill a list of key qualities that will underlie its vision for itself. The groups are then asked to generate a small set of provocative propositions about great teams and to fashion a guiding motto for themselves. They are asked to sign off on their vision and propositions to establish a psychological contract for the project. The energy rises dramatically again as we ask each team to introduce themselves to the class and share their ideals and motto. They know that they will be back on stage for a presentation later in the semester and they begin to see a real possibility in themselves and others for good performance and a rewarding experience. We want student teams to focus on the question of *"what would be great to do,"* and move away from the questions of "what is required" and "what the professor wants." This is how Sarah experienced this phase, as told in her own words.

> We used everything from our list of Best Team Characteristics. For example, we all agreed our team will be fun, productive, where we all learn a lot about ourselves and relevant topics. We actually made it happen. I have never been part of a team where the members talked and went out together outside of class . . . I would describe my team as caring, fun, productive, focused, open-minded . . . I learned a lot about both myself and topics discussed in class . . . rewarding, and insightful. I could say a lot more but I don't have enough space in the form.

Sarah's experience with her team is typical for many in her class. From observations of her team, it was clear that they started, like most, with fears and anxiety. Yet, when they were encouraged to rediscover their peak experiences of success and pride, they were able to dream of a great team that they could build together.

With a little imagination, it is possible to find opportunities for "dreaming" in many class topics and activities. In debriefing a corporate ethics role-play, we ask questions that raise moral leadership to greater prominence, vs. a focus of what not to do. Where did examples of moral leadership occur? What made these possible? Have there been times in life when we exercised a moral leadership at work or in other settings? What are the key factors necessary for personal and corporate moral leadership?

In a global simulation, following a round of regional goal setting and competitive bargaining, we ask the large group to collectively dream a picture of an ideal world. Not surprisingly, most people would like to see a world where all have adequate food to eat, with clean air and water, with basic education, and with sustainable and beneficial uses of technology. Asking the participants to work towards this dream dramatically transforms the next round of interaction between regions. Creativity, generosity, and trust flourish where 15 minutes before, manipulation and deception dominated. The contrasting spirit and behavior of the two rounds demonstrates the power of an overarching positive vision in the dynamics of human behavior and relationships.

Design and Destiny

The Dream step is a fertile soil for developing a "true" aim, ala Dewey. An aim which emerges from existing conditions is a stimulus to intelligence. The mind comes vibrantly alive in the planning and consequent actions that bring forth a complexity of unexpected conditions and connections with others. We like to isolate a vision or proposition from the dream step and identify the skills and know-how critical to success. In the team example, we often hear that a key factor in success was that "everyone agreed." What is agreement exactly? How did this happen? What was said? What skills do we need to insure agreement? As a team member, how can you make sure that a high level of agreement exists?

Continuing with the team example, we ask students to identify personal leadership behaviors to help their own team move towards the ideal. Throughout, we involve students in an ongoing reflection and action cycle based on their propositions and hopes for their team by asking individuals and groups to reflect (both worksheet and discussion) on questions such as: How are we doing so far in realizing our propositions and plans? What is going well? What have I done? What leadership or action is needed? What would be great to do? What is the first step to take from here, specifically? What will I do? Any resultant actions will be later reflected and hopefully lead to another cycle of action and reflection to further guide project activity. Class debriefing sessions during the semester and/or a final paper can identify current successes and pitfalls, and include further visioning and planning towards project completion. One group that was having difficulty in choosing a topic for their group project was encouraged to revisit their initial vision of a great group. In doing so, they realized that they were not "really listening" to each other. When they slowed down to listen, they not only found a topic that was exciting to everyone, they became a real team in the process.

The classroom reality differs in several important ways from a large organization. The ongoing organization is tied to an environment in short and long term ways. Common vision and collective action are critical to organizational survival and long term success, whereas the classroom is temporary and relatively closed to its environment. For visions that fall outside the course boundaries or do not involve collective action with others present, the responsibility for follow through rests on the individual.

The professor, however, may need to look creatively for ways that help support students pursuing their visions. When we debrief class experiences with a focus on what was done well, we can also add the design step by generalizing to work and life situations beyond the class. Assignments that encourage students to experiment and reflect are particularly helpful.

For example, MBA students are typically hesitant to initiate career discussions with higher ups, but at the same time they deeply desire to know where they stand and where they are going. Appreciative interviews with organizational leaders can focus on the exciting developments in their various industries and companies and the positive role that those pursuing and obtaining an education can play. Sharing this information in small groups and/or the larger class is always an option. Students are curious to hear these stories and there is great energy in processing them. There is genuine shock when they discover that organizations, which are paying the bill for an MBA, do not have plans for them. Some may discover that they will need to move on, while others have engaging conversations that instill hope and energize more initiatives. A surprising number discover that their appreciative inquiry was also a satisfying experience for the manager involved and created positive reverberations like new job assignments or promotions, often within weeks of the interview. The student learns that he or she also needs to creatively look for ways to reframe organizational or course activities to implement their vision.

A final note on the 4-D model. While these steps have been presented as a sequential model, there are not always clear lines between discovering, dreaming, designing, and delivering in practice. Inquiry and dialogue, particularly in groups, have a life of their own and are more of a dance, than a rigidly controlled prescription.

CONSEQUENCES OF APPRECIATIVE PEDAGOGY

We believe Appreciative Pedagogy to be a useful guide in organizing educational activities and a useful tool in tackling the mainstream content and activities of a typical management class. Moreover, additional benefits normally flow from this process of learning and relating to others. We believe that appreciative pedagogy has generated a number of healthy outcomes for our students. Some are immediate, some are cumulative (Yballe & O'Connor, 2001).

1a. *We have observed more energized and sustained interactions.* In contrast to the difficult moments of "pulling out" responses after a lecture, we are often faced with the question of when or whether to proceed to the next step due to the high energy level. One student commented, "This is the first time that I loved working in groups."

Freire notes that we must do everything to ensure an atmosphere in the classroom where teaching, learning, and studying are serious acts, but also ones that generate happiness. Only to the authoritarian mind can the act of education be seen as an adult task. Fredrickson (2001) notes that play builds enduring social resources, social-affective skills, increased levels of creativity, and fuels brain development. Happiness and play need not be restricted to the schoolyard. Dewey (1966) understands play and work as existing along the same continuum; both involve aims that require us to organize across time. The line between them is often fuzzy, particularly in creative endeavors such as brainstorming. Joy and fun can be and should be integral to education.

Several others themes constellate around this theme of energized and sustained interactions.

1b. *Students feel a sense of safety when publicly speaking up; they experience less fear and inhibition.* The positive focus "honors" their experiences. Students have reported: "This made it easy to talk to someone about my best performances," "I could talk for hours about my proudest moments," or "When I talk about failures, I cover up many facts, even from myself." Fredrickson (2001) posits that "the experience of positive emotion broadens people's momentary thought-action repertoires." For example, joy broadens the urge to play, push limits, and be creative. Interest broadens learning by creating the urge to explore, take in new information and experience, and expand the self in the process Fredrickson (2001). "Experiences of positive affect prompt individuals to engage with their environments and partake in activities."

1c. *A positive attitude emerges towards other students as knowledgeable, trustworthy, and real.* Appreciative Pedagogy helps to move the class through the early stages of group development and provides a foundation for a healthy and productive culture to emerge. Many students eagerly report that they have had experiences very similar to others in the class. There is surprise in discovering common ground with a stranger or a new insight into a friend. This deepens the conviction of the life-giving forces they uncovered, but also begins a bonding or identification with others and the class as a whole. In contrast with the traditional lecture culture and in spite of the initial wariness we all have of strangers and new situations, others become "real" and they come into focus as we listen, connect, show support, and work as partners.

1d. *Students gain a greater trust in self and heightened confidence in their experience.* Fredrickson (2001) suggests that

> the capacity to experience positive emotions may be a fundamental human strength central to the study of human flourishing . . .. Ancestors who succumbed to the urges sparked by positive emotions to play, explore, and so on would have by consequence accrued more personal resources.

Participation seems livelier and we attribute it to a greater trust and confidence in one's experience. Inner direction develops and drives further inquiry and this is a core element of a life worth living. Participation is fragile for younger students, because years of school have convinced many that the answers come from the book or the teacher. Pedagogy should "move students" from "beings for others" to "beings for themselves" (Freire, 1994).

1e. Many students have reported that they find it very comfortable to ask for feedback, request guidance, or chat with the professor on important challenges involving their teams or projects demonstrating a *positive attitude towards the professor as resource, guide, and helper*. While almost everyone reported an initial sense of skepticism and lack of understanding about what the professor is up to, they have also indicated that those feelings changed to trust.

2. *Concepts and insights are personally meaningful and relevant because they are firmly rooted in personal experiences.* Experiences are rich food for thought and learning. Appreciative Pedagogy reconnects ideas and thinking to experience, to outcomes, to others. Reports from subgroups are, in essence, "live cases" that can be used to springboard various discussions. Furthermore, topical coverage is rarely an issue. We have discovered that lists generated by undergraduates in very brief activities often contain a large percentage of the material reported by experts. This can help alleviate the distrust that some students have of experts and "book learning" as they find themselves on the same "page."

3a. *A "fuller" and hopeful view of the future (images of what students can be) emerges as an alternative to an "empty" view (what they should not be).* With focus on the positive, many wonder what happens to negative experience. After all, life isn't all roses. We believe that while negative experience may be useful in drawing attention to important issues, we ultimately learn best from what works well. Many part-time MBA's have had negative experiences in their organizations and in reaction to misguided change efforts. They feel frustrated by the constraints to initiative and growth and by the many subtle signs of disrespect they sense. Their anger is rooted in the fact that they have been hopeful and have expected better. Those who have begun to believe that nothing beyond their negative experience is possible in any organization are truly amazed to hear from classmates who love their jobs and bosses, who are challenged and empowered, and believe themselves to be in great organizations. They begin to wonder if maybe they could work in such a place or maybe carve out such a space right now. Some management innovations have actually worked. This kernel of possibility allows them to proceed, sometimes skeptically, with the work of the course. Some skepticism proves useful in deepening the learning process in ways that blind conversion may not.

3b. *Students begin to gain skill and confidence in Appreciative Inquiry as a creative alternative to objective analysis or problem solving.* Problem solving is a powerful activity that we believe works best in the context of Appreciative Inquiry. Going right to the problem often leaves us in the same frame of reference that we started with. Focusing on what was great and building a positive vision will often reframe the context of the problem and ultimately transform the system. Additionally, the appreciative process taps into the resource of personal experience and is sustained by the conviction of that experience, as well as the positive image. Approaching life as a miracle to be experienced rather than a problem to be solve is a dramatic and useful shift in perspective.

4. There have been *positive consequences for us, the professors*, when we have managed our classes with an appreciative stance. Certainly, the above outcomes (e.g. positive attitude, greater energy, participation, and interaction) make our teaching more enjoyable and easier. Practically, we have found it easier to guide students in developing their competencies because of the connection with personal experience.

We have also felt more alive in the process. The appreciative mindset awakens our desire and nurtures our curiosity to create and discover new possibilities that enrich our existence in class and give it new meaning and direction. We have also enjoyed a steady flow of success stories brought by students. This fresh material has stimulated our learning and has led to a deeper, more grounded connection with the values, concepts, and models we teach. Finally, their "aha!" experiences, the discovery of something valuable has renewed our hope and belief that we are on the right track.

Some Challenges

While the appreciative mindset has been a positive force in the classroom, this approach has not been without challenges. To do it right, the appreciative spirit must seep into every aspect of the course and it must penetrate the whole system. This teaching style will ultimately fail if it's tacked on like an experiential exercise at the end of a chapter in a textbook. We found that each experiment in Appreciative Pedagogy led us to new course adjustments or self confrontation on our values. Do we give students opportunities to read about what works well? Do assignments give students opportunities to experiment, practice, and reflect on what works well, and do they encourage the students to stretch to their highest level? Do our performance evaluations give students a sense of how much they have accomplished? Do papers help to clarify and integrate further each step in the 4-D model?

Younger students who have been deeply ingrained in "banking" methods will often find low structure or a personal focus unfamiliar and uncomfortable. Some may respond in self protective ways, e.g. "I've never had a success" or "I'm not really curious about anything." This requires some finesse in helping the individual draw upon their experience. More broadly, it requires some patience and consulting skill in respecting the resistance and working the class through some new ways of behaving and relating. Following Lewin's classic formulation, change (learning) occurs in a system (student) when we reduce resistance (through participation and ownership) and increase hope (through positive vision of the future).

As teachers, we feel "young" when we try something for the first time. The appreciative approach calls for a very different skill set than the traditional lecture style. Mistakes, uncertainty, resistance, and doubt are inevitable. Appreciative Pedagogy is a serious challenge. If you believe that it is possible, however, begin by looking for opportunities for small experiments. We believe that the positive results will kindle a long-term adventure for those willing to try. Still, one may experience pressure from peers and administrators who hear reports of too much noise in class, or lack of traditional structure, or who might misunderstand students' sense of comfort with the class as equivalent to lack of work or seriousness. Also, the steps we have outlined take considerable time and will raise issues of coverage. You will however, find ample opportunities to clarify one's values and purpose in the process of experimenting with an appreciative approach.

Stepping back from the class, we face the challenge of responsibility for our own educational experiences. As students or professors or trainers, personally and collectively, we must reflectively use an appreciative lens to examine our own best moments of learning and teaching as a basis for course adjustments, personal growth, and to better shape the educational settings we find ourselves in. A small example was an inquiry into best teaching moments at a small liberal arts school that led to a series of faculty led workshops on pedagogy.

As the appreciative method spreads through a course or curricula, inevitably one bumps into other limits of an institutional nature. Class size, room configuration, class time and length, coverage standards, and sequence of courses all pose challenges. Yet, ultimately, here also is an opportunity. It might be fun to imagine an entire school guided by appreciative values. We'd like to report such a success, but we are still dreaming.

Can we dare to imagine a boundary-less education where students connect to their experience, to others, across topics and disciplines, and to their organizations, families, and communities? Could an appreciative mission help bring this about and guide it? In fact, there are intriguing examples of this possibility already. In Chicago, young school children connected across generations to business and political leaders as they led appreciative interviews about the future of their city and the world. Students in a low performing urban school district in Cleveland found new learnings as they came to life in an appreciative inquiry involving themselves and school, business, church, and community leaders. Brazilian children learned about each other, poverty, and social economic class by having schools in wealthy and poor districts paired in appreciative interviews. We are limited only by our imagination. Students need not be just containers of knowledge, but can be partners in the re-creation and refinement of their society's knowledge and wisdom.

REFERENCES

Ackoff, R. (1974). *Redesigning the future: A systems approach to societal problems*. New York: Wiley.

Bennis, W. (1995). The four competencies of leadership. In: D. Kolb, J. Osland & I. Rubin (Eds), *The Organizational Behavior Reader* (pp. 395–400). Englewood Cliffs, NJ: Prentice-Hall.

Cooperrider, D. L. (2000). Positive image, positive action: The affirmative basis of organizing. In: D. Cooperrider & S. Srivastva (Eds), *Appreciative Inquiry: Rethinking Human Organization Toward a Positive Theory of Change*, 29–53.

Cooperrider, D. L. (2002). Foreword: The coming epidemic of positive change. In: R. Fry, F. Barrett, J. Seiling & D. Whitney (Eds), *Appreciative Inquiry and Organizational Transformation*. Connecticut: Quorum Books.

Dewey, J. (1966). *Democracy and education*. New York: Free Press.

Fredrickson, B. L. (2000). Cultivating positive emotions to optimize health and well-being. *Prevention and Treatment, 3*.

Fredrickson, B. L. (2001). The role of positive emotions in positive psychology: The broaden-and-build theory of positive emotions. *American Psychologist, 56*(3), 218–226.

Freire, P. (1970). *Pedagogy of the oppressed*. New York: Continuum.

Freire, P. (1994). *Pedagogy of hope*. New York: Continuum.

Friedman, T. (2000). *The Lexus and the olive tree*. New York: Anchor Books.

Goleman, D. (1995). *Emotional intelligence*. New York: Bantam Books.

Handy, C. (1998). *The hungry spirit*. New York: Broadway Books.

Kolb, D. (1984). *Experiential learning*. Englewood Cliffs, NJ: Prentice-Hall.

Maslow, A. (1976). *The farther reaches of human nature*. New York: Penguin Books.

McGregor, D. (1995). The human side of enterprise. In: D. Kolb, J. Osland & I. Rubin (Eds), *The Organizational Behavior Reader* (pp. 56–64). Englewood Cliffs, NJ: Prentice-Hall.

Shepard, H. (1995). On the realization of human potential: A path with a heart. In: D. Kolb, J. Osland & I. Rubin (Eds), *The Organizational Behavior Reader* (pp. 56–64). Englewood Cliffs, NJ: Prentice-Hall.

Yballe, L., & O'Connor, D. (2001). Appreciative pedagogy: Constructing positive models for learning. *Journal of Management Education, 24*(4), 474–483.

AP-PRAISE-AL: AN APPRECIATIVE APPROACH TO PROGRAM EVALUATION

Karen E. Norum, Marcy Wells, Michael R. Hoadley, Chris A. Geary and Ray Thompson

ABSTRACT

Conducting effective program evaluations such that all stakeholders benefit can be challenging. Appreciative inquiry provides a framework for seeking out the "goodness" of a program. By identifying what is being done "right," programs can be strengthened by keeping what is currently valued, discarding what is not valued, and creating what does not currently exist but is envisioned and desired by all stakeholders. This chapter explores the benefits of using an appreciative approach to program evaluation. It describes the process used to appraise the Technology for Education and Training graduate programs.

INTRODUCTION

When something new is introduced to a system, at some point, an assessment has to be made to determine if it is working. When a new education or training program is introduced to a system, this assessment is generally made by conducting a program evaluation. Program evaluation involves challenges of measurement and assessment (Senge et al., 1999). Typically, these systems of measurement and

Constructive Discourse and Human Organization
Advances in Appreciative Inquiry, Volume 1, 193–214
Copyright © 2004 by Elsevier Ltd.
ISSN: 1475-9152/doi:10.1016/S1475-9152(04)01009-9

assessment have evolved over the years and often, program evaluations begin with a focus on what is wrong. There seems to be an assumption that because there is no such thing as a "perfect" program, something will need to be fixed to make the program better. The process of program evaluation brings into question "the quality and effectiveness of stated purposes or intentions [of the program] by those in a position to render sound judgments" (Harrison, 2002, p. 80). Often, it is an appraisal of the program: an estimation of its quality or value; a determination of the worth of the effort (Roth, 1999). The focus is on problems and what is wrong with the program. We engage in a search for what we want less of with no assurance we will get more of what we do want (Ackoff, 1999). Based on the information received, we take actions to revise the world we live in accordingly. The revision often comes in the form of eliminating something we want less of, with no provision made to get more of what is working.

In this chapter, we seek to illustrate how an appreciative inquiry approach to program evaluation can provide an important contribution to program evaluation practices. According to Patton (1997), the purposes of traditional program evaluation are to judge a program's overall worth and merit, identify areas for improvement, and/or increase knowledge about the program. It is common for evaluators to collect data, plug it into a forumla, and produce a quantitative judgment (Roth, 1999). Such approaches tend to put the emphasis on the data and decisions rather than on the people involved (Patton, 1997). However, it is people who will use the information generated by the program evaluator.

An appreciative inquiry approach to evaluation shifts the focus away from data and problems into people and what is working in the current program. This chapter tells the story of how making the shift to examining what is working helped members of a division within a university to learn about our program in ways that benefited all stakeholders. The program evaluation became a program Ap-PRAISE-al as the goodness of the program was examined, with an emphasis on the "praise" in appraisal. Both students and faculty formed an Evaluation Team and engaged in a process that was a learning experience for all.

The learning experience unfolded as a graduate program in a higher education setting was ap-PRAISED. The students who were on the Evaluation Team found themselves engaged in a real evaluation project where they were stakeholders and would see the effect of their work. The faculty of the program being evaluated had to trust the students to conduct the evaluation. In the end, the faculty agreed the data obtained was rich and candid, perhaps more so than if the faculty had conducted the evaluation. All emerged with a far better view of what the Program was accomplishing, where it might be falling short, and what could make it even better. In informing each other through positive questions and responses, we became excited and energized to put forth our best efforts on all fronts toward achieving excellence. In this process, it became clear that the Program could be strengthened by keeping what was valued, discarding what was not valued, and creating what did not currently exist but was envisioned by both faculty and students.

The following pages explore the benefits of using an appreciative program evaluation approach as we describe the process used to appraise the Technology for Education and Training graduate programs.

SETTING THE CONTEXT

In Spring 2001, the Technology for Education and Training (TET) Division at the University of South Dakota assessed the status of the current degree offerings and programs. At this point, the Technology for Training and Development (TTD) Master's and Specialist degrees had been officially offered for two years. The Master's degree had two tracks within it: one with a K-12 emphasis and one with a Training and Development emphasis. The Program was created to appeal to both K-12 teachers and those from non-school settings. K-12 students might be attracted to the Program to sharpen their skills in technology to prepare for becoming technology coordinators in their schools or simply to learn how to better integrate technology into their curriculum. Students in the Training and Development track might be attracted to gain skills to become instructional designers, trainers, or organizational development specialists in business and industry.

At this two-year mark, the faculty determined an assessment of the status of the program offerings was in order. They sensed some confusion on the part of students as to what the program was really about. Was it technology skill development? Was it more conceptual than that? What did it mean to develop leaders in the appropriate use of technology in school and non-school settings?

At the suggestion of one of the faculty members, an Evaluation Team was created. The team consisted of eight students enrolled in Spring semester courses and two Division faculty members. The assessment became an action research project, engaging stakeholders (students and faculty) in the questioning, collection of data to address those questions, and sensemaking of the data collected (Reason & Bradbury, 2001).

An appreciative approach to this evaluation process was suggested. It would be an inquiry into discovering what was working well in the program offerings and how the offerings could be improved (Cooperrider & Whitney, 1999a). Rather than an inquiry into what wasn't working to determine what there should be less of, it became an inquiry into what was working and what there should be more of:

getting rid of what we do not want does not mean we will get what we do want (Ackoff, 1999).

At first, there was skepticism: by focusing on what was right, would real problems or flaws in the Program be discovered? After being assured concerns and issues students had with the Program would surface, the Evaluation Team agreed to an approach that would focus on what was working.

The Program faculty wanted to know what the students valued about the current program structure and offerings and what we should be doing "more" of. By using an appreciative evaluative approach that focused on what was working, information was gained about the strengths of the program; in turn, positive forward momentum was generated. The goal was to discover the best of what we had and use it to create a "collective image of a desired future," (Mohr et al., 2001, p. 292) engaging both faculty and student stakeholders.

Some significant background elements leading to the resulting success of the Program ap-PRAISE-al should be mentioned. The student members of the Evaluation Team were given a pertinent theoretical framework. One of the faculty Evaluation Team members introduced them to qualitative, action research and appreciative inquiry methodologies. Most of the students had already completed courses in change and transition and organization development required for their TTD majors, an innovative and relatively uncommon feature of educational technology programs. The other faculty Evaluation Team member was instrumental in motivating the group to relentlessly pursue their interviewing objectives in capturing all the data possible from a scattered and diverse student population. The student members thus felt grounded and supported in a time and energy consuming effort: e-mailing, phoning and making personal contact with classmates who often had tight schedules of work, classes, family obligations and community activities.

Thus, in spite of initial trepidations, all stakeholders involved were satisfied with the outcomes. We all learned something in ways that allowed us to engage in action to improve the existing program. Our specific learnings are described later in the chapter.

AP-PRAISE-ING THE PROGRAM

Patton (1997, p. 206) describes process evaluation as an approach that

> focuses on the internal dynamics and actual operations of a program in an attempt to understand its strengths and weaknesses. Process evaluations ask: What's happening and why? How do the parts of the program fit together? How do participants experience and perceive the program?

We had these basic questions but what set this apart from a typical process evaluation was that Appreciative Inquiry provided the framework for the program assessment, providing a structure for searching out the strengths of the program. Four basic types of questions are crafted when using the Appreciative Inquiry framework. The questions are crafted to elicit the "best of" the current system and to understand how these are life-giving and life-sustaining factors (Ludema et al., 2001). They are stated in the affirmative, using positive language; are presented as an invitation; evoke storytelling; are phrased in the vernacular; are sometimes ambiguous; and direct us to value what is (Cooperrider & Whitney, 1999b). The data collected comes primarily in the form of stories: we knew students (former and current) would have stories to share about their experiences in the Program and would be more likely to share them with a fellow student rather than a faculty member. Both the Division faculty and the students who conducted the actual assessment crafted the questions used for the program evaluation. Recognizing that the questions we asked would determine what we found, considerable attention was given to the wording of the questions. Expecting that decisions would be made and actions taken based on what we found, the questions would determine the future of the Program.

To set the storytelling mode, the first type of question asked in Appreciative Inquiry is a "deep story question" (Cooperrider & Whitney, 1999b). This question asks the interviewee to tell a story about a peak experience or high point. They are encouraged to describe who was involved, what made it a peak experience, what they did to make it a peak experience, what others contributed to make it a peak experience. We had two "deep story" questions:

(1) Why did you choose this program?
(2) Share a highlight of your time so far in the TTD Program. As you share your story, consider the following: What made it a high point? Who was involved? What did they do that made it a good experience? What did you do that made it a good experience?

The second type of question has to do with valuing the system (in this case, the Program) (Cooperrider & Whitney, 1999b). The interviewee is asked what they value about the system. The third type of question is the "core factors" or life-giving/life-sustaining question: What gives "life" to the system? (Cooperrider & Whitney, 1999b). This question elicits the specifics about what gives life to the system and seeks to understand why it gives life. Rather than identify the causes of a problem, this question asks the interviewee to ponder the best of the system and understand these factors as deeply as we typically understand what is wrong and why it is wrong. We crafted a question that captured both of these concepts: *Based on your experience so far, what do you value most about the Program?*

What would you define as core characteristics of the Program (without these, the Division and Program would not be what it is)? Please be specific.

The fourth type of question is the "future" question (Cooperrider & Whitney, 1999b). This is the question that invites people to dream about the ideal future of the system. To elicit these ideas, we asked, *If you were the "Student-in-Charge" of this Program and could have three wishes for the program granted, what would you wish? How would the Program be different if your three wishes were incorporated into the curriculum?*

We also had some practical concerns. For instance, some of the courses in this Program are delivered using distance technologies. We knew there was dissatisfaction among some of the students with the distance delivery of courses. We also knew that distance delivery of courses was not going away, so we wanted to find out how this could be improved. Hence, the questions all students were asked follow:

(1) Why did you choose this Program?
(2) Share a highlight of your time so far in the Program. As you share your story, consider the following: What made it a high point? Who was involved? What did they do that made it a good experience? What did you do that made it a good experience?
(3) Based on your experience so far, what do you value most about the Program? What would you define as core characteristics of the Program (without these, the Program and Division would not be what it is)? Please be specific.
(4) If you were the "Student-in-Charge" of the Program and could have three wishes for the program granted, what would you wish? How would the Program be different if your three wishes were incorporated into the curriculum?
(5) Many of the courses are delivered partially or fully using distance technologies such as Web CT and interactive video. What is it like to be in such a class? What courses have you had that are actually (or you believe would be) better delivered in a distance format? What role do you believe distance technologies should play in the future of the Program?

Through these questions, the Program would be ap-PRAISED. With an emphasis on the positive, it may appear we only wanted to hear good comments and not find out about actual problems students may be having with the Program. That was not our intent, and in fact, using the Appreciative Inquiry framework, we (the faculty and students) discovered

the richness of data gained from the four generic questions allows many more questions to be answered (Mohr et al., 2001, p. 313).

Particularly, as students described their wishes for the future of the Program, problems and criticisms surfaced. However, because the focus was on what was going right, it was easier to turn those problems and criticisms into positive recommendations. As Ludema et al. (2001) suggest, transformative dialogue and action were ignited and a creative, generative energy was engendered (Norum, 2001).

This was an action research project that employed qualitative research methods with an appreciative stance. Specifically, narrative inquiry methods were used. The interviews conducted were considered to be conversations with a purpose (Rossman & Rallis, 1998). The students conducting the evaluation were asking questions they and the faculty truly wanted answers to and they listened responsively to those answers. Data from a web-based questionnaire and interviews were analyzed by the students on the Evaluation Team. They identified themes and patterns that formed the basis of the evaluation report (Decker et al., 2001).

Each interview conducted yielded a narrative: a story about the person's experience so far with the Program, their hopes and wishes for its future, and perhaps their concerns. Thus, the Evaluation Team was engaged in narrative inquiry (Abma, 1999; Barone & Eisner, 1997; Clandinin & Connelly, 2000; Polkinghorne, 1995). This is a specific form of qualitative research and while narrative as research may be relatively new to education, it has been used in other disciplines such as sociology, psychology, literary theory, anthropology and history for some time (Casey, 1995–1996; Cortazzi, 1993; Josselson, 1993). It is quite natural for us to think narratively. Life is informed and formed by stories (Widdershoven, 1993). Narratives occur naturally (Cortazzi, 1993) and help us make meaning of life's episodes (Clandinin & Connelly, 1994; Connelly & Clandinin, 1990; Daloz, 1986; Polkinghorne, 1988, 1995; Reason & Hawkins, 1988; Simmons, 2001; Yaeger & Sorensen, 2001). It is quite common for people to explain their actions or relate an experience through telling a story. "We think and see in terms of stories because we are stories" (Feige, 1999, p. 87). Narrative inquiry is a heretical research method (Norum, 1998) because this method is a deliberate attempt to bring divergent points of view on issues to the forefront (Levin & Riffel, 1997). The form paints a different kind of picture, allowing for different and possibly new kinds of understandings to emerge (Barone & Eisner, 1997). By adding an appreciative stance as the foundation, the stories elicited provided clues as to what there could be more of, painting a picture of what was envisioned and desired for the Program by all stakeholders.

Because the practitioners were also the researchers, the Evaluation Team was also engaged in an action research project. Reason and Bradbury (2001) describe action research as a "participatory, democratic process concerned with developing practical knowing" (p. 1). The emphasis in action research methods is practical research based in (this case) qualitative methods. It takes everyday things in life and unpacks them (Noffke & Stevenson, 1995) by engaging people in a deeper understanding of their organization (Carr, 1997). A primary aim is to produce knowledge and action based on that knowledge that is directly useful to the group involved (Reason, 1998). Experiential knowledge is honored (Bray et al., 2000; Reason, 1998). It is a collaborative process: the people who were involved in collecting the data are also involved in disseminating and applying results (Quigley, 1997). Those who would directly feel the effects of changes in the system are involved in shaping what those changes might be. Stakeholders (in this case, students and faculty) are involved in the questioning, the collection of data to address those questions, and sensemaking of the data collected (Reason & Bradbury, 2001). In this process, Kemmis (2001, p. 92) suggests the stakeholders come to realize

> that we may want to improve our self-understandings, but also that our self-understandings may be shaped by collective misunderstandings about the nature and consequences of what we do.

This was true for us: we all gained new insights into what we understood and misunderstood about the program, what we expected from it, and how we envisioned its future.

In studying criteria of truth in action research Heikkinen et al. (2001) note that using pragmatism as a criterion of quality prompts the questions "Who has the power to determine a successful practice? Whose success are we interested in?" Faculty, staff and students alike found themselves asking new questions. What were we trying to achieve in the long run? Who was ultimately responsible for Program outcomes, and how could we collectively create success? We were beginning to understand we would live in the world our questions created.

While the Division faculty agreed to the ap-PRAISE-al process and drafted an initial set of interview questions, the Evaluation Team determined how the work would actually be done. In designing the process to be used, the students on the Evaluation Team suggested posting the questionnaire on the web and inviting former and current students to complete and submit it to a generic e-mail address. A generic e-mail address was used instead of a specific person's e-mail address: there was a concern that if the completed questionnaire went to someone specific, that might discourage some people from filling it out. We created a Program e-mail address. After receiving the completed questionnaires, the student Evaluation Team members followed up with a phone or face-to-face interview. The web-based questionnaire used the questions described earlier; these questions also provided the foundation for the follow up interviews.

An e-mail invitation to complete the web-based questionnaire and play a role in shaping the future of the Program was sent to 72 current and former Program students. Students who had graduated, those who had taken classes but were not currently enrolled, and current students were invited to participate in this ap-PRAISE-al of the Program. They were told that a current student would contact them whether they completed the questionnaire or not. If they did not want to be contacted, they had to let us know they were choosing not to participate. Less than six students asked to not be contacted. Some students could not be contacted – the contact information we had turned out not to be valid. In the end, 44 students participated in the Program ap-PRAISE-al.

One of the challenges with qualitative research is not so much in collecting the data, but what to do with it once you have it! Each of the eight on the Evaluation Team was assigned nine students to contact or follow up with. As mentioned above, some students could not be contacted and in the end, data was collected from 44 students (including the students conducting the Program evaluation). The task was to take the interview data from 44 people and move from individual stories to a co-created story. This was done by searching for themes and refrains (Lawrence-Lightfoot & Davis, 1997): an idea that runs through all or most of the data or one idea with heavy impact. Patterns were identified by looking for repeated relationships. Each of the eight students analyzed their interview data on an individual basis; then a group analysis of the data was conducted. The process was similar to that of reconstructing a jigsaw puzzle: puzzle pieces were identified within each individual data set and each data set became a piece of the overall evaluation project puzzle. The findings that emerged from this analysis provided the framework for the recommendations and report that were created.

All students on the Evaluation Team participated in writing the report. A smaller group of students presented the results of the report to the Division faculty. The Division Faculty met within a month of receiving the report recommendations and identified actions to take and commitments to make.

WHAT WE FOUND: THE THEMES

The questions asked and the stories shared created a world of recommendations. While some aspects of the Program were reaffirmed, new directions also emerged. The potential for the Program to be "more" was revealed. Each question and a summary of the responses are discussed below. The responses revealed stakeholders' desire to be "part of the positive history and positive future of the organization to which they belong[ed]" (Yaeger & Sorensen, 2001, p. 132).

Why did you choose the Program? A variety of answers were given to this question. The combination of education and technology, the emphasis on integrating technology and education in both school and non-school settings, increased employment opportunities for those who had such a background, and the scheduling of the classes such that the degree could be completed in four terms if desired were common themes. Although the satisfaction with the Program was high, disappointments were also voiced. These disappointments were related to a perception that students would receive more specific hands-on technology skills and experience. The philosophy of the Program was to emphasize concepts rather than specific technology skills or software, especially because the specifics change faster than the concepts behind the skills or software.

Share a highlight of your time so far in the Program. The answers to this question revolved around the Division faculty and staff. Time and time again, a faculty member or the assistance provided by the Division Secretary were mentioned in a story about a highlight experience. The passion of faculty who dedicated themselves to their knowledge field and student needs was cited as a core life-giving and life-sustaining characteristic of the Division. The high quality of the Division faculty and staff was noticed and appreciated by the students. In addition, creating opportunities for students to work with and learn from one another, as well as opportunities to apply theory in practical ways, were identified as strengths of the Program. Many felt that they were keeping on the cutting edge of technology and were excited about the group interactions they were having in both face-to-face and virtual settings.

Based on your experience so far, what do you value most about the Program? Related to the above question, the competence, professionalism, and support of the Division faculty were highly valued. In addition, students mentioned the feeling of community within the Division: they felt they were part of an academic community and the fact that their input was sought through this evaluation process solidified that perception. The offering of courses in a variety of formats (traditional face-to-face on campus classes, weekend classes, classes offered off campus, and Internet-supported or delivered) was noted, although the majority of students preferred face-to-face rather than distance delivery of courses. The constructivist orientation of the faculty was noticed in the design of the courses and assignments that were performance based and could be work-related. The opportunity to learn about how technology impacts organizations, society, and people and gaining perspectives on how to facilitate change in systems was also valued. Students remarked on the transferability and marketability of the skills and knowledge they were gaining through the Program.

If you were the "Student-in-Charge" of the Program and could have three wishes for the program granted, what would you wish? The responses to this question seemed to be dichotomous. Many students expressed a wish for more classes that introduced technical/application skills, while at the same time, many wished for more challenging, theory-oriented courses. Some wanted more courses that involved technical skills like setting up computers, networking, troubleshooting, and other application skills while the others felt these kinds of courses were not appropriate for a Graduate level program. This indicated the mission and goals of the Program needed to be re-evaluated and clarified so the intent of the program would be clearer to students.

What role do you believe distance technologies should play in the future of the Program? Students had varying degrees of experience with distance technologies used in the program. They may have had courses delivered by interactive video, Web CT as either an augmentation or primary mode of delivery, or both used conjunctively. While a live instructor and face-to-face interaction with classmates was usually preferred, there were many positive reactions to features of distance course tools. Students could work on assignments and communicate with the group at their convenience, fetch course materials online, and refer to an up-do-date syllabus, which the instructor could change or amplify to meet their needs. The conclusion seemed to be that distance-delivered courses should be an option, but not a requirement, and there should always be a face-to-face component to the delivery of the course. Students who would not otherwise be able to complete a graduate degree especially appreciated the Program's willingness to deliver courses in a variety of formats, including distance.

The ap-PRAISE-al revealed the Division was doing many things right and needed to continue to build on those strengths. It also revealed areas that were in need of improvement.

THE NEW TTD WORLD CREATED BY THE QUESTIONS ASKED

Several recommendations were made to the faculty. As a small group of student members of the Evaluation Team presented the findings and recommendations, the Division faculty listened attentively and inquisitively. They genuinely wanted to know what we should be doing more of and what improvements to the Program could be made. The faculty held a meeting approximately one month after receiving the report and recommendations (Decker et al., 2001). Several actions were taken and commitments were made based on recommendations reported by the Evaluation Team. A summary of the recommendations and actions follows.

Recommendation 1: Define the intent of the Program. The perception is that it is a combination of an MBA, Computer Science, and Education degree. Is the degree meant to be more skills-based or theory/concepts based? This needs to be well defined. Then, adequate pre-enrollment counseling needs to be provided so that students are well aware of what they realistically will and will not get out of the program. This could include advising students how to use their electives wisely to meet their personal goals for obtaining this graduate degree. If TTD continues its emphasis on concepts rather than skills, it needs to be clear to students that they will not receive "technical training" in the TET Programs.

In response to this recommendation, first and foremost, the mission statement of the Division was revisited and revised to reflect the continuing philosophy of teaching concepts over specific skills. The revised mission statement was shown to students in a 2001 summer course, all of who had conducted the Program evaluation or participated in it. They agreed the new statement did a better job of conveying the true intent of the Program.

Recommendation 2: Establish and maintain a "New Student Orientation" Program. When students are accepted into the program, they should receive a Student Handbook. The student's technology proficiency needs to be assessed and students advised as to what minimum skills they will need to be successful in the Program. An orientation to the labs used by the Program, as well as the hardware and software used by the Division, should be conducted. The minimum hardware and software they will need access to in order to complete courses could also be outlined for students; in addition, requirements for successfully participating in and completing distance-delivered courses should be outlined (i.e. students can be expected to use Web CT). An Orientation Program could also include a physical meeting one time each year where students in the Program meet one another as well as Division Faculty and Staff to maintain the feeling of community in the Division. Because students are accepted into the Programs throughout the year, a CD-ROM that introduces faculty and contains the above information could be sent to them to ensure greater consistency in the distribution of information.

In response to this recommendation, the Student Handbook was updated and is now given to all students entering the program. A CD-Rom was created in 2002 as a special project of students to introduce the faculty and the programs. The advising system was revised and updated to encourage more interaction between students and faculty. One faculty meeting each month focuses on advising issues and communication with students.

An orientation to technologies (hardware and software) is accomplished through classes and special projects. In addition to semester courses students can now enroll for free instruction in the university's Center for Instructional Design and Development Summer Tech program to enhance their skills and work toward personal mastery in technologies of their choosing (e.g. photo and video editing, Web page authoring, Palm computers, multimedia presentation, portfolio development and so on).

Recommendation 3: Advertise the program more using comments and "testimonials" from Program graduates and current students as a marketing tool for both the Master's and Specialist Degree Programs. To address this recommendation, the services of a marketing organization on campus were utilized in 2002 to create a brochure about TTD, which included comments from students and faculty. The marketing plan also included newspaper advertising in Rapid City, Sioux Falls, and Sioux City and providing more online information. In addition, the Division plans to try and establish one or two new cohorts of students each year.

Recommendation 4: Continue to hire high quality Faculty and Staff. Ascertain the technology proficiency of faculty. New faculty should be aware of the constructivist learning philosophy demonstrated by current faculty and be ready to assess learning outcomes via projects and papers vs. traditional tests.

Action on this recommendation includes ensuring that new faculty hired have a strong background in constructivist learning theory and they are technologically adept in some major area (e.g. multimedia, on-line learning, distance education, etc.). Performance-based evaluation through individual and group projects is being promoted. There is more emphasis on student portfolio development and presentation for instructional assessment.

Recommendation 5: Re-affirm a commitment to face-to-face delivery of courses. While students recognize that distance delivery of courses is a reality and they need to get used to it, they also value the face-to-face experience. The Program should not become a distance-delivered program only; the face-to-face experience should be part of most (if not all) courses. Courses that are distance delivered or have a distance delivery component need to be well designed and the instructors need to be well prepared if the experience is going to be positive for everyone involved.

To address this recommendation, all courses are to include some face-to-face component (even those offered solely by Web CT with an orientation session face-to-face via personal or virtual contact). There is a renewed and strengthened commitment of faculty to travel to remote sites to conduct a majority of class hours in their distance courses face-to-face, complemented by Web CT and other on-line components. The faculty work together in the creation of on-line courses and elicit input and feedback from students about instructional design and delivery of planned and ongoing courses. A cohort model will be used in an attempt to form groups of students at remote sites to strengthen support and collaboration and face-to-face student communication in distance courses.

Recommendation 6: Use a similar process, perhaps every two years, to conduct a thorough Program assessment. Students who conducted this assessment felt that other students were willing to voice their concerns about the Program, as well as share their positive experiences, because they were talking with a fellow student and would probably not be willing to share the same information with faculty directly. The process used for this assessment (Appreciative Inquiry, action research, interviewing, qualitative data analysis) provided richer data than would have been received from a standard survey; it also gave students a real project to apply evaluation and research methodologies to.

Based on this recommendation, it was agreed that the Program assessment would be conducted again in the near future to gain additional insights. The TTD faculty are teaching the same courses in a variety of delivery methods (face-to-face, completely on-line through Web CT or over the Internet, and some combination), and then being asked to evaluate them in terms of effectiveness. A similar type of Program assessment would help to determine the effectiveness of the various delivery methods.

Other impacts resulting from the assessment: More students are becoming involved in research and curriculum projects to learn more about the Program and its relationship to others working in the field. Portfolio development (conceptually and technically) has become a model for campus programs at the undergraduate and graduate levels.

The TTD Program was changed by the questions asked, the stories shared, and the Faculty response to the stories. These endeavors continue to be discussed and developed as the Division grows to maturity in the ever changing and expanding discipline of educational technology.

LIVING THE QUESTIONS: WHAT WE LEARNED

Ludema (2000) tells us that "social knowledge and organizational destiny are tightly intertwined ... all inquiry into organizational life should be collaborative" (p. 281). This project as a whole can be regarded as a collaborative effort at constructing knowledge of what the Division was attempting to achieve and how well program goals were being met by all involved. The student evaluators and students interviewed engaged in a dialogue from which new understanding was reached about their own and others' roles in making the Program a success. Employing the "art and science of asking powerful, positive, questions" (Cooperrider, 2000, p. 123) led us away from a path of negativity, criticism and "spiraling diagnosis" and to a path of "discovery, dream, and design" (Cooperrider, 2000, p. 124).

In discussing the generative potential of appreciative inquiry, Barrett and Cooperrider (2001) note belief, trust, and conviction as key elements. By creating an Evaluation Team consisting primarily of students, believing and trusting in the process, the faculty discovered space for new voices and new insights was forged. The students' candor and eagerness to participate in the ap-PRAISAL-al process was due in no small part to the relationships built up with the Division, leading them to trust that their voices would be heard by a faculty group that cared and was willing to take the risks involved in initiating change. A community of support for innovative action was engendered (Ludema et al., 2001). By demonstrating a good faith effort to act on the recommendations made, the students were validated. Empathy, hope, excitement, and social bonding among people around common desired values were generated (Barrett & Cooperrider, 2001). Positive relationships between students and faculty were deepened and the sense of community strengthened. A sense of respect for one another and partnership in the Program's continuing success intensified.

"People inform one another not through numbers, but through stories" (Johnson, 1999, p. 297). The combination of Appreciative Inquiry, narrative inquiry, and action research elicited a rich mosaic of opinions, impressions, and recommendations. Those who participated in the Program evaluation willingly shared their stories, exploring what the Program meant to them personally, and in the process, almost unconsciously raised additional questions, deepening the inquiry (Burchell & Dyson, 2000). Embedded in the stories were practical suggestions and recommendations for the stakeholders (faculty and students) of the Program. While serious issues surfaced and were addressed, valuable information, key insights, and pleasant surprises made this an evaluation report that was acted upon rather than relegated to a bookshelf to collect dust. As those involved in the ap-PRAISE-al process continue to reflect upon the experience, dialogue with others, and present our results in various ways (Norum et al., 2002), we are still reliving and retelling our own and others' stories. Perhaps this is evidence that supports Davenport and Prusak's statement: "Human beings learn best from stories" (1998, p. 81).

This is what we learned collectively. What we learned as each stakeholder group is discussed below.

Insights from the Student Perspective

The students on the Evaluation Team brought a fresh enthusiasm to a project with a novel methodology probably unlike any other evaluative process in which they had been involved. They had become acquainted with each other in various classes and had already participated in discussions about the emerging TTD program. They were full of questions of their own about the possible directions the Division could take in fulfilling its intended mission of developing leaders in educational technology. Students in the Program were on different career tracks: teaching and administration in K-12 to adult learning; training in medical sciences and corporate environments. Some were on their initial route through graduate studies and others were returning to seek a new degree after working in other fields.

The broad and diverse experience of the student Evaluation Team members and their familiarity with the Division student body was instrumental in helping to (re)formulate the interview questions from an original set of suggestions posed by the faculty. Each participant had opinions and questions of concern, which were freely given and discussed until consensus was reached on the final set for the interview process. Musings that may have remained unexpressed in a typical evaluation process were shared (Ludema et al., 2001). During these initial sessions, student Evaluation Team members started on a journey of enlightenment of their perceptions of what the Division was all about and their corresponding roles as its students. This journey would continue until the final reporting and beyond as new insights were gained on how each could contribute to improvements that would benefit all the stakeholders in this endeavor.

According to Liebler (1997),

> The process of doing the appreciative interviews is as important as the data collected, for it is through the doing that the internal conversations within organizations are changed.

The student members of the Evaluation Team themselves were changed in carrying out the interviews as they gained new knowledge of the how the interviewees felt about the TTD Program, and in turn examined how they themselves felt about it. "All life is in story so that, there, we find our experience confirmed, challenged and broadened," says storytelling advocate Maurice Lynch (cited in Burchell & Dyson, 2000, p. 437). The stories the student members heard about their fellow-students' peak experiences in the Program and how they were employing their current learning in their own life situations gave vitality and direction to the project, transforming it from a dry question and answer process to a live quest for truth. In the process of conducting it, the students found research "is a lived practice" that is shaped by and shapes the researcher (Sumara & Carson, 2001, p. xiii).

Although apprehensive at first (after all, why would someone want to share their experiences with someone they had never met?), the students conducting the evaluation were impressed and delighted by the stories they heard, especially those about peak experiences in the Program and how learning was already enhancing daily lives. For example, one current student was directly applying the methodology she had learned to a corporate training program in a national travel firm. Others were using the concepts and techniques in their leadership efforts in introducing and enhancing computer-based learning in K-12 classrooms. The student evaluators' mental models were being changed and elaborated with each story, and the Program became more of a living system in relation to real-life projects and processes. Students connected with each other and with their course work more and more as the interviews proceeded, and the appreciative nature of the investigation brought forth positive feelings and perceptions that otherwise may not have been so strongly sensed and expressed.

The Evaluation Team was learning how to ask the "best" questions, which was half the battle in evaluating the current state of things and effecting positive change where called for. Were most students benefiting from the Program in such a way that they were currently using or planned to use what they were learning in their particular setting? Would they recommend the program to others? Are the courses offering what they expected or were they led to expect something entirely different (by whatever route they had come to the Program)? And underlying the practical considerations was a philosophical one: should the Program be producing leaders to serve larger society as it is, or to be changing "what is" to make it better?

The team was getting a notion of what it would be like to live in the world our questions created.

Insights from the Faculty Perspective

The Program ap-PRAISE-al had unearthed student views the faculty had not before heard with regard to some aspects of the program: advantages and limitations of distance classes, significance of hands-on experience in various technologies, the dichotomous wishes for technical training vs. theory in a Graduate level program. The very meaning of "educational technology" in general could widely vary among students who had entered the Program with differing knowledge levels and objectives.

While the faculty had committed from the outset to not allow the Report to sit on a shelf, regardless of the findings, they were delighted to hear affirmations. The strength of the faculty and sense of community extended to the students were revealed in comments such as:

> I think that a highlight of this program has been the opportunity to receive new ideas and be able to contemplate them in my perspective of the world. In each of my classes so far, the professors have provided me with a myriad of new ideas that I have been able to contemplate and construct meaning to in my own world. The readings and projects have been productive and insightful both intrinsically and extrinsically. They have given me new mental challenges as well as the right to express my own viewpoints. They have accepted my viewpoints as legitimate, allowed me my errors to find for myself, and create a new idea of what I think.

> I value the faculty and students. The faculty is very willing to help. The core characteristic is the feeling of community, the closeness like a family between the faculty, staff, and the students.

At the same time, concerns were also voiced. They were illuminated most frequently through students' wishes for the Program. While some of the wishes echoed concerns faculty suspected would be unearthed, other concerns were unexpected.

> More face to face classes than on-line. I didn't come here from another country to take classes on the Internet.

> There would be a complete separation of the K-12 and corporate track. Although I could apply some of the situations and theories discussed in the courses that had a K-12 focus, it was difficult to be in the minority.

> I thought the program would include more "hands-on" technology rather than theory.

> The majority of the class should be conducted in face-to-face situations. I do not think that courses should be completely distance based. You get so much more out of face-to-face classes.

The Program Ap-PRAISE-al revealed the Division was doing many things right and needed to continue to build on those strengths. Most of the students felt they were truly benefiting from what the Program offered and wanted more of it. Especially heartening were the many specific stories of how a faculty member had effected a student – as teachers, we know we have the potential to impact and change lives but do not always hear those kinds of stories.

The report also revealed areas that were in need of improvement. As the Program continues to evolve, the intent is to get more of what was identified as positive through the Program ap-PRAISE-al.

THE "PRAISE" IN AP-PRAISE-AL

On the surface, it appears that by framing questions positively problems and concerns will be glossed over. However, that is not the case. In this process, we found that when students had a concern, they voiced it. By focusing on the "praise" in appraisal, instead of dwelling on the "problem," the conversation focuses on suggestions for what could be done about it. A generative energy is created as possibilities unfold.

We live in the worlds our questions create. What we choose to question, study and measure in the evaluation process is a sign of what is valued in the system. We typically use the evaluation process to identify what we need less rather than more of. As described here, program ap-PRAISE-al inquires into a program's successes and in practice, is an inquiry into discovering what gives life and sustains it in that system. A basic tenet of Appreciative Inquiry is that a system will move in the direction of what it is studying. If this is true, what we choose to evaluate and how we evaluate it becomes fateful:

> When we inquire into the things in our organisations that are life giving, we begin to understand that we can choose to focus on those qualities. Through asking others to join in our inquiry, we can have a considerable impact on the image of our organisation and, ultimately, on the way it functions (Mohr et al., 2001, p. 315).

Program evaluation is something that we are all called upon to do in many settings. Often, the evaluation focuses on problems and what is wrong with the program. It becomes a search for what we want less of with no assurance we will get more of what we do want (Ackoff, 1999). We then use the data generated from the questions we asked to judge a program's overall worth and merit, identify areas for improvement, and/or increase our knowledge about a program (Patton, 1997). In turn, we take actions to revise the world we live in accordingly. The revision often comes in the form of eliminating something we want less of, with no provision made to get more of what is working. Because evaluation can be an intimidating prospect for all stakeholders, it can be challenging to conduct evaluations where everyone benefits.

"Changing the way we measure changes everything" (Meador, 1999, p. 299). Program ap-PRAISE-al offers an approach that highlights what the program is doing right and what it could be doing "more" of. Concerns and problems will still be identified. The refreshing aspect is that instead of dwelling on those "problems," a creative, generative energy is engendered, reducing the challenges typically found in program evaluation. Instead, ". . . constructive organizational understandings that open new possibilities for human organizing and action" (Ludema, 2000, p. 284) are discovered. By identifying what is being done "right," programs can be strengthened by keeping what is currently valued, discarding what is not valued, and creating what does not currently exist but is envisioned and desired by all stakeholders. An appreciative approach to program evaluation opens the door for the evaluation process to be positive, valuable and energizing for all involved.

REFERENCES

Abma, T. A. (1999). Powerful stories: The role of stories in sustaining and transforming professional practice within a mental hospital. In: R. Josselson & A. Lieblich (Eds), *Making Meaning of Narratives* (Vol. 6, pp. 169–195). Thousand Oaks, CA: Sage.

Ackoff, R. L. (1999). *Re-creating the corporation: A design of organizations for the 21st century.* NY: Oxford University Press.

Barone, T., & Eisner, E. (1997). Arts-Based educational research. In: R. M. Jaeger (Ed.), *Complementary Methods for Research in Education* (2nd ed., pp. 70–116). Washington, DC: American Educational Research Association.

Barrett, F. J., & Cooperrider, D. L. (2001). Generative metaphor intervention: A new approach for working with systems divided by conflict and caught in defensive perception. In: D. L. Cooperrider, P. F. Sorensen, Jr., T. F. Yaeger & D. Whitney (Eds), *Appreciative Inquiry: An Emerging Direction for Organization Development* (pp. 147–174). Champaign, IL: Stipes Publishing L. L. C.

Bray, J. N., Lee, J., Smith, L. L., & Yorks, L. (2000). *Collaborative inquiry in practice: Action, reflection, and making meaning.* Thousand Oaks, CA: Sage.

Burchell, H., & Dyson, J. (2000). Just a little story: The use of stories to aid reflection on teaching in higher education. *Educational Action Research, 8*(3), 435–446.

Carr, A. A. (1997). User-design in the creation of human learning systems. *Educational Technology Research and Development, 45*(3), 5–22.

Casey, K. (1995–1996). The new narrative research in education. In: M. W. Apple (Ed.), *Review of Research in Education* (Vol. 21, pp. 211–253). Washington, DC: American Educational Research Association.

Clandinin D. J., & Connelly F. M. (1994). Personal experience methods. In: N. K. Denzin & Y. S. Lincoln (Eds), *Handbook of Qualitative Research* (pp. 413–427). Thousand Oaks, CA: Sage.

Clandinin, D. J., & Connelly, F. M. (2000). *Narrative inquiry: Experience and story in qualitative research.* San Francisco: Jossey-Bass.

Connelly, F. M., & Clandinin, D. J. (1990). Stories of experience and narrative inquiry. *Educational Researcher, 19*(5), 2–14.

Cooperrider, D. L. (2000). The "child" as agent of inquiry. In: D. L. Cooperrider, P. F. Sorensen, D. Whitney & T. F. Yaeger (Eds), *Appreciative Inquiry: Rethinking Human Organization Toward a Positive Theory of Change* (pp. 123–129). Champaign, IL: Stipes Publishing L. L. C.

Cooperrider, D. L., & Whitney, D. (1999a). *Appreciative inquiry.* San Francisco: Berrett-Koehler.

Cooperrider, D. L., & Whitney, D. (1999b). *Appreciative inquiry: A constructive approach to organization development and social change (A Workshop).* Taos, NM: Corporation for positive change.

Cortazzi, M. (1993). *Narrative analysis.* London: Falmer Press.

Daloz, L. A. (1986). *Effective teaching and mentoring: Realizing the transformational power of adult learning experiences.* San Francisco: Jossey-Bass.

Davenport, T. H., & Prusak, L. (1998). *Working knowledge: How organizations manage what they know.* Boston: Harvard Business School Press.

Decker, R., Geary, C. A., Glander, C., Korn, K., Lee, S., Lin, L., Moody, L., Wells, M., Norum, K. E., & Thompson, R. (2001). *Technology for training and development program assessment.* Vermillion, SD: University of South Dakota, School of Education.

Feige, D. M. (1999). The legacy of Gregory Bateson: Envisioning aesthetic epistemologies and praxis. In: J. Kane (Ed.), *Education, Information, and Transformation: Essays on Learning and Thinking* (pp. 77–109). Upper Saddle River, NJ: Prentice-Hall.

Harrison, M. D. (2002). *Narrative Based Evaluation.* New York: Peter Lang Publishing.

Heikkinen, H., Kakkaori, L., & Huttunen, R. (2001). This is my truth, tell me yours: Some aspects of action research quality in the light of truth theories. *Educational Action Research, 9*(1). Retrieved May 30, 2002 from http://www.triangle.co.uk/ear/.

Johnson, H. T. (1999). Moving upstream from measurement. In: P. Senge, A. Kleiner, C. Roberts, R. Ross, G. Roth & B. Smith (Eds), *The Dance of Change* (pp. 291–298). New York: Doubleday/Currency Publishing.

Josselson, R. (1993). A narrative introduction. In: R. Josselson & A. Lieblich (Eds), *The Narrative Study of Lives* (Vol. 1, pp. ix–xv). Thousand Oaks, CA: Sage.

Lawrence-Lightfoot, S., & Davis, J. H. (1997). *The art and science of portraiture.* San Francisco: Jossey-Bass.

Levin, B., & Riffel, J. A. (1997). *Schools and the changing world: Struggling toward the future.* London: Falmer Press.

Liebler, C. J. (1997, Summer). Getting comfortable with appreciative inquiry: Questions and answers. Global Social Innovations, Journal of the GEM Initiative. *Case Western Reserve University, 1*(2), 30–40. Retrieved February 23, 2001 from http://www.geminitiative.org/getting.html.

Ludema, J. D. (2000). From deficit discourse to vocabularies of hope: The power of appreciation. In: D. L. Cooperrider, P. F. Sorensen, D. Whitney & T. F. Yaeger (Eds), *Appreciative Inquiry: Rethinking Human Organization Toward a Positive Theory of Change* (pp. 265–287). Champaign, IL: Stipes Publishing L. L. C.

Ludema, J. D., Cooperrider, D. L., & Barrett, F. J. (2001). Appreciative Inquiry: The power of the unconditional positive question. In: P. Reason & H. Bradbury (Eds), *Handbook of Action Research* (pp. 189–199). London: Sage.

Meador, D. (1999). Measuring to report . . . or to learn? In: P. Senge, A. Kleiner, C. Roberts, R. Ross, G. Roth & B. Smith (Eds), *The Dance of Change* (pp. 298–302). New York: Doubleday/Currency Publishing.

Mohr, B. J., Smith, E., & Watkins, J. M. (2001). Appreciative inquiry and learning assessment: An embedded evaluation process in a transnational pharmaceutical company. In: D. L. Cooperrider, P. F. Sorensen, Jr., T. F. Yaeger & D. Whitney (Eds), *Appreciative Inquiry: An Emerging Direction for Organization Development* (pp. 291–315). Champaign, IL: Stipes Publishing L. L. C.

Noffke, S. E., & Stevenson, R. B. (Eds) (1995). *Educational action research: Becoming practically critical.* New York: Teachers College Press.

Norum, K. E. (1998). *Hearing voices of difference: Stories of erasure and heretical research methods.* (ERIC Document Reproduction Service No. ED 419 215.)

Norum, K. E. (2001). Appreciative Design. *Systems Research and Behavioral Science, 18*(4), 323–333.

Norum, K. E., Wells, M., Hoadley, M. R., & Geary, C. A. (2002). Appreciative program evaluation: A qualitative action research project. Paper presented at the American Educational Research Association Annual Meeting, April 1–5, New Orleans, LA.

Patton, M. Q. (1997). *Utilization-focused evaluation: The new century text* (3rd ed.). Thousand Oaks, CA: Sage.

Polkinghorne, D. E. (1988). *Narrative knowing and the human sciences.* Albany: State University of New York Press.

Polkinghorne, D. E. (1995). Narrative configuration in qualitative analysis. In: J. A. Hatch & R. Wisniewski (Eds), *Life History and Narrative* (pp. 5–23). London: Falmer Press.

Quigley, B. A. (1997). The role of research in the practice of adult education. In: B. A. Quigley & G. W. Kuhne (Eds), *Creating Practical Knowledge Through Action Research: Posing Problems, Solving Problems, and Improving Daily Practice* (pp. 3–22). San Francisco: Jossey-Bass.

Reason, P. (1998). Three approaches to participative inquiry. In: N. K. Denzin & Y. S. Lincoln (Eds), *Strategies of Qualitative Inquiry* (pp. 261–291). Thousand Oaks, CA: Sage.

Reason, P., & Bradbury, H. (2001). Introduction. In: P. Reason & H. Bradbury (Eds), *Handbook of Action Research* (pp. 1–14). London: Sage.

Reason, P., & Hawkins, P. (1988). Storytelling as inquiry. In: P. Reason (Ed.), *Human Inquiry in Action* (pp. 79–101). London: Sage.

Rossman, G. B., & Rallis, S. F. (1998) *Learning in the field: An introduction to qualitative research.* Thousand Oaks, CA: Sage.

Roth, G. (1999). Cracking the "black box" of a learning initiative assessment. In: P. Senge, A. Kleiner, C. Roberts, R. Ross, G. Roth & B. Smith (Eds), *The Dance of Change* (pp. 303–311). New York: Doubleday/Currency Publishing.

Senge, P., Kleiner, A., Roberts, C., Ross, R., Roth, G., & Smith, B. (1999). Assessment and measurement: The challenge. In: P. Senge, A. Kleiner, C. Roberts, R. Ross, G. Roth & B. Smith (Eds), *The Dance of Change* (pp. 281–291). New York: Doubleday/Currency Publishing.

Simmons, A. (2001). *The story factor.* NY: Perseus Publishing.

Sumara, D., & Carson, T. R. (2001). Reconceptualizing action research as a living practice. In: T. R. Carson & D. Sumara (Eds), *Action Research as a Living Practice* (pp. xiii–xxxv). New York: Peter Lang Publishing.

Widdershoven, G. A. M. (1993). The story of life: Hermeneutic perspectives on the relationship between narrative and life history. In: R. Josselson & A. Lieblich (Eds), *The Narrative Study of Lives* (Vol. 1, pp. 1–20). Thousand Oaks, CA: Sage.

Yaeger, T. F., & Sorensen, P. F., Jr. (2001). What matters most in appreciative inquiry: Review and thematic assessment. In: D. L. Cooperrider, P. F. Sorensen, Jr., T. F. Yaeger & D. Whitney (Eds), *Appreciative Inquiry: An Emerging Direction for Organization Development* (pp. 129–142). Champaign, IL: Stipes Publishing L. L. C.

PART III:
NEW METAPHORS OF
POSITIVE CHANGE

THE PSYCHOPHYSIOLOGY OF APPRECIATION IN THE WORKPLACE

Leslie E. Sekerka and Rollin McCraty

ABSTRACT

This chapter reviews literature in support of a model that predicts the effects of Appreciative Inquiry on physical health in the workplace. Studies that demonstrate the physiological correlates associated with the experience of appreciation are examined. A model of emotion is proposed that shows how the heart, in concert with the brain, nervous, and hormonal systems, are fundamental components of a dynamic network from which emotional experience emerges. The authors demonstrate how favorable affective experiences and appreciative processes go hand in hand – and suggest the need for further empirical investigations in the field of positive organizational change practices.

INTRODUCTION

The heart has often been associated with wisdom and emotional experience, particularly with regard to other-centered, positive emotions such as love, care, compassion, gratitude, and appreciation. Current research provides evidence our heart plays a role in the generation of emotional experience, suggesting the associations are more than mere metaphor.

In this chapter, we review literature in support of a model that predicts effects of Appreciative Inquiry on physical health (Cooperrider & Srivastva, 1999). Research that identifies physiological correlates associated with the experience

Constructive Discourse and Human Organization
Advances in Appreciative Inquiry, Volume 1, 217–239
© 2004 Published by Elsevier Ltd.
ISSN: 1475-9152/doi:10.1016/S1475-9152(04)01010-5

of appreciation is examined. We propose a model of emotion that suggests the heart, in concert with the brain, nervous, and hormonal systems, are fundamental components of a dynamic network from which emotional experience emerges. Studies supporting our contention that favorable affective experiences and appreciative processes go hand in hand are described. The need for further empirical investigations examining the emotional impacts of positive organizational change practices such as Appreciative Inquiry is discussed. Finally, questions and propositions for future research to advance Appreciative Inquiry theory and positive organizational scholarship are offered – areas that we believe require further investigation.

VIEWING APPRECIATIVE INQUIRY THROUGH AN EMPIRICAL LENS

Techniques that use positive experiences as organizational development frameworks to foster change are no longer missing from the palate of practitioner options. A major shift in both research and practice has occurred. Recent emphasis has redirected the focus, toward the positive, in both organizational and psychological inquiry. Many scholars realized that we know a great deal about dysfunctional process. After decades of focusing on what is wrong, identifying the illnesses and aliments within our organizations through problem-solution based frameworks, we became experts at identifying what is wrong. Today, however, there is a tremendous shift toward the examination of what is right – what does it look like to thrive, achieve, and be well? As a result, recent efforts have altered the direction of research with inquiry shifting to examine what it looks like when we are at our best (Gillham, 2000).

Recognizing the influences that organizational change practices can have on participants' well-being is now considered essential. Toward that end, this chapter moves to explicate what happens physiologically as individuals embrace positive change approaches. We discuss how favorable emotional experiences from such techniques can lead to beneficial outcomes such as reduced stress and enhanced performance. Assumptions in the field, which suggest appreciative processes are conducive to generating favorable emotions, are now supported with empirical evidence. Given that psychophysiological consequences are associated with emotional experiences (Salovey, Rothman, Detweiler & Steward, 2000), it is important to extend examination of organizational development processes such as Appreciative Inquiry, where one's state of appreciation may influence physical health positively.

Formed in the womb of social constructionism, Appreciative Inquiry came from theoretical bedrock where reality is not out there to be found, but continuously co-created. There are no hard and fast laws or axioms of social interaction within this framework because from this stance we create truth by what we perceive, believe, and bring into our personal schema via the world around us. To understand the psychophysiological impacts of the process, however, a departure from Appreciative Inquiry's theoretical roots is required. While truths of social interaction are emergent, the science of human physiology is guided in large part by the laws of biological science. Hence, the traditions, language, and methods of normative science are also embraced and applied to create knowledge. By combining different ways of knowing and holding multiple assumptions, we hope to petition interest, debate, and curiosity.

Coming from a modernist perspective, the world around us is reflected objectively by observing what is out there. Here, causal relations are described by researchers and observers as they communicate findings via the use of language systems. By adopting the use of conventional methods to convey one's ideas, researchers become participants in the use of traditional "textual genre" or "linguistic forestructure" to interpret their observations (Gergen, 2001, p. 807). While empirical investigations into appreciation have adopted preexisting protocols to express the interpretation of data, there is equal respect for postmodern constructionism. The assumption is that scientific exploration will contribute to our understanding and provide evidence that mirrors reality – a reflection of our shared experience.

Our ambition is not to find an ultimate truth, but to seek cultural meaning in organizational contexts. By presenting a model of the psychophysiological underpinnings of appreciation as an emotional process, the intention is to exercise theory in a way that kindles our mutual construction of the world while also focusing on the individual's organizational experience. Perhaps our framing will seem paradoxical, as we choose to use a logical positivist lens to advance our understanding of a postmodern technique. While it may be awkward to hold multiple assumptions, the overarching goal is to create a bridge for dialogue. We believe Appreciative Inquiry is a practice that seeks to enable dialogue in order to "traverse boundaries of difference" (Gergen, 2001, p. 807). Our intention is to extend knowledge of how positive emotions, such as appreciation, affect individuals in the workplace – and to spark conversation among people who make sense of the world holding different assumptions. We hope to stimulate dialogue among academics, practitioners, and organizational members and, as such, new knowledge will emerge. As Bohr (1967) suggests, it is our belief that truth is found not by breaking the world into either-ors, but by embracing both-and. Referring to this concept,

Palmer (1998) writes: "...truth is a paradoxical joining of apparent opposites, and if we want to know that truth, we must learn to embrace those opposites as one" (p. 63).

LANGUAGE AND EMOTIONS

To understand the relationship between Appreciative Inquiry and the emotional experience, researchers must address the role that language plays in this process. Knowledge, in the form of feelings, emotions, thoughts, and perceptions, comes to us by way of language (Anderson, 1997). What we know is formed, takes shape in, and is communicated via language. Meanings are assigned to events constructed from language. As an interpretative device, language is the nucleus for forming our reality. What we experience as real is actually based upon metaphorical cognitions that, when believed, contribute to our perceptions of what is real (Madison, 1988).

Meaning, however, is not found in language per se – words themselves do not hold intention, emotion, or feeling – people do! In short, words are platforms used to conjure up underlying recollections of understood intentionality. Language is an ongoing unfoldment of patterns of relationships, associations that contribute to our ability to stay connected – creating our world in concert with others (Gergen, 1988). As a result, the relationship between thoughts and words continues to be a living, evolving, and an emergent process (Vygotsky, 1986).

Advances in applied developmental psychology support that language is the basic condition for humans to become agentive and make active and productive sense of their world (Bamburg, 2000). Highly relevant to the emotional experience is one's schema for interpretation of events. In short, how we translate and make meaning of our experience has the propensity to influence the various components of our emotional response triad – feelings, expression, and physiology (Frijda, 1986; Johnstone & Scherer, 2000). For example, if one assesses a situation using an internal script based upon opportunity, an emotional response and expression of that encounter will be very different than if that same situation is translated and experienced as a problem, a concern to be overcome.

With language serving as a cognitive interpreter and conduit for emotional experience, how we create reality is determined by the language schemas we call upon internally and use in concert with others. Gergen (1994) takes the communal aspect of knowledge creation further, suggesting human reality is actually the product of social dialogue. Our exchanges and interactions represent an agreement between people. Therefore, accounts (realities) hold up when we find them useful, and not because they are necessarily true (as cited in Anderson, 1997). This implies that psychological knowledge is guided by our shared construction of the world and not by the objective validity of its truth. Holding the aforementioned assumptions, we contend that the reality of our emotional experience can be favorably altered, depending upon the nature of the dialogue we choose to socially construct in concert with others. We suggest that if the dialogue within an organization shifts to one that focuses on its positive core through appreciation, this shared reality in the workplace can transform individual and organizational well-being.

In Maturana's *Biology of Language: The Epistemology of Reality*, the scholar provides insight on the association between the process of cognition (language formation and use) and emotion (1978). Much like Gergen, he considers language as a coupling activity, based upon the establishment of consensuality between recursive interactions among self and others. He views expression as being linked to "isomorphic physiological responses" that relate to "consensual domains" of relating and understanding (pp. 50–53). In other words, we constitute the reality of our moments with the transaction of both cognitive and biological interactions that occur both within and between individuals. Further, participants in conversation undergo structural changes as a result of their shared interaction, which lead to feelings and behavior. While communication is not necessarily a result of physiology, the determination of the capacity for recursive structural coupling is *dependent upon the nervous system*. That is, internal structures on which linguistic interactions operate serve as triggers for "perturbations" that fuel recursive interactions (p. 52).

Implications of Maturana's thesis are that knowledge (i.e. assertion) implies interaction has transpired, which can lead to additional interactions. Further, the extent of what we can do is determined by our contained internal structure and its organization – actions from within this structure create our cognitions. While knowledge implies prior interaction, we cannot step out of our mind. Therefore, we live in a domain of subject-dependent knowledge. As Maturana states, "We literally create the world we live in by living it" (p. 53). The reality of what we know and feel is created by our internal and external ongoing and recursive flow of interactions. In summary, language and the subsequent new knowledge are formed between self and others. It is both a cognitive and biologically-based activity and the context of dialogue is determined as organisms experience interactions at both the individual and dyadic level. Taken together, these theoretical assumptions support the contention that there is potential to alter emotional experience favorably, depending upon what reality is constructed. If our internal and external dialogue focuses on appreciation, our emergent reality has the capacity to favorably transform both individual and organizational well-being in the workplace.

APPRECIATION AND POSITIVE EMOTIONS

As noted by practitioners and participants alike in a variety of circumstances, individuals engaged in Appreciative Inquiry report that the stimulation of positive conversations between themselves and other organizational members serves as a catalyst for creating positive change in their organization. In the initial phase of Appreciative Inquiry, interviews are conducted where members from all levels of the organization come together to converse with one another. During these dialogues, people have been observed to shift to a more positive, lively, and engaged stance. The process of asking people to think about and share the "best of" their organizational experiences with a fellow organizational member appears to energize participants (Sekerka & Cooperrider, 2001). As they reflect on positive encounters, exchange stories, and listen, they appear to become more hopeful, enthusiastic, and interested – cynicism gives way to idea generation. The recognition of the best in something or someone seems to instill an energetic quality that is uplifting.

The optimism generated by participating in an appreciative dialogue has been observed in a broad milieu of situations. The Appreciative Inquiry *Discovery Phase*, as described above, brings people together and is an important step toward tapping the positive core of the organization (Sekerka, Cooperrider & Wilken, 2001). We believe that this process moves organizational systems away from entrenched negative mental models (Senge, 1990) and single-loop learning (Argyris, Putnam & McLain Smith, 1985) toward more flexible and broader thinking. Given consistent reports from practitioners about how participants experience positive emotions in Appreciative Inquiry (Cooperrider & Whitney, 1999, 2000; Magruder & Mohr, 2001; Whitney & Shau, 1998), research that explores this technique at the psychophysiological level is warranted in order to understand the phenomena and outcomes more fully.

For centuries, religious scholars, artists, scientists, medical practitioners, and lay authors have written about the transformative power of positive emotions. Presently, a growing body of research is beginning to provide objective evidence that positive emotions may indeed be key to well-being, enhancing nearly all spheres of human experience. Positive emotions have been demonstrated to improve health and increase longevity (Blakeslee, 1997; Danner, Snowdon & Friesen, 2001; Goldman, Kraemer & Salovey, 1996; Russek & Schwartz, 1997), increase cognitive flexibility and creativity (Ashby, Isen & Turken, 1999; Isen, 1999), facilitate broad-minded coping and innovative problem solving (Aspinwall, 1998; Fredrickson, 2002; Isen, Daubman & Nowicki, 1987), and promote helpfulness, generosity, and effective cooperation (Isen, 1987). Fredrickson's work with the broaden-and-build theory suggests that positive emotions have reparative functions, which serve to bolster recovery from negative encounters (2001). Current research has also elucidated emotion-related changes in the body, including changes in the patterns of the heart's rhythmic activity. Researchers have recently moved to investigate this unique relationship between the heart and brain, finding that the interaction affects physiological, cognitive, and emotional processes.

THE HEART'S ROLE

Throughout the 1990s, increasing evidence has accrued to support the view that the brain and body work in conjunction in order for perceptions, thoughts, and emotions to emerge. This perspective has gained momentum and is now widely accepted. The brain is considered an analog processor that relates whole concepts to one another and looks for similarities, differences, or relationships between them. Longstanding assumptions, that emotions were purely mental expressions generated by the brain alone, have been set aside. Emotions have as much to do with the body as with the brain, and the heart plays a particularly important role in the emotional system. Emotions are thus a product of the brain, heart, and body acting in concert.

Recent work in the field of neurocardiology has firmly established that the heart is a sensory organ and a sophisticated information encoding and processing center, with an extensive intrinsic nervous system sufficiently sophisticated to qualify as a *heart brain*. Its circuitry enables it to learn, remember, and make functional decisions independent of the cranial brain (Armour, 2003; Armour & Ardell, 1994). Moreover, numerous experiments have demonstrated that patterns of cardiac afferent neurological input to the brain not only affect autonomic regulatory centers, but also influence higher brain centers involved in perception and emotional processing (Frysinger & Harper, 1990; McCraty, 2003; Sandman, Walker & Berka, 1982).

One tool that has proven valuable in examining heart-brain interactions is heart rate variability analysis. Heart rate variability (HRV), derived from the electrocardiogram (ECG), is a measure of the naturally occurring beat-to-beat changes in heart rate. The analysis of HRV, or *heart rhythms*, provides a powerful, noninvasive measure of neurocardiac function that reflects heart-brain interactions and autonomic nervous system dynamics, which are particularly sensitive to changes in emotional states (McCraty, Atkinson, Tiller, Reiu & Watkins, 1995; Tiller, McCraty & Atkinson, 1996). Research conducted by the Institute of Heart-Math, along with that of others, suggests an important link between emotions and changes in the patterns of both efferent (descending) and afferent (ascending) autonomic activity (Collet, Vernet-Maury, Delhomme & Dittmar, 1997; Ekman, Levenson & Friesen, 1983; McCraty, 2003; McCraty et al., 1995; McCraty, Barrios-Choplin, Rozman, Atkinson & Watkins, 1998; Tiller et al., 1996).

Changes in autonomic activity lead to dramatic changes in the *pattern* of the heart's rhythm, often without any change in the *amount* of heart rate variability. Specifically, researchers have found that during the experience of emotions such as anger, frustration, or anxiety, heart rhythms become more erratic and disordered, indicating less synchronization in the reciprocal action that ensues between the parasympathetic and sympathetic branches of the autonomic nervous system (ANS) (McCraty et al., 1995). In contrast, sustained positive emotions, such as appreciation, love, or compassion, are associated with highly ordered or *coherent* patterns in the heart rhythms, reflecting greater synchronization between the two branches of the ANS, and a shift in autonomic balance toward increased parasympathetic activity (Fig. 1) (McCraty et al., 1995, 1998; McCraty, Atkinson, Tomasino, Goelitz & Mayrovitz, 1999; Tiller et al., 1996).

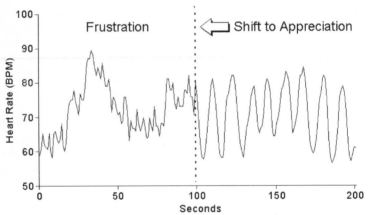

Fig. 1. Emotions Are Reflected in Our Heart Rhythm Patterns. *Note:* Real-time heart rate variability (heart rhythm) pattern of an individual making an intentional shift from a self-induced state of frustration to genuine feeling of appreciation by using a HeartMath positive emotion refocusing technique (Freeze-Frame). It is of note that when the recording is analyzed statistically, the *amount* of heart rate variability is found to remain virtually the same during the two different emotional states; however, the *pattern* of the heart rhythm changes distinctly. Note the immediate shift from an erratic, disordered heart rhythm pattern associated with frustration to a smooth, harmonious, sine wave-like (coherent) pattern as the individual uses the positive emotion refocusing technique and self-generates heartfelt feelings of appreciation.

Earlier research on conversations that flow from the heart and body to the brain provided evidence that afferent input from the cardiovascular system could significantly affect *perception and behavior* (J. I. Lacey & Lacey, 1970; Rosenfeld, 1977). Behavioral and neurophysiological data suggested that sensory-motor integration could be modified by cardiovascular activity (B. C. Lacey & Lacey, 1974; J. I. Lacey & Lacey, 1970). The research also established relationships between the heart's afferent signals and reaction times, showing that decreasing heart rate in the anticipatory period of reaction time experiments quickens reaction times, while increasing heart rate slows reaction times (J. I. Lacey & Lacey, 1970).

To date, extensive experimental data have been gathered documenting the role played by afferent input from the heart in modulating such varied processes as pain perception (Randich & Gebhart, 1992), hormone production (Drinkhill & Mary, 1989), electrocortical activity, and cognitive functions (Rau, Pauli, Brody & Elbert, 1993; Rosenfeld, 1977; Sandman et al., 1982; van der Molen, Somsen & Orlebeke, 1985). In addition, scientists now have a framework for understanding how patterns of afferent input and emotional processes go hand in hand, which provides support for a systems-oriented model of emotion. This model includes the heart, brain, and the nervous and hormonal systems as fundamental components of a dynamic, interactive network that underlies the emergence of emotional experience (McCraty, 2003; McCraty et al., 1998).

The model builds on the theory of emotion proposed by Pribram (Pribram & Melges, 1969) where the brain serves as a pattern identification and matching system. From this view, past experiences build an internal set of familiar patterns, which are maintained in the neural architecture. Inputs to the brain from both the external and internal environments contribute to the maintenance of these patterns. Throughout the body, many processes provide constant rhythmic inputs with which the brain becomes familiar. This includes the heart's rhythmic activity; digestive, respiratory and hormonal rhythms; and patterns of muscular tension, particularly facial expressions. Such inputs are continuously monitored by the brain to organize perception, feelings, and behavior. When an input pattern is sufficiently different from the familiar reference pattern, this *mismatch*, or *departure from the familiar*, underlies the generation of feelings and emotions (McCraty, 2003).

When inputs do not match the existing program, an adjustment must be made in an attempt to achieve control and return to stability. One way to reestablish control is by taking an outward action. We run away or fight if threatened or do something to draw attention if feeling ignored. We can also reestablish stability by making an internal adjustment (without any overt action). For example, a confrontation at work may lead to feelings of anger, which can prompt inappropriate behavior (e.g. shouting). However, through internal adjustments, we can *self-manage* our feelings in order to inhibit these responses, reestablish stability, and maintain our composure.

We observe two sets of emotions; those that reflect current order and those that reflect expectation of future order. Emotions, signals of perturbation and its cessation, and the initiation of processes necessary to reestablish control, can thus be divided into *concurrent* and *prospective* encounters. The concurrent reflects the degree of match or mismatch between the current inputs and the reference pattern in the here-and-now (Pribram & Melges, 1969). A mismatch creates arousal, with an achievement of regaining a match or control characterized by gratification. The prospective affects can be either optimistic or pessimistic. Inputs to the neural system are appraised and compared to memories of past outcomes associated with similar inputs or situations. If the historical outcomes of similar situations are positive, an optimistic affect results (e.g. interest, confidence, or hope). If, however, the memory of past outcomes has led to the expectation of failure to achieve control, the current inputs are accompanied by pessimistic feelings regarding the future (e.g. annoyance, apprehension, hopelessness, or depression).

It is through practice and experience that inputs become appraised as relevant or irrelevant, hopeful or hopeless, appreciated or unappreciated. As we encounter new situations, experience new inputs, and learn how to gain or maintain control, we expand our repertoire of successful outcomes. The more repertoires available, the more likely a new input will be assessed as optimistic with a high probability of success in maintaining control. Organization of sequences of input patterns and behaviors into hierarchically arranged programs give a person flexibility and adaptability.

Once a stable baseline pattern or program is established, the neural systems attempt to maintain a match between the baseline pattern and current inputs and the outcomes of projected future behaviors. If the baseline pattern becomes maladapted, the system will still strive to maintain a match to that pattern, even though it is not in our best interest. There are many examples of maladaptation. For example, one may adapt to a convenience to the point of it becoming an *expectancy*. Something is then taken for granted – rather than truly appreciated. Therefore, if an individual does not get what he/she wants or expects, a mismatch occurs and there is emotional discord.

Monitoring the alterations in the rates, rhythms, and patterns of afferent traffic is a key function of the cortical and emotional systems in the brain. Thus, input originating from many different bodily organs and systems is ultimately involved in determining our emotional experience. The heart, however, as a primary and consistent generator of rhythmic information patterns in the human body, and possessing more extensive afferent communication with the brain than other organs, plays a particularly important role (McCraty, 2003; McCraty & Atkinson, 2003). With each beat, dynamic patterns of neurological, hormonal, pressure, and electromagnetic information are sent to the brain. Cardiovascular afferent signals play a major part in establishing the dynamics of the baseline pattern or *set point* against which our current experience is compared. At lower brain levels, the heart's input is compared to references or set points that control blood pressure, affect respiration rate, and gate the flow of activity in the descending branches of the autonomic system (Langhorst, Schulz & Lambertz, 1983). From there, these signals cascade up to a number of subcortical or limbic areas that are involved in the processing of emotion (Oppenheimer & Hopkins, 1994; Rau et al., 1993).

Several lines of research support the perspective that changes in bodily states, particularly those mediated by the ANS, are crucial to emotional experience. One area of research has found that an absence of afferent feedback concerning autonomically generated bodily states is associated with impairments in emotional response (Critchley, Mathias & Dolan, 2001). Validation also comes from studies that examine effects of afferent input on the amygdaloid complex – the amygdala and associated nuclei, which play a pivotal role in storing and processing emotional memory and in attaching emotional significance to sensory stimuli (LeDoux, 1993). For example, neural activity in the central nucleus of the amygdala is synchronized to the cardiac cycle and is modulated by cardiovascular afferent input (Frysinger & Harper, 1990; Zhang, Harper & Frysinger, 1986).

The importance of changes in the pattern of afferent cardiac information is also evidenced in many cases of panic disorder. For example, one study found that DSM-IV criteria for panic disorder were fulfilled in more than two-thirds of patients with undiagnosed sudden-onset cardiac arrhythmias (Lessmeier et al., 1997). Arrhythmias generate a sudden change in the pattern of afferent information sent to the brain, which is detected as a mismatch, which results in feelings of anxiety and panic. When heart rhythms from this type of arrhythmia are compared to incoherent heart rhythm patterns produced by strong feelings of anxiety in an otherwise healthy individual, the plots are similar. By contrast, coherent heart rhythm patterns associated with sincere positive emotions are recognized as familiar and evoke feelings of security and well-being.

Our contention is that techniques capable of shifting the pattern of the heart's rhythmic activity actually modify one's emotional state. In fact, people commonly use just such an intervention – simply altering their breathing rhythm by taking several slow, deep breaths. Most people do not realize, however, that the reason breathing techniques are effective in helping to shift one's emotional state is because changing one's breathing rhythm modulates the heart's rhythmic activity (Hirsch & Bishop, 1981).

PHYSIOLOGICAL COHERENCE

Our research on emotion has identified distinct physiological correlates of heartfelt positive affective states. We have introduced the term *physiological coherence* to describe a functional mode encompassing a number of related physiological phenomena that are frequently associated with feelings of appreciation. In physics, the term *coherence* is used to describe the ordered or constructive distribution of power within a waveform. The more stable the frequency and shape of the waveform, the higher the coherence.

An example of a coherent wave is the sine wave. The term *autocoherence* denotes this kind of coherence. In physiological systems this type of coherence describes the degree of order and stability in the rhythmic activity generated by a single oscillatory system. Coherence also describes two or more waves that are either phase or frequency-locked. A common example is the laser, in which multiple waves phase-lock together, producing a coherent energy wave. In physiology, coherence is used to describe a functional mode in which two or more of the body's oscillatory systems, such as respiration and heart rhythms, become *entrained* and oscillate at the same frequency. The term *cross-coherence* is used to specify this type of coherence.

Interestingly, all the above apply to the study of emotional physiology. We have found that sincere positive emotions such as appreciation are associated with a higher degree of coherence *within* the heart's rhythmic activity (autocoherence). During such states there also tends to be increased coherence *between* different physiological oscillatory systems (cross-coherence/entrainment) (Tiller et al., 1996). Typically, entrainment is observed between heart rhythms, respiratory rhythms, and blood pressure oscillations. That stated, other biological oscillators, including very low frequency brain rhythms, craniosacral rhythms, electrical potentials measured across the skin, and rhythms in the digestive system, can also become entrained (McCraty & Atkinson, 2003).

A related phenomenon that can also occur during physiological coherence is *resonance*. In physics, resonance refers to a phenomenon whereby an abnormally large vibration is produced in a system in response to a stimulus whose frequency is the same as, or nearly the same as, the natural vibratory frequency of the system. The frequency of the vibration produced in such a state is said to be the *resonant frequency* of the system. When the human system is operating in the coherent mode, increased synchronization occurs between the sympathetic and parasympathetic branches of the ANS, and entrainment between the heart rhythms, respiration,

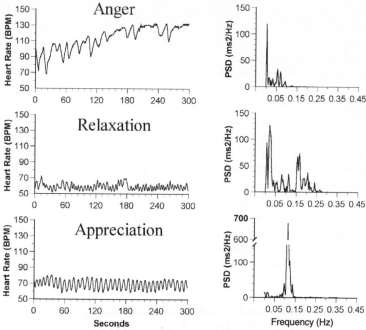

Fig. 2. Heart Rhythm Patterns During Different Psychophysiological States. *Note:* Heart rate tachograms, showing beat-to-beat changes in heart rate (left) and heart rate variability power spectra (right) typical of different emotional/psychophysiological states. Anger (top) is characterized by a lower frequency, disordered heart rhythm pattern and increasing mean heart rate. As can be seen in the power spectrum, the rhythm is primarily in the very low frequency band, which is associated with sympathetic nervous system activity. Relaxation (center) results in a higher frequency, lower-amplitude rhythm, indicating reduced auto- nomic outflow. In this case, increased power in the high frequency band of the power spec- trum is observed, reflecting increased parasympathetic activity (the relaxation response). In contrast, sustained positive emotions such as appreciation (bottom) are associated with a highly ordered, smooth, sine wave-like heart rhythm pattern (coherence). As can be seen in the power spectrum, this physiological mode is associated with a large, narrow peak in the low frequency band centered around 0.1 Hz. This indicates system-wide resonance, increased synchronization between the sympathetic and parasympathetic branches of the nervous system, and entrainment between the heart rhythm pattern, respiration, and blood pressure rhythms. The coherent mode is also associated with increased parasympathetic ac- tivity, thus encompassing a key element of the relaxation response, yet it is physiologically distinct from relaxation because the system is oscillating at its resonant frequency and there is increased harmony and synchronization in nervous system and heart-brain dynamics. In addition, the coherent mode does not necessarily involve a lowering of heart *rate* per se, or a change in the *amount* of variability, but rather, a change in heart rhythm *pattern*. Also, note the scale difference in the amplitude of the spectral peak during the coherent mode.

and blood pressure oscillations is observed. This occurs because these oscillatory subsystems are all vibrating at the resonant frequency of the system (~0.1 hertz). Thus, in the coherent mode, the power spectrum of the heart rhythm displays an abnormally large peak around 0.1 hertz (see Fig. 2).

Most models show the resonant frequency of the human cardiovascular system is determined by the feedback loops between the heart and brain (Baselli et al., 1994; deBoer, Karemaker & Strackee, 1987). The system especially vibrates at its resonant frequency when an individual is actively feeling appreciation or some other positive emotion (McCraty et al., 1995). In terms of physiological functioning, resonance confers a number of benefits to the system, which result in system-wide energy efficiency and metabolic energy savings (Langhorst, Schulz & Lambertz, 1984; Siegel et al., 1984). This provides a link between positive emotions and increased physiological efficiency, which may explain the growing number of correlations documented between positive emotions, improved health, and increased longevity. In addition, data suggest this functional mode also improves the cognitive processing of sensory information (McCraty, 2002; McCraty & Atkinson, 2003).

APPRECIATION: HEART AND BRAIN IN HARMONY

Physiological coherence is also associated with increased *synchronization* between the heartbeat and alpha rhythms in the electroencephalogram (EEG). In experiments measuring heartbeat-evoked potentials, it was found that the brain's alpha wave activity (8–12 hertz frequency range) is naturally synchronized to the cardiac cycle. However, when subjects used a positive emotion-focused technique to self-induce a feeling of appreciation, their heart rhythm coherence significantly increased, as did the ratio of the alpha rhythm that was synchronized to the heart (McCraty, 2002; McCraty & Atkinson, 2003).

Further research demonstrated that increased heart rhythm coherence correlates with significant improvements in cognitive performance in auditory discrimination tasks, which require subjects to focus and pay attention, discriminate subtle tone differences, and react quickly and accurately. Not only did increases in heart rhythm coherence accompany increased cognitive performance, but also the degree of coherence correlated with task performance across all subjects during all tasks (McCraty, 2002; McCraty & Atkinson, 2003). Such research provides support for the concept that the *pattern* of cardiac afferent input reaching the brain can inhibit or facilitate cortical function significantly beyond the micro-rhythm of inhibition/facilitation associated with simple changes in heart rate that was documented by earlier research. Thus, findings continue to point to a potential physiological link between appreciation and improvements in faculties such as motor skills, focused attention, and discrimination.

In summary, we use the term *coherence* to describe a physiological mode that encompasses entrainment, resonance and synchronization – distinct but related phenomena, all of which emerge from the harmonious interactions of the body's subsystems. Correlates of physiological coherence include: increased synchronization between the two branches of the ANS, a shift in autonomic balance toward increased parasympathetic activity, increased heart-brain syn-chronization, increased vascular resonance, and entrainment between diverse physiological oscillatory systems. The coherent mode is reflected by a smooth, sine wave-like pattern in the heart rhythms, and a narrow-band, high-amplitude peak in the low frequency range of the HRV power spectrum, at a frequency of about 0.1 hertz.

RESEARCH WITH APPRECIATION IN ORGANIZATIONS

To explore how participants experience the Appreciative Inquiry process on a psychophysiological level, a research study was conducted at the Department of Veterans Affairs Medical Center in Washington, DC (Sekerka, 2002). Two hundred twenty-four employees took part in a study examining their emotional experience as a result of their engagement in different organizational change processes. Participants reflected on their work situation with either an appreciative or problem-based focus. As in the *Discovery Phase* of the Appreciative Inquiry process, those in appreciative conditions were asked to recall a time when things were at their best on the job or with their organization. Conversely, those in a problem-based approach were asked to recall a time when things were not at their best on the job or with their organization.

While participants in the problem-based approach showed no change, employees in the appreciative conditions experienced a reduction in negative affect and lowered heart rate. Further, a significant increase in HRV was specifically attributable to those who reflected on appreciative thoughts about their organization. This finding was of particular interest because it suggests that outward-focused appreciation may have more pronounced links to positive psychophysiological effects than inward-focused appreciation. The results of this study suggest that individuals engaged in Appreciative Inquiry – focusing appreciatively on their organization – became less negative, more relaxed, and less stressed (Sekerka, 2002).

Interestingly, the indicators reflecting increases in HRV occurred during the act of reflection as opposed to after the Appreciative Inquiry experimental encounter. Given these results, it appears that *the act or process of positive reflection outside of self* is where beneficial impacts may be the most prominent. That is, it is the actual process of thinking appreciatively about the organization that may be the entry point for inducing favorable shifts in one's psychophysiological health and well-being. We see that when individuals' cognitive focus is centered on appreciation beyond the self, this leads to a shift in feeling, whereupon beneficial physiological changes can occur. With a lowered heart rate reflecting a change in autonomic balance towards decreased sympathetic and increased parasympathetic activity, the use of Appreciative Inquiry can now be predicted to be associated with other competencies such as improved cognitive task performance and increased accuracy of perception and reaction time (B. C. Lacey & Lacey, 1974; J. I. Lacey & Lacey, 1970; Sandman, Walker & Berka, 1982).

In summary, research has documented that participating in the *Discovery Phase* of Appreciative Inquiry, focusing on the best of one's organization, leads to a favorable change in psychophysiological well-being. Unlike individuals focusing on what is wrong, the deficits or problems in their organization or with their jobs, those who look to the best of their organization experience decreased negative affect and favorable shifts in ANS activity (Sekerka, 2002). Short-term increases in HRV, present in the appreciative approach, indicate less mental workload during that period (Jorna, 1992). While these benefits were short-term, we see engagement in the initial phase of the Appreciative Inquiry reduces negative emotions and helps employees relax. These findings demonstrate the potential for health benefits for those engaging in Appreciative Inquiry in workplace settings and corroborate the beneficial health outcomes associated with the use of the positive emotion-focused techniques (McCraty, Atkinson & Tomasino, 2001; McCraty & Childre, 2002).

FURTHER INQUIRY

While the research described here documents favorable outcomes of Appreciative Inquiry, numerous of unanswered questions remain. One issue, the sustainability of positive emotions, is of particular importance. How can organizational members create a state of psychophysiological coherence and positive emotion after an Appreciative Inquiry encounter? How can the Appreciative Inquiry dialogue be prolonged in an organization long after the practitioner leaves and members need to move forward with the next steps? How can we help individuals to respond positively to change on a daily basis, specifically helping them to reframe negative mindsets and create long-term health and well-being over time?

One efficient and effective avenue of intervention may be to provide training for organizational members in the use of positive emotion-focused techniques designed to help individuals reduce stress, increase positive affect, and improve performance in real time. A number of heart-based refocusing and emotional restructuring tools and techniques developed by the Institute of HeartMath have been demonstrated to yield measurable improvements in heath, emotional well-being, and performance at both the individual and organizational levels (Childre & Cryer, 2000; McCraty et al., 2001). Organization-relevant outcomes associated with the practice of these techniques include increases in productivity, goal clarity, job satisfaction, communication effectiveness, and reductions in employee turnover (Barrios-Choplin, McCraty & Cryer, 1997; Barrios-Choplin, McCraty, Sundram & Atkinson, 1999; McCraty, Atkinson & Tomasino, 2003; McCraty, Atkinson, Tomasino & Sundram, 1999).

We believe positive emotion-focused techniques are effective in helping to *build back energy* that has been depleted by persistent mental processing or negative emotional arousal, thereby enhancing health and favorably impacting numerous domains of performance. Further research is needed to investigate both short-term and long-term health, organizational, and quality of life benefits associated with the use of positive emotion-focused techniques in conjunction with Appreciative Inquiry. Refocusing and emotional restructuring techniques such as *Freeze-Frame* and *Heart Lock-In* (Childre, 1998; Childre & Cryer, 2000; Childre & Martin, 1999; Childre & Rozman, 2002), which help individuals self-generate and sustain feelings of appreciation, can be used in association with Appreciative Inquiry to complement one another.[1]

To advance this sustainability inquiry, researchers can compare workplace settings, those with and without established daily appreciative practices, to determine differences in health and well-being over time. Only by employing techniques on a regular basis will we be able to examine the long-term *quality of life* repercussions. Designing longitudinal studies will be an important next step in Appreciative Inquiry's practice and theoretical development. In addition, we recommend that current deficit-based assessment programs, tools, and techniques be augmented with strength-based appreciative approaches. It is important to create learning and development programs that focus on the positive to harvest both short and long-term benefits.

By moving Appreciative Inquiry beyond its current scope, coupling the best of this process with positive emotion refocusing and emotional restructuring tools, organizations have the potential to enhance health and well-being, performance, and *quality of life* in the workplace on an ongoing basis. Studies that validate these propositions will help expand the capabilities of Appreciative Inquiry and promote interventions that foster appreciation on a sustained basis in the workplace. Equally important are investigations that link positive emotion-based approaches with favorable modifications of key organization-relevant outcomes such as productivity, creativity and innovation, sales, key performance indicators, absenteeism, turnover, and customer satisfaction. Additional questions must examine organizational climate: does Appreciative Inquiry influence communication, social support, relationships between employees, and between employees and customers?

CONCLUSION

Research is beginning to substantiate what many have intuitively known – positive emotions not only feel good at the subjective level, but also bolster one's ability to meet life's challenges, optimize one's cognitive capacities, sustain constructive and meaningful relationships with others, and foster good health. We have identified and characterized a distinct mode of physiological functioning associated with the emotion of appreciation. Physiological coherence encompasses a number of related phenomena including entrainment, synchronization, and resonance. These favorable processes result from efficient and harmonious interactions of the body's subsystems. We suggest the coherent mode provides a potential physiological link between positive emotions and a range of favorable health-related, cognitive, and psychosocial outcomes that have been associated with positive emotional experience.

We have outlined how the brain functions as a pattern identification and matching system, and highlighted the role of afferent bodily input in establishing the familiar references critical in determining emotional experience. As a principal source of rhythmic information patterns that influence the physiological, cognitive, and emotional systems, the heart plays an important role in the generation and perception of emotion. Therefore, shifts in heart rhythm patterns can bring about significant changes in perception and emotional experience.

Appreciative Inquiry and positive emotion-focused techniques serve to help shift the heart's rhythmic patterns with self-induced feelings of appreciation. Independently, these processes have been shown to be an effective means to reduce stress and negative emotions in the moment. With sustained appreciative practices, such efforts will instill more positive perceptions, expression, emotions, and behaviors. As a result, a positive transformation of our shared and emergent realities can be created on both the individual and collective organizational level.

Appreciative approaches not only significantly reduce stress, but also lead to enduring positive changes in attitude, relationships, and worldview.

How we choose to experience the world contributes to our reality. We see that we can alter our emotional experience and, in so doing, can generate favorable outcomes. With interactions focused on what we appreciate, the workplace can be an environment for positive transformation, serving to contribute to both individual and collective well-being.

NOTE

1. HeartMath, Heart Lock-In, and Freeze-Frame are registered trademarks of the Institute of HeartMath.

ACKNOWLEDGMENTS

Special thanks go to the Yellow Roadway Corporation, who helped to fund the VA research. Our appreciation is also extended to Rob Kolodner, Evelyn Grigsby, and those who participated in the study. Finally, we thank Mike Atkinson and Dana Tomasino, who have been tremendously helpful throughout our extended research process.

REFERENCES

Anderson, H. (1997). *Conversation, language, and possibilities: A postmodern approach to therapy.* New York: Basic Books.

Argyris, C., Putnam, R., & McLain Smith, D. (1985). *Action science.* San Francisco: Jossey-Bass.

Armour, J. A. (2003). *Neurocardiology – Anatomical and functional principles.* Boulder Creek, CA: HeartMath Research Center, Institute of HeartMath, Publication No. 03-011.

Armour, J., & Ardell, J. (Eds) (1994). *Neurocardiology.* New York: Oxford University Press.

Ashby, F. G., Isen, A. M., & Turken, A. U. (1999). A neuropsychological theory of positive affect and its influence on cognition. *Psychological Review, 106*, 529–550.

Aspinwall, L. (1998). Rethinking the role of positive affect in self-regulation. *Motivation and Emotion, 22*, 1–32.

Bamburg, M. (2000). Language and communication – What develops? Determining the role of language practices for a theory of development. In: N. Budwig & I. C. Uzgiris et al. (Eds), *Communication: An Arena of Development* (pp. 55–77). Westport, CT: Ablex Publishing.

Barrios-Choplin, B., McCraty, R., & Cryer, B. (1997). An inner quality approach to reducing stress and improving physical and emotional wellbeing at work. *Stress Medicine, 13*, 193–201.

Barrios-Choplin, B., McCraty, R., Sundram, J., & Atkinson, M. (1999). The effect of employee self-management training on personal and organizational quality. Boulder Creek, CA: HeartMath Research Center, Institute of HeartMath, Publication No. 99-083.

Baselli, G., Cerutti, S., Badilini, F., Biancardi, L., Porta, A., Pagani, M., Lombardi, F., Rimoldi, O., Furlan, R., & Malliani, A. (1994). Model for the assessment of heart period variability interactions of respiration influences. *Medical and Biological Engineering and Computing*, *32*, 143–152.

Blakeslee, T. (1997). *The attitude factor: Extend your life by changing the way you think*. London: Thorsons/HarperCollins.

Bohr, H. (1967). My father. In: S. Rozental (Ed.), *Niels Bohr: His Life and Work as Seen by His Friends and Colleagues*. New York: Wiley.

Childre, D. (1998). *Freeze-Frame: A scientifically proven technique for clear decision making and improved health*. Boulder Creek, CA: Planetary.

Childre, D., & Cryer, B. (2000). *From chaos to coherence: The power to change performance*. Boulder Creek, CA: Planetary.

Childre, D., & Martin, H. (1999). *The HeartMath solution*. San Francisco: HarperSanFrancisco.

Childre, D., & Rozman, D. (2002). *Overcoming emotional chaos: Eliminate anxiety, lift depression and create security in your life*. San Diego: Jodere Group.

Collet, C., Vernet-Maury, E., Delhomme, G,, & Dittmar, A. (1997). Autonomic nervous system response patterns specificity to basic emotions. *Journal of the Autonomic Nervous System*, *62*, 45–57.

Cooperrider, D. L., & Srivastva, S. (1999). Appreciative Inquiry in organizational life. In: S. Srivastva & D. L. Cooperrider (Eds), *Appreciative Management and Leadership: The Power of Positive Thought and Action in Organization* (Rev. ed., pp. 401–441). Cleveland, OH: Lakeshore Communications.

Cooperrider, D. L., & Whitney, D. (1999). Appreciative inquiry: A positive revolution in change. In: P. Holman & T. Devane (Eds), *The Change Handbook: Group Methods for Shaping the Future*. San Francisco: Berrett-Koehler Publishers.

Cooperrider, D. L., & Whitney (2000). A positive revolution in change: Appreciative inquiry. In: R. T. Golembiewski (Ed.), *Handbook of Organizational Behavior* (2nd ed., pp. 611–629). New York: Marcel Dekker.

Critchley, H. D., Mathias, C. J., & Dolan, R. J. (2001). Neuroanatomical basis for first- and second-order representations of bodily states. *Nature Neuroscience*, *4*, 207–212.

Danner, D. D., Snowdon, D. A., & Friesen, W. V. (2001). Positive emotions in early life and longevity: Findings from the nun study. *Journal of Personality and Social Psychology*, *80*, 804–813.

deBoer, R. W., Karemaker, J. M., & Strackee, J. (1987). Hemodynamic fluctuations and baroreflex sensitivity in humans: A beat-to-beat model. *American Journal of Physiology*, *253*, H680–H689.

Drinkhill, M. J., & Mary, D. A. (1989). The effect of stimulation of the atrial receptors on plasma cortisol level in the dog. *Journal of Physiology*, *413*, 299–313.

Ekman, P., Levenson, R. W., & Friesen, W. V. (1983). Autonomic nervous system activity distinguishes among emotions. *Science*, *221*, 1208–1210.

Fredrickson, B. L. (2001). The role of positive emotions in positive psychology: The broaden-and-build theory of positive emotions. *American Psychologist*, *56*(3), 218–226.

Fredrickson, B. L. (2002). Positive emotions. In: C. R. Snyder & S. J. Lopez (Eds), *Handbook of Positive Psychology*. (pp. 120–134). New York: Oxford University Press.

Frijda, N. H. (1986). *The emotions*. Cambridge, England: Cambridge University Press.

Frysinger, R. C., & Harper, R. M. (1990). Cardiac and respiratory correlations with unit discharge in epileptic human temporal lobe. *Epilepsia*, *31*, 162–171.

Gergen, K. J. (1988). If persons are texts. In: S. B. Messer, L. A. Sass & R. L. Woolfolk (Eds), *Hermeneutics and Psychology Theory* (pp. 28–51). New Brunswick, NJ: Rutgers University Press.

Gergen, K. J. (1994). *Realities and relationships: Soundings in social construction*. Cambridge, MA: Harvard University Press.

Gergen, K. J. (2001). Psychological science in a postmodern context. *American Psychologist, 56*(10), 803–813.

Gillham, J. E. (2000). *The science of optimism and hope: Research essays in honor of Martin E. P. Seligman*. Philadelphia: Templeton Foundation Press.

Goldman, S. L., Kraemer, D. T., & Salovey, P. (1996). Beliefs about mood moderate the relationship of stress to illness and symptom reporting. *Journal of Psychosomatic Research, 41*, 115–128.

Hirsch, J. A., & Bishop, B. (1981). Respiratory sinus arrhythmia in humans: How breathing pattern modulates heart rate. *American Journal of Physiology, 241*, H620–H629.

Isen, A. M. (1987). Positive affect, cognitive processes, and social behavior. *Advances in Experimental Social Psychology, 20*, 203–253.

Isen, A. M. (1999). Positive affect. In: T. Dalgleish & M. Power (Eds), *Handbook of Cognition and Emotion* (pp. 522–539). New York: Wiley.

Isen, A. M., Daubman, K. A., & Nowicki, G. P. (1987). Positive affect facilitates creative problem solving. *Journal of Personality and Social Psychology, 52*, 1122–1131.

Johnstone, T., & Scherer, K. R. (2000). Vocal communication of emotion. In: M. Lewis & J. M. Haviland-Jones (Eds), *Handbook of Emotions* (2nd ed., pp. 220–235). New York: Guilford Press.

Jorna, P. G. A. M. (1992). Spectral analysis of heart rate and psychological state: A review of its validity as a workload index. *Biological Psychology, 34*, 237–257.

Lacey, B. C., & Lacey, J. I. (1974). Studies of heart rate and other bodily processes in sensorimotor behavior. In: P. Obrist, A. Black, J. Brener & L. DiCara (Eds), *Cardiovascular Psychophysiology* (pp. 538–564). Chicago: Aldine.

Lacey, J. I., & Lacey, B. C. (1970). Some autonomic-central nervous system interrelationships. In: P. Black (Ed.), *Physiological Correlates of Emotion* (pp. 205–227). New York: Academic Press.

Langhorst, P., Schulz, G., & Lambertz, M. (1983). Integrative control mechanisms for cardiorespiratory and somatomotor functions in the reticular formation of the lower brain stem. In: P. Grossman, K. H. L. Janssen & D. Vaitl (Eds), *Cardiorespiratory and Cardiosomatic Psychophysiology* (pp. 9–39). New York and London: Plenum Press.

Langhorst, P., Schulz, G., & Lambertz, M. (1984). Oscillating neuronal network of the "common brainstem system." In: K. Miyakawa, H. Koepchen & C. Polosa (Eds), *Mechanisms of Blood Pressure Waves* (pp. 257–275). Tokyo: Japan Scientific Societies Press.

LeDoux, J. E. (1993). Emotional memory systems in the brain. *Behavioural Brain Research, 58*, 69–79.

Lessmeier, T. J., Gamperling, D., Johnson-Liddon, V., Fromm, B. S., Steinman, R. T., Meissner, M. D., & Lehmann, M. H. (1997). Unrecognized paroxysmal supraventricular tachycardia: Potential for misdiagnosis as panic disorder. *Archives of Internal Medicine, 157*, 537–543.

Madison, G. B. (1988). *The hermeneutics of postmodernity*. Bloomington, IN: Indiana University Press.

Magruder, W. J., & Mohr, B. J. (2001). *Appreciative inquiry: Change at the speed of imagination*. San Francisco, CA: Jossey-Bass/Pfeiffer.

McCraty, R. (2002). Influence of cardiac afferent input on heart-brain synchronization and cognitive performance. *International Journal of Psychophysiology, 45*(1–2), 72–73.

McCraty, R. (2003). *Heart-brain neurodynamics: The making of emotions*. Boulder Creek, CA: HeartMath Research Center, Institute of HeartMath, Publication No. 03-015.

McCraty, R., & Atkinson, M. (2003). *Psychophysiological coherence*. Boulder Creek, CA: HeartMath
    Research Center, Institute of HeartMath, Publication No. 03-016.
McCraty, R., Atkinson, M., Tiller, W. A., Rein, G., & Watkins, A. D. (1995). The effects of emotions
    on short term heart rate variability using power spectrum analysis. *American Journal of
    Cardiology, 76*, 1089–1093.
McCraty, R., Atkinson, M., & Tomasino, D. (2001). *Science of the heart*. Boulder Creek, CA:
    HeartMath Research Center, Institute of HeartMath, Publication No. 01-001.
McCraty, R., Atkinson, M., & Tomasino, D. (2003). Impact of a workplace stress reduction program
    on blood pressure and emotional health in hypertensive employees. *Journal of Alternative and
    Complementary Medicine, 9*(3), 355–369.
McCraty, R., Atkinson, M., Tomasino, D., Goelitz, J., & Mayrovitz, H. N. (1999). The impact of an
    emotional self-management skills course on psychosocial functioning and autonomic recovery
    to stress in middle school children. *Integrative Physiological and Behavioral Science, 34*,
    246–268.
McCraty, R., Barrios-Choplin, B., Rozman, D., Atkinson, M., & Watkins, A. D. (1998). The impact of
    a new emotional self-management program on stress, emotions, heart rate variability, DHEA
    and cortisol. *Integrative Physiological and Behavioral Science, 33*, 151–170.
McCraty, R., & Childre, D. (2002). *The appreciative heart: The psychophysiology of positive
    emotions and optimal functioning*. Boulder Creek, CA: HeartMath Research Center, Institute
    of HeartMath, Publication No. 02-026.
McCraty, R., Tomasino, D., Atkinson, M., & Sundram, J. (1999). Impact of the HeartMath self-
    management skills program on physiological and psychological stress in police officers.
    Boulder Creek, CA: HeartMath Research Center, Institute of HeartMath, Publication
    No. 99-075.
Oppenheimer, S., & Hopkins, D. (1994). Suprabulbar neuronal regulation of the heart. In: J. A. Armour
    & J. L. Ardell (Eds), *Neurocardiology* (pp. 309–341). New York: Oxford University Press.
Palmer, P. (1998). *The courage to teach*. San Francisco, CA: Jossey-Bass.
Pribram, K. H., & Melges, F. T. (1969). Psychophysiological basis of emotion. In: P. J. Vinken &
    G. W. Bruyn (Eds), *Handbook of Clinical Neurology* (Vol. 3, pp. 316–341). Amsterdam:
    North-Holland.
Randich, A., & Gebhart, G. (1992). Vagal afferent modulation of nociception. *Brain Research Reviews,
    17*, 77–99.
Rau, H., Pauli, P., Brody, S., & Elbert, T. (1993). Baroreceptor stimulation alters cortical activity.
    Psychophysiology, 30, 322–325.
Rosenfeld, S. A. (1977). *Conversations between heart and brain*. Rockville, MD: National Institute
    of Mental Health.
Russek, L. G., & Schwartz, G. E. (1997). Feelings of parental caring predict health status in midlife:
    A 35-year follow-up of the Harvard Mastery of Stress Study. *Journal of Behavioral Medicine,
    20*, 1–13.
Salovey, P., Rothman, A. J., Detweiler, J. B., & Steward, W. T. (2000). Emotional states and physical
    health. *American Psychologist, 55*(1), 110–121.
Sandman, C. A., Walker, B. B., & Berka, C. (1982). Influence of afferent cardiovascular feedback on
    behavior and the cortical evoked potential. In: J. T. Cacioppo & R. E. Petty (Eds), *Perspectives
    in Cardiovascular Psychophysiology* (pp. 189–222). New York: Guilford Press.
Sekerka, L. E. (2002). *Exploring appreciative inquiry: A comparison of positive and problem based
    organizational change and development approaches in the workplace*. Unpublished doctoral
    dissertation, Case Western Reserve University, Cleveland, OH.

Sekerka, L. E., & Cooperrider, D. L. (2001). The appreciative inquiry conversation and its impact on affect, view of self, and creativity. Paper presented at the Academy of Management Annual Meeting, August, Washington, DC.

Sekerka, L. E., Cooperrider, D. L., & Wilken, J. (2001). An appreciative organizational development intervention: Positive emotions set the stage for change. Poster Session presented at the Positive Psychology Summit, October, Washington, DC.

Senge, P. M. (1990). *The fifth discipline: The art and practice of the learning organization.* New York: Doubleday.

Siegel, G., Ebeling, B. J., Hofer, H. W., Nolte, J., Roedel, H., & Klubendorf, D. (1984). Vascular smooth muscle rhythmicity. In: K. Miyakawa, H. Koepchen & C. Polosa (Eds), *Mechanisms of Blood Pressure Waves* (pp. 319–338). Tokyo: Japan Scientific Societies Press.

Tiller, W. A., McCraty, R., & Atkinson, M. (1996). Cardiac coherence: A new, noninvasive measure of autonomic nervous system order. *Alternative Therapies in Health and Medicine, 2*, 52–65.

van der Molen, M. W., Somsen, R. J. M., & Orlebeke, J. F. (1985). The rhythm of the heart beat in information processing. In: P. Ackles, J. R. Jennings & M. G. H. Coles (Eds), *Advances in Psychophysiology* (Vol. 1, pp. 89–165). London: JAI Press.

Vygotsky, L. S. (1986). *Thought and language* (Rev. ed.). A. Kozulin (Trans.). Cambridge, MA: MIT Press. (Original work published 1934.)

Whitney, D., & Shau, C. (1998). Appreciative inquiry: An innovative process or organization change. *Employment Relations Today, 25*(1), 11–28.

Zhang, J., Harper, R. M., & Frysinger, R. C. (1986). Respiratory modulation for neuronal discharge in the central nucleus of the amygdala during sleep and waking states. *Experimental Neurology, 91*, 193–207.

UNDERLYING RITUAL PRACTICES OF THE APPRECIATIVE INQUIRY SUMMIT: TOWARD A THEORY OF SUSTAINED APPRECIATIVE CHANGE

Edward H. Powley

ABSTRACT

This paper presents a framework to study organizational change using the metaphor of ritual. Concepts of myth and ritual facilitate understanding of change interventions. A qualitative study of Appreciative Inquiry helped answer the question: what mechanisms or processes explain the effect of the Appreciative Inquiry Summit? Four mechanisms, based on qualitative interviews and anthropological and sociological theory, explain why the AI Summit produces organizational change: (1) internal dialogue: recognizing a positive dimension and new vocabulary at the individual, interpersonal, and organizational levels of analysis; (2) communitas: the mechanism whereby new relationships form due to relational anti-structure; (3) commitment: how organization members cognitively and cathectically commit to the organization; and (4) longitudinal repetition: how sustained and continuous change involves repetition of ritual practices and the recognition.

Constructive Discourse and Human Organization
Advances in Appreciative Inquiry, Volume 1, 241–261
Copyright © 2004 by Elsevier Ltd.
All rights of reproduction in any form reserved
ISSN: 1475-9152/doi:10.1016/S1475-9152(04)01011-7

INTRODUCTION

Rituals exist to transform individuals and their societies and communities (Turner, 1967; Van Gennep, 1908/1960). For example, from a religious perspective, rituals are instrumental for transformational, sacred experiences, and in traditional or primitive societies, ritual plays a central role in daily tribal and religious life (Turner, 1967). Depending on the cultural group, a wide range of rituals exists. Some establish social order during conflict, marriage, birth, or death. Others transform youth into adults, men into husbands, and women into mothers. Because rituals focus on transformation, the study of ritual is of potential importance to the study of organizational change.

Multiple parallels exist between ritual and organizational change. We know from the study of ritual that rituals and rites of passage are powerful mechanisms for change at the individual, group, and cultural level, and rituals abound in the daily life of primitive societies. Rituals function to strengthen social relations, instill values and beliefs, and transform the young into responsible adults. Similar to ancient and primitive rituals documented by anthropologists (Eliade, 1967; Turner, 1967), organizational change, including the Appreciative Inquiry (AI) Summit (Whitney & Cooperrider, 1998, 2000), shapes lives and organizations using stories, symbolism, and ritual processes. Through organizational development and change, relationships are often stronger, organizational values and beliefs are taught, and individuals and organizations are transformed.

This chapter describes the juxtaposition of organizational change and rites of passage and also illustrates similarities between the AI Summit and a specific aspect of ritual, namely liminality. I argue that because organizational change and AI in particular have strong parallels to ritual practices, their effects should also be similar. I recast Appreciative Inquiry as a ritual of positive organizational change (Cooperrider & Sekerka, 2003), presenting first, a comparison between rites of passage and organizational development and change, and second, a comparison with a specific aspect of ritual and AI. Finally, I explore processes derived from qualitative interviews and literature from the field of anthropology to present mechanisms that explain why organizational development and AI produce change.

TRANSFORMATION THROUGH
RITUAL AND CHANGE

Literature on ritual and rites is relatively unexplored in the organizational domain. In order to familiarize the organizational scholar to this literature, I make a note on rites and rituals. Distinguished from rites, rituals are "prescribed formal behaviors for occasions not given to technological routine, having reference to beliefs in mystical beings or powers" (Turner, 1967, p. 19). Rites on the other hand, are singular, solemn, ceremonial moments, "elaborate, dramatic, planned set of activities" (Beyer & Trice, 1987, p. 6) within ritual which are coupled with symbols – "objects, activities, relationships, events, gestures, and spatial units in a ritual situation" (Beyer & Trice, 1987, p. 19). A rite of passage is a ritual with three specific phases or series of rites – rites of separation, rites of initiation (liminality), and rites of aggregation (reincorporation) (Van Gennep, 1908/1960). These phases correspond with the three phases of organizational change introduced by Kurt Lewin (1951) (unfreezing, moving, and refreezing), which have since become the trademark of organizational change.

Analysis of change as a ritual practice has received little attention in the field of organizational development and change. A few scholars have described rites and ceremony to classify types of change processes in organizations and groups (Beyer & Trice, 1987; Trice & Beyer, 1984). Their attempt to see similarities between ritual and change overlooks ritual as efficacious, indicating that it "seldom [produces] intended, practical consequences of any importance," and defines them as "a standardized, detailed set of techniques and behaviors that [manage] anxieties" (Beyer & Trice, 1987, p. 6). They postulate that *rites* serve a more practical function: to "combine various forms of cultural expressions and that often has both practical and expressive consequences" (Beyer & Trice, 1987, p. 6). From this perspective, rites of passage function as a transformational process with practical consequences, and, as we shall see, the rites of initiation or liminality play an important role in the Appreciative Inquiry change process, combining cultural expressions and fantastic shapes and forms.

Beyer and Trice's (1987; Trice & Beyer, 1984) analysis assumes that rituals are not intended to produce change. This may be attributed to three primary functions of ritual: (1) to define relationships between individuals and social groups; (2) to clarify boundaries, role hierarchy, and status; and (3) to impart knowledge regarding the importance of myths and traditions (Hocart, 1903). These purposes give the impression that ritual maintains the status quo rather than initiating change; however change implies movement between states such that in the transforming process, relationships are redefined, status roles are clarified, social structure is anchored, and ritual participants acquire new knowledge about themselves and their system. Said differently, rites of passage *do* transform, indeed, that is their very intent. Consistent with this paradox between stability and change, Srivastva and Fry (1992) note that "continuity is necessary to accomplish change that is transformational" (Srivastra & Fry, 1992, p. 3) and it is established by managing change to ensure long-term, sustainable effects.

Furthermore, rites and ritual restore order and social well-being to the members of a culture (Van Gennep, 1908/1960) by sharing and enacting creation myths during ritual – narratives about the origins of society, the earth, or a particular culture (Eliade, 1954, 1959, 1963, 1967). Such myths provide a renewing effect on the members such that they are strengthened as a corporate body. In this sense, "myth narrates a sacred history" and, is always an account of a "creation" (Eliade, 1963, pp. 5–6) because rituals are the source of life-giving creation and individual and cultural change. The restorative nature of change does not return participants to a former state, but propels them forward with new knowledge, new status, new roles, and new identity.

This chapter argues that the AI Summit produces positive organizational change precisely because of its inherent ritual nature. What will be shown here is more than the striking comparisons between Appreciative Inquiry and ritual practices. It attempts to uncover the underlying mechanism of organizational change processes that explain why a change effort like the AI Summit produces change in an organizational system.

RITES OF PASSAGE AND ORGANIZATIONAL CHANGE

The study of organizational development and change has a long tradition (Cummings & Worley, 1993; Grieves, 2000; Kleiner, 1996). Contemporary approaches to change include participatory action research (Greenwood, Whyte, & Harkavy, 1993; Reason & Bradbury, 2001), action learning (Morgan & Ramirez, 1984), action science (Argyris, Putnam & Smith, 1985), or self-design (Mohrman & Cummings, 1989). Among other change models (Beckhard, 1969; Beckhard & Harris, 1987; Bridges, 1980; Weisbord, 1991), Kurt Lewin (1951; Marrow, 1969) is well known for his unfreeze-movement-refreeze model. The parallels between Lewin's work and the anthropological literature on rites and ritual (Van Gennep, 1908/1960) are unmistakable (see Table 1).

Separation-Unfreezing

First, a person is removed from what is familiar, both in time and in space, from the known world, from common experiences. An initiate separates from kinship and other social relationships, and later stripped of identity and relations as well as the material world. In terms of the temporal, the individual transports to "mythical time" (Eliade, 1954). This temporal dimension is based on the belief that when

Table 1. Comparison of Rites of Passage and Lewin's Change Model.

Rites of Passage	Lewin's Change Model
Separation • "Symbolic. . . detachment of the individual or group either from a fixed point in social structure or a set of cultural conditions (a 'state')" • Accomplished when ritual subjects (individual or group) are separated from structural positions, kinship ties, and other social relationships	Unfreezing • Reduction of restraining forces maintaining equilibrium • Accomplished by introducing information that shows discrepancies between currently exhibited and desired behaviors
Initiation (Liminality) • Transition between stable states: ritual subjects are passengers through unknown territory where significant knowledge is revealed through sacred stories • Accomplished when ritual subjects acquire new identity and new norms to be adopted upon reincorporation	Moving (Changing) • A shift in "the behavior of the organization, department, or individual [toward] a new level" • Accomplished by developing "new behaviors, values, and attitudes"
Aggregation (Reincorporation) • "The passage is consummated": ritual subjects are "in a stable state once more" • Accomplished by ensuring that the newly initiated can function as a full member of society	Refreezing • Stabilization of "the organization at a new state of equilibrium" • Accomplished by implementing "[support] mechanisms" (i.e. "organizational culture, norms, policies, and structures") that reinforce the new state
Turner (1967, pp. 93–94), Van Gennep (1908/1960)	Cummings and Worley (1993, p. 27)

rituals, in this case rituals of initiation, are performed, the person is transported to primordial time, a time of creation, or the creation of the cosmos. Separation temporally and spatially induces conditions where initiation takes place. From a Lewinain system's perspective, there is a reduction in restraining forces that maintain equilibrium. The person is "unfrozen" from previous ideals held in balance within the organization. This is accomplished by introducing information demonstrative of discrepancies between currently held and desired values and behaviors.

Initiation-Moving

The second phase is initiation or liminality. It represents the unknown, death, or transition into a new life. Fear, ambiguity, danger, and risk characterize this phase wherein initiates question previously held assumptions. Individuals in this phase do not outwardly display rank or status. More importantly however, during this period, significant knowledge is imparted; that knowledge comes in the form of myths or stories: creation myths (narratives describing origins), ceremonial rites, or other events. During the initiation, the individual transforms into a new person with a new identity and new norms for relating and being, preparatory to their reestablishment within the collective, society, or group. This represents a shift in behavior of the organization, department, or individual, and is accomplished by developing behaviors and values consistent with the newly acquired knowledge.

Aggregation-Refreezing

Following liminality is aggregation or reincorporation, which ensures that the newly initiated can function as a full member of society. Upon completion of their initiation, individuals return to the group with a higher status and with the expectation that they will act according to established norms. With reincorporation come changes in roles, identity, and status: individuals take on a transformed identity with new possibilities and expectations as they are transported intellectually (due to new knowledge) and emotionally (due to changes in status and identity) to a new space (physical and non-physical). In Lewin's model, this phase represents a stabilizing process, returning the organization to a new level, a new state of equilibrium. This is accomplished through the application of mechanisms and processes that support a new culture, new policies, or new structures.

Lewin's three-step model for organizational change has influenced the social and behavioral sciences over the past 40 years; in particular, it has been established in the organizational sciences as a foundational process for change (Cummings & Worley, 1993). As an outgrowth of his change model, there exist processes of change that encourage large-scale participation to foster ownership among organizational members who further develop the organization (Cooperrider, 1999; Senge, 1990). Appreciative Inquiry is one innovative approach to large-system organizational change that focuses on the positive aspects of organizational life. As such, AI is a process of organizational transformation, a contemporary model for organizational development (Cummings & Worley, 1993), or a type of action research (Reason & Bradbury, 2001). In the context of rites and ritual, the Appreciative Inquiry Summit is the ritualized form of AI.

LIMINALITY AND APPRECIATIVE INQUIRY

The AI Summit applies Appreciative Inquiry in a large group, whole system context (Powley, Cooperrider & Fry, 2002; Weisbord & Janoff, 1995; Whitney &

Cooperrider, 1998, 2000) vs. small group strategic organizational change based on agreement and collaboration among executives or senior managers (Burke, 1987; Cummings & Worley, 1993). Furthermore, AI focuses on the positive and appreciative organizational histories, whereas other change interventions view organizations through a deficiency-oriented lens. AI appreciates, values, and recognizes the best in people and organizations by affirming strengths, successes, and potential. It also involves exploration and discovery through inquiry, a cooperative search for the best in people, organizations, and larger integrated systems (Cooperrider, 1999). During the AI Summit, participants search out goodness in others and in their organizations to facilitate change and develop others within those structures (Barrett & Cooperrider, 1990; Cooperrider & Srivastra, 1987).

In the language of rites of passage, the AI Summit represents a liminal experience for organizational members and the whole organization. Turner (1967) further developed the second phase of rites of passage, initiation or liminality. The term liminality derives from the Latin *limen*, meaning threshold, or between two statuses. Turner describes this phase in more detail, explaining the characteristics and elements of liminality. This liminal space, as the center of ritual practice, serves to heighten the awareness and importance of change. This is also true of the AI Summit process; the Summit represents the space between organizational realities in which organizational members carry the organization to a different level. Table 2 highlights the comparisons between liminality and the Appreciative Inquiry intervention.

Individuals pass through the liminal phase in order to take on new identities, new status, new commitments, and new relationships. During liminality, participants and organizations are "betwixt and between." Turner (1969) notes:

> Liminal entities are neither here nor there; they are betwixt and between the positions assigned and arrayed by law, custom, convention, and ceremonial. As such, their ambiguous and indeterminate attributes are expressed by a rich variety of symbols . . . Liminal entities . . . may be represented as possessing nothing . . . [indicating] that as liminal beings they have no status, property, insignia (p. 95).

Here, Turner highlights two important features of liminality relating to change and transformation in organizations. First, in the context of organizational change, both individuals and organizations are considered liminal entities (or ritual participants). This is based on the premise that individual action is foundational for social organizing. While the intent of this chapter is not to define levels of analysis and the structural aspects of change processes that differ by those levels, it is important to understand the structural relationship between individual and organizational level phenomena. On the one hand, the processes and

Table 2. Comparison of Liminality and Appreciative Inquiry.

Liminality	Appreciative Inquiry
Reduction of Culture • "[Reduce] the culture into recognized components or factors" • Make explicit the core values, and expected norms and behaviors of a group	Discovery • Uncover high point stories or peak moments of the organization's history through appreciative interviews • Identify the root causes of success, positive core, and proudest prouds
Dramatization • Characterize the core factors in "fantastic or monstrous patterns and shapes" • Exaggerate culture (i.e. values, behaviors, norms) by personifying mythical monsters or animals	Dream • Envision positive changes since the time of the Summit: what is new, better, or different • Perform images of the future organization: imagine and portray the most desirable culture
Cultural Reconstruction • Recombine cultural factors and exaggerations to make sense of the ritual experience • Prepare ritual subjects for the new state and status upon their reincorporation	Design • Develop provocative propositions (aspiration statements) that outline the future organization • Outline proposals for working toward 3-year aspirations
Turner (1967, p. 106)	Whitney and Cooperrider (1998)

manifestations at the organizational level are different from the individual level of analysis. Yet, to discuss the individual without implicating the organization runs the risk of reducing the potential for deeper understanding and appreciation of ritual in organizational life.

The second feature of liminality is the role of ambiguity amidst change. During rites of initiation, liminal entities are metaphorically (and sometimes physically) stripped of structural markers: status, rank, and position, representing equality between participants. This state is characterized as ambiguous, wherein the ritual subject "passes through a realm that has few or none of the attributes of the past or coming state" (Turner, 1969, p. 94). Individuals are neither here nor there; they are between states. At the organizational level, an organization's identity is called into question: what will be the organization's new strategy, what will relationships between management and labor look like, or what is the mission and vision of the organization?

The Appreciative Inquiry Summit adheres to patterns of myth, ritual, and transformation, derived from the anthropological literature. Appreciative Inquiry attempts to break from history (Powley et al., 2002) – an organizational history which is often viewed from a deficiency-orientation. AI re-discovers the rites and practices that are the basis for the creation (or re-creation) of a new history based in a new life-giving "mythology" (Eliade, 1967; Hocart, 1903). During the change process, individuals reach into the best of the past to discover the most life-giving properties, and that which amplifies human and organizational potential. The result is a new "mythology."

Liminality, the second phase of a rite of passage, forms the basis for communicating sacred symbols and conveying important messages regarding change to ritual participants and organizational members broadly. The liminal phase of ritual involves three processes: reducing the culture to its core factors, recombining those factors in "fantastic" patterns and shapes, and reconstructing an image of the future state and status (Turner, 1967). A comparison of these liminal processes to the Appreciative Inquiry Summit is helpful. The first three parts of the Summit – Discovery, Dream, and Design – correspond to Turner's description of liminal processes. Both represent a series of events and experiential activities that communicate information regarding change. They also involve a space where change is encouraged and valued. During these moments, Summit facilitators communicate the "sacra" (Turner, 1967, p. 106) and other important information in order to guide the participants toward their images of the future.

Discovery: Reducing Culture to Core Factors

The first phase "is the reduction of the culture into recognized components or factors" (Turner, 1967, p. 106) or those factors that characterize the organization's core essence. During the Discovery phase of the Summit, participants uncover and uplift the root causes of success, the positive core, the proudest prouds, and that which gives life to the organization, or those factors that describe the organization when it is operating at its best. These organizational characteristics are posted on flip charts around the room, shared among participants, and referred to throughout the Summit. This "reduction of the culture" allows a participant to see clearly their organization in its most generative sense.

Additionally, the positive factors, stories, or creation myths represent the organization's sacred history or its core identity. Moreover, an organization's identity is bound up in the corporate myths and stories told about the organization. These stories come from a myriad of sources: customers, suppliers, employees, historical records (newspaper articles, magazine articles, etc.), and financial records (annual reports, etc.). All internal and external factors shape the core organizational myths and therefore its identity. These factors describe the organization by appreciating the organization when it is at its best, but not until the second phase do the participants make explicit their image of the organization in its current and future state.

Dream and Dramatization: Fantastic Patterns and Shapes

Once participants have shared the positive factors of the organization, those things
that they do well, and those things they will carry forward as they imagine the
organization in the future, they turn to the Dream phase of the Summit. Turner's
corresponding phase is the "recombination [of these core factors] in fantastic or
monstrous patterns and shapes" (Turner, 1967, p. 106). The term "monstrous,"
derived from Turner's fieldwork observations of tribal rituals among the Ndembu,
refers to masks that personify monsters or other animals or spirits. He indicates
that the purpose of such masks and their monstrous display during the ritual is
to exaggerate reality, in order to "encourage the observer to think about . . . [their]
qualities, metaphorical properties, religious significance, and so on" (Turner, 1967,
p. 106). They are to make the participants "vividly and rapidly aware of . . . the
'factors' of their culture" (Turner, 1967, p. 105).

Similarly, Summit participants perform skits and visions of the future. These
caricatures of a future organizational reality might be "unrealistic" – during the
presentation of a skit, participants at the summits often laugh and half-jokingly
say, "Oh, that'll never happen here." Yet, these ritual performances bring to the
forefront in participants' minds, through an emotive process, those characteristics
that are most important to strive for in the future. In other words, the dramatization
of myths in ritual helps to teach the value of the myth, and participants remember
the profane representations and out-of-the-ordinary symbols better when they
are dramatized. Dramatization is also the present enactment of a future state;
while in tribal rituals, the dramatizations often look back in time to creation,
in Appreciative Inquiry, the skits symbolize forward-looking representations.
MacAloon (1984) indicates that cultural performances are "occasions in which
as a culture we reflect upon and define ourselves, dramatize our collective myths
and history, present ourselves with alternatives, and eventually change in some
ways while remaining the same in others" (MacAloon, 1984, p. 1). That is, the
performance of fantastic images enables organization members to construct a
new reality.

Design: Cultural Reconstruction

The final phase of liminality consists of the "recombination [of the core factors]
in ways that make sense with regard to the new state and status that the neophytes
will enter" (Turner, 1967, p. 106). In this phase, the Design phase, the participants
begin to make sense of their ritual experiences; they begin to connect the
meaning of symbols and events to the ritual performances, social organization,

and the core factors of the culture in the form of actionable projects. At the Summit, participants turn to the challenge of developing provocative statements or aspiration statements and identify which ideas to develop. They then form teams around key challenges and opportunities and begin developing projects to change organizational processes or functions.

It is important to note that the locus of change may or may not be during the liminal phase. Change is not something that starts and stops, but rather is continuous and discontinuous (Nadler, 1988), always moving. While planned or intentional change is guided, it is not something that stops once the intervention has ended. Using ritual as a metaphor, as I have done, is instructive on this point: rituals raise awareness, share knowledge through myths, and create opportunities to alter relationships, but when the rituals end, change continues. It is by virtue of the ritual that change occurs after the ritual in the direction of the intended intervention, even though the outcomes may not be predictable at the outset.

PROCESSES OF RITUAL ORGANIZATIONAL CHANGE

Thus far, I have drawn parallels between ritual and Appreciative Inquiry in order to argue that ritual is a useful frame to study organizational change. I turn now to an analysis of the Appreciative Inquiry Summit to show that this organizational change process follows patterns of ritual practice. More than comparing similar change processes, existing knowledge on ritual and transformation provide one explanation for why the AI Summit has a powerful effect on organizational members. I present four constructs based on a qualitative research study that respond to the question: What mechanisms, factors, or processes based on documented examples of ritual practices underlie the Appreciative Inquiry Summit that lead to effective, regenerative, and embedded organizational change? Understanding what happens during liminality (i.e. the Summit) establishes a point of departure to analyze post-Summit activity and effectiveness, and these themes establish grounding for a theory of sustained and continuous appreciative change.

In the qualitative study, employees from one organization that has held successive AI Summits responded to questions about the Summit and its effect in the company. The research site for this paper was a nationwide freight carrier. The company's leadership learned about Appreciative Inquiry as a way to improve relationships between management and labor, drive down costs, and increase revenues, and believing that the Summits would be one vehicle to empower company employees, in August 2000, senior executives initiated a corporate-wide leadership development program involving AI.

The mechanisms, processes, and activities during the Summit set in motion effective post-Summit implementation. These processes include, first, *internal dialogue* which represents the predominant language of organizational members and by extension, organizations themselves. The Summit initiates for some a new way to communicate with each other, thereby shifting their internal dialogue from negative to positive. Second *communitas* develops. The presence of communitas involves: (1) deeply forged relationships that form during the organizational change process; and (2) relational anti-structure characterized by leadership's approachability and a sense of equality across organizational levels during the intervention. *Commitment* refers to the process to generate greater loyalty to the organization and deeper, emotional-spiritual commitment to organizational goals. Finally, *longitudinal repetition* refers to a long-term commitment to making the process work with the recognition that this type of change takes time.

Internal Dialogue: Shifting from Negative to Positive

Internal dialogue refers to the language patterns and vocabularies used inside the company by individuals, among co-workers, and the organization. Appreciative Inquiry starts with the assumption that systems evolve in the direction of their inquiry and the inquiry unambiguously appreciates the full range of human emotion and experience, good or bad, positive or negative. It is characterized by some as being unequivocally focused on the positive (Barge & Oliver, 2003). But AI is more than this. Through the AI Summit, organizational members develop new vocabularies for developing an appreciative eye, such that a shift in internal dialogue from negative to positive does not negate the presence of challenges, tensions, and difficulties at the interpersonal and organizational level. Rather, where negative language is predominant in the culture, recognizing the positive dimension is an important step because it has the potential to increase the capacity to form cooperative relationships across traditional boundaries.

Employees who were interviewed after the Summit talked about the difference in attitude and conversations on the dock, in the yard, and in the terminal office. The conversations concerning the company have been, as one employee of 22 years said, "predominantly negative. This is a negative place to work at." He continued: "And I've said this for years as well, is that the biggest challenge of working here at [this company] is maintaining a positive attitude. That's the biggest challenge." Yet, given the change intervention used, Appreciative Inquiry, which seeks to value and discover what works well, using a new vocabulary and language, the Summit initiated a shift from deficit-oriented organizational dialogue.

There are several dimensions of this shift toward the recognition and practice of abundance-oriented vocabularies. First, at the individual level, employees as well as managers were presented with a decision to shift their frame, to choose new language and vocabularies of the positive. The Summit demonstrated to people that a shift could take place, despite the historically strained relationships among workers and management. Second, at the interpersonal level, there exists a positive peer pressure to speak positively with one another. Co-workers remind co-workers about the Summit, to be positive, and not to talk down about the company. They use phrases such as: "That ain't any way to talk," "We're supposed to be positive," "We're supposed to have a positive attitude out here, and we don't need to hear that negative stuff," or "If you don't have anything positive to say, don't say anything at all." Incorporating an alternative internal dialogue on the dock or the yard had implications for how work was accomplished in teams and in different functional areas. At the organizational level, there was a reputation of measuring and analyzing every data point possible using a deficiency vocabulary. During the Summit, participants were encouraged to think about different kinds of measures that would shift the internal dialogue positively: instead of focusing on the one or two missed deliveries, one manager suggested that the company measure, discover, or determine why the majority of deliveries went right.

Communitas: Relationship and Ritual Status

Turner introduced the term "communitas," which emerges in the liminal period where social structure is absent (Turner, 1969) and differs from structured, differentiated, and hierarchical systems in that these make distinctions of "more" or "less" (Turner, 1969, p. 96). Ritual liminality, the space where communitas forms, presents a "moment in and out of time" and "in and out of secular social structure" which exposes an underlying social bond that no longer exists and is not completely undone (Turner, 1969, p. 96). This phase is "not a matter of giving a general stamp of legitimacy to a society's structural positions" but rather gives a recognition that without this "generic human bond" there would be "*no* society" such that "the high could not be high unless the low existed, and he who is high must experience what it is like to be low" (Turner, 1969, p. 97). Turner argues that ritual moments create a space wherein social structure and their relationships are recognized. Thus, communitas is an experience of anti-structure where ritual participants come out of structured roles to form equal, homogenous, and deeply connected relationships. This begins at the Summit, but continues well beyond. Examples of communitas abound: during a meeting where employees made a presentation to senior and mid-level managers from across the company, the COO approached one of the truck drivers to talk personally. The truck driver said to the COO: "If it wasn't for these Summits, I would never have had the opportunity to meet you, and get to know you at this level."

There are two primary aspects of communitas: (1) deeply forged relationships, what Turner refers to as comradeship (1969), which form during the organizational change process; and (2) relational anti-structure, equality of ritual participants, or homogeneity. These are built into the structure of the Summit through symbols. The layout of the Summit, for example, includes round tables with seating for 6 to 8 people. Summit organizers assign participants to tables, mixing employees. This creates equality: it is not atypical to find the dockworkers sitting at the same table with senior managers. The leadership does not make speeches "down to" employees; there is no center stage platform where the leadership sit; everyone participates (there are no bystanders); and all individuals are encouraged to share ideas during open microphone times. These structural aspects create the experience of anti-structure.

Communitas involves the emergence of a common language that organization members begin to enact on the dock, in team meetings, or with those who have not attended the Summit. Moreover, the use of positive language between co-workers on the dock or between management and labor facilitates trusting relationships. Other anti-structural forms are characterized by leadership's approachability and equality across organizational levels. Communitas also includes the development of new levels of cooperation, the inclusion of multiple stakeholder voices in decision-making teams, and system-wide awareness of organizational functions. In this case, communitas takes on new meaning: the unification of organization members around a shared goal or objective while simultaneously developing a cooperative mental model.

Referring to the Turner's discussion of liminality, ritual participants carry neither rank, insignia, or markings as to their status. Managers and supervisors are known to be structurally higher organizational members, but new and positive, internal dialogue disrupts previous structural forms in order to create an alternating and juxtaposing process between communitas and structure (Turner, 1969). This give and take plays a critical role in the ritual process. Even though a hierarchical structure exists between organizational levels (and members), the Summit initiates a dialectical process between existing structural forms and newly created communitas. Turner (1969) describes the dialectic thus:

> The immediacy of communitas gives way to the mediacy of structure, while, in *rites de passage*, men are released from structure into communitas only to return to structure revitalized by their experience of communitas . . . Communitas cannot stand alone if the material and organizational needs of human beings are to be adequately met. Maximization of communitas

provokes maximization of structure, which in its turn produces revolutionary strivings for renewed communitas (p. 129).

While Turner sets structure and communitas at opposites end of a continuum, they function more as a polarity (Johnson, 1992), oscillating back and forth such that the dialectical process fosters potential for new organizational forms. Thus, the dialectical process dictates the "fate of communitas" (Deflem, 1991), which is a "decline and fall into structure and law" (Turner, 1969, p. 132), and after which a new form of communitas may rise again (Turner, 1974). This dialectic introduces the concepts of commitment and repetition. While communitas is about the relationships formed during the liminal period, these relationships are based on commitment to the process and other participants. Relationships between organizational levels become equal through the Appreciative Inquiry Summit because the process fosters the development of more connected relationships. Furthermore, this temporarily established equality, or what Turner refers to as anti-structure, reappears after the Summits.

Commitment: Cognitive and Cathectic

Appreciative Inquiry is more than coming up with an innovative idea and developing a new strategy. It is more than cognitive and rational processes for gaining knowledge that enhance organizations. More than relationship building and equality between organization members, the Appreciative Inquiry Summit develops in participants a profound commitment to the organization and to their newly formed relationships. Appreciative Inquiry is about fostering positive change because AI Summits create conditions where organizational commitment is encouraged and strengthened.

Liminality functions as a critical step in developing commitment in the change process. It is within this phase that the potential for change is highest. In order for rituals to have lasting meaning and significance for the individuals, cultures, groups, or organizations involved, commitment to change is tantamount. New identity, new roles, new commitment, and new status for participants are contingent upon the level of commitment one makes during the liminal period. That is, the success of a rite is dependent upon the frame of mind and emotionality in which it is received, how seriously it is received, and how ritual participants perceive the importance of the rite. In order for the ritual to have the desired effect in the lives of the initiates, it must be coupled with the significance of the change (i.e. a business case for an AI Summit). This is a primary reason that rites are seriously fearful, ambiguous, dangerous, and risky (Turner, 1967). That said each individual participant must choose whether he or she will accept the new knowledge, shift his or her thinking, and become renewed and changed.

There are two aspects of commitment apparent in this analysis: cognitive and cathectic. The cognitive aspect refers to a logical-rational frame which focuses on the rational aspects of the change: what new ideas are considered, what new ways to think about the problem are brought to light, what are new ways to deal with current challenges. Commitment to the change focuses on the idea related to the topic of the Summit. Highly cognitive activities during the Summit include listening to stories and generating logical categories of themes. Likewise, prior to the Summits, a steering committee designs the Summit topic that incorporates the business case.

Ritual practice adds a cathectic dimension (Parsons, 1951) to change processes. When participants interact with each other during the Summit activities, they have conversations, share stories, and talk about their experiences related to the topic. It is through this engagement process where affective feelings are created. At first, many are skeptical of the process, but through conversations and hearing others' stories, conversations shift toward possibilities, and non-verbal and verbal expressions change. This dimension adds deep emotional, affective, or enduring energy: it bridges the cognitive-rational aspects of a change process with the affective and emotional connection associated with the change process and its desired effect, such that a combination of affect (i.e. attitudinal changes due to "positive" framing and inquiry, high point questions) and cognition (i.e. awareness of the on-the-dock implications for the topic) promotes a deeper commitment to the proposed change. Moreover, the second phase of liminality, dramatization of the culture via monstrous and fantastic re-creations and reconstruction, is a moment of instruction that combines cognitive-rational, as well as drama and relationship, which are emotional and affective. This is an example of the bridge between cognitive and emotional commitment, resulting in a deeper form what I call cathectic commitment. This connection suggests that a deep and enduring commitment occurs when both are present (Hallinger & Murphy, 1985).

The AI Summit involves both types of commitment. In the cognitive-rational area, newly formed teams educate themselves regarding business processes, learning what needs to be done to address particular challenges. For example, teams develop specific technical or socio-technical projects to improve work processes or find a new way to measure an aspect of the work. The shift from cognitive to cathectic commitment is readily seen in comments like: "I came out really positive." "If I can change some things I used to do better myself, then I might better the business." Participants at the Summit developed a stronger purpose at work because they possessed more knowledge about the company, the industry and the business. In this sense, cathectic commitment is related to having pride in one's work (seeing company trucks going down the road) and sense of responsibility (knowledge that the equipment is clean and is in exceptional condition).

These dimensions are not linear. Summit participants do not change on both the cognitive and cathectic dimensions simultaneously. Piderit (2000) indicates committing cognitively to a change may come before cathectic change: individuals may shift their mental models prior to developing a deep commitment to the process. Furthermore, cathectic commitment may occur well-after a Summit when an individual notices changes in relationships with co-workers. Or cognitive change may take place when a breakthrough is made on a challenging problem. Overall, cognitive and cathectic shifts solidify employees' commitment to organizational goals and to the success of AI. Furthermore, organization members that have a cathectic commitment will personally dedicate time and energy beyond their daily work to improve the organization.

Longitudinal Repetition: Repeatable Ritual Practice

The fourth construct, repeatable ritual practice, is the outcome of shifting internal dialogue, communitas, and cathectic commitment. As organizations continually engage in repeated rituals over time, these processes are adopted into the organizational ethos. Longitudinal repetition is an upward spiraling motion: inherently positive language techniques beget positive language; deeply forged relationships among ritual participants produce stronger relational ties; emotional and cognitive commitment leads to more commitment.

Repeatable ritual practice is derived from the literature on creation myths, ceremonial rites, and other myths; the sharing of those myths or stories in the Summit instills new positive language. The stories also represent one aspect of cognitive commitment. Ritual, according to Eliade, is most efficacious when repeated through time via creation myths (Eliade, 1959). In his terms, society and the Cosmos are regenerated when they reoccur on an episodic or periodic basis:

> ... myths serve as a model for ceremonies that periodically reactualize the tremendous events that occurred at the beginning of time. The myths preserve and transmit the paradigms, the exemplary models, for all the responsible activities in which men engage. By virtue of the paradigmatic models revealed to men in mythical times, the Cosmos and society are periodically regenerated (p. xiv).

The AI Summit represents a mythical time where the stories or myths generated before and during the Summit describe the origins and the foundations of life that give meaning and inform identity for the organization and its members.

Eliade continues: "the effects that this faithful reproduction of paradigms and this ritual repetition of mythical events" (Eliade, 1959, p. xiv) have on participants is critical. The emerging stories, experiences, and actions from the discovery phase constitute the underlying organizational creation myths. But it is not enough to "*know* the origin myth, one must *recite* it" (Eliade, 1963, p. 17). The power these myths or sacred stories grant to enact a social reality that portrays the organization's finest moments lies in the repetition of the stories and myths. Teams that re-share stories and aspirations during weekly, bi-weekly, or monthly meetings perpetuate an reality based on those stories, thus playing a role in constructing organizational history and identity over time. As teams do this, they symbolically step back to Summit experiences, yet are propelled into the future as they continue to design and carry out their previously designed action steps. Such a return to the positive core, to the aspiration statements, and personal experiences is one key energizing force of post-Summit activity. Ritual repetition however, is not "ritualistic"; that is, telling stories or sharing experiences are not taken-for-granted activities. Rituals are not *just* ritualistic; they are regenerative, such that through the process of repetition, the organization is enacted anew.

When organizations engage in AI type ritual interventions and create consistent patterns around repeatable ritual practices, then practices are transferred and become embedded in the workings of the organization. This is an example of re-living communitas on a periodic basis so that the relational anti-structure is preserved beyond the Summit. Ritual is not simply superficial in its effects – it does not occur once and for all in order to magically transform an organization. Rather, regular and repeatable rituals such as the AI Summit, allow organizations to sustain change over time.

CONCLUSION

Appreciative Inquiry is an organizational change process grounded in ritual patterns and characteristics, which are linked through the ritual moments of liminality: reduction of culture to core factors, dramatization of myths and sacred stories through ritual performances, and recombination of futuristic aspirations. Based on this connection, ritual, including liminality, is important in any study of organizational change interventions. Four underlying processes (internal dialogue, communitas, commitment, and longitudinal repetition) of ritual are manifested in the AI Summit and afterward, thus providing one explanation for why the AI Summit produces change. Because of the Summit, internal dialogue shifts from negative to positive, deeper relationships are created across organizational levels, greater commitment is created at a cathectic level, and teams continue long after the Summit. These are the key factors to success of the Appreciative Inquiry intervention.

Rituals are powerful mechanisms in primitive cultures to create individual and cultural change. Similarly, organizational change, and appreciative inquiry specifically, patterned after rituals produce change. If patterns of ritual are found across cultures to be effective in producing change, and if AI or organizational change in general are similar to ritual, then a ritual lens should inform the craft of organizational development such that practitioners would include elements of ritual in the interventions they use. In practice then, applying the ritual metaphor to organizational development and change has great potential as a new language to understand organizational change.

REFERENCES

Argyris, C., Putnam, R., & Smith, D. (1985). *Action science*. San Francisco: Jossey-Bass.

Barge, K. J., & Oliver, C. (2003). Working with appreciation in managerial practice. *Academy of Management Review, 28*(1), 124–142.

Barrett, F. J., & Cooperrider, D. L. (1990). Generative metaphor intervention: A new approach for working with systems divided by conflict and caught in defensive perception. *Journal of Applied Behavioral Sciences, 26*(2), 219–239.

Beckhard, R. (1969). *Organizational development: Strategies and models*. Reading, MA: Addison-Wesley.

Beckhard, R., & Harris, R. (1987). *Organizational transitions: Managing complex change* (2nd ed.). Reading, MA: Addison-Wesley.

Beyer, J. M., & Trice, H. M. (1987). How an organization's rites reveal its culture. *Organizational Dynamics, 15*(4), 5–24.

Bridges, W. (1980). *Transitions: Making sense of life's changes*. Reading, MA: Addison-Wesley.

Burke, W. (1987). *Organization development: A normative view*. Reading, MA: Addison-Wesley.

Cooperrider, D. L. (1999). Positive image, positive action: The affirming basis of organizing. In: S. Srivastra & D. L. Cooperrider (Eds), *Appreciative Management and Leadership* (pp. 91–125). Euclid, OH: Williams Custom Publishing.

Cooperrider, D. L., & Sekerka, L. E. (2003). Toward a theory of positive organizational change. In: K. S. Cameron, J. E. Dutton & R. E. Quinn (Eds), *Positive Organizational Scholarship: Foundations of a New Discipline*. San Francisco: Berrett-Koehler.

Cooperrider, D. L., & Srivastra, S. (1987). Appreciative inquiry in organizational life. *Research in Organizational Change and Development, 1*, 129–169.

Cummings, T. G., & Worley, C. G. (1993). *Organization development and change* (6th ed.). Cincinnati, OH: West Publishing Company.

Deflem, M. (1991). Ritual, anti-structure, and religion: A discussion of Victor Turner's processual symbolic analysis. *Journal for the Scientific Study of Religion, 30*(1), 1–25.

Eliade, M. E. (1954). *The myth of the eternal return, or cosmos and history*. Princeton, NJ: Princeton University Press.

Eliade, M. E. (1959). *The sacred and the profane: The nature of religion*. New York: Harcourt Brace.

Eliade, M. E. (1963). *Myth and reality*. New York: Harper & Row.

Eliade, M. E. (1967). *Gods, goddesses, and myths of creation*. New York: Harper & Row.

Greenwood, D., Whyte, W., & Harkavy, I. (1993). Participatory action research as process and as goal. *Human Relations, 46*(2), 175–192.

Grieves, J. (2000). Introduction: The origins of organizational development. *Journal of Management Development, 19*(5), 345–351.

Hallinger, P., & Murphy, J. F. (1985). Assessing the instructional management behavior of principals. *Elementary School Journal, 86*(2), 217–247.

Hocart, A. M. (1903). *The life-giving myth*. New York: Grove Press.

Johnson, B. (1992). *Polarity management: Identifying and managing unsolvable problems*. Amherst, NH: HRD Press.

Kleiner, A. (1996). *The age of heretics: Heroes, outlaws, and the forerunners of corporate change*. New York: Doubleday.

Lewin, K. (1951). *Field theory in social science*. New York: Harper.

MacAloon, J. J. (1984). *Rite, drama, festival, spectacle: Rehearsals towards a theory of performance*. Philadelphia: Institute for the Study of Human Issues.

Marrow, A. (1969). *The practical theorist: The life and work of Kurt Lewin*. New York: Basic Books.

Mohrman, S., & Cummings, T. (1989). *Self-designing organizations: Learning how to create high performance*. Reading, MA: Addison-Wesley.

Morgan, G., & Ramirez, R. (1984). Action learning: A holographic metaphor for guiding social change. *Human Relations, 37*, 1–28.

Nadler, D. (1988). Organization frame-bending: Types of change in the complex organization. In: R. Kilmann & T. Covin (Eds), *Corporate Transformation*. San Francisco: Jossey-Bass.

Parsons, T. (1951). *The social system*. Glencoe, IL: Free Press.

Piderit, S. K. (2000). Rethinking resistance and recognizing ambivalence: A multidimensional view of attitudes toward an organizational change. *Academy of Management Review, 25*(4), 783–794.

Powley, E. H., Cooperrider, D. L., & Fry, R. E. (2002). Appreciative inquiry: A revolutionary approach to strategic change. In: P. Goett (Ed.), *Handbook of Business Strategy* (pp. 165–172). New York: EC Media Group.

Reason, P., & Bradbury, H. (Eds) (2001). *Handbook of action research: Participative inquiry and practice*. London: Sage.

Senge, P. M. (1990). *The fifth discipline: The art and practice of the learning organization*. New York: Doubleday.

Srivastva, S., & Fry, R. E. (1992). *Executive and organizational continuity: Managing the paradoxes of stability and change*. San Francisco: Jossey-Bass.

Trice, H. M., & Beyer, J. M. (1984). Studying organizational cultures through rites and ceremonials. *Academy of Management Review, 9*(4), 633–669.

Turner, V. W. (1967). *The forest of symbols*. Ithaca, NY: Cornell University Press.

Turner, V. W. (1969). *The ritual process: Structure and anti-structure*. Ithaca, NY: Cornell University Press.

Turner, V. W. (1974). *Dramas, fields, and metaphors: Symbolic action in human society*. Ithaca, NY: Cornell University Press.

Van Gennep, A. (1908/1960). *The rites of passage*. Chicago: University of Chicago Press.

Weisbord, M. R. (1991). *Productive workplaces: Organizing and managing for dignity, meaning, and community*. San Francisco: Jossey-Bass.

Weisbord, M. R., & Janoff, S. (1995). *Future search: An action guide to finding common ground for action in organizations and communities* (1st ed.). San Francisco: Berrett-Koehler.

Whitney, D., & Cooperrider, D. L. (1998). The appreciative inquiry summit: Overview and applications. *Employment Relations Today, 25*(2), 17–29.

Whitney, D., & Cooperrider, D. L. (2000). The appreciative inquiry summit: An emerging methodology for whole system positive change. *OD Practitioner, 32*(1), 13–26.

FEEDBACK FROM THE POSITIVE QUESTION – THE INTEGRATION OF APPRECIATIVE INQUIRY WITH SURVEY FEEDBACK: FROM CORPORATE TO GLOBAL CULTURES

Peter F. Sorensen Jr. and Therese F. Yaeger

ABSTRACT

This chapter proposes a synergy and integration between OD's long tradition of "survey guided development" and the rapidly emerging new directions offered by Appreciative Inquiry. Both Appreciative Inquiry and the survey-guided development approaches have a common shared commitment to the Lewinian call to Action Research. The chapter traces the movement from Action Research to "survey guided development," and then to the emergence of Appreciative inquiry. Several illustrations of Appreciative Inquiry combined with Survey Guided Organization Development are presented for U.S. and international applications. Findings illustrated in the chapter present the possibility of a third new and powerful perspective on the driving forces and dynamics of change. In addition, the international illustrations raise the question of and strengthen the argument for a common universal human experience.

Constructive Discourse and Human Organization
Advances in Appreciative Inquiry, Volume 1, 263–281
© 2004 Published by Elsevier Ltd.
ISSN: 1475-9152/doi:10.1016/S1475-9152(04)01012-9

INTRODUCTION

A major theme presented in this chapter is that the application of peak organizational experiences, the foundation of Appreciative Inquiry, is universal in nature and transcends national cultural boundaries. Specifically, it deals with the adaptation of a major Organization Development intervention, Survey Feedback, in a manner designed to build on the strengths and contributions to organization health and performance offered by both Survey Feedback and Appreciative Inquiry.

The paper introduces several new findings and concepts that we believe have critical implications. Historically, Organization Development has employed discrepancy based, or gap analysis, as a catalyst for change. More recently, future visioning has been widely adopted as the change catalyst. Findings presented in this paper suggest a powerful third alternative to change – the existence of a latent past culture, or a positive high point history.

A second major finding presented deals with the question of the universality of Organization Development, an argument which has been central to the applicability of Organization Development internationally. One of the basic questions here is whether OD is culturally specific – specific to the cultural values in which it is being practiced or whether there are approaches which are universal in application, based on fundamental organizational human needs and values.

This chapter is organized into eight sections. In the first section we define the nature, content and organization of the chapter. We then describe Appreciative Inquiry, Action Research and Survey Feedback (data based change) and set forth the historical context reviewing the origins of Action Research, and the history of Survey Feedback as a special form of Action Research. This section includes the paradigm-shifting call to reconsider Action Research as set forth by Cooperrider and Srivastva (1987) and the adaptations and integration of Appreciative Inquiry and Survey Feedback as a response to the Cooperrider and Srivastva invitation to re-think Action Research. The third section sets forth a model of Survey Feedback and the extension of Survey Feedback based on Appreciative Inquiry. The Instrumentation section then describes the Organization Culture Inventory, the instrument used in the application of the Appreciative Inquiry/Survey Feedback model. The next section presents illustrations representing a variety of organizations ranging from Fortune 500 financial and manufacturing organizations, to health care and governmental agencies. This section also extends Appreciative Inquiry and Survey Feedback to international settings. Finally the chapter provides a discussion and considerations for future research.

ACTION RESEARCH, APPRECIATIVE INQUIRY, AND SURVEY FEEDBACK

Action Research

Action Research has been a major part of the field of Organization Development and has its origins in the initial work of Kurt Lewin (French & Bell, 1999; Weisbord, 1987). Lewin presented Action Research as a means for addressing several needs simultaneously: the pressing need for greater knowledge about the causes and dynamics of social ills; the need to understand the laws of social change; the need for greater collaboration and joint inquiry between scientists and practitioners; the need for "richer" data about real-world problems; the need to discover workable, practical solutions to problems; and the need to discover general laws explaining complex social phenomena (French & Bell, 1999).

The Action Research process is described as consisting of problem identification, consultation with a behavioral science expert, data gathering, and preliminary diagnosis, feedback to a key client or group, joint diagnosis to the problem, joint action planning, action and data gathering after action. The process is described as being continuous with cyclical learning from and modification of action after each cycle (French & Bell, 1999).

Appreciative Inquiry

In 1987 one of the most important, if not the most important article on Appreciative Inquiry, appeared in the Woodman and Pasmore *Research in Organization Change and Development* annual series. In this article, Cooperrider and Srivastva stated for action-research to reach its potential as a vehicle for social innovation it needs to begin advancing theoretical knowledge of consequence . . . that *appreciative inquiry* represents a viable complement to conventional forms of action-research (p. 129).

Survey Feedback

Survey Feedback represents a form of Action Research and like Action Research is part of the core tradition of Organization Development and has been described along with laboratory training as one of two major stems in the development of the field (French & Bell, 1999). Early Survey Feedback work is associated with the work of Rensis Likert and the Institute for Survey Research at the University of Michigan. Likert's work is probably best remembered for the four systems of management and the profile of organization characteristics. The profile of organization characteristics served as an important introduction to discrepancy-based change – the use of differences between the actual and the ideal organization as described by respondents as a catalyst for change (Likert, 1962, 1967). In 1973 in a study of organizational change approaches, Survey Feedback was reported to be the most effective change technique when compared with a number of other Organization Development interventions (Bowers, 1972, 1973).

SURVEY FEEDBACK MODEL

One of the most comprehensive and systematic presentations of Survey Feedback is David Nadler's *Feedback and Organization Development: Using Data-based Methods* (1977). In his description and conceptual model Nadler is concerned with a number of aspects of its process. The following is a summary of the four phases of the Nadler model, followed by a more detailed integration with Appreciative Inquiry. The first phase is concerned with determining the nature of data to be collected. In Nadler's model the data to be collected is determined by knowledge of organizations (in general), combined with knowledge of a client organization (specifically). A second fundamental aspect of Nadler's model is the creation and amount of energy through Survey Feedback. In the Nadler model, energy is created through rewards and the amount of energy is determined by the act of data collection itself, the perceived accuracy of the data, and the perception of how data is to be used by relevant power groups (management). A third element of Nadler's model is the criteria for effective feedback which include the following: relevant, understandable, descriptive, verifiable, limited, impactful, comparative, and unfinalized. The fourth and final element of Nadler's model is the structure and composition of feedback meetings which include the following seven approaches: family group, cascading groups, subordinate groups, peer groups-intergroup, intergroup, collateral groups, and ad hoc collateral groups.

Linking Appreciative Inquiry to Nadler's Model

The following section elaborates on the integration of Appreciative Inquiry with each of the four phases in Nadler's Survey Feedback model. First, determining the nature of data to be collected. General knowledge of organizational functioning is provided by a combination of the principles of Appreciative Inquiry and the model provided by the Organizational Culture Inventory (to be presented in the next section). Sources of specific knowledge pertaining to the organization are generated by both individual and group responses to the Organization Culture Inventory. The second focus becomes the creation of energy. A fundamental aspect of Nadler's model is the creation of energy; in fact, it is a fundamental aspect of Organization Development. In Appreciative Inquiry energy is created through intrinsic reward – the sharing and re-creation of peak experiences. Peak experiences by definition represent intrinsic rewards. In Appreciative Inquiry, the amount of energy is created through data collection itself which is consistent with the Appreciative Inquiry principle of simultaneity and through the perceived accuracy of the data in which there is little motivation to fabricate peak experiences. Finally, the amount of energy is determined by one's perception of how it will be used by relevant power groups (management). In the Appreciative Inquiry process, it becomes critical that power groups are perceived as highly invested in both the initial process and the sustainability of the process.

With regards to the third element of Nadler's model, creating effective feedback, Nadler argues the process must be perceived as:

(1) Relevant – the identification of peak experiences is of central importance to most organization members.
(2) Descriptive – "for feedback to generate energy, the receiver must be able to relate the data to real-life events in his world." The identification and elaboration of stories described in peak experiences reinforces the relevance for the individual, and by definition, peak experiences are part of the respondent's lived world.
(3) Understandable – reporting of peak experiences and stories of peak experiences are almost always understandable.
(4) Verifiable – data must be valid and accurate. Although there might be some reason for not providing accurate data on the existing organization little or no motivation exists for fabricating participant-generated peak experiences.
(5) Limited – avoidance of information overload. In our experience peak experiences reporting is focused and clear.
(6) Impactable – data needs to deal with issues under the control of the participants – this issue which is dependent on the structuring of the Appreciative Inquiry session and implementation strategy. This is a critical issue in Appreciative Inquiry. Does Appreciative Inquiry serve as a "front-end" intervention, or "catalyst" or as an integrated part of the overall change process. This issue is commented on later.
(7) Comparative – providing part of the comparison or benchmarks. The peak experiences serve as the benchmark. A benchmark which has particular

relevance since it is based on the respondent's own organization and own experiences within the organization.

(8) Unfinalized – The initial session is not the completion but beginning of the process of generating additional data and action planning. To the extent that Appreciative Inquiry is Action Research, Action Research is continuous. However, this part of the Appreciative Inquiry literature is not complete and the continuous role of Appreciative Inquiry over time in an Action Research model is not at all clear and is in fact an area of debate.

With regard to the fourth element of Nadler's model, structure and composition of feedback groups, Appreciative Inquiry/Survey Feedback may utilize any of these feedback groups. Our own experience has been with each of the groups except collateral group. An eighth category would of course, be large groups, or the Appreciative Inquiry Summit. It has been our experience that each of these formats work well and selection is a function of the overall intent of the intervention. Finally, Nadler's model also addresses the direction of energy – toward the creation of: (1) productive; or (2) non-productive behavior.

Traditional data feedback is vulnerable to the intentional withholding of data, providing misleading data (purposely inaccurate responses), misdirected behavior – an over-concern for numbers, or defensive behavior reflected in efforts to discredit the process due to fear of surfacing negative data. Causes of productive or non-productive behaviors are a function of participants' expectations of how the information is to be used based on past experience.

Appreciative Inquiry/Survey Feedback appears to be uniquely oriented toward the creation of productive outcomes. In fact, Appreciative Inquiry/Survey Feedback provides a unique opportunity for the creation of positive outcomes if there is trust and confidence in the sustainability in support on the part of power groups (management).

INSTRUMENTATION

The Organization Culture Inventory

The Survey Feedback process described here refers to the use of questions based on well documented and supported theories of organizational characteristics and performance.

The Organization Culture Inventory (OCI) reflects over 50 years of organizational behavior research ranging from McClelland (1953), Hersey (1957), Horney (1954), Maslow (1954) and Stodgill (1963), to Cooke and Rousseau

(1983), Lawrence and Lorsch (1969), Litwin and Stringer (1968), Nadler (1977), Friedlander and Margulies (1969) and more recently Thomas Head et al. (2001). For information on the Organization Culture Instrument, contact Human Synergistics at www.hscar.com.

The Organization Culture Inventory addresses a concept central to the field of Organization Development and change and in fact Organization Development as culture change was one of the first definitions of the field put forth by Warner Burke (1987) in his original Addison-Wesley series book. The Organization Culture Inventory has been employed extensively by the authors in educational settings with students, managers and executives as well as field studies and change projects. Our experience has been that the Organization Culture Inventory clearly differentiates between organizational cultures associated with high and low performance.

The Organization Culture Inventory assesses the culture based on responses to a set of 120 questions. These responses are then presented in the form of a circumplex comprised of twelve styles (see Fig. 1).

(1) *Humanistic-Helpful Culture:* Managed in a participative and person-centered way. Members are expected to be supportive and constructive, and open to influence in their dealings with one another.

(2) *Affiliative Culture:* High priority is placed on constructive interpersonal relationships. Members are expected to be friendly, open, and sensitive to their work group and also sharing feelings and thoughts.

(3) *Approval Culture:* Conflicts are avoided and interpersonal conflicts are pleasant – at least superficially. Members feel like they should agree with, gain the approval of, and be liked by others.

(4) *Conventional Culture:* Conservative, traditional and bureaucratically controlled. Members are expected to conform, follow the rules, make good impressions and always follow policies and practices.

(5) *Dependent Culture:* Hierarchically controlled and non-participative. Centralized decision making leads members to do only as they are told, clear all decisions with superiors, doing what is expected and pleasing those in positions of authority.

(6) *Avoidance Culture:* Fail to reward success but nevertheless punish mistakes. The negative reward system leads members to shift responsibilities to others, avoid any possibility of being blamed, wait for others to act first, and take few chances.

(7) *Oppositional Culture:* Confrontation prevails and negativism is rewarded. Members gain status and influence by being critical and thus reinforced to oppose the ideas of others, make safe decisions, pointing out flaws and are hard to impress.

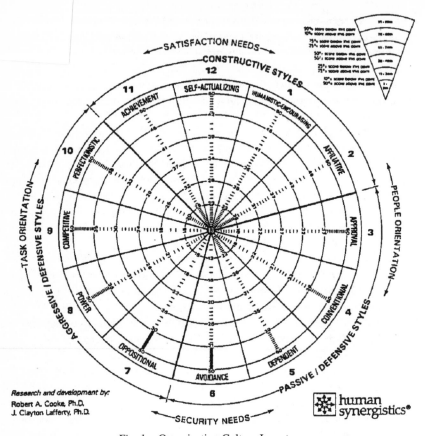

Fig. 1. Organization Culture Inventory.

(8) *Power Culture:* Non-participative organizations structured on the basis of authority inherent in members' positions. Members believe they will be rewarded for taking charge, controlling subordinates while being responsive to demands of superiors.

(9) *Competitive Culture:* Winning is valued and members are rewarded for out-performing one another. Members operate in a win-lose framework and believe they must work against, not with, their peers.

(10) *Competence/Perfectionist Culture:* Perfectionism, persistence and hard work are valued. Members feel they must avoid all mistakes, keep track of everything, work long hours to attain narrowly defined objectives.

(11) *Achievement Culture:* Do things well and value members who accomplish goals. Members set challenging but realistic goals, establish plans to reach them and pursue them with enthusiasm.

(12) *Self-Actualization Culture:* Value creativity, quality over quantity and both task accomplishment and individual growth. Members are encouraged to gain enjoyment from their work, develop themselves and take on interesting activities.

Research using the Organization Culture Inventory addressing the issue of culture and performance reports a positive relationship between higher levels of organization performance and "top of the clock" (styles 11, 12, 1 and 2) and lower performance for "bottom of the clock" styles (styles 3 through 10). These relationships are also supported by other similar measures of organization characteristics such as Likert's Four Systems (1967) and Harrison's Four Culture Types (1992).

In the Appreciative Inquiry approach to Survey Feedback, the Organization Culture Inventory is modified to ask the respondent to reflect on and describe peak experiences within the organization – experiences that are drawn from that time when the respondents and the organization were working at their best. Use of peak experience draws on the literature concerning the importance of the positive question (Yaeger & Sorensen, 2001).

ILLUSTRATIONS

Oceanside Hospital

This study is the first to dramatically contrast the traditional deficiency-based culture pattern with the peak experience pattern, and was in fact awarded the Best OD Project of the Year Worldwide Award in 1998 by the OD Institute.

The first study reporting the use of Appreciative Inquiry with the Organization Culture Inventory was in a large private hospital in which cultural assessment data was used in terms of initiating a strategic change process. The session was attended by over 50 members of the top administrative staff.

Within the same session, administrators were asked to describe the existing Organization Culture Inventory pattern for the organization, followed by the Organization Culture Inventory pattern based on peak experiences. The different patterns are presented in Figs 2 and 3. Figure 2 presents the organization culture as it was perceived at the present time while Fig. 3 represents the peak

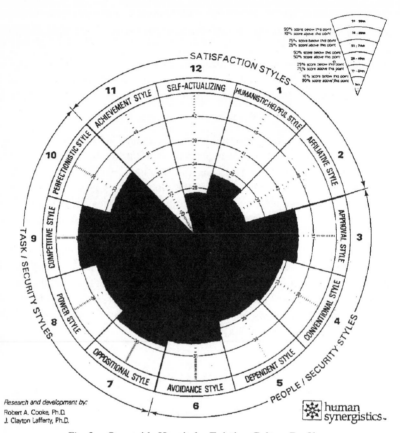

Fig. 2.   Oceanside Hospital – Existing Culture Profile.

experience culture. This striking difference is a pattern, which has been repeated consistently. As discussed later in this chapter, theme analyses of peak experiences consistently reflect experiences characterized by task accomplishment under adverse conditions, adverse conditions that create the need for high levels of collaborative efforts.

These distinctive patterns reflect in a dramatic way one of David Cooperrider's initial experiences in what has now become a classic case in the literature of Appreciative Inquiry – the story of the transformation of the Medic Inn – a Best Paper at the Academy of Management in 1988.

The major learning from the Oceanside Hospital case involves the reconfirmation of the dramatic case of Medic Inn that perceptions and descriptions of an organization are a function of the nature of the inquiry or questions asked and

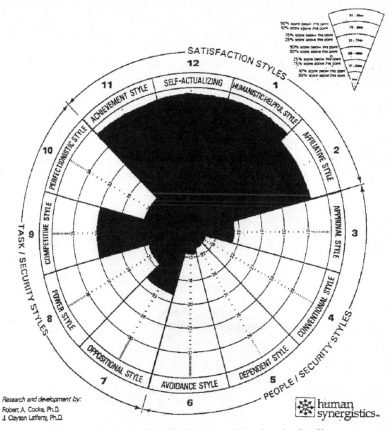

Fig. 3. Oceanside Hospital – Appreciative Inquiry Profile.

that the organization profiles resulting from these questions have the dramatic potential for the development of shared positive energy and a common bond for moving the organization forward.

U.S. Postal Service Case

The key learnings from the U.S. Postal Service illustration is the identification of latent cultures. In a study using Appreciative Inquiry/Organization Culture Inventory in several sites of the U.S. Postal Service existing and Appreciative Inquiry or peak experience patterns were again dramatically similar to the patterns experienced in the Oceanside Hospital case.

In this case the concept of "latent" cultures was first experienced. One of the postal sites had been at one time a premier site – the peak experiences profile served to trigger and recall the values and memories of the site when it had been widely recognized for its exceptional performance. The resurfacing of the latent high performance culture resulted in performance improvements indicated by the movement from the 97% in performance to the top 10% (Akinyele, Yaeger & Sorensen, 2001).

The key learning from the U.S. Postal Service case revolves around the fact that Appreciative Inquiry is a powerful means for resurfacing positive latent cultures and that the recollection of these previous cultures serves as a powerful means for creating strong organization identity and renewed pride as a catalyst for positive

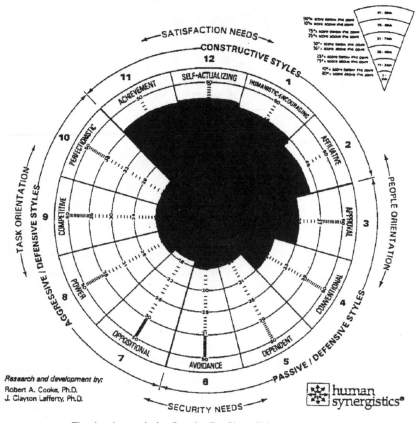

Fig. 4. Appreciative Inquiry Profile – Chinese Executives.

change. It is difficult to adequately portray or describe the experiences as employees relate and share the accomplishment that one time characterized the organization. In this case the Postal site had deteriorated from an organization characterized by its "firsts" – first to have a minority postal director, to first performance, into an organization which made the front page of local newspapers for its exceptionally poor performance. The resurfacing of histories of exceptional performance are themes that occur repeatedly in the application of Appreciative Inquiry and Survey Feedback.

A second major learning from the U.S. Postal Service case was the identification of characteristics and themes associated with peak organization characteristics. Based on themes which were identified in employee discussions

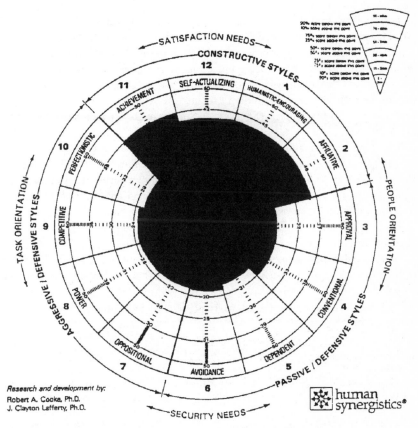

Fig. 5. Appreciative Inquiry Profile – U.S. Executives.

of peak experiences during feedback sessions, employees were asked to relate and describe stories of their peak experience. Content analysis of these stories reconfirmed dominant themes identified in the feedback session. Consistently, peak experiences are described as characterized by major task accomplishment under highly adverse conditions, requiring high levels of collaboration.

Appreciative Inquiry/Organization Culture Inventory – International

Recently the Appreciative Inquiry/Organization Culture Inventory approach has been used with two international groups – groups of international executives from the U.S., India and Japan as part of a Fortune 50 global organization, and a group of Chinese executives.

The application of the peak experience concept to Japan and India represents an extension to cultures, which differ sharply from the U.S. Both Japan and India differ sharply for instance from the U.S. on all four of Hofstede's (1980) cultural dimensions of: Power, Uncertainty Avoidance, Individualism, and Masculinity. Consequently, it is of note that the Organization Culture Inquiry profile for both Japanese and Indian executives is almost identical to the profiles reported by U.S. executives (Sharkey & Sorensen, 2002) indicating top of the clock responses.

The Appreciative Inquiry/Organization Culture Inventory peak experience model has also recently been used with over 100 Chinese executives studying in the U.S. A special form of the Organization Culture Inventory translated into Mandarin and a U.S.-Ph.D. student of Chinese background helped to facilitate understanding and discussion. A comparison of one group of 25 Chinese executives is presented in Fig. 4, and compared with a group of 25 U.S. executives. See Fig. 5.

Again, peak experience profiles from these two groups of executives from very different cultures provide strikingly similar peak experience profiles (Lu, Yaeger

Table 1. Themes from Peak Experience – U.S. and Chinese Comparison.

U.S. Executives	Chinese Executives
1. Task accomplishment 83%	1.Task accomplishment 82%
2. Teamwork 72%	2. Teamwork 66%
3. Leadership 64%	3. Leadership 54%
4. Org. culture 15%	4. Friendship 48%
5. Friendship 15%	5. Org. culture 42%
6. Personal development 10%	6. Top mgmt support 40%

& Sorensen, 2002; Sorensen, Yaeger, Keogh & Bengtsson, 2003). Theme analyses from stories given by respondents from each group are presented in Table 1.

Again we see the recurring themes of task accomplishment and interpersonal support.

DISCUSSION

This discussion concerns the following topics: Appreciative Inquiry/Survey Feedback vs. discrepancy-based change, the concept of latent cultures, the recall of peak experiences, and the issue of sustainability.

Survey Feedback is frequently characterized by the identification by respondents of the existing state and the ideal state. The discrepancy between the actual or existing and the ideal serves to unfreeze the organization, or as a catalyst for change (Beckhard, 1987; Likert, 1962). The disadvantage of discrepancy based models and procedures is that the ideal is frequently a model which the respondents have not experienced and remains an abstract concept with difficulties in implementing and operationalizing through concrete action plans.

Appreciative Inquiry on the other hand captures a potential future that is in fact based on the respondent's personal experience. This emerging model of the desired state, because it is based on actual experiences, facilitates the development of operationalizing concrete, specific action plans and addresses many of the issues of resistance to change addressed by Thomas Head, presented in Table 2.

The concept of latent positive cultures is a powerful catalyst for recapturing a once-successful and effective organization. This concept of latent culture however also raises the question of whether latent culture characteristics are related to another time, when the culture was better suited to the task and environment of a previous time and that a previously successful culture may not address issues in the current environment. Our experience has been that the latent culture concept is more closely related to more fundamental concepts – the fundamental need for accomplishment and supportive interpersonal relations. The latent culture concept also throws into sharper focus not only the characteristics of the high performance culture experienced at a previous time but also the identification of forces which have served to depress that culture. For example, in one health care organization studied, it had been a premier organization in the past, discussion of peak experiences helped the organization focus on the changes in the environment which had a strong negative impact. This awareness then served as a means for developing a specific strategy and mechanism for dealing with these changes.

Table 2.   How Appreciative Inquiry Undermines Resistance to Change.

Reason for Employee Resistance	How does AI Reduce Resistance
Fear of the unknown – we know what we have, but we don't know what change will bring. Employees like the old system.	AI works from the known – the organization is trying to "recapture" the already experienced peaks. AI begins with what employees like most about the existing system – making the peak experiences the norm. The implication is that at the same time non peak experiences will be adjusted/removed.
Change can cause the employee to question his/her self-image – "Can I do the new task?"	Because AI builds upon what already has been experienced by the employee he/she already knows the "new" can be done. There is no self doubt – in fact, because of tapping into peak experiences, the "new" will probably focus upon issues, which cause the employee to experience personal growth and self esteem.
The employees feel imposed upon – they have to do all the work for the change, but only the "organization" will reap the benefits.	AI clearly puts the "gain" into personal terms. The process focuses on how to permit each employee to constantly experience the personal satisfaction that occurred during the "peak experiences."
The employees view this change process as another "fad" – "why adopt anything new when management is going to forget it in a couple of weeks anyway?"	AI does not appear to be a revolutionary concept. Its goal can be seen as making "what is going on now" better. It is logical, and fits into the current paradigms – managers are always trying to get the current system to be more effective and efficient.

Since this approach is based on recall of peak experience it is conceivable that an organization is either too new to have history or has been so decimated that those with knowledge of the organization have left. This has not been our experience – even a small number of respondents with knowledge of history can be given opportunity to share their peak experiences creating a shared knowledge of when the organization was at its best.

It may also be that an organization has been so traumatized that the recent traumatic events are so dominant that they preclude any recall of peak experience. This again has not been our experience. However, use of Appreciative Inquiry/Organization Culture Inventory with the intent to selfishly exploit the power of Appreciative Inquiry would conceivably lead to cynicism and discredit management, the consultant, and Appreciative Inquiry. In these circumstances it would be particularly important to get a good "read" on management's intent and sincerity before the consultant enters into a contract.

One of the critical questions which continues to confront the field of Organization Development is the question of sustainability. The question of sustainability is also relevant to Appreciative Inquiry. In fact, the question comes into sharper focus, as Appreciative Inquiry appears to move predominantly toward the use of the Appreciative Inquiry Summit. There is increasing discussion regarding large group interventions. Some large-scale interventions such as Future Search and to some extent the Appreciative Inquiry Summit serve as "front end" interventions. As a catalyst for change large-group interventions serve as powerful and effective catalysts. Other approaches using large groups have more integrated approaches to other Organization Development technologies; for example, the integration of large groups with work process redesign in Dick Axelrod's (2000) conference model.

SUMMARY

The application of Appreciative Inquiry concepts to Survey Feedback represents an extension of Appreciative Inquiry to an additional Organization Development methodology and integration of Appreciative Inquiry with more traditional approaches to Organization Development. In fact, the application of Appreciative Inquiry to data-based change and Survey Feedback represents the wedding of Appreciative Inquiry with one of the most powerful and widely used Organization Development methods which has long been at the core of Organization Development.

This chapter has set forth the conceptual modification of Survey Feedback using Appreciative Inquiry. The article also presents an illustration of the use of a particular survey instrument, the Organization Culture Inventory. The Organization Culture Inventory represents a well-conceptualized and constructed instrument that addresses a core concept in organization change – the concept of organization culture. The Organization Culture Inventory reflects over 50 years of behavioral science research and parallels in many respects earlier instruments developed at the University of Michigan Survey Research Center.

The use of the Organization Culture Inventory has the advantage of placing Appreciative Inquiry within a broader conceptual framework which provides the opportunity for dialogue and action planning based not only on the concepts of Appreciative Inquiry but on concepts supported by more generalized behavioral science literature.

The chapter provides illustrations of applications in a variety of organizational settings. Responses to peak experience questions reveals a strikingly consistent pattern. Regardless of the organizational setting peak experiences are consistently associated with "top of the clock" patterns.

Most dramatic is the pattern of similarity across national cultures – that respondents from highly diverse cultures respond with highly similar patterns. It certainly can be argued that the respondents from each of the various countries represent special populations that may share a more common perspective with U.S. executives than the general population. Nevertheless it raises the ongoing question, is Organization Development more universal than culture specific in its application (Golembiewski, 1989; Hofstede, 1980; Jaeger, 1986; Yaeger, 2001). Even more so, is Appreciative Inquiry universal in its application? (Sharkey & Sorensen, 2001).

FUTURE RESEARCH

The dramatic consistency in the manner in which peak experiences are described across highly diverse cultures and the identification of latent positive cultures provides an important additional perspective for the practice of Appreciative Inquiry and Organization Development. The power of these experiences was recently again reinforced with a group of executives with which we had the opportunity of discussing peak experiences. One executive from the Federal Aviation Administration (FAA) attempted to relate her highly emotional experience involving the worldwide grounding of all planes on 9–11, a crucial task that required critical and exceptionally high levels of global collaboration. This was a dramatic illustration of task accomplishment and collaboration under exceptionally adverse conditions.

We feel that instrumented change-Survey Feedback offers a major additional approach to positive change. We also feel that it is critical to continue to try to understand the conditions which contribute to sustainability. It is also critical to expand or complement our understanding through rigorous analysis which extends beyond the important learnings from case studies. Survey Feedback is a data based process which has significant potential for increasing our understanding of positive change.

Several years ago Bob Golembiewski effectively demonstrated that OD works. It is now clear that AI works. We need to understand more about WHY it works.

REFERENCES

Akinyele, A., Sorensen, P., & Yaeger, T. (2001). Recreating high performance cultures with appreciative inquiry. Paper presented at the First International Conference on Appreciative Inquiry, Baltimore, MD.

Axelrod, R. H. (2000). *Terms of engagement: Changing the way we change organizations.* San Francisco: Berrett-Koehler.

Bowers, D. G. (1973). OD techniques and their results in 23 organizations: The Michigan ICL study. *Journal of Applied Behavioral Science, 9*, 21–43.

Burke, W. (1987). *Organization development: A process of learning and changing*. Reading, MA: Addison-Wesley.

Cooperrider, D. L., & Srivastva, S. (1987). Appreciative inquiry in organizational life. In: W. Pasmore & R. Woodman (Eds), *Research in Organization Change and Development* (Vol. 1, pp. 129–169). Greenwich, CT: JAI Press.

French, W. L., & Bell, C. H. (1999). *Organization development: Behavioral science interventions for organization improvement*. Upper Saddle River, NJ: Prentice-Hall.

Friedlander, R., & Margulies, N. (1969). Multiple impacts of organizational Climate and individual value systems upon job satisfaction. *Personnel Psychology*, *22*, 171–183.

Golembiewski, R. T. (1989). *Organization development: Ideas and issues*. New Brunswick: Transaction.

Head, T., Sorensen, P., Preston, J., & Yaeger, T. (2001). Is appreciative inquiry the philosopher's stone? In: D. L. Cooperrider, P. F. Sorensen, D. Whitney & T. F. Yaeger (Eds), *Appreciative Inquiry: Rethinking Human Organization Toward a Positive Theory of Change*. Stipes Publishing L.L.C.

Hofstede, G. (1980). *Culture's consequences*. London: Sage.

Horney, K. (1954). *Our inner conflicts*. New York: Norton.

Jaeger, A. (1986). Organization development and national culture: Where's the fit? *Academy of Management Review*, *11*, 178–190.

Lawrence, P. R., & Lorsch, J. W. (1969). *Organization and environment*. Homewood, IL: Irwin.

Likert, R. (1962). *New patterns of management*. New York: McGraw-Hill.

Likert, R. (1967). *The human organization*. New York: McGraw-Hill.

Litwin, G., & Stringer, R. (1968). *Motivation and organizational climate*. Boston Harvard University Press.

Lu, L., Sorensen, P., & Yaeger, T. (2002). The role of appreciative inquiry and corporate culture in the sustained growth of the Chinese economy. Paper presented at First International Chinese conference on economic growth, ZheJiang University, ZheJiang, China.

Maslow, A. H. (1954). *Motivation and personality*. New York: Harper & Row.

Nadler, D. A. (1977). *Feedback and organization development: Using data-based methods*. Addison-Wesley series on Organization Development. Addison-Wesley.

Organizational Culture Inventory, by R. A. Cooke & J. C. Lafferty, 1983, 1986, 1987, 1989, Plymouth, MI: Human Synergistics. Copyright 1989 by Human Synergistics.

Sharkey, L., & Sorensen, P. F. (2002). Survey feedback: An alternative to a classic intervention experience in the U.S., Japan and India. *Organization Development Practitioner*, *34*(1), 43–46.

Sorensen, P., Yaeger, T., Keogh, D., & Bengtsson, U. (2003). Preliminary findings on the international application of appreciative inquiry as an illustration of integrating local and global approaches to management research and practice: A three-country study. Presented at the European Academy of Management Conference, Milan, Italy.

Stodgill, R. M. (1963). *Manual for the leader behavior description questionnaire – Form XII*. Columbus: Bureau of Business Research, Ohio State University.

Weisbord, M. R. (1987). *Productive workplaces*. San Francisco: Jossey-Bass.

Yaeger, T., & Sorensen, P. (2001). What matters most in appreciative inquiry: Review and thematic assessment. In: D. Cooperrider, P. Sorensen, T. Yaeger & D. Whitney (Eds), *Appreciative Inquiry: An Emerging Direction for Organization Development*. Champaign: Stipes.

THE 'ARTFUL CREATION' OF POSITIVE ANTICIPATORY IMAGERY IN APPRECIATIVE INQUIRY: UNDERSTANDING THE 'ART OF' APPRECIATIVE INQUIRY AS AESTHETIC DISCOURSE

Nick Nissley

ABSTRACT

While Cooperrider (2001, p. 32) suggests that appreciative inquiry is about "the artful creation of positive imagery," most of the literature that describes the process of artful creation explains it as one in which the organizational members simply talk about these new images, vs. actually engaging in the creation of artistic representations of the desired future. This chapter moves the appreciative inquiry literature beyond the metaphorical understanding of the "art of" appreciative inquiry in order to reveal and explain how practitioners are actually engaging organizations in the artful creation of positive anticipatory imagery. In this chapter, the literature that labels and describes the process of artful creation in organizations is reviewed, described, and synthesized into five propositions – ultimately creating a framework for understanding artful creation as a unique organizational

Constructive Discourse and Human Organization
Advances in Appreciative Inquiry, Volume 1, 283–307
Copyright © 2004 by Elsevier Ltd.
All rights of reproduction in any form reserved
ISSN: 1475-9152/doi:10.1016/S1475-9152(04)01013-0

discourse: an aesthetic discourse. These five propositions reveal the common characteristics of artful creation: (1) presentational knowledge/language; (2) mediated dialogue; (3) symbolic constructions that act as metaphorical representation; (4) collaborative inquiry/co-creation; and (5) window to the unconscious. The chapter concludes by addressing the implications, seeking to answer the question "What is the value of an organization engaging with the process of artful creation?" Finally, the chapter suggests that the five propositions may guide future research in two areas: (a) the practice of the artful creation of positive anticipatory imagery in appreciative inquiry; and (b) the further development of a theoretical framework for understanding the "art of" appreciative inquiry as aesthetic discourse.

INTRODUCTION

Appreciative inquiry (AI) is grounded in what Cooperrider (2001, p. 32) refers to as "the artful creation of positive imagery," asserting, "The artful creation of positive imagery on a collective basis may well be the most prolific activity that individuals and organizations can engage in if their aim is to help bring to fruition a positive and humanly significant future." Yet very little literature on appreciative inquiry describes this process of "artful creation," except, for example, Watkins and Mohr (2001, p. 134), De Jong (2001, pp. 109–112), Johnson and Ludema (1997, p. 82) and Ludema, Mohr, Whitney and Griffin (2003). Instead, the literature is filled with metaphorical references to the "art of" appreciative inquiry. For example, Cooperrider (2000) metaphorically speaks of the "art of" appreciative inquiry when discussing anticipatory images: "These guiding images are not detailed objectives but are paintings created with a larger brush stroke," referring to them as "poetic images." In addition, Watkins and Mohr (2001) state, "These stories [referring to stories surfaced during the 'discover' phase] are used like an artist's paintbrush to create a vibrant image of the future" (p. 134).

This chapter moves beyond the metaphorical understanding of the "art of" appreciative inquiry in order to reveal and explain how practitioners are *actually* engaging organizations in the artful creation of positive anticipatory imagery. While very little literature in appreciative inquiry describes this process of artful creation, within the broader organizational studies framework, a descriptive, practitioner-based understanding of the use of artful creations is emerging. Consider, for example, the following labels and descriptions of artful creation in organizations: Barry's (1996) "artful inquiry," Palus and Drath's (2002) "mediated dialogue," Heron and Reason's (2001) "presentational knowledge,"

Table 1. Ways of Talking About Artful Creation.

Labels	References
Artful creation	Cooperrider (2000)
Artful inquiry	Barry (1996)
Mediated dialogue	Palus and Drath (2002)
Presentational knowledge/language	Heron and Reason (2001), Gagliardi (1996)
Metaphorming	Siler (1999, 2002)
Cognitive sculpting	Sims and Doyle (1995)
Analogically mediated inquiry	Barry (1994)
Imaging	Palus and Horth (2002)
Creating shared vision	Parker (1990)
Seeing the voice	Zaltman and Coulter (1995)
Arts-based learning	Nissley (2002a), Nissley and Jusela (2002)
Aesthetic discourse	Strati (1992)
Aesthetic communication	Gagliardi (1996)
Expressive arts consulting and education	California Institute of Integral Studies (2001)

Siler's (1999, 2002; Nissley & Jusela, 2002) "metaphorming," Sims and Doyle's (1995) "cognitive sculpting," Barry's (1994) "analogically mediated inquiry," Palus and Horth's (2002) "imaging," Parker's (1990) "creating shared vision," and Nissley's (2002a; Nissley & Jusela, 2002) "arts-based learning." These can be understood as specific, practice-based examples of artful creation, or what Strati (1992, p. 575) more generally and theoretically refers to as "aesthetic discourse," and what Gagliardi (1996, p. 574) refers to as "aesthetic communication" and "presentational language" (see Table 1). In addition, to moving beyond the metaphorical understanding of the "art of" appreciative inquiry, to reveal and explain how practitioners are *actually* engaging organizations in the artful creation of positive anticipatory imagery, this chapter seeks to expand on Ludema, Wilmot and Srivastava's (1997) assertion that "words create worlds" – to also *show* how "art creates worlds."

It should be noted that these modern examples of artful creation in organizations have a history – not in organization development, but in organizational folklore. Lockwood (1984) and Dewhurst (1984) both describe the phenomenon of "homers," artful creations from the workplace. Lockwood (1984, p. 203) refers to "homers" as "aesthetic creations secretly produced by workers on the job for their own pleasure with the tools and materials of their jobs," continuing, "They are produced by workers who use their work experiences and skills with the machines, tools, and materials of their jobs in alternative, aesthetic ways…. Thus, workers apply job skills to extra-occupational activity and consciously create art forms" (p. 205). Lockwood notes that the worker's creation of a homer serves as an expression that reflects the organizational culture: thus, the "study of homers aims at increasing our understanding of occupational culture by broadening our knowledge about workplace behavior" (p. 203). Similarly, Dewhurst (1984) examines examples of homers. He describes a Michigan auto manufacturing facility where workers create jewelry from scrap materials in paint rooms: catching the excess drippings of car paints on to pieces of scrap metal, which they craft into jewelry. He describes another example of artful creation in the workplace: the assembly line worker at a Michigan foundry who created an ongoing visual dialogue with fellow workers. The dialogue took the form of a series of drawings, jokes, and commentary on the life of the assembly line workers – all chronicled on the rubber conveyor belt of the assembly line.

The organizational folklorist has identified these artful creations from the workplace as potentially valuable artifacts for the organizational studies researcher interested in the artful representation of organizational life. Similarly, today, the organization development practitioner is becoming more aware of the significance of artful creations in the organization environment, and specifically within the context of organization development (see Table 1). More specifically, organization development practitioners and practitioners of appreciative inquiry are actively engaging organizations in the actual making of artful creations – where these cultural expressions afford insights to the organization.

This chapter contributes to our understanding of this emerging phenomenon of artful creation, seeking to better understand it as a unique discourse – an aesthetic discourse (Strati, 1992). Strati's (1992) notion of aesthetic discourse allows us to see appreciative inquiry as a process of creative inquiry that permits us to move beyond words alone: one in which visual images (or other artful creations) are used as a mediate for discovering and communicating shared meaning – the artful creation of positive imagery.

The chapter should be regarded as an exploratory discussion, rather than a finished philosophical framework for understanding artful creations/aesthetic discourse in appreciative inquiry. My hope is that we may learn more about artful creations and the practice of aesthetic discourse in appreciative inquiry by naming and seeking to explain this emerging phenomenon. The resultant framework allows us to see this emerging phenomenon of artful creation as an aesthetic discourse – the way it is practiced in organization development and appreciative inquiry. It is not intended to be an exhaustive look; the examples are meant to be representative. Most fundamentally, the framework allows us to move beyond the metaphorical conceptualization of the "art of" appreciative inquiry. Instead, this framework allows us to view artful creations as generative metaphor *and* as an *actual* representation of positive imagery.

THE ARTFUL CREATION OF POSITIVE ANTICIPATORY IMAGERY IN APPRECIATIVE INQUIRY

Throughout history and from a diversity of perspectives, the image has been considered to play a powerful role in shaping action. Cooperrider (2000) views this phenomenon through the lens of organizational theory, seeking to make sense of the role of the image in relation to organizational action; and even more specifically, from within the framework of appreciative inquiry, he articulates the idea that positive anticipatory images guide organizational action.

Practitioners of appreciative inquiry assert that organizations' imaginative projections are key to their actions, and that for an organization to seek to change its present actions, present images must be replaced with images of a better future (e.g. Cooperrider, 2000, p. 47). Yet the literature gives little detail about the *process of how organizations create* these anticipatory images, aside from accounts in Barrett and Cooperrider (2001). Such windows onto the process of positive anticipatory image creation mostly reveal stories of a process that is grounded in the logico-rational paradigm. That is, they reveal a process grounded in rational discourse – dialogue – to generate new knowledge and new images of possibility. In other words, most of the literature describes the process as one where the organizational members *simply talk about* these new images, vs. *actually engaging in the creation of* visual representations of the new images. While practitioners of appreciative inquiry *are* engaging in the actual artful creation of positive imagery (see Table 2), the literature has not remained as current as the practice. This chapter seeks to help the literature "catch up" with the practitioner – to report the advances in the practice and theory of artful creation.

Table 2.   References to the Practice of Artful Creation in Appreciative Inquiry.

Examples	References
Enacting/enlivening the dreams; dramatic dream enactments	Ludema, Mohr, Whitney and Griffin (2003)
Use of song/music in provocative propositions	De Jong (2001, p. 111)
Positive core map (in discovery)	Ludema, Mohr, Whitney and Griffin (2003)
Generally describe the process of creating a shared image of the preferred future	Watkins and Mohr (2001, p. 134)
Use of drama to promote dialogue in the appreciative inquiry process	Johnson and Ludema (1997, p. 82)
A "unity quilt" was created by participants during the dream phase	Pratt (2002, pp. 112–113)

Beyond the appreciative inquiry literature, within the larger body of organization studies literature, emerging case stories describe the process of how practitioners are actually engaging with the artful creation process (e.g. Nissley, 2002a). The following examples, from appreciative inquiry and the more general organization development context, describe *how* practitioners are actually engaging organizations in the artful creation of positive anticipatory imagery, or aesthetic discourse.

Offering a context for the reader to see what artful creation looks like, these examples are intended to serve as snapshots – a sampling of pictures – of how artful creation in organizations is being practiced. More importantly, these examples show the diversity of applications of artful creation in organizational life. After these snapshots of the process of artful creation are presented, a more detailed examination of aesthetic discourse is undertaken, seeking to inform the practice and theory of artful creation in appreciative inquiry.

"Dreaming" with Artful Creations

In the appreciative inquiry literature, Watkins and Mohr (2001, pp. 134–135) offer one of the only examples found that explains the process of artful creation. They describe the "dreaming" phase of appreciative inquiry, noting that after undergoing a process of discovery (of what gives life to an organization), participants may then take this new knowledge and actually develop an image of how the organization might look at some future point. In describing the process of creating a shared image of the preferred future, they explicitly state that the organization may create expressions or visual images (e.g. songs, skits, collages, etc.) that describe the larger vision for the organization. From these images, a written statement, called a "provocative proposition" or "possibility statement," is developed. The provocative proposition/possibility statement poetically describes the image/vision of the organization's desired future; or, alternatively, the image helps to describe the written statements. In addition, Ludema, Mohr, Whitney and Griffin (2003) explain the "dream" phase and the specific process of "enlivening the dreams," where small groups discuss specific, tangible examples of their dream and create metaphorical, creative presentations (artful creations). Ludema et al. describe "enacting the dreams," where groups present dramatic dream enactments to the large group.

Marjory Parker (1990) describes a strategic visioning process (a similar process, although not AI) at Europe's largest producer of aluminum, Norway's Hydro Aluminum Karmøy Fabrikker. In *Creating Shared Vision: The Story of a Pioneer Approach to Organizational Revitalization*, Parker describes how she helped the company to create a shared vision using an aesthetic approach. The final vision statement, co-created by nearly every employee over a two-year period, was not a piece of writing at all – instead, it was an extraordinary mural of a flourishing garden. The mural, in which every plant and element embodied rich metaphorical meaning, served as an artful creation – a positive anticipatory image of the organization's vision.

Another example of organizations' engaging with artful creation in the strategic visioning process can be found in the future search conference (Weisbord, 1992; Weisbord & Janoff, 1995). Weisbord and Janoff describe the section of the future search design that asks participants to focus on the desired future and to imagine that they have made their dreams come true. Participants create and present scenarios. The creative presentations might be a drama, a visual arts work, a musical performance, or other art form.

Murphy (1997) discusses four functions of art and specifically suggests a "revisioning" function, characterized by creating a new awareness for and casting different perspectives on familiar, everyday phenomena that have become invisible. The use of artful creation in the dreaming phase of appreciative inquiry appears to serve such a function – i.e. the artful creation creates a new awareness for the organization. Also, by using a presentational/aesthetic form of representation, each organization member can connect to and reflect on the strategy/vision in his or her own way, one that resonates for him or her as an individual (this is the inherent subjectivity of art) as opposed to the unitary meaning of a more discursive form that is based in intellectual/propositional knowledge.

"Discovery" with Artful Creations

Like Watkins and Mohr (2001), Ludema, Mohr, Whitney and Griffin (2003) explain the "discover" phase and the specific use of the "positive core map" in the Appreciative Inquiry Summit methodology – a large group process that allows for the *illustration* of the organization's positive core. Similar to the "positive core map" idea – but coming from outside of AI – Root Learning (2001), an Ohio, USA-based organizational consulting business, has developed a learning technology they refer to as "learning maps." Learning maps are pictorial representations of organizational life and issues, created jointly by Root Learning artists and the contracting organization. These maps serve as a means of focusing and stimulating dialogue, as well as serving as an artful representation of organizational life and desired futures. Similarly, Applied Learning Labs (2003) has created a "knowledge map" process – a visual representation of organizational life for use with their clients.

Similar to Root Learning's learning maps and Applied Learning Labs's knowledge maps, Mintzberg and Van der Heyden (1999) describe "organigraphs":

drawings that show how organizations work. They refer to the potential of organizational charts as the "picture albums" (p. 87) of organizations. They propose to overcome what they see as the shortcomings of the traditional organizational chart by proposing the organigraph as a creative new approach to the way we look at organizations. Organigraphs, they assert, can be used to stimulate conversations in organizations, thereby facilitating a sort of image-initiated dialogue.

"Learning maps," "organigraphs," "knowledge maps," and "positive core maps" are examples of the emerging bridge between visual arts and organization studies. In an emerging practice specialty within facilitation, referred to as "visual practitioners," facilitators capture ideas and synthesize conversations on large paper, creating a colorful mural from words and images. There are diverse styles, and practitioners have coined many names to identify and differentiate their work: graphic recording, graphic facilitation, reflective graphics, mindscaping, visual thinking, information architects, visual synthesis, graphic translation, group graphics, and ideation specialists (see the International Forum of Visual Practitioners website: *www.hnl-consulting.com/ifvp.html*). These visual practitioners translate the lived experience of the meeting into a presentational form, thereby making from the experience an object on which the organizational members can reflect, or a mediate used to channel their inquiry. These are all examples of how organizations are beginning to use pictorial representations of organizational life to develop positive anticipatory images.

Beyond the above-mentioned general descriptions of the process of artful creation, few examples exist that more specifically detail the *practice* of artful creation in appreciative inquiry. For example, De Jong (2001, p. 111) describes a case study of Syntegra Netherlands, a daughter company of British Telecom, in which the client organization was asked to express provocative propositions not only in words but also in music and dance. De Jong asserts, "The combination of words, music, and dance proved to be extremely successful during the presentation of the provocative propositions to the other groups" (p. 111). Also, Pratt (2002, pp. 112–113) describes a case study where participants created a "unity quilt" during the "dream" phase. Pratt had individual participants design a personal swatch, a representation of the individual, that later became part of a "unity quilt" that incorporated all of the individual swatches. Thus, a collage of individual expressions formed the unified whole quilt.

All of these examples, from both the practice of appreciative inquiry and the more traditional practice of organization development, reveal that practitioners are beginning to engage with artful creation with organizations in order to create positive anticipatory images. Murphy (1997), discussing four functions of art, suggests a "visionary/utopic" function, characterized by the creation of new positive images. The process of artful creation in appreciative inquiry appears to be an example of such a function of art (artful creations).

Next, we'll move beyond the practitioner-based understanding of artful creations to a richer theoretical understanding of these examples as a unique form of discourse: aesthetic discourse.

UNDERSTANDING ARTFUL CREATION AS AESTHETIC DISCOURSE

Grant, Keenoy and Oswick (1998) assert that organization "is articulated by and through the deployment of discursive resources" (p. 12). With the emergence of social semiotics and postmodern semiotics, it has been argued that the definition of "text" can be further broadened to include cultural artifacts such as art, architecture, and music (Gottdiener, 1995; Hodge & Kress, 1988; Kress & Van Leeuwen, 1990). This chapter asserts that artful creations – like novels (e.g. Brawer, 1998; Czarniawska-Joerges & Guillet de Monthoux, 1994), poetry (e.g. Windle, 1994), songs (Nissley, 2002b; Nissley, Taylor & Butler, 2002), and plays (e.g. Taylor, 2001, 2000) – can be considered a form of organizational discourse. Thus, artful creations – if understood as a form of organizational discourse – may powerfully shape the creation of positive anticipatory imagery in organizations. To better understand this unique form of organizational discourse, let's turn to the organizational aesthetics literature.

Strati (1996) describes the history of aesthetic epistemology and the development of organizational aesthetics. Recalling that the German philosopher Alexander Gottlieb Baumgarten developed the field of inquiry we refer to as "aesthetics" during the mid-eighteenth century, in response to the emphasis on rationality and intellectual knowledge extending back to Descartes, Strati notes,

> Baumgarten conceived of aesthetics as one of the two components of the theory of knowledge or gnoseology: on the one hand, logic, which investigates intellectual knowledge; on the other, aesthetics, as both the theory of the beautiful and of the arts, which investigate sense knowledge (p. 216).

Strati (1999) develops this idea of aesthetic epistemology within the organizational studies framework. According to Strati, aesthetics in organizational life "concerns a form of human knowledge; and specifically the knowledge yielded by the perceptive faculties" (p. 2). Strati argues "that it is possible to gain aesthetic, rather than logico-rational, understanding of organizational life" (p. 7). More specifically, Strati (1992, p. 575) describes "aesthetic discourse"; similarly, Gagliardi (1996, p. 574) describes "aesthetic communication." Yet the literature does not elaborate

Table 3. A Framework for Understanding Artful Creation.

Characteristics of Artful Creations	Description	References in the Literature
1. Presentational knowledge/language	A means of representing knowing and expressing meaning, through expressive forms (e.g. visual images, drama, song, dance) – allowing us to see what we're thinking.	Heron (1992, 1996a, b), Heron and Reason (2001), Gagliardi (1996), Watkins and Mohr (2001)
2. Mediated dialogue	The creation of an analog to mediate an inquiry into organizational life, where the analog acts as a means through which insights may be elicited.	Barry (1994), Palus and Drath (2002), Johnson and Ludema (1997, p. 82)
3. Symbolic constructions that act as metaphorical representations	An approach that uses artlike representation (e.g. photos, sculpture, drawings) to elicit, reveal, and transform existing sensemaking frameworks.	Sims and Doyle (1995), Barry (1996), Siler (1997, 1999, 2002)
4. Process of collaborative inquiry/co-creation	Using the process of artful creation for the development of shared sens making, where the artful creation is co-created by organization members and their inquiry is self-guided (socially constructed), not relying on expert interpretation.	Barry (1996), Parker (1990), Watkins and Mohr (2001)
5. Window to the unconscious	Engaging the artful inquiry process as a means to make hidden thoughts more discussable – where the artful creation acts as a vehicle for gaining insight by externalizing unconscious or tacit thinking.	Barry (1994, 1996), Siler (2002)

upon what characterizes aesthetic discourse, nor does it provide examples, aside from works such as Nissley's (2002b; Nissley, Taylor & Butler, 2002) consideration of organizational song as a form of aesthetic discourseaesthetic communication.

In the next section, the literature that labels and describes artful creation in organizations is reviewed, described, and synthesized into propositions and a framework for understanding artful creation as an aesthetic discourse. The framework that emerged from the review of literature outlined in Tables 1 and 2 is presented in Table 3. This framework (a) names the common characteristics of artful creation (presentational knowledge/language, mediated dialogue, symbolic constructions that act as metaphorical representation, collaborative inquiry/co-creation, and window to the unconscious) that were found in the emerging literature; and (b) suggests propositions.

ADVANCING OUR UNDERSTANDING OF ARTFUL CREATIONS

Proposition 1: Artful Creations are Expressions of Presentational Knowledge/Language

Strati (1999) asserts "that it is possible to gain aesthetic, rather than logico-rational, understanding of organizational life" (p. 7). Heron (1992, 1996a, b) and Heron and Reason (2001), in their extended epistemology, define four ways of knowing, moving beyond the logico-rational orthodoxy: experiential, presentational, propositional, and practical. Heron and Reason acknowledge the aesthetic way of knowing that Strati asserts, naming it "presentational knowing." They explain the four ways of knowing as follows:

> *Experiential knowing* is through direct face-to-face encounter with person, place or thing; it is knowing through the immediacy of perceiving, through empathy or resonance. *Presentational knowing* emerges from experiential knowing, and provides the first form of expressing meaning and significance through drawing on expressive forms of imagery through movement, dance, sound, music, drawing, painting, sculpture, poetry, story, drama, and so on. *Propositional knowing* 'about' something, is knowing through ideas and theories, expressed in informative statements. *Practical knowing* is knowing 'how to' do something and is expressed in a skill, knack or competence (Heron & Reason, 2001, p. 183).

Specifically, the making of artful creations often begins with direct *experience*. Then one moves on to representing that experience with *presentational* or aesthetic forms (e.g. images, song, dance, story, drama) and then to expressing that experience through *propositional* knowing, such as ideas and theories. Finally, *pragmatic* knowing is expressed in action. The presentational form of knowing (which may take the form of artistic expressions) allows one to see what one is thinking and to inquire into that thinking. Simply put, art (presentational knowing) and logic (propositional knowing) provide different ways of expressing oneself.

Yet are we limiting our potential to inquire into organizational life if we only consider propositional knowing? Gourlay (1984), the music anthropologist, writes that we create new forms of expression when speech is inadequate and we want communication to attain a new level of intensity. Might artful creations then serve as such a new form of expression?

Heron and Reason's (2001) epistemological framework follows Langer's (1942) ideas about the role of art. Langer suggested that tacit knowledge can be represented through artistic, presentational, or symbolic forms and that explicit knowledge can be expressed through discursive forms. The idea that different ways of knowing are suited to different forms of expression – and in particular, that tacit knowing may best be expressed through art forms – is a challenge to the dominant, intellectual forms of knowledge (such as those expressed in this book and in most organizations). Palus and Horth (1996) go so far as to assert the following:

> In attempting to make sense of their challenges, organizations have become overly reliant on rational-analytical competencies, such as deductive reasoning employed within a set of accepted paradigms, numeric criteria and formulae, compartmentalizing problems, and standard operating procedures. Rational-analytical competencies are obviously valuable but, we argue, insufficient by themselves. The full repertoire of competencies for effective co-inquiry includes what we call *aesthetic competencies* (p. x).

Palus and Horth (1996, 2002) name the "aesthetic competencies" that move leaders beyond the orthodoxy of rational-analytical competencies. Specifically, they assert that one of those competencies, "imaging," allows leaders to go beyond the limits of discursive language. They refer to imaging as "the ability to make sense of information, construct ideas, and communicate effectively through the use of images" (2002, p. 71). They more boldly proclaim,

> The world is in the midst of an image revolution. Pictures, stories, metaphors, and visual arts animate the language of the New Economy. The palette of communication options and, more important, of idea making is expanding enormously, transforming the way people think. For today's creative leadership a new kind of literacy is required: a literacy of images (p. 71).

What I find in artful creation in organizations is that such an aesthetic form of knowing calls upon a combination of presentational knowing (the imaginal mode of knowing in which a literacy of images resides) *and* propositional knowing (the conceptual mode of knowing expressed in intellectual statements). As we saw in the earlier examples, artful creations help organizational members to show *and* tell their ideas, or engage in presentational *and* propositional knowing.

Thus, in the "showing" of the artful creation, the organization member engages in presentational knowing; and in the "telling," the member engages in propositional knowing. Watkins and Mohr (2001, p. 134) describe this show-*and*-tell process in the context of appreciative inquiry. They note that the creation of the shared visual image of the organization's preferred future (*show*) is followed by a written statement (provocative proposition/possibility statement) that describes the image (*tell*).

The literature reveals that the artful creations are not merely "left to speak for themselves." Rather, a facilitator ensures that the "showing" of the artful creations is also combined with a collective "telling," where the organizations inquire into the meanings. Specifically, consider the example of the Center for Creative Leadership's Visual Explorer process, which engages participants in "mediated dialogue" (Palus & Drath, 2002). Palus and Horth (1996, 1998, 2002) have described their use of this artful creation process – Visual Explorer – which they employ at the Center for Creative Leadership. Visual Explorer, a tool consisting of more than 200 printed images, is designed to help people in organizations make sense of complex challenges. The use of visual media results in a process called "mediated dialogue" (Palus & Drath, 2002). In the Visual Explorer process, each person in the group selects at least one image that he or she thinks represents some important aspect of a complex challenge he or she faces. Each person then takes a turn at putting his or her image in the middle of the dialogue. The first person (named "Pat," let's say) starts by describing the image itself – the details, the whole scene. What is clear in it? What is mysterious? Next, Pat describes her challenge and how it relates to the image she chose. Each person in the group then reflects on Pat's image and challenge: first reflecting on the image itself, and then relating it to the challenge, using language such as "what I am noticing about that image and your challenge is ..." or "if that were my image ...." After the entire group has had a chance to speak, Pat has the last word, "taking back" her image, challenge, and interpretations from the group. Each person in the group follows the same steps. From this foundation, the group is encouraged to continue the dialogue and reflection on their own terms, to look for patterns and build shared meaning. Thus, the emphasis is on dialogue (propositional knowing grounded in discourse); yet a mediated dialogue is also present, in which presentational knowing and non-discursive expressions (artful creations – e.g. the Visual Explorer images) may shape the collective inquiry.

Thus, the artful creation process is really a combination of presentational *and* propositional knowing, discourse *and* non-discursive expressions – show *and* tell. I suggest that the organizational inquiry process is made richer through artful creations, offering more than one way of thinking about the subject of inquiry by including propositional *and* presentational ways of knowing. Examples of such artful creations acting as presentational knowing can be found in the literature (see Table 4) and encompass all art forms, including theater, poetry, song, visual art, sculpture, and drawing.

Table 4. Examples of Artful Creations Acting as Presentational Knowing.

Presentational or Aesthetic Form of Knowledge	References
Drawing	Barry (1996), Orr (2003)
Sculpture	Sims and Doyle (1995), Nissley and Jusela (2002)
Drama	Oshry (2001), von Krogh, Ichijo and Nonaka (2000, p. 96), Taylor (2000, 2001)
Visual Art	Parker (1990), Pratt (2002, pp. 112–113)
Music	Seifter and Economy (2001), Nissley (2002b), Nissley, Taylor and Butler (in press), De Jong (2001, p. 111)
Poetry	Palus and Horth (2002, pp. 95–98)

Proposition 2: Artful Creations Act as a Mediate
for Organizational Inquiry

Barry (1994) describes a process that he names "analogically mediated inquiry" (AMI). In AMI, the client organization creates an analog of the subject of the inquiry. Analogs can take a variety of forms (e.g. collages, drawings, sculptures, stories, psychodramas, and other artistic expressions) and can be created around many phenomena (e.g. a client can create an analog of her job, her team, her organization, a conflict, or a vision). The analog mediates the inquiry/reflection process and becomes a means through which insights may be elicited.

Barry's description of analogically mediated inquiry is similar to Palus and Drath's (2002) description of "mediated dialogue": placing a mediating object (e.g. artful creation) in the middle of a dialogue to enhance the participants' experience of the dialogue. They describe two techniques for facilitating a mediated dialogue – "Visual Explorer" and "Movie Making" – that make use of pictorial metaphors and storytelling. Palus and Drath assert, "Mediated dialogue means building artistic bridges for communication" (p. 37). They go on to describe a three-stage process, or model of how mediated dialogue works: (a) bring meaning to the *surface* by attaching significance to an object (e.g. artful creation); (b) *display* it, by placing it at the center of dialogue for public view; and then (c) *inquire* into its various meanings.

Isaacs (2002) reminds us that mediated dialogue resembles Schrage's (2000) notion of the importance of prototyping to stimulate innovation. He goes on to say that mediating objects can stimulate dialogue and act like "conversational proto-types" that help people give form to unformed or unarticulated ideas. Similarly, Nissley and Jusela (2002) describe artful representations as prototypes. What I've found in the process of artful creation in organizations is that the organization's inquiry is not "direct," but is rather "mediated" – where the mediates (artful creations) act as a means to focus inquiry and elicit insights. In the process of artful creation in organizations, the artful creation itself acts as the mediate or object of the inquiry.

In both cases previously mentioned, an artful creation helped to "focus" the organization's inquiry: at Norway's Hydro Aluminum Karmøy Fabrikker, a mural; visual images at the Center for Creative Leadership and Root Learning. In either case, the organization's inquiry was not only organized by propositional knowledge but also was mediated through artful creations. In addition, VanGundy and Naiman (2003) offer examples from practitioners of how artful creation can mediate organizational inquiry.

Proposition 3: Artful Creations Serve as Symbolic Constructions that Act as Metaphorical Representations of Organizational Life

Rather than simply referring to an artful creation as a mediate, the more specific description of artful creations as symbolic constructions that act as metaphorical representations may be more descriptive and helpful in creating understanding of this unique characteristic of artful creations. Sims and Doyle (1995) define "cognitive sculpting" as "a collection of symbols to represent the part of the world that they have been talking about" (p. 118). They describe how the technique can help managers to talk through and develop a view of difficult and complex organizational issues. Managers can express the issues by organizing a collection of symbolically rich objects in an expression, or sculpture (three-dimensional model making). Like the work of Nissley and Jusela (2002) and Di Ciantis (1995), Sims and Doyle's technique follows the tradition of elicitation techniques, such as cognitive mapping, in that it encourages a person or group to dialogue with a physical and/or metaphorical representation of their ideas. The Lego Corporation (Serious Play, 2002) has created a similar three-dimensional approach to working with business organizations: engaging organizational members with Legos as artful creation, for the purpose of uncovering insights. In other words, organizational members create three-dimensional symbolic constructions that act as metaphorical representations of organizational life issues.

Similar to Sims and Doyle's (1995) cognitive sculpting, Barry (1996), building on Clifford Geertz's (1980) work, describes "symbolic constructivism" in what he refers to as "artful inquiry," which he describes as an approach that uses art-like representation (e.g. sculpture, photographs, drawings, dramatization, etc.) to elicit, reveal, and transform existing sensemaking frameworks. Barry describes three kinds of inquiry/reflective practice: eliciting, revealing, and transforming. *Eliciting* is the use of visual images (such as sculpture, photographs, drawings, etc.) to evoke descriptive tellings. Images used in this way evoke ideas, draw one out, and get one to say more than he or she would otherwise. *Revealing* allows one to discern what is not being said: the tacit or unconscious aspects of a situation. Barry asserts that uncovering repressed meaning is critical for creating and maintaining organizational functionality and is central to the practice of organization development. *Transforming*, according to Barry (1996), is especially appropriate where the inquirer is a change agent or where the change project has a liberationist bent. In other words, "transformation requires not only description and revelation but also the development of imaginative and compelling alternatives" (p. 428).

This specific type of inquiry – transformation – seems to best describe how artful creation is used in the provocative proposition phase of appreciative inquiry.

Ludema (2000, p. 282), referring to the provocative principle, asserts, "The most powerful images of the future are those that stretch, challenge, or interrupt the status quo," also stating that "such images are rarely strictly rational" (p. 282). Ludema thus acknowledges a place for something other than the logico-rational discourse: the positive possibility of aesthetic discourse.

Also, Siler (1999, 2002) describes a model that he calls "The Five Dimensions of Communication." His model suggests that greater understanding and shared vision can be achieved when communication combines words, images, structures, motion, and symbolism. Siler engages participants in this five-dimensional model building process, allowing them to physically represent their ideas in a sculpture-like creation or prototype. The prototype displays knowledge in physical form. Siler calls this transformation of imagination and ideas "Metaphorming," a process in which the participants' unconscious (tacit) ideas may become conscious (explicit). Specifically, participants are given a variety of materials (e.g. yarn, Styrofoam forms, pipe cleaners, magazine photographs) so they can create a five-dimensional model. It is a process of making ideas physical (similar to prototyping, but more freeform and free-associative). This process involves what Siler refers to as the "five dimensions of communication": words, images, structures, motion, and symbols. Siler (2002) elaborates, "I coined the word *Metaphorming* to describe the act of transforming one thing (a word, image, object, idea, expression, piece of information or knowledge) into something with a new meaning, purpose, and use" (p. 16). Siler has been using this approach to facilitate innovative thinking for the past 25 years.

Within the field of marketing, one can find similar work by Richard Zaltman (Pink, 1998; Zaltman & Coulter, 1995) at the Harvard Business School. Zaltman has developed a creative use of pictorial metaphor for marketing professionals: the Zaltman Metaphor Elicitation Technique (ZMET). Zaltman's work is framed by the idea that thoughts travel as images. The ZMET uses images as a means of getting at consumers' underlying relationships with products. ZMET is a form of inquiry where product marketers help consumers to describe their experiences with a product through the use of images and visual metaphor.

In the previously mentioned examples, the organizational inquiry process was facilitated by the creation of symbolic constructions that act as metaphorical representations. For example, Norway's Hydro Aluminum Karmøy Fabrikker used the garden metaphor; with the Center for Creative Leadership's Visual Explorer and Root Learning's learning maps, a visual metaphor was generated. Thus, in organizations, artful creations serve as symbolic constructions that act as metaphorical representations, allowing an organization to literally "see" the subject of inquiry.

Proposition 4: Artful Creations are Realized Through Collaborative
Inquiry/Co-Creation

Barry (1996) asserts that, unlike most art-based methods that rely on expert interpretation, artful inquiry with organizations and the specific practice of symbolic constructivism stress the development of shared sensemaking – and thus compose a process of collaborative inquiry/co-creation. This process is found throughout the practice of artful creation (e.g. Palus & Drath, 2002; Palus & Horth, 2002; Parker, 1990; Sims & Doyle, 1995). Similarly, within the field of qualitative research, Lawrence-Lightfoot and Davis (1997) describe a collaborative form of image-based co-inquiry that they refer to as "portraiture," and Noble and Jones (2001) within the organization studies framework describe "photography as participative action research."

Specifically, by collaborative inquiry/co-creation, I mean the following: using the process of artful creation for the development of shared sensemaking, where the artful creation is co-created by organization members and where their inquiry is self-guided, not relying on expert interpretation (socially constructed).

However, there are examples where artful creation is not collaborative or co-created, especially in the area of musical arts. For example, the musicians of Orpheus Chamber Orchestra (2001), an orchestra without a conductor, have engaged with business organizations who seek to learn how the Orpheus orchestra's way of creating music may serve as a model for their own organization (Lieber, 2000; Lubins, 1999; Seifter, 2001; Traub, 1996). Harvey Seifter, the executive director of the Orpheus Chamber Orchestra, and Peter Economy (2001) have co-authored a book about the "Orpheus Process" – how the Orpheus model of organizing may help other organizations to re-create this model of collaborative leadership. In this example, the collective reflection is collaborative; however, the participants do not co-create the music – alone, the orchestra musicians create it. In a second example, *The Music Paradigm* (2001) brings business organizations together with orchestra musicians, as the business organization seeks to learn different ways to "look at" organizational life. After participating in a "Music Paradigm" experience (conducted by Stamford [Connecticut] Symphony Orchestra conductor Roger Nierenberg), Paul Charron, chairman and CEO of Liz Claibourne, called it an extremely effective learning experience, noting, "I think we gained new valuable insights by our ability to look at the concepts of leadership, communication, and collaboration through the lens of a different medium" (Gershman, 2000).

Thus, commonly, in the process of artful creation in organizations, the creative process (i.e. the mediate, symbolic constructions that act as metaphorical representation, presentational language) is often a collaborative process, although not exclusively so. In addition, there are some examples where the organization members do not actually co-create a physical representation (e.g. the previously mentioned example of Visual Explorer at the Center for Creative Leadership) but instead use "pre-made" art forms (e.g. the images used in the Visual Explorer process) or engage as an audience: observing the art form (e.g. a performance of the Orpheus Chamber Orchestra) as a starting point to focus inquiry and construct meaning.

When working with images, one must remember that they naturally have multiple interpretations. Palus and Horth (2002) remind us that this quality is what makes images so helpful in our inquiry of organizational life and its complexity. Specifically, images are polysemous: that is, they lend themselves to multiple meanings. Thus, when working with artful creations, two people most likely see different things. They can then talk about the differences and similarities in what they see. Palus and Horth (2002, p. 86) assert that this polysemous nature of images is a wonderful antidote to tunnel vision in organizations.

Proposition 5: Artful Creations Serve as Windows to the Unconscious

Barry (1994) asserts that discovery systems in organization development presume that high levels of consciousness exist – that people in organizations know what they think or feel, even if those thoughts are not openly expressed. He describes analogically mediated inquiry (AMI) – a type of artful creation process – as a means to make hidden thoughts more discussable and to uncover the organizational unconscious. Similarly, discussing the "metaphorming" process, Siler (2002, p. 17) states, "These models allow you actually to see what you're thinking and what others think, to make tangible all the intangible thoughts and viewpoints that tend to remain hidden from view and uncommunicated." Morgan (1993) has shown that when participants combine metaphor with artlike creation, powerful vehicles for change tend to result: the images created can serve as both "mirrors and windows" – devices that reflect back who we are and simultaneously suggest new horizons (pp. 215–233, 288–294).

From the field of knowledge creation we find examples of the usefulness of artful creations to express tacit knowledge. For example, Nonaka and Konno (1998) describe a model of knowledge creation, with four steps (socialization, externalization, combination, and internalization) in the knowledge conversion process. Externalization, they note, requires the expression of tacit knowledge and its translation into comprehensible forms that can be understood by others. They suggest, "The articulation of tacit knowledge – that is, the conversion of tacit into explicit knowledge – involves techniques that help to express one's ideas or images as words, concepts, figurative language (such as metaphors, analogies, or narratives), and visuals" (p. 44).

What is obvious to the practitioner who engages in the process of artful creation is that artful creations invite creative inquiry into the thought process that moves us well beyond words alone. The imagery of the artful creations acts as a vehicle for reflecting and discovering meanings that emerge – a way of gaining insight. Artful creation appears to probe beneath the level of the rational mind, revealing what cannot be known from that perspective alone. It allows an organization to make "hidden" (unconscious) thoughts more discussable by externalizing unconscious or tacit thinking – thereby making it available for reflection. I suggest that much of what an organization needs to reflect on is unconscious, and artful creation is one way to get at this.

CONCLUSION

Barry and Elmes (1997) ask, "What form will strategic narratives take next?" Many (e.g. Cooperrider & Whitney, 2000; Ludema, 2000) have already asserted that appreciative inquiry is a "next" form of strategic narrative – moving from "deficit discourse to vocabularies of hope" (Ludema, 2000, p. 265). This chapter suggests, more specifically, that within the practice of appreciative inquiry, artful creation or aesthetic discourse is a "next" form of strategic narrative.

This chapter moves the appreciative inquiry literature beyond the metaphorical understanding of the "art of" appreciative inquiry in order to reveal and explain how practitioners are actually engaging organizations in the artful creation of positive anticipatory imagery. While very little literature in appreciative inquiry describes this process of artful creation, a descriptive, practitioner-based understanding of the use of artful creations is emerging within the broader organization studies framework. Table 1 labels the diverse ways of talking about artful creation in organizations.

Then, the literature that labels and describes artful creation in organizations was reviewed, described, and developed into a framework for understanding artful creation as a unique organizational discourse: an aesthetic discourse. A framework that emerged from this literature review – presented in Table 3 – names and describes the five common characteristics of artful creation that were found in the emerging literature: (1) presentational knowledge/language; (2) mediated dialogue; (3) symbolic constructions that act as metaphorical representation; (4) collaborative inquiry/co-creation; and (5) window to the unconscious. Third, the chapter discusses these characteristics, moving us beyond the practitioner-focused understanding of artful creations that dominate the organization studies literature, and including a theoretical understanding of artful creation.

As mentioned previously, most of the literature on artful creation describes it as a process where the organizational members *simply talk about* these new images, vs. *actually engaging in the creation of* visual representations of the new images. This chapter shows that practitioners are engaging in the actual artful creation of positive imagery; however, the literature has not remained as current as the practice. This chapter helps the literature to "catch up" with the practitioner by reporting advances in the practice and theory of artful creation.

Finally, Ludema (2000, p. 282) hints, referring to provocative propositions, that "the most powerful images of the future are those that stretch, challenge or interrupt the status quo." Ludema continues, "Such images are rarely strictly rational" – to which we can say, "Yes, and . . .." *Yes*, they are rarely strictly rational; *and* they may be a form of aesthetic discourse, moving us beyond the limitations of strictly relying on rational forms of expression. As Cooperrider (2001, p. 32) and these propositions suggest, appreciative inquiry is actually about "the artful creation of positive imagery."

Implications

What is the value of an organization's engaging with the process of artful creation? Based on this initial exploration into the subject, two major benefits are possible. First, in the context of organizational learning, we appear to be limiting our potential to inquire into organizational life if we only consider propositional knowing. Presentational forms of knowing (e.g. artful creations) allow us to "see what we're thinking" and to inquire into that knowing. Simply put, artful creations (presentational knowing) and logic (propositional knowing) provide different ways of expressing ourselves, thus offering a richer way of knowing organizational life.

Second, through the lens of organizational effectiveness, given the growing complexity of organizational life, we must continue to seek ways that will allow us to make sense of that growing complexity. Dr. Thomas Bechtler, CEO of Hesta AG, Zug reflected on the functional value of corporate art during an interview with Marjory Jacobson (1993, p. 170): "A work of art is always a condensation of the complex reality. So, art can be a means through which one learns to perceive an intricate solution through a simplified image." I suggest that, like corporate art, artful creations may serve as condensations of the complex realities of organizational life, allowing us to perceive an intricate solution through a simplified image.

Future Research Directions

First, while this chapter asserts that the process of artful creation moves organizational members beyond *simply talking about* new images of the future by *actually engaging them in the creation of* positive anticipatory images, no research speaks to the effectiveness of such inquiry – aside from the emerging work of Orr (2003), which specifically addresses artful creations, and the more general assertions of Schein (2001), which address the value of the arts in organizational inquiry. Second, while this "exploratory" chapter suggests a heuristic – a framework for understanding artful creation in organizations – it should be viewed as a beginning. The characteristics of artful creation that are identified should be further developed and challenged. For example, artful creations may also allow us greater access to emotions and may offer deeper insights to subjects of inquiry. Artful creations provide a means to represent and give meaning to "inner experiences," serving as non-discursive expressions of what one thinks *and* feels. The art therapy literature may offer additional insights into the emotion-knowing connection. Third, Murphy (1997), discussing four functions of art, suggests a "visionary/utopic" function, characterized by the creation of new positive images. I have suggested that the process of artful creation in appreciative inquiry appears to be an example of such a function of art (artful creations). Another function that Murphy discusses is the "dystopic" function of art, whereby art serves to criticize the present and provide cautionary tales about the future. Further inquiry into this juxtaposition of the "utopic" and "dystopic" functions of art/artful creations may deepen our understanding of how artful creation functions in the creation of positive anticipatory images.

ACKNOWLEDGMENTS

I would like to acknowledge and thank the following individuals who have helped shape my ideas and passion of artful creation in organizational life: Paul Nelson, who "turned me on to" artful creation in my M. A. studies; Jim Ludema, whose manuscript review, comments, and encouragement were invaluable; David Barry and fellow ACORNers, who have always offered insight and encouragement; and my clients and students (especially my Spring 2002 Change Agent Skills Laboratory), who actually engaged in the artful creation process! And, finally, to my always caring and encouraging wife, Elise – who also encouraged me to complete this manuscript so that I could share time with my newborn daughter, Isabel.

REFERENCES

Applied Learning Labs (2003). *Applied Learning Labs home page*. Retrieved 25 May 2003 from http://www.appliedlearninglabs.com/kmaps/overview.html.

Barrett, F., & Cooperrider, D. (2001). Generative metaphor intervention: A new approach for working with systems divided by conflict and caught in defensive perception. In: D. Cooperrider, P. Sorensen, T. Yaeger & D. Whitney (Eds), *Appreciative Inquiry: An Emerging Direction for Organization Development*. Champaign, IL: Stipes.

Barry, D. (1994). Making the invisible visible: Using analogically-based methods to surface the organizational unconscious. *Organizational Development Journal, 12*(4), 37–48.

Barry, D. (1996). Artful inquiry: A symbolic constructivist approach to social science research. *Qualitative Inquiry, 2*(4), 411–438.

Barry, D., & Elmes, M. (1997). Strategy retold: Toward a narrative view of strategic discourse. *Academy of Management Review, 22*(2), 429–452.

Brawer, R. (1998). *Fictions of business: Insights on management from great literature*. New York: Wiley.

California Institute of Integral Studies (2001). *California Institute of Integral Studies home page*. Retrieved 7 May 2001 from http://www.ciis.edu/catalog/exacertificate.html.

Cooperrider, D. (2000). Positive image, positive action: The affirmative basis of organizing. In: D. Cooperrider, P. Sorensen, D. Whitney & T. Yaeger (Eds), *Appreciative Inquiry: Rethinking Human Organization Toward a Positive Theory of Change* (pp. 29–53). Champaign, IL: Stipes.

Cooperrider, D. (2001). Positive image: Positive action. In: D. Cooperrider, P. Sorenson, T. Yaeger & D. Whitney (Eds), *Appreciative Inquiry: An Emerging Direction for Organization Development*. Champaign, IL: Stipes.

Cooperrider, D., & Whitney, D. (2000). A positive revolution in change: Appreciative inquiry. In: D. Cooperrider, P. Sorensen, D. Whitney & T. Yaeger (Eds), *Appreciative Inquiry: Rethinking Human Organization Toward a Positive Theory of Change* (pp. 3–27). Champaign, IL: Stipes.

Czarniawska-Joerges, B., & Guillet de Monthoux, P. (1994). *Good novels, better management: Reading organisational realities in fiction*. Chur, Switzerland: Harwood Academic Press.

De Jong, J. (2001). Case study: Syntegra. In: J. Watkins & B. Mohr (Eds), *Appreciative Inquiry: Change at the Speed of Imagination* (pp. 109–112). San Francisco, CA: Jossey-Bass/Pfeiffer.

Dewhurst, C. (1984). The arts of working: Manipulating the urban work environment. *Western Folklore, 43*, 192–202.

Di Ciantis, C. (1995). *Using an art technique to facilitate leadership development*. Greensboro, NC: Center for Creative Leadership.

Gagliardi, P. (1996). Exploring the aesthetic side of organizational life. In: S. Clegg, C. Hardy & W. Nord (Eds), *Handbook of Organizational Studies*. London: Sage.

Geertz, C. (1980). Blurred genres: The refiguration of social thought. *The American Scholar, 49*(2), 165–179.

Gottdiener, M. (1995). *Postmodern semiotics: Material culture and the forms of postmodern life*. Cambridge, MA: Blackwell.

Gourlay, K. (1984). The non-universality of music and the universality of non-music. *The World of Music, 28*(2).

Grant, D., Keenoy, T., & Oswick, C. (1998). Introduction: Organizational discourse: Of diversity, dichotomy, and multi-disciplinarity. In: D. Grant, T. Keenoy & C. Oswick (Eds), *Discourse and Organization* (pp. 1–13). London: Sage.

Heron, J. (1992). *Feeling and personhood: Psychology in another key*. Newbury Park, CA: Sage.

Heron, J. (1996a). *Cooperative inquiry: Research into the human condition*. Thousand Oaks, CA: Sage.

Heron, J. (1996b). Helping whole people learn. In: D. Boud & N. Miller (Eds), *Working with Experience* (pp. 75–91). London: Routledge.

Heron, J., & Reason, P. (2001). The practice of co-operative inquiry: Research 'with' rather than 'on' people. In: P. Reason & H. Bradbury (Eds), *Handbook of Action Research: Participative Inquiry and Practice* (pp. 179–188). London: Sage.

Hodge, R., & Kress, G. (1988). *Social semiotics*. Cambridge: Polity Press.

International Forum of Visual Practitioners (2002). *International Forum of Visual Practitioners home page*. Retrieved 1 July 2002 from http://www.hnl-consulting.com/ifvp.html.

Isaacs, W. (2002). Commentary [Putting something in the middle: An approach to dialogue]. *Reflections*, *3*(2), 37–38.

Jacobson, M. (1993). *Art for work: The new renaissance in corporate collecting*. Boston, MA: Harvard Business School Press.

Johnson, S., & Ludema, J. (1997). *Partnering to build and measure organizational capacity*. Grand Rapids, MI: Christian World Relief Committee.

Kress, G., & Van Leeuwen, T. (1990). *Reading images*. Geelon, Australia: Deakin University Press.

Langer, S. (1942). *Philosophy in a new key*. Cambridge, MA: Harvard University Press.

Lawrence-Lightfoot, S., & Davis, J. (1997). *The art and science of portraiture*. San Francisco: Jossey-Bass.

Lieber, R. (2000). Leadership ensemble. *Fast Company*, *34*(May), 286–291.

Lockwood, Y. (1984). The joy of labor. *Western Folklore*, *43*, 202–211.

Lubins, P. (1999). Orchestrating success. In: R. Rehm (Ed.), *People in Charge: Creating Self Managing Workplaces*. Gloucestershire, UK: Hawthorne Press.

Ludema, J. (2000). From deficit discourse to vocabularies of hope: The power of appreciation. In: D. Cooperrider, P. Sorensen, D. Whitney & T. Yaeger (Eds), *Appreciative Inquiry: Rethinking Human Organization Toward a Positive Theory of Change* (pp. 265–287). Champaign, IL: Stipes.

Ludema, J., Mohr, B., Whitney, D., & Griffin, T. (2003). *The appreciative inquiry summit: A practitioner's guide for leading positive large-group change*. San Francisco: Berrett-Kohler.

Ludema, J., Wilmot, T., & Srivastava, S. (1997). Organizational hope: Reaffirming the constructive task of social and organizational inquiry. *Human Relations Journal*, *50*(8), 1015–1038.

Mintzberg, H., & Van der Heyden, L. (1999). Organigraphs: Drawing how companies really work. *Harvard Business Review*, *77*(5), 87–94.

Morgan, G. (1993). *Imaginization: The art of creative management*. London: Sage.

Murphy, P. (1997). Art and the natural environment. *Organization and Environment*, *10*(1), 18–19.

Nissley, N. (2002a). Art-based learning in management education. In: B. DeFillippi & C. Wankel (Eds), *Rethinking Management Education in the 21st Century* (pp. 27–61). Greenwich, CT: Information Age Press.

Nissley, N. (2002b). Tuning-in to organizational song as aesthetic discourse. *Culture and Organization*, *8*(1), 51–68.

Nissley, N., & Jusela, G. (2002). Using arts-based learning to facilitate knowledge creation: The art of intellectual capital at Equiva Services. In: J. Phillips (Ed.), *Measuring and Monitoring Intellectual Capital*. Alexandria, VA: American Society for Training and Development.

Nissley, N., Taylor, S., & Butler, O. (2002). The power of organizational song: An organizational discourse and aesthetic expression of organizational culture. *Tamara: Journal of Critical Postmodern Organization Science*, *2*(1), 47–62.

Noble, A., & Jones, D. (2001). 'Hey look at this': Photography as participatory action research. In: S. Sankaran, B. Dick, R. Passfield & P. Swepson (Eds), *Effective Change Management Using Action Learning and Action Research: Concepts, Frameworks, Processes and Applications* (pp. 133–147). Lismore, New South Wales: Southern Cross University Press.

Nonaka, I., & Konno, N. (1998). The concept of '*ba*': Building a foundation for knowledge creation. *California Management Review, 40*(3), 40–54.

Orpheus Chamber Orchestra (2001). *The Orpheus web page.* Retrieved 15 February 2001 from http://orpheusnyc.com.

Orr, D. (2003). Aesthetic practice: The power of artistic expression to transform organizations. Unpublished doctoral dissertation, Benedictine University, Chicago, IL.

Palus, C., & Drath, W. (2002). Putting something in the middle: An approach to dialogue. *Reflections, 3*(2), 28–39.

Palus, C., & Horth, D. (1996). Leading creatively: The art of making sense. *The Journal of Aesthetic Education, 30*(4).

Palus, C., & Horth, D. (1998). Leading creatively. *Leadership in Action, 18*(2), 1–8.

Palus, C., & Horth, D. (2002). *The leader's edge: Six creative competencies for navigating complex challenges.* San Francisco: Jossey-Bass.

Parker, M. (1990). *Creating shared vision: The story of a pioneering approach to organizational revitalization.* Oslo, Norway: Norwegian Center for Leadership Development.

Pink, D. (1998). Metaphor marketing. *Fast Company, 14,* 214–220.

Pratt, C. (2002). Creating unity from competing integrities: A case study in appreciative inquiry methodology. In: R. Fry, F. Barrett, J. Seiling & D. Whitney (Eds), *Appreciative Inquiry and Organizational Transformation: Reports from the Field* (pp. 99–120). Westport, CT: Quorum Books.

Root Learning (2001). *Root Learning home page.* Retrieved 14 February 2001 from http://www.rootlearning.com.

Schein, E. (2001). The role of art and the artist. *Reflections (Journal of the Society for Organizational Learning), 4*(2), 81–83.

Schrage, M. (2000). *Serious play: How the world's best companies stimulate to innovate.* Boston, MA: Harvard Business School Press.

Seifter, H. (2001). The conductor-less orchestra. *Leader to Leader* (Summer), 38–44.

Seifter, H., & Economy, P. (2001). *Leadership ensemble: Lessons in collaborative management from the world's only conductorless orchestra.* New York: Henry Holt and Company.

Serious Play (2002). *Serious Play home page.* Retrieved 1 July 2002 from http://www.seriousplay.com.

Siler, T. (1999). Think like a genius process. In: P. Holman & T. Devane (Eds), *The Change Handbook: Group Methods for Shaping the Future* (pp. 279–294). San Francisco: Berrett-Koehler.

Siler, T. (2002). Metaphorming your organization. *Leader to Leader, 24,* 15–19.

Sims, D., & Doyle, J. (1995). Cognitive sculpting as a means of working with managers' metaphors. *Omega International Journal of Management Science, 23*(2), 117–124.

Strati, A. (1992). Aesthetic understanding of organizational life. *Academy of Management Review, 17*(3), 568–581.

Strati, A. (1996). Organizations viewed through the lens of aesthetics. *Organization, 3*(2), 209–218.

Strati, A. (1999). *Organization and aesthetics.* London: Sage.

Taylor, S. (2000). Aesthetic knowledge in academia: Capitalist pigs at the Academy of Management. *Journal of Management Inquiry.*

Taylor, S. (Writer and Director) (2001). *Soft targets* [Play].

Traub, J. (1996, September 2). Passing the baton: What CEOs could learn from the Orpheus Chamber Orchestra. *New Yorker,* 100–105.

VanGundy, A., & Naiman, L. (2003). *Orchestrating collaboration at work: Using music, improv, storytelling, and other arts to improve teamwork.* San Francisco: Jossey-Bass.

von Krogh, G., Ichijo, G., & Nonaka, I. (2000). *Enabling knowledge creation: How to unlock the mystery of tacit knowledge and release the power of innovation.* New York: Oxford University Press.

Watkins, J., & Mohr, B. (2001). *Appreciative inquiry: Change at the speed of imagination.* San Francisco, CA: Jossey-Bass/Pfeiffer.

Weisbord, M. (1992). *Discovering common ground: How future search conferences bring people together to achieve breakthrough innovation, empowerment, shared vision, and collaborative action.* San Francisco: Berrett-Koehler.

Weisbord, M., & Janoff, S. (1995). *Future search: Finding common ground for action in organizations and communities.* San Francisco: Berrett-Koehler.

Windle, R. (1994). *The poetry of business life: An anthology.* San Francisco: Berrett-Koehler.

Zaltman, J., & Coulter, R. (1995). Seeing the voice of the customer: Metaphor-based advertising research. *Journal of Advertising Research, 35*(4), 35–51.

SUSTAINING POSITIVE CHANGE: INVITING CONVERSATIONAL CONVERGENCE THROUGH APPRECIATIVE LEADERSHIP AND ORGANIZATION DESIGN

Michael J. Mantel and James D. Ludema

ABSTRACT

This chapter explores the power of appreciative inquiry in moving beyond a one-time intervention technique to sustaining positive change by creating on-going "conversational convergence" around continuously evolving futures and directions for an organization. A conversational map was created from nine years of change data revealing the centrality of language in creating and sustaining change. Awareness of the corporate conversational streams and the intentional influencing of these streams helped sustain the positive change process over this extended period. This influence was applied at the individual level by developing a commitment for appreciative leadership principles and at the corporate level by incorporating appreciative design elements into the organization's social architecture.

Constructive Discourse and Human Organization
Advances in Appreciative Inquiry, Volume 1, 309–336
© 2004 Published by Elsevier Ltd.
ISSN: 1475-9152/doi:10.1016/S1475-9152(04)01014-2

INTRODUCTION

The authors of this chapter worked together for over nine years (Mike primarily as an organizational "insider" and Jim as an organizational "outsider") on the formation and expansion of a joint venture called Vision Chicago, which was formed to understand and encourage the processes that enable large collaborative partnerships to address domain-level issues in urban contexts such as housing, education, employment and violence in the city of Chicago. The context for the research is World Vision, a large, private, volunteer organization (PVO) operating relief and development efforts that impact 85 million people in nearly 100 countries. Like many PVOs, World Vision's mission is to bring relief to areas experiencing intense suffering from war, famine, genocide and natural disasters, and to develop the capacity of communities interested in extending their reach to sustainable agriculture, health, education and financial self-sufficiency. Success in these environments requires collaboration across dividing lines of culture, religion, geography, sector, and economic status. Consequently, PVOs like World Vision are ideal organizations in which to study innovative approaches to system-wide change in diverse, complex environments. In this sense the case meets the criteria for an "extreme case" (Dutton & Dukerich, 1991; Eisenhardt, 1989).

Background

During its first nine years, Vision Chicago mobilized a network of over 1,500 organizations resulting in more than $6 million in direct aid, $13 million in donated products, and 12,000 volunteers to invest in the health and development of the City of Chicago. In June 1994, Vision Chicago was recognized by the Council of Foundations as one of eight "Models of Hope" for its pioneering work in rebuilding America's cities and in June 1999, won the "Best Practices Award" by the U.S. Department of Housing and Urban Development.

Very early on, Vision Chicago became a significant success story, and World Vision began to replicate the model in other U.S. cities (New York, Los Angeles, Minneapolis/St. Paul, and Seattle). The influence of Vision Chicago and these other *Vision Cities* began to be felt in World Vision's corporate offices in Seattle when World Vision's CEO called for a new "regional structure" to support the promise of the Vision Cities. World Vision used appreciative inquiry in many ways throughout the formation of Vision Chicago, the Vision Cities, and the new regional structure. We were amazed to see the power appreciative inquiry had in this highly complex environment to unify people around a common direction for the future. It brought together people that were rich and poor, black and white, northerners and southerners, close to home and far away to discover one another's strengths and to find agreement for collective action.

Yet, a few years after World Vision launched the initial appreciative inquiry process, they discovered that implementing the organizational vision initiated by appreciative inquiry became more difficult. They began to experience relational stress and staff fatigue. At times it seemed as if they were going backward rather than forward. Among the different parties involved, words such as "war" and "camps" began to replace "invitation" and "hospitality." Exclusion competed with inclusion. What was wrong began to get more attention than what was right. Before long, critics were heard saying that while appreciative inquiry is a potent force to help people find common ground and envision a shared future, it does not sustain forward movement. People at World Vision were faced with the questions: If appreciative inquiry is so good, so effective, why is change so hard? They had experienced the amazing power of appreciative inquiry, but was it sustainable? Nothing they had ever experienced could move a complex organization forward like appreciative inquiry, but could it stay the course?

Sustaining Positive Change

While much research and literature has been completed on appreciative inquiry as an intervention (Barrett, 1995; Bushe, 1998, 1999; Bushe & Coetzer, 1995; Cooperrider, Sorensen, Yaeger & Whitney, 2001; Cooperrider & Srivastva, 1987; Fry,Barrett, Seiling & Whitney, 2002; Ludema, Cooperrider & Barrett, 2001; Ludema, Whitney, Mohr & Griffin, 2003; Whitney & Trosten-Bloom, 2003), none has explored the specific topic of *sustainability of change* that is launched by an appreciative intervention. Throughout the literature about organizational change, one continues to find the question, "How is a change sustained?" A summary of the literature suggests that change is sustained by a focus on vision (Nutt & Backoff, 1997), or on Schneider and Brief's three conditions (1996) of challenge, participation and mutual trust, or on multilevel conversational management (Deazin, Glynn & Kazanjian's, 1999), or on Moss Kanter's circle of change encouragement, change knowledge, collaboration, and innovation (1999). Bate, Khan and Pye go on to show that collaboration and participative inquiry will lead to sensemaking of loose-jointed structures (2000). Quinn, Spreitzer and Brown turn our attention to the individual's role in sustaining change (2000). What all of these perspectives share is the understanding that change is continuous, evolving, and incremental and that it is influenced, directed and "sustained" through conversations (Weick & Quinn, 1999).

We concur with this perspective. An organization no sooner sets its course than the conversation shifts, diverges, grows or diminishes; the initial map of change is no longer valid. As natural systems tend toward entropy, social systems in a linguistic framework tend toward cacophony. Organizations dream and work toward positive futures, but no person can predict the precise moment when that vision will be realized or the exact shape the vision will take. When it does emerge, it is not possible to know how long it will be a valid present. Sustained movement towards an ever-evolving future requires continuous appreciative engagement. Consequently, *sustaining change* in this study is an intentional moving toward a collectively and continually defined future while remaining poised and responsive to the surprises of the present.

Summary of Findings

Findings in this case study reveal that appreciative change was sustained by developing an awareness of the corporate conversational streams and by intentionally and positively influencing those streams through inquiry at the individual level and at the corporate level.

A number of practices have been identified that enabled change agents to shape conversations at both of these levels. At the individual level, organization members incorporated a number of appreciative concepts into their own personal intentions and commitments throughout the study. At the organizational level, change agents utilized design concepts that strengthened the change effort over the long term by building appreciative principles and interventions into the social architecture of the organization.

METHODOLOGY

This was a unique project that drew from a variety of methodological streams. First and foremost it was an appreciative inquiry (Cooperrider & Srivastva, 1987) that resulted in the creation of "generative theory" (Gergen, 1982) about the influence of conversational convergence on sustaining positive organization change. It was an appreciative inquiry in the sense that we (the authors) used appreciative inquiry as an OD intervention methodology with the client system (World Vision) throughout the full nine years of the project. For example, in 1993–1994 we, along with members of World Vision, conducted dozens of appreciative inquiry interviews and held a series of large-group appreciative inquiry summit meetings in both Chicago and Los Angeles to create Vision Chicago. We did the same in Minneapolis/St.

Paul to create Vision Twin Cities in 1995–1996. From 1997 to 2001, we used a similar appreciative inquiry "intervention" process to help World Vision design and implement a "regionalized" nation-wide organizational structure.

It was not just the intervention strategy, however, that made this an appreciative inquiry project. It was also an appreciative inquiry in the sense that throughout the project, at every step along the way, the responses to the appreciative questions that were posed by us and by the members of World Vision generated reams of "data" (stories, quotes, themes, dreams, aspirations) that were collected in the form of transcripts, field notes, and other forms of communication media (reports, memos, emails, videotapes, etc.). These data were collected, analyzed, and used as the basis for the generative theory developed in this chapter and in other publications (Ludema, 1996, 2001; Ludema, Wilmot & Srivastva, 1997; Mantel, 2001; Mantel & Ludema, 2000).

Insider/Outsider Research Team

Although our study was fundamentally an appreciative inquiry leading to generative theory, it drew from other methodological approaches. We used an insider/outsider research team (Bartunek & Louis, 1996) to counter one of the main criticisms of qualitative research in organizations that no matter how carefully and faithfully done, the study always represents the interpreting perspective of only one single observer, and is thus subject to idiosyncrasies. Using two perspectives mitigated this problem. It also served to expand our access to data. Mike's role as an organizational insider (line manager and doctoral student) gave him direct experience with information, meanings, and perspectives unattainable to anyone from the outside. Jim's role as an organizational outsider (consultant and academic) allowed him to appreciate Mike's experience and to compare it with that of several other informants and data sources.

Data Collection

The story of how conversational convergence led to sustainable positive change over time was built from four data sources collected over a nine-year period from 1992 to 2001: (1) semi-structured interviews with 197 people connected to the World Vision initiatives (42 from Vision Chicago; 30 from Vision Twin Cities; 125 from the Regionalization initiative); (2) over 10,000 pages of historical documents such as memos, letters, faxes, emails, concept papers, strategy documents, meeting minutes, magazine and newspaper articles, and promotional brochures; (3) notes from a series of large-group appreciative inquiry summit meetings held with World Vision over the period of the study; and (4) participant observation (Spradley, 1980) and field notes from formal and informal meetings and conversations with dozens of people involved with Vision Chicago, Vision Twin Cities, and the Regionalization effort during the entire nine-year period. The participants/informants for the study included a wide range of people from the World Vision board, corporate offices, regional offices, partner organizations, and the donor community.

Data Analysis

One of the foundational principles of appreciative inquiry is that organizations move in the direction of their most compelling guiding images of the future (Cooperrider, 1990). From a social constructionist perspective, guiding images of the future are nothing more or less than patterns of conversations or stories that organizations tell themselves about what to expect from the future. Thus, our interest in this study was to track the content of conversations at World Vision from 1992 to 2001 to discover the implicit images of the future that were guiding the actions and directions of organization members. To do this, we developed a methodology that we have chosen to label "*conversational mapping*" to track the patterns of change at World Vision. Once we built the conversational map, "World Vision 1992–2001," we analyzed it and used the conventions of grounded theory (Glaser & Strauss, 1967; Strauss & Corbin, 1990) and generative theory (Gergen, 1982) to develop our explanation of how positive organization change can be sustained by managing the corporate conversation through acts of appreciative leadership and appreciative organization design.

To develop the conversational map we reviewed the historical documents and summarized them in various grids and charts for further analysis. Events from the nine years of data that received significant attention or energy in the thematic conversations were highlighted (Jick, 1979), grouped, themed and charted to create a conversational map of the corporate conversations. Time was represented on the horizontal axis by year (see Appendix). Using second-order analysis (Van Maanen, 1979), we looked across the conversational streams at particular moments in time to see how an individual corporate conversation may have influenced other conversations. Time periods with major directional shifts were identified and named to reflect the conversational character of the period. The timeline reflected five conversational epochs: (1) cacophony; (2) creation; (3) divergence; (4) competition; and (5) convergence. We selected key moments (i.e. highs, lows, twists, turns, trends, and events) from the timeline that measurably moved World Vision toward philosophical and structural change.

We created narratives for these moments by following a procedure similar to that of the open coding technique of grounded theory research (Strauss & Corbin, 1990). Open coding is the part of analysis that pertains specifically to the naming and categorizing of phenomena through close examination of data. The purpose of open coding is to identify and name concepts or themes and then to make propositions about these themes and relationships to other themes, thereby advancing the development of theoretical knowledge (Strauss & Corbin, 1990).

While similar to open coding, the procedure used in this study differed in two significant ways. First, consistent with a commitment to appreciation and generative theory, the themes that were sought were those that reflected the most powerful and compelling hopes and aspirations of program participants. Instead of searching for "just any old theme," the search was guided by the generative-theoretical questions: "What is striking, intriguing, compelling, and hopeful about this data? What new possibilities for social-organizational theory and practice does it invite? What fresh vistas and vocabularies can be discovered that make a transformative contribution to human thought and action?" Second, the purpose of the coding was not to develop a grounded theory as such, but to generate a series of narratives that would tell the story of sustaining appreciative change in a compelling and generative way and "enrich the range of theoretical discourse with the particular hope of expanding the potential for human practices" (Gergen, 1994).

The narratives were used to create stories for four of the five epochs. (The first epoch, cacophony, was the condition of the corporate conversation prior to the initial appreciative interventions.) Following each story we developed a mini-method section on the specific appreciative inquiry intervention(s) used during the time period. Observations from each epoch were woven together to produce an initial framework for sustainability of appreciative change. These epochs were not intended to be endpoints that conveyed dynamic equilibrium along a linear path but rather terms designed to illustrate the conversational character of the specific time periods of the longitudinal study from which this chapter's principles for sustainability were drawn.

POWER OF CONVERSATIONAL CONVERGENCE

When we began to analyze the research data, we found the "corporate conversation" went through a series of phases over time – cacophony, creation, divergence, competition, and convergence – and that these conversational phases served as harbingers of decisions and actions to come (see Table 1). While each of the phases or *epochs* continued to have conversational elements of the other epochs, they were named to reflect their dominant characteristic. It is important to point out

Table 1. Story Observations.

Creation	Divergence	Competition	Convergence
Invitation & hospitality	Challenge of the dominant discourse	Words for competitive advantage	Leadership
Continual engagement	Meaning of words	Back to problem solving	Inclusion
Expanding dialogue	Balanced dialogue	Exclusion	Shared meaning
Continual innovation	Organizational design	Change agent fatigue	Organizational design
	Change agents	Focus on the best	

here that the naming of these conversational epochs is a product of our retrospective sensemaking. They reflect our interpretation (based on multiple data sources) of what occurred at World Vision during the nine years of this study. We do not mean to suggest that these epochs are in any way inevitable or that one leads to the next in a predictable pattern. In fact, we are proposing just the opposite. Our study shows that throughout the process with World Vision, appreciative inquiry led to conversational creation and convergence, whereas more deficit-based approaches led to conversational divergence and competition.

At first, there was "conversational cacophony" with multiple voices talking over one another with no seeming coherence. Analysis of the conversations highlighted issues of identity, sustainability, survival, opportunity, fear, risk, mistrust, curiosity, hope, compassion, service, ownership, and creativity. There were as many agendas as there were participants in the conversations: a large national organization, small community-based ministries, urban and suburban churches, local staff, national staff, African-Americans, Latinos, and Whites. Although all were collectively looking to a shared future, each privately expressed concerns that others were ready to misuse the relationship: take the money, take the ownership, take the recognition, take advantage of the rich, take advantage of the poor, and then walk away.

In the cacophony, organization members experienced immobilization. No one knew how to get started. As appreciative inquiry was introduced and voices were brought into the conversation, connected, and amplified, an epoch characterized primarily by "conversational creation" began in which relationships were strengthened and a common image of the future began to emerge (see Fig. 1).

The participants began to see some real value in their discussions: potential for exchanging resources among stakeholders in addition to meeting personal agendas; the possibility of a symbiotic relationship between volunteers and pastors; ways to bring new resources into the city rather than competing within the city for existing resources. Organization members began to believe that collaboration

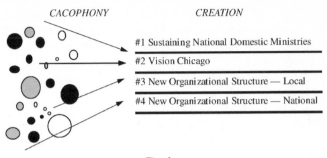

CACOPHONY   CREATION

#1 Sustaining National Domestic Ministries

#2 Vision Chicago

#3 New Organizational Structure — Local

#4 New Organizational Structure — National

Fig. 1.

would produce positive rather than competitive exposure. This led to a virtual explosion of cooperation, action, financial resources, and organizing at multiple levels and locations.

Four major conversational streams became visible that encompassed the multiple organizational levels and locations. They were: (1) sustaining national domestic ministries; (2) creating a local partnership called Vision Chicago to increase ministry impact; (3) visions of a new local organizational structure; and (4) visions of a new national organizational structure. Positive change was being accomplished at each of these four levels in the initial three years of the study.

Over time, however, environmental forces, organizational distractions, personal factors, and the normal ups-and-downs of organizational life began to divert the organization's attention, and the language of *creation* gave way to "conversational divergence." Conversation that had previously begun to focus on a shared, preferred future took on new, unshared meaning, and people began to pursue divergent directions. An analysis of the data suggests that these four conversational streams diverged into two primary flows (see Fig. 2).

The first flow focused on sustaining national domestic programs, combining the first three conversation streams to the exclusion of the fourth. This stream

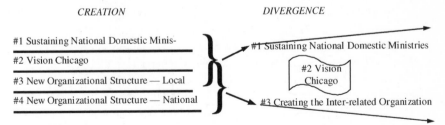

CREATION   DIVERGENCE

#1 Sustaining National Domestic Minis-

#2 Vision Chicago

#3 New Organizational Structure — Local

#4 New Organizational Structure — National

#1 Sustaining National Domestic Ministries

#2 Vision Chicago

#3 Creating the Inter-related Organization

Fig. 2.

primarily found its source in the national headquarters. The other conversational flow focused on creating an inter-related organizational structure, combining the last three conversational streams to the exclusion of the first. This stream found its source in Chicago.

The term "vision cities," when uttered by staff at the national office, referred to efforts to sustain national, domestic ministries. The same term, "vision cities," when uttered by staff in the Chicago office, referred to a national effort to create local independent business units that were supported by an integrated marketing and ministry effort in the national offices. The Chicago office expressed the belief that Vision Chicago was the model that would be used, via the Vision Cities Strategy, to develop locally managed vision cities in other major cities and that World Vision would rally its divisional resources to extend its marketing reach to expand the local ministries of Vision Chicago. On the other hand, the national office used its resources to develop national ministries in other locations and explored national fundraising techniques to fund its national office and to invest in new field locations. For the Chicago office, the new inter-related organizational structure was seen as the means that would enable Vision Chicago to flourish through collective efforts with national fundraising efforts. For the national office, Vision Chicago became an example of a potentially sustainable "field program" that could fund itself locally while receiving the benefit of a national structure.

The conversational streams continued to diverge to the point that they separated totally and began to develop independently. The activity in Chicago (i.e. Vision Chicago and new local organization structure) was a part of both conversational streams but was interpreted by one group in the context of sustaining national domestic ministries and by the other in the context of creating an inter-related organizational structure. As these two primary conversational flows continued to bifurcate and the divergence went unchecked, the conditions of "conversational competition" began to develop (see Fig. 3). The divergent voices grew louder and louder and, in multiple ways, attempted to silence the others.

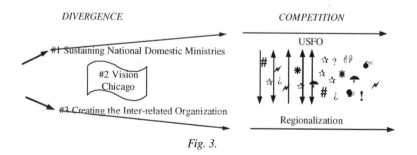

Fig. 3.

The events, issues, successes and failures that framed Vision Chicago during the years of conversational divergence were re-interpreted during this period of conversational competition by both "camps" to strengthen or weaken their arguments for a structural model. Arguments developed over the intent of the 1995 Vision City proposal. Both sides questioned the financial efficiencies, responsibilities, identity and loyalties of the other. Both pointed to the limited fundraising success of the other. Competition burgeoned over ownership for the successful or hopeful initiatives. Both camps initiated personnel, leadership or financial audits on the other.

The former "model of hope," Vision Chicago, was now referred to as "the conflict in Chicago" or, derisively, just plain "Chicago." During this phase, rivalries for access, resources, and legitimacy occurred, and many previous gains began to erode.

Finally, an epoch characterized by "conversational convergence" emerged when the organization reinvested in appreciative processes, specifically appreciative approaches to leadership and organization design (see Fig. 4). These processes, offered in this chapter, were formulated and promoted by the authors during the competition epoch. At that point in the case study, while developing the conversational map, we began to see the organization as streams of conversations that rise and fall, grow and diminish. As we gained awareness of the corporate conversation we began to shape it by applying our emerging principles of sustainability. This led to a new flourish of cooperation, action and organizing around a common image of the future. We discovered that once awareness of the conversational streams was developed, appreciative change could be maintained by intentionally and positively influencing those streams.

We suggest that appreciative organizational change took root for World Vision as its change agents re-embraced appreciative leadership and intentionally worked to bring convergence to the corporate conversational streams. This convergence, in turn, produced enough corporate attention, will, engagement, and resources for organizational (re)design. But, the change at World Vision, like change in

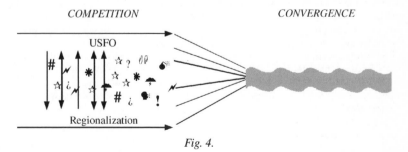

Fig. 4.

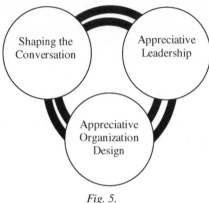

Fig. 5.

any organization, was not linear or predictable. It was continuous, evolving, and incremental and could be "sustained" only by re-enlivening positive conversations through the use of appreciative inquiry. When these positive conversations died, it led to divergence and competition. When they were revitalized, it created new possibilities for convergence. Sustaining positive change at World Vision required an unrelenting commitment to: (1) shaping the conversation; (2) engaging in appreciative leadership; and (3) applying appreciative principles to organization design (see Fig. 5).

These three factors influence each other in a mutually reinforcing way. Conversational convergence is realized through shaping the corporate conversation. Appreciative leadership builds a greater capacity throughout an organization to

Table 2. Principles for Sustainability.

Shaping the Conversation	Appreciative Leadership	Appreciative Organizational Design
1. Listen to the conversational streams	1. Believe in the possible	1. Use processes to develop shared vision & goals
2. Join conversations of possibility & opportunity	2. Approach others with unconditional positive regard	2. Develop appreciative leadership
3. Attend to conversational cross-influence & balance	3. Radically include others	3. Design for structural inclusion
4. Enfold voices of the whole system	4. Continuously move toward others	4. Use processes for continual appreciative inquiry
5. Pursue continual meaning-making		
6. Expand conversations with written documents		

see and shape conversations. In a similar way appreciative organization design extends the shaping ability into the social architecture of the organization.

It is to an explanation of these three factors that we now turn. They are summarized in Table 2 and discussed below.

SHAPING THE CONVERSATION

Listen to the Dominant Discourse and Other Conversational Streams

The sustainability of appreciative change begins with the social constructionist perspective that "words create worlds" (Ludema, Wilmot & Srivastva, 1997). Worlds were emerging and evolving as people entered and left conversations. The conversational streams that were flowing within and around the organization revealed a sense of the world that was evolving for Vision Chicago. By identifying the sources and paths of various streams, exploring conversational capillaries that influence the streams, and interpreting their directions and relative strengths, change agents were able to recognize the vision, the obstacles, the direction, and the development of the change process.

The dominant discourse at World Vision for five of the years covered by this study was the relocation of its national office and the transition of its president. These conversations consumed the organization, as existing and new staff worked to define their roles within these transitions. They overshadowed the Vision Chicago conversations about a new locally integrated structure (i.e. the inter-related organization), which began to be interpreted differently by members of various divisions as they made sense of them in isolation. Ultimately, confusion and competition resulted in hindered movement toward the positive vision that had, at one time, been shared. Being cognizant earlier of the conversational streams would have allowed organization members to choose which dialogue to join, influence, connect to, strengthen or redirect (Ford & Ford, 1995; Ludema, 2001) in order to affect the desired outcome. Understanding the continuous ebb and flow of conversations urges the appreciative leader to remain watchful, anticipating that shared meaning can only be achieved for a short period of time and requires perpetual engagement.

Join Conversations of Possibility and Opportunity

The questions a person asks and the dialogues in which he or she engages are fateful (Ludema et al., 2001). People choose the conversational streams in which they participate. At least, they choose the manner in which they engage in dialogue. When organization members chose to focus on deficits, to engage in the negative, deconstructive conversational streams, they tended toward problem solving and competition. During the epoch of conversational competition, Vision Chicago had devolved from a model of hope to one of conflict. Both sides were painting a picture of the failing "other." Hospitality, creative conversations and shared planning summits were abandoned in favor of formal audits and email announcements. These activities broadened and deepened the negative dialogue and focused creative energy on raising concerns of personal competence, loyalty, and ongoing involvement of the participants.

On the other hand, when people focused on the best, engaging in conversations of success, hope and possibility, they tended to move in the direction of their desired future, attracting others to the vision, drawing out imagination and creativity. Even during the conversational competition epoch, there was a shared investment in certain programs. When personal engagement was exercised with positive and generative conversations, people imagined, created and moved in the direction of the shared vision of what can and should be. This positive movement forward was not in a straight line but followed the course of the conversational stream. An appreciative leader is always evaluating conversations, refocusing the limited resources of personal and organizational attention from diverging, competitive, and destructive conversations to those that focus on "the best."

Identify and Attend to Conversational Cross-Influence and Balance

The analysis of the historical data revealed four primary conversational streams that were created, connected and amplified. These began to divert, compete and then converge during the period of this study. The conversational map also revealed that these conversational streams, while developing somewhat independently, influenced each other to bring about greater convergence or divergence for appreciative change. Had organization members been attending to these conversational cross-influences at the time, they would have been able to positively affect them towards convergence, rather than allowing divergence to deepen into competition.

Conversational balance is a paradox. In a discussion around the notion of paradoxes in organizations, Smith and Berg (Berg, 1987) suggest that typically when people in organizations are confronted with something different than themselves or disagreeable to themselves, they separate that entity and fight against it. This results in an even stronger reassertion of the different entity. The intensity of this conflict escalates as the push back and forth continues and shifts energy from the desired end to a battle of the present means. Conversational balance calls for a deliberate resistance to such antagonism.

Put simply, the paradox is, "Talk softly, to be louder." In order to move the organization forward, the conversational stream of change needed to be amplified enough to become the dominant discourse, or at least a major discourse, of the organization without drowning out voices of other, perhaps divergent, conversations. Efforts to strengthen one conversation that created antagonistic reactions in other streams invited a spirit of competition rather than one of co-creation.

Continuously Enfold the Voices of the Whole System

Movement from conversational competition towards conversational convergence in this study was expedited when four appreciative processes were brought together, bringing over 125 people into the conversation. The first was an appreciative inquiry summit orchestrated at the senior management level. The second was a "walk-about," an informal set of appreciative interviews with the national administrative leadership who had previously not participated in the dialogue. The third was a series of appreciative inquiry summits with 20 new staff and 70 stakeholders from across Chicago. The fourth was a series of working meetings with 40 "SWAT" teams from across the divisions at World Vision's national office to design a new organizational structure.

Including the voices of the whole system (Levine & Mohr, 1998) into the change conversation enables participants to: (1) build an understanding of the need for change; (2) analyze the current reality and determine what should be changed; (3) generate ideas about how to change the existing processes; and (4) begin to implement and support the change efforts. Including a broad spectrum of stakeholders and building shared meaning, provides access to more information and moves the organization more quickly while building commitment and pursuing innovation (Deazin, Glynn & Kazanjian, 1999; Jick, 1995).

Continually Pursue Shared Meaning-Making as People Join and Leave Conversations

Including the voices of the whole system into the change conversation sustained and enriched it. Organization members collectively developed a new meaning for regionalization. It moved from being a Vision City, to a strategy for regionalization, to a metro strategy. The participants in the dialogue shared this meaning. In order to achieve a shared meaning, those that had been in the conversation for a period of time needed to make space for new participants by giving up authorship of old ideas and embracing new ideas. To develop a shared meaning, the conversation could not be allowed into a mode of "been there, done that." The process to affirm and build a shared understanding required patience and self-sacrifice and a lot of up-front time, but greatly improved the quality of the ideas and the efficiency of their implementation.

Continual meaning-making (Nutt & Backoff, 1997b) sustains appreciative change as people come and go in organizational life. As voices enter or leave a conversational stream, meaning changes for those involved and must be recreated for the participants. Enfolding an ever-increasing number of voices improves the quality of change (Dannemiller & Jacobs, 1992; Deazin et al., 1999; Nutt & Backoff, 1997a) but requires on-going efforts as large numbers of people join and leave an organization over multiple years.

Expand Conversations with Written Documents

Written communication pieces extend the conversation even further. The position papers and business plans for Vision Chicago and regionalization created words and images, which were presented to people who had not previously been included in the conversations. When all of these documents were gathered into an anthology, the dialogue was extended to still more participants. Also, written communication sparked additional dialogue. A new comprehensive vocabulary and set of images and ideas were created and action followed language for a period of time. In this case, even over the long process of change.

CONVERSATIONAL CONVERGENCE THROUGH APPRECIATIVE LEADERSHIP

Shaping the corporate conversation toward convergence requires both appreciative leadership and appreciative organization design. When we refer to appreciative leadership we mean an on-going individual commitment to value and develop the gifts and capacities of others, to engage others, to ask positive questions, to join with others in imagining a world of positive potential, and to build constructive futures. Management theorist Peter Drucker has said that "the central task of leadership is to create an alignment of strengths such that weaknesses are no longer relevant (Drucker, 2002)." An appreciative leader is able to see the best in people and leverage their strengths to achieve significant and mutually valued goals. The authors suggest this case study revealed four principles that guide the development of individual appreciative leadership (see Table 3).

Table 3. Factors Influencing Appreciative Leadership.

Appreciative Leadership Principles

1. Believe in the possible
2. Approach others with unconditional positive regard
3. Radically include others
4. Continuously move toward others

Believe in the Possible

Belief in the possible is at the core of sustaining appreciative change. The shape and source of belief in the possible varies, but its existence enables movement toward the deepest level of a person's understanding of life. Participants in the Vision Chicago case intensely believed that they would be able to span the divisions of class, creed, and color to create mutually beneficial relationships and programs. When they actively and continually immersed themselves in values such as love, personal relationships, creativity and completeness they were imbued with those very same qualities. When they consciously connected to their ultimate values, these values became part of them and spilled out horizontally in their actions and organizational relationships.

Hopeful images, in turn, are powerful catalysts for change and transformation. The appreciative change agent lives and acts out of a sense of excited anticipation of the unexpected. By means of inquiry into the life-giving dimensions of the organization, the change agent stimulates collective imagination and aspirations to create images of new possibilities that guide his or her actions (Ludema et al., 1997).

View Others with Unconditional Positive Regard

Unconditional positive regard (Rogers, 1980) flows out of a belief that all people have intrinsic worth. As a participant in the organization, each person *can* provide a valuable contribution to the development of a shared vision. In the Vision Chicago story, some of the best program innovations and marketing approaches were sparked from conversations far outside the mainstream of corporate conversations. The people that generated these ideas lived in "impoverished" Lawndale, pastored a suburban church, or were living out retirement on the North Shore. They contributed because they felt that they would be heard.

As Quinn, Spreitzer & Brown put it, "the leader attracts others by maintaining reverence for them and an awareness of their highest potential self" (2000). Unconditional positive regard grows out of a closely held belief, a positive world-and-life view. Practicing the words of appreciation contribute to the development of a deeper, genuine appreciation for each individual. However, using appreciative language as a means to reduce resistance to change or to manipulate organization members into accepting a top-down change will not strengthen sustainability. In other words, to avoid the short-lived, cynicism-inducing change interventions described in Molinsky's (1999) or Rousseau and Tijoriwala's (1999) hospital case studies, appreciation has to be talked *and* walked. As Groucho joked, "Authenticity cannot be faked" (Bennis, 1999). Deep appreciation engenders trust, which enriches the conversational stream that creates the future into which the organization begins to live.

Appreciative inquiry is a radically inclusive approach that draws in a wide range of people and inspires human action in the service of the widest possible good. This case study revealed striking similarity of ultimate concerns among people regardless of race, culture, religion or geographical location. The focus on such shared concerns compelled collective action.

Radically Include Others (Into the Conversational Stream)

Inclusion of *the other* into processes, teams, or conversations controlled by each organizational member must be a continuous act because people enter and leave organizational life. Inclusion requires an invitation. Some people enter into the conversational stream with a simple invitation; others require an engaging courtship. The courtship is often personal and requires considerable time to convince the other of your intentions. This is especially true when an organization, like Vision Chicago, is built across the social dividing lines of race, culture, geography, and wealth. These dividing lines were crafted in a long history of different language and perspective, steeped in misunderstanding and mistrust. Personal hospitality, affirmation, and respect based on an unconditional positive regard were fundamental to move people toward significant involvement in the corporate conversational streams.

Inclusion that is radical is carried to its farthest limit: including people when it goes beyond the cost of time to the cost of self-sacrifice. Some people were not fun to include; sometimes the return on investment was not immediately evident. Personal self-sacrifice was required to build trust and to communicate that the mission of the organization is of greater significance than a personal agenda. People are more likely to contribute selflessly when a role model is acting in an altruistic fashion (Quinn et al., 2000).

In the real world, radical inclusion may seem foolishly optimistic. There were people who did not respond to ongoing invitations for inclusion in Vision Chicago, and there were times throughout this study that organization members were convinced they just needed to cut their losses with certain people. Although limited resources, time, and energy must be balanced with overcoming barriers to inclusion and a reasonable return on the relational investment, they were often surprised by a person that turned from an aggressive competitor to a valuable partner.

Continuous engagement and continual meaning making are important because people come and people go in organizational life. Also, the broader the diversity among stakeholders, the more the need for on-going interpretation, translation and re-interpretation. People's languages, backgrounds and approaches are so different that misunderstandings emerge when they are brought into relationship. Vision has to be continuously revisited, re-imagined and re-crafted. As new people joined in (with new ideas, resources, agendas, aspirations, and hopes) they had to be negotiated into the whole. In order to achieve a shared meaning, those that had been in the conversation for a period of time made space for new participants by giving up authorship of "old" ideas and embracing "new" ideas even if the old and the new were virtually the same idea.

Continuously Move Toward Others with Positive Inquiry, Even in Conflict

Despite differences, continually refocusing on the value of the other and inquiring into their "best" offers a platform from which to recreate meaning and collective action. Conflict and discomfort are inherent in human relationships, particularly across dividing lines, but appreciative inquiry provides organization members with a radically simple method to navigate through conflict.

Critics of appreciative inquiry purport that it is only about feeling good. In stark contrast to this position, members of Vision Chicago experienced discomfort and conflict throughout the process. The intervention itself and the action it inspired created a type of pressure cooker. Other perspectives, other stories, beckoned their attention, drowning out hope for constructive change. It was difficult for change agents to maintain a positive posture. Sometimes they failed. Their courage flagged, isolation beset them, and the voices became confusing. This occurred despite their first-hand observations of the positive power of being in the discovery process with others, uncertain of the outcome, yet creating something together. Only by moving into the conflict – re-engaging with appreciative questions into the best of the past and the excellent, shared futures – were they able to remove themselves from deficit-based, problem-focused mire.

Conversely, efforts to exclude participants from conversations broadened divergence and created an environment for competition. As competition for resources, visibility, and personal position grew, the potential for cooperative movement forward eroded and people became worn out.

When a struggle became personalized and devaluing, participants spent more time with those that agreed with them and began to create meaning within more limited contexts. This pushed the other even further away. The other descended from being a person with a different perspective to being a person who is evil, intending to inflict personal harm. Once a relational posture of competition set in, competing camps were inevitable, leading to fragmentation. Yet it was a gradual evolution. At first, focusing on a difference created a little distance. Then, focusing on the distance revealed more differences and greater distance. Finally, camps were entrenched against one another, planning for war. Continuously moving toward others, even in conflict reversed the movement toward fragmentation.

CONVERSATIONAL CONVERGENCE THROUGH ORGANIZATION DESIGN

Finally, the authors suggest that organizations can sustain appreciative change by incorporating appreciative design elements into their organizational structures. The design elements we suggest are maintaining openness to shared vision and goals; developing appreciative leadership; developing intentional, structural inclusion; and committing to regular, on-going appreciative inquiry into its positive core (see Table 4).

Table 4. Appreciative Organizational Design.

1. Shared vision and goals
2. Develop appreciative leadership
3. Structural inclusion
   - Develop a shared knowledge web
   - Go local
   - Balance openness with control
   - Discover and strengthen change agents
   - Construct relational on-ramps
   - Negotiate and create balanced scorecards
4. Continual appreciative inquiry

Processes for Developing Shared Vision and Goals

A rich organizational vision, created through a collaborative process, is much more likely to be implemented and sustained (Bate, Khan & Pye, 2000; Coghlan, 1998; Nutt & Backoff, 1997a; Quinn et al., 2000; Schneider, Brief & Guzzo, 1996). The most compelling vision is one that people have constructed themselves and, therefore, feel passionate about implementing. Cross-level and cross-divisional creativity (Deazin et al., 1999) attracts the largest possible number of voices, producing a rich and textured vision that improves sustainability. Traditional business practice leans toward the notion that vision is penned by senior leadership and then rolled out to line management to be implemented on the ground. This was not the experience of Vision Chicago. Rather, they sought to draw in all stakeholders (from custodians to corporate officers) into an ever-expanding circle of dialogue accessing a more complete body of knowledge and enjoying a higher level of commitment for implementation (Tenkasi, 2000).

This movement was facilitated by a continual search for the life-giving capacities of everyone that was participating in the organization through creating summits that evolved more and more sophisticated positive questions, which deepened the capacity of the whole system to connect to its positive core.

Efforts to Develop Appreciative Leadership

Appreciative leadership is essential to sustaining appreciative change (Bennis, 1999). Appreciative leadership reaches out to include a wide range of stakeholders in conversations to explore the best of the past, utilize processes to develop a shared vision, and engage in the difficult task of organizational design. Appreciative leaders have a sense of the conversational streams within an organization and invest in positive conversations of opportunity while maintaining balance across the conversational streams. They seek to develop their own belief in the possible, maintain an unconditional positive regard toward others, practice radical inclusion and continually move toward others, even during conflict, with positive inquiry.

Appreciative leadership may exist at many levels within an organization, but when it is embraced by top-level leaders, appreciative change is much easier to sustain. Throughout this story, leaders brought together the organization to imagine and move toward a preferred future. This was done when they convened the Vision Chicago Management Team to commission the original appreciative inquiry into Vision Chicago, promoted the Vision Cities initiative, organized the Regionalization Cross-functional Team, and led the business planning process for metro-centers. These leaders did not attempt to drive a predetermined strategy but rather harnessed the innovation that existed throughout the organization, which led to the formation of new strategies.

Organizational Structure that Encourages Inclusion

With reference to one case study, Burke noted, "The big picture work was done. The devil was now in the details. These details involved improving the systems (especially the information system), eliminating unneeded paperwork, and changing the reward systems. It was a matter of providing support and removing barriers" (Burke, 1995). The integration of systems into a change initiative is commonly a challenge. However, personal regard and radical inclusion extend into an organization through a set of appreciative design elements for structural inclusion. Structural inclusion facilitates cross-level, cross-divisional participation in corporate conversational streams (Deazin et al., 1999). We found the appreciative organization design to be most powerful when it was locally-rooted, self-organizing, and coupled with some capacity for wholeness – a shared deepening of learning, common purpose, and principles.

This result was achieved by periodically hosting global summits or whole-systems planning processes and by creating a shared knowledge web to experience, assess, and share the total strength of the system while empowering the local entity with its own self-management practices and decision-making. To this end, a number of design elements emerged during the period of this study.

Go local. Appreciative inquiry unleashed freedom and local initiative that enabled sustainable solutions. By pushing the decision-making point as far out from the central leadership as possible, appreciative inquiry liberated local staff to innovate, energized by the strengths, assets, and resources they had identified in themselves. It allowed people to dream and design their organizations and their social reality at the local level. It affirmed local culture, tradition, and ways of doing things. This has proven to be essential in the context of international organization development where local solutions are the most appropriate for local situations and where respect for cultures, differences, and global variety is a required ingredient for change.

Maintain openness to discovery rather than attempting to predetermine or control the outcome. A number of unexpected programmatic innovations emerged for Vision Chicago. These included a building materials distribution center, a city-wide network to distribute humanitarian goods and the Vision Chicago partnership itself. Such openness may appear organizationally inefficient, but its value lies in the readiness to sport whatever form is required under the local circumstances. The members of these teams were busy improvising and tinkering (Ciborra, 1996).

Discover and strengthen the change agents and adopt processes to transfer this role from individuals to whole systems. Unless the change agents are affirmed, either by giving them authority or by someone who does have authority backing them, they burn out over time. It takes time to build into the social architecture of an organization the principles of complex systems, relational interaction, discovery and construction in such a way that it can run itself in a healthy way. The change agents of Vision Chicago had to stay positively engaged until the dominant discourse of the organization enfolded the conversation of change. As the circle of dialogue was expanded through cross-divisional visioning, new change agents emerged from various arenas. The greater the number of change agents as the change process developed, the less vulnerable the initiative was to change agent burnout.

Construct relational "on-ramps" and other systems that bring participants into on-going relational proximity. In this case study, urban vision trips made it possible for suburbanites to build relationships with urban residents. Steering committees and task forces enabled business leaders to use their skills to strengthen World Vision's operations and those of its partners. The act of collaborative visioning was an on-ramp by itself. Appreciative summits and follow-up activity were also effective on-ramps. Participation at an appreciative inquiry summit is, by design, diverse and inclusive of all the organization's stakeholders (Whitney & Cooperrider, 1998). Team building around specific projects allows for the interrelation of organization members. The concept of relational competence should be promoted, recognized, applauded.

Negotiate and create balanced scorecards (Burke, 1995) *for team members that clearly define and measure the key activities required to move the mission and goals of the organization forward.* Adding scorecards to other communication tools measures and extends conversations of success. To sustain appreciative change, organizations need to develop the competencies of summarizing and communicating the *relational* bottom-line of their operations as clearly and aggressively as they do their financial bottom-line. Developing the means to measure relational trends and to identify areas of success and opportunity for investment strengthened the relational fabric of Vision Chicago and yielded greater appreciative sustainability.

Processes for Continual Inquiry into the Positive Core

From a structural vantage point, the four phases of appreciative inquiry need to be extended into the continuous cycles of the organization with repeated formal and informal interventions. Organization members need to be vigilant about providing "booster shots" for appreciative interventions after the initial launch (Burke, 1995).

These help current participants avoid reverting to a problem-solving approach as well as enfold new voices. Vision, goals and processes were in flux as they reflected the collective vision of the conversationalists while remaining true to the intent of the organization and the practicalities of daily organizational life. Regular inquiries into the highest ideals of the organization informed and included those new to the dialogue and spun off fresh creativity to feed the forming vision and design an appropriate structure.

Including people in the conversation shifts power relationships and generates enthusiasm by putting the locus of inquiry in the hands of all members of the organization and by inviting an affirmation of the positive change core in each. Traditional deficit-based approaches to organization development are notorious for generating high levels of resistance to change. As Kanter (1992) points out, this is true for many reasons, not the least of which is a lack of involvement on the part of organization members. Problems are identified and solutions designed "behind closed doors" and then imposed on the majority of the organization. This approach, of course, violates the age-old organizational development maxim that "people support what they help to create" (Weisbord & Janoff, 1995). Inclusion developed a greater commitment to responsibility or accountability for results. When organization members were engaged in the process, they were motivated to invest uncommon energy into envisioning and designing strategies for implementation and action. What was needed at the whole system level in terms of organization design was a rapid sharing of strengths, capacity, and learning coupled with periodic summits for dialogue around the deeper meaning and purpose of work, which creates shared meaning. When this was in place, the organization was able to let go and allow self-organizing to happen in terms of projects, approaches, and action.

Radical inclusion and continual meaning-making lead to continuous innovations and require a flexible structure (Ciborra, 1996). The eventual decentralized organizational model of Vision Chicago allowed for each unit to develop its own goals, deliverables, partnerships, etc. while continuing to work toward the goals of the whole organization. The citywide network to distribute goods and the building distribution center were examples of innovative dreams that could be realized because of a flexible organizational structure.

Appreciative inquiry produces cooperation and innovation because it simultaneously addresses strategy, process, and implementation. It affirms that inquiry *is* intervention, that there is a self-reinforcing, synergistic relationship between creating strategy, learning through the process, and producing the results. As people ask themselves unconditional positive questions, they generate new learning about the resources that make their organizing and action possible. They strengthen the relational bonds needed to translate vision into reality, and through the process they create new levels of commitment to action. Consequently, process and results are maximized in the same moment, and results are achieved much more quickly.

The appreciative change process was sustained as participants in the organization remained cognizant of the conversational streams and sought to influence them at the levels of both relational leadership and organizational design by applying the appreciative principles suggested in this chapter. These general principles applied in the context of the organization in which the authors worked and studied, but we believe they are generalizable and may be applied to other organizations. We are eager to "compare notes" with other organizations who have been able to sustain positive change in environments where corporate politics, control structures, bottom-lines and never-perfect conditions abound.

REFERENCES

Barrett, F. J. (1995). Creating appreciative learning cultures. *Organizational Dynamics, 24*(2), 6–49.

Bartunek, J., & Louis, M. R. (1996). *Insider/outsider team research* (Vol. 40). Thousand Oaks, CA: Sage.

Bate, P., Khan, R., & Pye, A. (2000). Towards a culturally sensitive approach to organization structuring: Where organization design meets organization development. *Organization Science, 11*(2), 197–211.

Bennis, W. (1999). The end of leadership: Exemplary leadership is impossible without full inclusion, initiatives, and cooperation of followers. *Organizational Dynamics, 27*(1), 71.

Berg, S. (1987). *Paradoxes of group life*. San Francisco: Jossey-Bass.

Burke, W. W. (1995). Organization change: What we know, What we need to know. *Journal of Management Inquiry, 4*(2), 158–171.

Bushe, G. R. (1998). Appreciative inquiry with teams. *Organization Development Journal, 16*(3), 41–50.

Bushe, G. R. (1999). Advances in appreciative inquiry as an organization development intervention. *Organization Development Journal, 17*(2), 61–68.

Bushe, G. R., & Coetzer, G. (1995). Appreciative inquiry as a team-development intervention: A controlled experiment. *Journal of Applied Behavioral Science, 31*(1), 13–30.

Ciborra, C. U. (1996). The platform organization: Recombining strategies, structures, and surprises. *Organization Science, 7*(2), 103.

Coghlan, D. (1998). The process of change through interlevel dynamics in a large-group intervention for a religious organization. *Journal of Applied Behavioral Science, 34*(1), 105(115).

Cooperrider, D. L., Sorensen, P. F., Yaeger, T. F., & Whitney, D. (Eds) (2001). *Appreciative inquiry: An emerging direction for organization development*. Champaign, IL: Stipes.

Cooperrider, D. L., & Srivastva, S. (1987). Appreciative inquiry in organizational life. In: W. A. Pasmore & R. W. Woodman (Eds), *Research in Organizational Change and Development* (Vol. 1, pp. 129–169). Greenwich, CT: JAI Press.

Dannemiller, K. D., & Jacobs, R. W. (1992). Changing the way organizations change: A revolution of common sense. *Journal of Applied Behavioral Science, 28*(4), 480–498.

Deazin, R., Glynn, M. A., & Kazanjian, R. K. (1999). Multilevel theorizing about creativity in organizations: A sensemaking perspective. *Academy of Management Review, 24*(2), 286(282).

Drucker, P. F. (2002). *The effective executive*. New York: HarperBusiness.

Dutton, J. E., & Dukerich, J. (1991). Keeping an eye on the mirror: The role of image and identity in organizational adaptation. *Academy of Management Journal, 34*(3), 517–554.

Eisenhardt, K. M. (1989). Building theory from case study research. *Academy of Management Review, 14*, 532–550.

Ford, J. D., & Ford, L. W. (1995). The role of conversations in producing intentional change in organizations. *Academy of Management Review, 20*(3), 541–570.

Fry, R., Barrett, F. J., Seiling, J., & Whitney, D. (Eds) (2002). *Appreciative inquiry and organizational transformation: Reports from the field*. Westport, CN: Quorum Books.

Gergen, K. J. (1982). *Toward transformation in social knowledge*. New York: Sprinter-Verlag.

Gergen, K. J. (1994). *Realities and relationships: Soundings in social construction*. Cambridge, MA: Harvard University Press.

Glaser, B. G., & Strauss, A. L. (1967). *The discovery of grounded theory: Strategies for qualitative research*. New York: Aldine de Gruyter.

Jick, T. (1995). Accelerating change for competitive advantage. *Organizational Dynamics, 24*(1), 77–82.

Jick, T. D. (1979). Mixing qualitative and quantitative methods: Triangulation in action. *Administrative Science Quarterly, 24*, 602–661.

Levine, L., & Mohr, B. J. (1998). Whole system design (WSD): The shifting focus of attention and the threshold challenge. *Journal of Applied Behavioral Science, 34*(3), 305(322).

Ludema, J. D. (1996). *Narrative Inquiry: Collective storytelling as a source of hope, knowledge, and action in organizational life*. Unpublished doctoral dissertation, Case Western Reserve University.

Ludema, J. D. (2001). Appreciative storytelling: A narrative approach to organization development and change. In: R. Fry, F. J. Barrett, J. Sellig & D. Whitney (Eds), *Appreciative Inquiry and Organization Transformation*. Westport, CT: Greenwood Publishing Group.

Ludema, J. D., Cooperrider, D. L., & Barrett, F. J. (2001). Appreciative inquiry: The power of the unconditional positive question. In: P. Reason & H. Bradbury (Eds), *Handbook of Action Research*. Thousand Oaks: Sage.

Ludema, J. D., Whitney, D., Mohr, B. J., & Griffin, T. J. (2003). *The appreciative inquiry summit: A practitioner's guide for leading large group change*. San Francisco: Berrett-Koehler.

Ludema, J. D., Wilmot, T. B., & Srivastva, S. (1997). Organizational hope: Reaffirming the constructive task of social and organizational inquiry. *Human Relations Journal, 50*(8), 1015(1038).

Mantel, M. J. (2001). *Sustaining appreciative change: Inviting conversational convergence through relational leadership and organization design*. Unpublished doctoral dissertation, Benedictine University.

Mantel, M. J., & Ludema, J. D. (2000). From local conversations to global change: Experiencing the worldwide web effect of appreciative inquiry. *Organizational Development Journal, 18*(12), 42–53.

Molinsky, A. L. (1999). Sanding down the edges: Paradoxical impediments to organizational change. *Journal of Applied Behavioral Science, 35*(1), 8(1).

Nutt, P., & Backoff, R. (1997a). Crafting Vision. *Journal of Management Inquiry, 6*(4), 308–328.

Nutt, P., & Backoff, R. (1997b). Organizational transformation. *Journal of Management Inquiry, 6*(3), 235–254.

Quinn, R. E., Spreitzer, G. M., & Brown, M. V. (2000). Changing others through changing ourselves: The transformation of human systems. *Journal of Management Inquiry, 9*(2), 147–164.

Rogers, C. (1980). *A way of being*. Boston: Houghton Mifflin.

Rousseau, D. M., & Tijoriwala, S. A. (1999). What's a good reason to change? Motivated reasoning and social accounts in promoting organizational change. *Journal of Applied Psychology, 84*(4), 514(515).

Schneider, B., Brief, A. P., & Guzzo, R. A. (1996). Creating a climate and culture for sustainable organizational change. *Organizational Dynamics,* 7.

Strauss, A., & Corbin, J. (1990). *Basics of qualitative research: Grounded theory procedures and technigques.* Newbury Park: Sage.

Tenkasi, R. V. (2000). The dynamics of cultural knowledge and learning in creating viable theories of global change and action. *Organization Development Journal, 18*(2), 74–87.

Van Maanen, J. (1979). The fact of fiction in organizational ethnography. *Administrative Science Quarterly, 24,* 539–550.

Weick, K. E., & Quinn, R. E. (1999). Organizational change and development. In: J. T. Spence, J. M. Darley & D. J. Foss (Eds), *Annual Review of Psychology* (Vol. 50, pp. 361–386). Palo Alto, CA: Annual Reviews.

Weisbord, M. R., & Janoff, S. (1995). *Future search: An action guide to finding common ground in organizations and communities.* San Francisco: Berrett-Koehler.

Whitney, D., & Cooperrider, D. L. (1998). The appreciative inquiry summit: Overview and applications. *Employment Relations Today, 25*(2), 17(12).

Whitney, D., & Trosten-Bloom, A. (2003). *The power of appreciative inquiry: A practical guide to positive change.* San Francisco: Berrett-Koehler.

APPENDIX

Corporate Conversational Map – Streams & Cross-Influence

CONVERSATIONAL	CACOPHONY	CONVERSATIONAL CREATION, CONNECTION & AMPLIFICATION			CONVERSATIONAL DIVERGENCE			CONVERSATIONAL COMPETITION		CONVERSATIONAL CONVERGENCE
	FY92	FY93	FY94	FY95	FY96	FY97	FY98	FY99	FY00	FY01
Sustaining U.S. Ministries										
Marketing			Target Cities	Vision Cities, USFO, Hope USA	Standards	NI – Mail	2yr test results	Mail		
Leadership	Visionaries go		Sr. VP goes	AI to Board			Church Rel	Review Lead		New VP
Nat'l programs in Chicago										
Urban Churches	NURMP	NURMP			Grants end					
Suburban	NURMP									
GIK	Cash grants		GIKNET			NFT-PA	Merge w/ SH			
Vision Chicago										
Grants	Cash Grants	Cash Grants			Grants end	NIF account	No incubation subsidy			
Urban churches	NURMP	CMC, C1	C2, Hope House	New CMC, C3		NURMP ends, MLF CDC				
New programs	LoveINC			Jobs collab						
Trans. programs	CityLINC	PIQE test			Training	CD team, P$, PIQE test				
Urban/suburban	5 Yr. plan					Schools		Merge w/ SH	New staff	WV DBA
Strategic Alliance		Roles debate		VC Structure	Task forces, Media	Individuals, Kits = Need	Merge GIK-NFT, Kohler			WV DBA
Storehouse			Storehouse	SH staff		Streams, role	2yr test results			
Marketing	Resource dev. staff. Vision trips	Integr. plan, Pres. kick-off media, mag.	Magazine, Council of Fnds, Mobil, Mac. WCCC	2yr. test mail, Mag. cover		MR contract		SH campaign	SH campaign	WV DBA
Major Donors			Mac. WCCC	Mac, WCCC, FZ, local hire	SH fees. Dept of Fd	WCCC shift, FZ, SH Fnds	New OH allocations, Rump group	Bud. reports, audit, SH own	Poor reporting	New Sr. VP
Finance	Bud. cap. split OH. 0 growth			Budgets not integrated	Reserve, no growth					
Leadership	Visionaries go		VCMT, Sr. VP goes							
AI – boundary spanning	VC scope	VC Integrated plan #1	VC midterm	VC to Board	VTC plan	MWG plan	Regional plan	La Gente plan	CFT process	WVC plan
Regional Org. Efforts	Visionaries go	VC Integrated plan #1	VC Integrated plan #2	VC Integrated comm. plan	Vision Twin Cities, MWG	MWG, Integr. plan, Mkting prox	Regional plan, RTC, Cabinet	La Gente, RTF, Vision NY	Regional CFT, Crane, S/rel. issues	New Sr. VP HQ/VC tour, RITF

APPRECIATIVE INQUIRY IN TRANSFORMATIVE PUBLIC DIALOGUE

Judy Rodgers

ABSTRACT

The use of dialogues within and across organizations is on the rise. This increase is a tacit acknowledgement of the relational foundations from which new meaning is created and social innovations emerge. However, coming together for a dialogue doesn't assure constructive conversation or transformative engagement. Dialogue participants, even when they are asked to "suspend assumptions," are generally still embedded in the mental models and familiar frameworks that distance them from one another and prevent real generativity and novelty.

This paper proposes Appreciative Inquiry as an approach particularly conducive to creating public dialogues that are generative and transformative. It suggests that a community is best served by inquiry into strengths, assets and past successes. It further proposes that this mode of inquiry tends to produce positive emotional states, which expand the resources and pro-social inclinations of those in the dialogue. It offers five conditions that support generative and transformative public dialogue and explains how Appreciative Inquiry creates these conditions.

Constructive Discourse and Human Organization
Advances in Appreciative Inquiry, Volume 1, 337–357
ISSN: 1475-9152/doi:10.1016/S1475-9152(04)01015-4

THE RISE OF DIALOGUE WITHIN
AND ACROSS ORGANIZATIONS

The idea of using public forums to create understanding, consider new possibilities, and arrive at consensus is as old as civilization itself. The ancient Greeks, many of the North American native civilizations and other indigenous societies turned regularly to these kinds of dialogues to address challenges faced by the community and to determine a future course of action.

So, in some ways the rise of dialogic methods to address 21st century challenges and search for consensus is nothing new. However the recent explosion in the use of public dialogue has created renewed interest in the possibilities it poses for creating real social innovation.

Public dialogues are rapidly becoming one of the most widely used methods for convening stakeholders around issues of public interest. The World Bank and the Archbishop of Canterbury have turned to public dialogue in an unlikely partnership to bring the international development community and the faith community together to share learnings (Marshall). Barnet Pearce and Kim Pearce have documented their use of dialogue in the civic affairs of Cupertino, California (Pearce and Pearce). The Public Conversation Project in Boston, Massachusetts, convened leaders on both sides of the abortion debate for six years (Fowler et al., 2001). The list of public dialogue initiatives is a long one ranging from the Arts and Civic Dialogue project of Anna Devere Smith (2000) to the Business as Agent of World Benefit inquiry convened by the Weatherhead School of Management at Case Western Reserve University.

The use of dialogues inside of organizations has increased dramatically as well, which is drawing interest from management scholars. The study of public dialogues can benefit from the study of dialogue as an organizational practice as both applications of dialogic methods operate from the same premise. Barge and Oliver explain, "The postmodern turn in management theory shifts our conception of organizations toward a more dynamic relational conception, where organization 'is produced in contextually embedded social discourse and used to interpret the social world' " (Boje, Gephart & Thatchenkery, 1996, p. 2). The same can be said of subsets of society or communities of interest that choose to engage in a dialogue around a shared area of interest.

There are three fundamental differences between dialogues convened within organizations and those convened across organizational boundaries. First, within organizations, people can be required to participate, whereas in public dialogue participants come and leave by choice. Second, within organizations participants are fluent in the same organizational discourse, whereas in public dialogue, there are generally multiple discourses or subsets of a discourse present in the dialogue. Third, within organizations the field of action is boundaried, making it easier to observe changes in thought and action within the system. Whereas in a public dialogue the field of action of those participating is more dispersed, making it more difficult to track transformation in the life and work of participants.

Those differences notwithstanding, two approaches detailed by Barge and Oliver provide a useful frame for considering the ways that both types of dialogues produce high-quality conversation that fosters social innovation. The approach proposed by Isaacs and Senge focuses on creating conversational patterns that facilitate detailed collective inquiry into the underlying assumptions, values, beliefs, and contexts that compose organizational activity in order to create new patterns of actions. The approach preferred by proponents of Appreciative Inquiry contends that the foundation for affirmative change is fostered in conversation that inquires into the life-generating experiences, core values, and moments of excellence in organizational life. Barge and Oliver explain that dialogue as described by Isaacs and Senge facilitates an exploration into the problems and challenges confronting organizational members as well as their hopes, visions, and dreams for what the organization might become. Appreciative Inquiry emphasizes that inquiry should confine itself to what works well within organizational life, eschewing organization talk on problem solving, problem identification, cause analysis, possible solutions and action planning as unconstructive.

Barge and Oliver agree that conversational practices aimed at creating learning, change and innovation should be life generating, but take issue with the correlation of "appreciative" with "positive" believing that it "dismisses and discounts other equally important and appropriate types of conversation and emotionality within organizations that may foster learning and change." They find it ironic that Appreciative Inquiry is positioned as a postmodern approach to management and yet "limits conversation to a particular set of discussable topics." They argue for reconceptualizing the notion of appreciation in conversational practice to broaden its use to a variety of conversational topics and to embrace different types of emotion in organizational life (p. 125).

While Appreciative Inquiry doesn't limit the conversation to a particular set of discussable subjects, it does focus inquiry into that which gives life. This method is tethered to a search for the positive, which we believe explains its dramatic impact in public dialogue, characterized by high levels of idea generation, relationship building, and real social innovation. Some of the recent research on positive emotion sheds light on why Appreciative Inquiry dialogues have the effect of being so highly motivational.

APPRECIATIVE INQUIRY AND PUBLIC DIALOGUE

Public dialogue presents an opportunity to convene those with a stake in a particular issue in a process of mutual co-construction of a genuinely new way of looking at the subject. When public dialogues start by looking at the history of problems and challenges, they miss this opportunity. Participants are reinforced in their familiar discourse, reconfirming old frameworks and meaning making and frequently find themselves back at the impasse that caused them to convene the dialogue in the first place. When this happens, public dialogue deteriorates into public debate with everyone in the room gravitating to familiar positions and old adversarial clichés. However, there is another way to approach public dialogue that allows a whole system to collectively construct fresh and creative frameworks for familiar issues.

Public dialogue can be truly generative and deeply transformative – a remarkable kind of improvisational community theatre. This happens when those engaged in the dialogue make a conscious choice to inquire into what gives life to their community and to the issues about which they care so deeply. One of the best ways to do this is to use Appreciative Inquiry as a kind of search engine at the heart of public dialogue, because Appreciative Inquiry (AI) is by definition an inquiry into what gives life to a system (Cooperrider & Srivastva, p. 131). There are five elements to an AI dialogue that lead to generativity and transformation. When these five conditions are applied in designing and convening a dialogue, they infuse the dialogue with a sense of surprise and newness. Rather than old enemies taking their stations in a familiar battle, a whole system of people with endless resources comes together to co-construct new relationships and new spaces of meaning.

To show this approach to public dialogue, I will use a system whose approaches to world issues are notoriously deficit focused and increasingly formulaic, the media. One might say that the powerful world media community is continuously at the center of public discourse. The films, newscasts, magazines, television sitcoms and Internet portals that interlace the world today are perpetually constructing a story of the world. The reportable world is so vast and the spaces of commentary so limited, that choices must be made. Increasingly over the past twenty years, those choices have reflected the convictions of the owners of media businesses – that their audiences become most engaged (and loyal) when media focus on conflict and breakdown.

"Images and Voices of Hope: A Question of Choice" is a public dialogue among media professionals, journalists and artists that considers the question, "What does it mean for media to be agents of world benefit?" Convened by three organizations, it began in 1999 with a single dialogue in New York City. By 2003 dialogues have taken place in over 20 cities around the world. We will look at two of these dialogues: one in Miami, Florida and the annual Summit that includes representatives of dialogues from around the world. Images and Voices of Hope (IV of Hope) uses Appreciative Inquiry in most of its dialogues.

These dialogues with journalists, media professionals and artists are convened in hopes of intervening in the cultural drift of the media community towards sensationalism for the sake of profit alone. They are created to engage the whole system in a shift of thinking – a consideration of what it might look like if media were to be agents of benefit to that community and to the world. IV of Hope is not intended to dichotomize profit and philanthropy, but to involve the very creative minds of the media community in examining the assumptions that underlie the current patterns of thought and action and in socially constructing some new patterns of relationship in hopes that they will produce even more public engagement with their work, and hopefully no less profit.

I have chosen Miami, because, now in its fourth year, it is the longest running single IV of Hope dialogue. I have chosen to look at the World Summit that took place in 2002 because it included representatives from dialogues all over the world and so embraces very different cultures and nationalities.

Aside from the great gain to humanity if media were to foster public discourse that generated new and life-giving ideas to the world, the most important point in offering these examples is *to provide a* perspective on public dialogue as an opportunity for real social innovation, creating new spaces of meaning and transformation in the patterns of thought and action in a community of interest. The aim is not to provide a specific model for conducting public dialogue.

GENERATIVITY IN PUBLIC DIALOGUE

Public dialogue at its best is an attempt to intervene in the drift of public discourse towards fractiousness and stalemate and to turn it in an entirely new direction. The key to creating this shift is to light the fire of generativity in the room, to engage the public imagination, the spirit of community, and a feeling of generosity.

Gergen, Gergen and Barrett describe dialogue as discursive coordination (2003, p. 2). When they speak about generative dialogue, they place their central focus on the various "dialogic moves" that bring realities and ethics into being and bind them to particular patterns of action (2003, p. 9). We apply the notion of generativity as that which enlarges the cognitive context in which we are thinking, increasing creative thinking, and expanding the field of available thought and action.

There has always been a veil of mystery about the sources of generativity. Poets talk about their muses. Creatives have as many superstitious rituals as baseball pitchers. However recent research into positive emotion sheds some important new light on the notion of generativity. Barbara Fredrickson suggests that the positive emotions of joy, interest, contentment and love share the feature of broadening an individual's momentary thought-action repertoire, and also appear to build an individual's personal resources – physical, intellectual, and social. Especially important for sustaining the outcomes of public dialogue into the arena of new patterns of action is Fredrickson's further proposition that these resources are durable, ultimately building the individual's personal resources for use over time (Fredrickson, 1998). Specifically then, generativity in the context of public dialogue might be experienced by participants as a broadened scope of attention, of cognition, and of action and by a building of physical, intellectual and social resources over time.

Jon Haidt of the University of Virginia has looked in depth at the emotion of elevation, noting that those who are witness to acts of generosity and altruism are themselves moved to an uplifted emotional state and propelled to generous action (Haidt, 2000). It is as if these positive emotional states are contagious and can be "caught" by merely witnessing good and generous action, causing one to become "infected" with generosity and altruism oneself. While there is much more research to be done on the relationship between positive emotional states and generativity, it is a useful direction for inquiry. Applied to public dialogue, it suggests that when dialogues are created in such a way that they elicit positive emotional states, they are more likely to be generative, creating real social change.

Our proposition is simple: that a community is better served by inquiring into strengths, assets and past successes than by pouring over an inventory of *challenges and* failures. The former moves us into positive emotional states, expands our personal resources, and takes us towards possibility. While the latter constricts us, leading us to default to the familiar dictum that "we already tried that and it didn't work." Common sense says that this approach doesn't have an ascending trajectory.

For real transformation to happen in a public dialogue, there must be an affirmative, constructive climate in which to work. Dialogue participants must feel a fire of possible new ideas kindled within themselves. This fire of possibility is often lit by a high-point memory or an image of the future that opens in them an awareness of new horizons. This shift in awareness affects the vision. It is as if a light dawns on a previously dim scene and they see an old landscape in a new way. There are possibilities in this familiar landscape that they had overlooked before – new connections to be made, new approaches to be tried, new markets to be tapped. The sequence of new feeling, new awareness, new vision, and new action in turn creates a new world. But it has to start with intention. Generativity in a public dialogue space doesn't just happen, even if the conveners have picked the right room, the right day and the right subject. It requires a certain kind of intention in the convening.

There are five conditions for a generative dialogue: (a) intention; (b) questions that guide a search for the positive; (c) whole system; (d) relational space; and (e) reflection. They are important first, because they locate us as fellows seeking towards common and beneficial ends; we are predisposed to work together towards something that will benefit all of us. More important, they create the conditions for generativity and for real transformation.

A generative dialogue improves the likelihood that real transformation will occur. Ken and Mary Gergen and Frank Barrett describe transformative dialogues as those where something new is created as a result of the dialogue. "Transformative dialogue is essentially aimed at facilitating the collaborative construction of new realities . . . It is a relational accomplishment that creates new spaces of meaning" (2003, p. 22). In transformative public dialogues participants collectively create new spaces of meaning and form new relationships as "communities of inquiry." Though dialogues are not always concerned with implementing specific actions, they frequently lead to new actions engendered by the new spaces of meaning and new relationships. Even if the group that came together for the dialogue doesn't engage in a particular kind of coordinated action, the individuals in the dialogue frequently undertake new actions in their lives and work because of the new spaces of meaning opened in the dialogue.

THE FIVE CONDITIONS FOR GENERATIVE AND TRANSFORMATIVE DIALOGUE

If a public dialogue is to intervene in the drift of public discourse, it should engage participants from the moment in which they first hear about the dialogue through to the end, when they have left the room and are back in the midst of their life and work. Furthermore their engagement must be at a very deep level, at the level of the inner reflective dimension where we churn our understandings and make meaning of what is happening to us. Transformative dialogues require an open and trusting engagement where we enter into a repartee of meaning making with others willing to create something new together. There are five conditions for this kind of dialogue.

(1) *Intention to locate what gives life.* Participants in a public dialogue are not neutral. They are part of a society, and therefore part of the cultural drift of that society and the public discourse in which the society is continuously engaged.

If we come into the dialogue with no purpose, the pull of the familiar discourse will keep us in our traditional mental models and patterns of meaning making. AI dialogues have the purpose of locating that which is life-giving, past and present successes, and the root causes of success. This distinguishes AI dialogues from many approaches. For example, in writing about dialogue David Bohm counseled, "We need a place where there is no authority, no hierarchy, no special purpose – sort of an empty place where we can let anything be talked about" (Bohm, p. 42). However, experience tells us that what appears to be an empty place is rarely truly empty. We bring into a dialogue the history of our experiences, our intellectual constructs and assumptions in which we are embedded. It isn't until we sign on with an intention of looking more deeply, of searching specifically for that which is life-giving, that a new space of possibility opens. This condition is critical to a truly generative dialogue.

(2) *Questions that guide a search for the positive and the life affirming*. David Cooperrider, the creator of the Appreciative Inquiry theory and method, frequently says, "We live in worlds our questions create." The power of the right question is that it carries the seeds of the new discovery. One of the most famous examples of the creative power of a question is Einstein's question that allegedly led him to his Theory of Relativity: What would it be like to be riding on a beam of light? Each question of course enfolds hundreds and thousands of other questions, of images, memories, and related ideas. The right question is like a box of seeds being sent from the "nursery of the future."

(3) *Whole system in the room*. Public dialogue is never something created by a committee on high somewhere and shipped to the society with operating instructions. It is generated in the interactions among those gathered in the room. If we intend to intervene in the drift of public discourse, we do well to have the whole system – or representatives of the whole system – in the room. The reason for this is not a commitment to fairness so much as an awareness that societies are subtle networks of relationships that we never fully understand. Public discourse is generated, modified and passed along in thousands of venues by all the people of a society – in barber shops and diners, in schools and churches, at dinner tables and bus stops. When all of these different parts of a society are present in the room, it increases the probability that a diverse range of insights will inform the dialogue and that the new spaces of meaning created in the dialogue will be carried back by participants and woven into the larger fabric of public discourse.

(4) *Relational space of trust and affirmation*. As mentioned above, there is no such thing as an empty space. Spaces are charged in ways that make

them conducive to certain kinds of interactions. And of course we begin to transform those spaces the moment we enter the room. In his book on the powerful Truth and Reconciliation hearings in South Africa, the Archbishop Desmond Tutu spoke about the tangible impact of space: "We can sense that a home is happy even before anyone tells us because we are able to catch the 'vibes' – it is in the very stones. We know when a church is redolent of sanctity, of holiness; when it has been prayed in. We can almost catch the odor of holiness and sense the energy and reverence of those many who have gone before. It is there in the atmosphere, in the very fabric. A prayed-in church is qualitatively different from one that has the atmosphere of a concert hall." Rooms that are filled with the kinds of vibes the Archbishop is talking about produce different dialogues, different spaces of meaning than those that aren't. One important way to generate relational spaces of trust and affirmation is to give each voice equal weight in the design and facilitation of the dialogue. In this we agree with Bohm, that we need a place where there is no authority, no hierarchy.

(5) *Reflection*. This final condition is not an intrinsic part of the AI theory and method. We adopted it from the practices of the Brahma Kumaris World Spiritual Organization, one of the convening partners of the IV of Hope dialogues, with very positive results. There are many ways to introduce a space for reflection, with periods of silence, with periods of music conducive to reflection, or with a guided meditation. We have experimented with all three with positive results. We have also experimented with dialogues that had no reflective space and been disappointed with the results. Reflective space in a dialogue provides participants with an opening to consider the inner space in which their dialogue is running. It provides an interruption, a pause in which they can notice what they are experiencing, incorporate new ideas, and examine automatic responses. It is an opportunity to connect the inner patterns of thought of the individual with those of the collective. Silence, in particular, seems to offer an opportunity to notice the subtle threads of community that are being laid in place. We have found that once silence has been introduced as a norm in a dialogue, if we forget to take time for it, dialogue participants will often challenge us, asking for the silence to be observed.

HOW APPRECIATIVE INQUIRY PRODUCES THE CONDITIONS FOR GENERATIVE DIALOGUE

Appreciative Inquiry (AI) is a systematic search for what gives life to a human system. It can be applied to the micro-system of a couple or to vast systems like

Roadways Express, the largest L. T. L. trucking company in the U.S. Starting with a one-on-one interview, AI-designed interviews ask each person in the room to search his or her past for high point experiences, for successes, for moments of inspiration. They are then asked to unpack that memory, to bring it to life in full living color. For reasons that recent research in psychology is helping us to understand, a highpoint moment, remembered and relived, brings with it the physiology, emotional chemistry, and intellectual activity of the original experience. We become life-filled and idea-filled again.

Another distinctive conversational act in the AI interview is the creation of a concrete image of the future, as you would most like it to be. Interviewees are not asked to imagine the future so much as they are asked to step into this future as a lived experience. This experience of putting attention on a positive and inspirational image of the future has what Cooperrider has dubbed a "heliotropic" effect. "When presented with the option, organizations will move more rapidly and effectively in the direction of affirmative imagery (moving towards light) than in the opposite direction of negative imagery (moving against light or towards 'overpowering darkness'). Existing in a dynamic field of images, it can be argued that organizations move along the path of least resistance (Fritz, 1984) toward those images that are judged to represent the organization's highest possibilities – those images that are the brightest, most purposeful, or most highly valued. Positive images whose prophetic, poetic, and normative aspects are congruent will show the greatest self-fulfilling potential" (Cooperrider, 1990, p. 93).

The interviews characteristically end either with wishes for the future or with a consideration of actions one might be willing to take. After both people have interviewed one another, they join a small group of two or three other pairs where they introduce their interview partner to the group, sharing a high point story, images of the future and future actions. So, why does this approach have such a powerful impact on organizations, or in the cases we're considering, on those gathered for a public dialogue?

First, it shifts the defining metaphor of the conversational space. Rather than convening around society as a problem to be solved, it posits a relational network of infinite capacity. The metaphor itself opens the conversational scope to emergent possibilities and to the mystery and the miracle of our existence.

Second, dialogues exist in the micro-social world of relationships. Dialogues that invite us to locate past failure and breakdown, amplify the critical voice, reify constrictive emotional states and discourage relational connection. Alternatively AI calls for an appreciative eye, which serves as a virtual "grow-light" for relational connection, sowing seeds of possibility, inviting those in dialogue to join together in creating new images and ultimately new designs and actions for the future.

Third, AI dialogues draw strength from the power of wholeness. Conveners are urged to have all stakeholders in the room or, if that is not possible, to have a representation of all stakeholders in the room. When it is time to begin the initial interview, participants are asked to seek out an interview partner they do not know very well. As "two's" merge into "eight's," and then into a plenary gathering of up to hundreds or even thousands, they experience the scalability of intimacy and empathy. (The national convention of the American Red Cross in June of 1999 included an AI interview among all 2500 attendees.) They have seen themselves reflected in the other and find there is common ground. This happened in a dialogue among religious leaders convened by His Holiness the Dalai Lama. At one point in this dialogue a Russian Orthodox cleric was introducing his interview partner a bishop from the Roman Catholic faith. He stood to introduce his partner, and opened his introduction by exclaiming, "I like this man!" (Cooperrider, 2000).

These three factors utterly transform the relational space in which the dialogues unfold. Limitation gives way to infinite possibility. Criticism yields to appreciation. A microcosm of the social system is created, but this time with a presumption of fellowship. We recall our past joy; we co-create images of the futures we hope to share; and we begin to lay the groundwork for the road ahead. Our past positions and previous future scenarios seem limited, pale, and two-dimensional in comparison with the vital, living possibilities we are co-creating. There is the wonder of new discovery, the pull towards concrete dreams of the future and the growing confidence that comes of making designs to move ahead together.

IMAGES AND VOICES OF HOPE:
A QUESTION OF CHOICE

Images & Voices of Hope (www.ivofhope.org) began in 1999 with a public dialogue in New York City of 180 journalists, media professionals, and artists. Our intention in putting together the invitation list was to bring together in one room representatives of the entire system of media – producers, distributors, and consumers of public images and messages. Peter Max, the artist renowned for his psychedelic art in the 1960s was there, and so was Jamie Raab, publisher of Warner Books. Justine Toms, who with her husband produces *New Dimensions Radio*, Sharon Green of National Public Radio, Richard Kilberg of the Fred

Friendly seminars, actor Clark Peters, David Finn of the PR agency Ruder Finn, John Pavlik of the Columbia University Program on New Media and so on.

We had come together to look at the impact of public image making and public story telling on society. The conveners were the SIGMA (Social Innovations in Global Management) program at Case Western Reserve University, the Brahma Kumaris World Spiritual Organization, and the Visions of a Better World Foundation. We used a set of Appreciative Inquiry questions starting with a question, "Tell me about a time when you were genuinely moved by an image or a story you encountered in the media." The dialogue lasted for four and a half hours, beginning with a one-on-one interview, moving to small group conversations, and culminating in a plenary dialogue so powerful that people were still lined up at microphones around the room at the time we were supposed to be bringing the dialogue to a close. The next day the phones and fax machines started ringing. Much to our surprise we had hit a nerve. People wanted very much to engage in this particular dialogue and they wanted to know what we were going to do for a second act. At that moment we had no second act. It had taken all of our collective resources to plan and execute the first act and we did not have the infrastructure in place for a second. However, what happened next was interesting. People in different cities began calling on us to help them organize their own dialogues, which began to spring up in multiple locations. The complementarities of the partners helped here. The Brahma Kumaris had a presence in major cities in over 85 countries in the world, so they provided many of the places to convene the conversations. SIGMA had a Ph.D. student, Danielle Zandee, who was researching generativity and who was happy to provide expertise on AI. The Visions Foundation offered the administrative center for the dialogues.

IMAGES AND VOICES OF HOPE – MIAMI

The first dialogue following the initial one in New York was in Miami, Florida. One of the Brahma Kumaris in Miami, Meredith Porte, is a television producer at WLRN television. She called on David Lawrence, former publisher of the *Miami Herald*, to host the initial dialogue, which was held in a studio at WLRN. Over 100 people attended that dialogue, which was covered that evening on the 6 o'clock news.

Since then a core team in Miami has organized a dialogue every year. By 2002, they had attracted the attention of local celebrities such as Robin Gibb of the Bee Gees and his wife Dwina, Univision news anchor and author, Jorge Ramos, as well as artists, galleries, the Miami City Ballet, all of the television networks, and the publisher of the best selling *Chicken Soup for the Soul* series. It had also drawn the Mayor of South Miami Beach and the president of Facts About Cuban Exiles (FACE). Many of those in the room in 2002 had become loyal to the dialogue, returning every year since 2000.

At the 2002 IV of Hope dialogue in Miami, a number of interesting things happened. Jorge Ramos addressed participants to say that he was looking at his work as a reporter in new ways: he was seeing that the way he had pre-loaded his questions to interview subjects may have predisposed the interview to head in a deficit and defensive direction. He was considering how he might take the awareness he had gleaned from the dialogue back to his work. Fox News anchor, Laurie Jennings, told the room how aware she was becoming of the way that headlines in a news story ("John Walker Lind, most hated man in America?") could unnecessarily create negativity around the news viewing experience. Claire Mitchell of the *Miami Herald* talked about how she was working to shift the way people in South Florida thought about aging. Ralph de la Cruz, columnist for the *South Florida Sun Sentinel*, was touched by the reflective component of the dialogue and subsequently wrote a story about it called "Looking for the Good in Bad News" (De la Cruz, 2002).

The 2002 dialogue in Miami points to the way that a public dialogue becomes generative and can begin to transform a community. Recalling the criteria for transformative dialogues proposed by the Gergens and Barrett, it "facilitated the collaborative construction of new realities" – new spaces of meaning, new communities of interest, and from these, new actions. In the case of the IV of Hope Dialogues our goal is not to orchestrate collective action by the entire community in the room (although a number of collective undertakings have come of these dialogues in the past). Our interest is in the shifts in awareness that take place in those in the room and how their new awareness affects what they see and subsequently report when they look at the world.

The actions in which we are most interested are the thousands of choices made in their lives and work: this photo or that photo, this headline or that headline, this artist or that one, and so on. With the Miami dialogue we have seen new actions taken by those in the IV of Hope dialogue community, a film festival on Hope created by Susan Schein and a television series conceived of by Meredith Porte. When the FCC held their ascertainment hearings in South Florida after the first IV of Hope dialogue in 2000, IV of Hope was cited three times as an example of the media community coming together around community interest. When a Miami schoolteacher who attended the 2002 dialogue accepted an award from the Florida Department of Education as "Teacher of the Year," she spoke in her acceptance speech about finding images of hope in her children. Clearly this growing community is collaborating in the construction of new realities – including of course the tangible creation of the community itself.

In the case of the Miami IV of Hope dialogue, all five conditions for transformative dialogue were there. The stated *intention* was to search for what gives life. Here is an excerpt from the letter of invitation from David Lawrence, ". . . In such times, people look to the media and to community leaders – and yes, to each other – for information about what's going on and for help in interpreting the significance of what is taking place. These times present new opportunities for greater awareness, and new possibilities for making a positive difference in the world."

The *questions* were a guide to what is affirmative and life giving:

Journalists, Media Professionals, Artists, and Educators as Agents of World Benefit.

Part One: Moments of Magnified Meaning Making.
All of us, at some level, wonder what possible good, what new understandings, awareness, energies, relationships, insights and perspectives will come out of this time.

1a. Will you share with your partner, one story, image or powerful quote – either from the news or from your own experience over the last few months – something that provided you with a precious image, understanding or appreciation of what we, as human beings, in the positive sense, are capable of?

1b. What draws you to be here today?

Part Two: Exploring a high point moment from you life.
You, as well as everybody here, have been part of many change initiatives in organizations, in communities, in your personal and professional lives, etc. Certainly there have been ups and downs, high points and low points, etc.

2a. Can you share a story about a time you felt engaged in something meaningful, a time you felt effective, alive and found yourself learning new things about change? Please share the story. What happened, when, where, etc? Tell us about the experience, your feelings, and some of your insights.

Your vision of a better world and your images of communicators as agents of world benefit.

2b. What do you see in your own vision of communicators as agents of world benefit? Visualize media organizations, educators, artists and even businesses of the future and the kinds of approaches they might take that might be of world benefit. What do they look like? Can you imagine and list some of the ways they might serve to benefit the world and the variety and types of contributions they might offer?

Part Three: Leading exemplars that are offering images of possibility and strengths that you might want to magnify.

3a. As you think about your vision, you probably already know of some examples within the areas of communication, arts and sciences, that are already pioneering ways of being agents of world benefit – organizations that are creating practices that nurture the human spirit, or are serving as catalysts for social and world benefit. Can you share a story of one "golden innovation" that you see somewhere emerging in one of the many fields of communication – publishing, music, advertising, filmmaking, graphic design, arts, etc.?

3b. If anything we can imagine is possible, what is the smallest step you can imagine that we might take if our aim is to set in motion an epidemic of positive change of communicators as agents of world benefit?

3c. Now, can you share with us some of the steps that might be possible in your own life that you can commit to attaining or at least beginning, during the weeks and months ahead?

The dialogue generated by these questions transcended fractious debate and brought those in the room into collective consideration of their shared aspiration for South Florida and how they and the media community of which they are a part can help.

The *whole system* or at least a representative sample of it was in the room. The ages ranged from those in their twenties to those in their eighties. A rich representation of the South Florida ethnic communities was in attendance. Representatives from the major television networks, galleries, theatre groups, journalism programs, and newspapers were there as well as a healthy mix of interested consumers and social activists.

The *relational space of trust and affirmation* is harder to quantify, although you can see it and hear it when you look at the videotape that was shot that day and you could definitely feel it in the room. Some of this came from simple hospitality, the personal welcomes of everyone at the door, the food made by the Brahma Kumaris, the seating of everyone at small tables, the generous contributions of area galleries and of the Miami City Ballet who offered the space. But most of it was created by the good will and shared high purpose of those who had come together in the room. The high quality of the dialogue emerged from this relational space of trust.

The *reflective element* was provided by Gayatri Naraine, the Brahma Kumaris representative to the United Nations, who has performed the same service for each of the dialogues since 2000. At a certain point in the dialogue, she invited everyone in the room to put down their notes, set aside their questions and take their minds to a space of reflection on what was going on for them. *Sun Sentinel* reporter Ralph de la Cruz said later that it was this experience that caused him to set aside his normal skepticism and open himself to the possibility that something truly transformative might happen in a dialogue such as this.

One might say that these conditions are more likely to be transformative and produce new realities when it occurs in a community where the participants are from the same location. So for contrast, we can look at the annual Summit of Images and Voices of Hope that took place in October of 2002 in upstate New York.

THE IMAGES AND VOICES
OF HOPE WORLD SUMMIT

In October of 2002 over 90 people checked in to a retreat center of the Brahma Kumaris in the tiny village of Haines Falls, New York for the third World Summit of Images and Voices of Hope. They were advertising executives, screenwriters, radio producers, investigative journalists, television producers and filmmakers and they had arrived from virtually every corner of the world. They came from Jordan, Israel, Argentina, Chile, and Brazil. They came from the Northwest Territories of Canada, from Warsaw, from Birmingham, England and the Philippines.

Again all of the conditions for transformative dialogue were met. The *intention* was clear. When the group came together on opening night, I read to them from a letter I had written with them in mind: "Images and Voices of Hope is a call for engagement in the life-giving work of creating images and stories of possibility and hope.... This is not about happy talk – about pretending that bad things don't happen. It is about cultivating minds that have a quality of compassion and generosity and vision that can see what's best in the world – even in difficult situations. It is about being wise enough to recognize that cynicism often passes for sophistication and it is about being courageous enough to know that creating images and voices of hope is what gives life to our world... We have come together for a dialogue among colleagues to reflect on the impact of media in the world and to think together about what we might do to be agents of benefit, so the societies we serve might cultivate strength and imagination for the road ahead."

The topic for the Summit was "Media that Moves Us..." The *questions* explored the many ways in which media move societies. Here are the topics around which questions were crafted:

- "When media shifts the way we see the world" recalled how Stewart Brand, founder of the original *Whole Earth Catalogue* campaigned to NASA for the opportunity for everyone to be able to see the pictures of the Earth from space that those inside NASA had seen.
- "When media catalyzes a movement for truth and hope against all odds" cited the example of how Veran Matic kept B-92 radio alive in Serbia as a voice of freedom in the world.
- "When media amplifies the impact of transformative partnerships" referred to the role played by the international media community in amplifying the work being done by Nelson Mandela and F. W. de Klerk in ending apartheid.
- "When media makes cooperation possible," retold the story of Bob Geldof's wildly successful creation of the "Live Aid" concert and album, which raised over 100 million British pounds to feed people in Africa.

- "When media changed the course of history" asked dialogue participants to imagine that "you have survived a dark and difficult period in the world and find yourself on the other side of it all. The world is so different . . . transformed beyond recognition. The sense of love and unity is palpable and the natural beauty and harmony is the first thing you notice . . . you find one old woman who remembers how this all came to be and she tells you that it was precipitated by an event in the media of the world at that time. What," the question asks, "is the story that the old woman tells you?"

The Summit became an incubator for a microcosm of the world media community. As they engaged in interviews, screened each other's films and advertisements, and met together for meals they began to talk about ways they could influence the societies from which they came. The *relational space* among participants was one of trust and affirmation of one another's work.

Because the Summit was held at a retreat center, the opportunities for *reflection* didn't just come occasionally, but throughout the Summit, from early morning at 4 am to evening at 7, and many people took advantage of the times of silence to be together and reflect.

Many things were created over the four days of that Summit. Robert Baskin, a "20/20" producer for ABC, who has won practically every award in journalism including the Peabody and Dupont, said that she realized she had spent her entire career focused on stories of corporate corruption and greed, and wondered aloud what might happen if she applied the same journalistic intensity and access to locating the stories of extraordinary imagination and generosity. Paul Andrews, who had produced the first two films in a series on cooperation across conflict divides called "Improbable Pairs," facilitated a two-day meeting of those from the Middle East to look at ways that media might support new approaches to peace making in the Middle East and other war torn areas. A number of people came together to see how they might influence the upcoming UN World Summit on the Information Society. Participants from St. Thomas University in South Florida decided to create a dialogue between seasoned journalists and journalism students in South Florida.

As always the most important creations were the relationships and networking that happened in screening rooms, walks and over meals. This is a group whose influence spanned four continents. Their potential for transforming media in the societies in which they live and work is considerable.

These two cases are highlights of an extraordinary, vibrant, transformative public dialogue. With no funding and the thinnest collaborative infrastructure, Images & Voices of Hope has expanded to reach a worldwide media community of thousands.

It stands in stark contrast to dialogues on the abhorrent effects of violence or those burdened inquiries into "responsible media." While both of these frames are valid rational constructs for public discourse, they are missing the seeds of generativity that have allowed IV of Hope to find fertile soil in media communities across cultures.

We know how many efforts there have been to shift the media and how helpless people feel about the climate generated by deficit media, but when we use deficit methods to appeal for life-affirming media, we defeat ourselves before we even begin. The means and the ends of the dialogue need to be congruent.

Karl Weick makes this point about congruence of the means and the ends in his case about the ways that the Workers Defense Committee in Poland in 1976 set about creating freedom. They did not convene to regret their lack of freedom or even to talk about creating freedom, they lived freedom: "What if a group began to publish a newsletter in which factory conditions were truthfully described?" What if people did social work and gave direct, medical, financial, and legal aid to those who needed it?... Notice that every act proved to be a test of just how much liberty they might have . . . The guiding principle was simple, but radical:

> Start doing the things you think should be done, and . . . start being what you think society should become. Do you believe in freedom of speech? Then speak freely. Do you love the truth? Then tell it. Do you believe in a decent and humane society? Then behave decently and humanely . . . (Weick, pp. 50–51).

The Gergens and Barrett address a related concept when they propose that dialogue is generative to the degree that it fosters relational coordination (2003, p. 8). They cite acts of affirmation, elements of conversational coherence, and narrative and temporal integration as the dialogic moves that heighten relational coordination.

The means and the ends of the dialogue must be the same. A Workers Defense Committee that meets and acts in freedom creates freedom. A public dialogue that meets in generative engagement creates generative communities and new actions. A public dialogue doesn't merely talk about actions; it is public action, and the kind of public dialogue in which we engage affects the world we create. It is no surprise that many came away from the U.N. Conference on Racism, Racial Discrimination, Xenophobia, and Related Intolerance feeling more despondent about the prevalence of racism and all kinds of discrimination and hopeless about ever moving ahead.

In Appreciative Inquiry theory, there is a principle called "The Principle of Simultaneity," which explains why inquiry and action are inseparable moments: "Here it is recognized that inquiry and change are not truly separate moments, but are simultaneous. Inquiry is intervention. The seeds of change – that is, the things people think and talk about, the things people discover and learn, and the things that inform dialogue and inspire images of the future – are implicit in the very first questions we ask" (Cooperrider & Srivastva, 1987).

Images and Voices of Hope is a crucible of life affirming messages. Jennifer Valoppi, evening news anchor for WTVJ NBC 6 engaged in an IV of Hope dialogue in the afternoon and then, hours later, spoke on camera about her experience on the six o'clock news in Miami. This is the possibility of public dialogue. It is the public lived experience of a new way of being: we are, as Gandhi said, "being the change we want to see in the world."

CONCLUSION

Public dialogue presents an opportunity to intervene in public discourse that is apathetic or openly hostile about an issue and to transform it into a generative space where new realities can emerge, new spaces of meaning, new configurations of relationships, and new kinds of actions. This happens most consistently when five conditions are present:

- Intention or purpose to search for what gives life to this issue or community.
- Questions to guide a search for the best in the past and present, for strengths, talents, assets, successes and so on.
- Representation of the whole system in the dialogue.
- A relational space of trust and respect.
- An opportunity for reflection.

The theory and approach to public dialogue most likely to produce these five conditions is Appreciative Inquiry. Though AI is most often applied to organizational change, it is remarkably powerful at producing constructive change in public dialogue settings.

In Images and Voices of Hope, media communities convene to consider how they might be agents of benefit. When new Images and Voices of Hope dialogues open, participants generally bring with them to the dialogue space their familiar constructs and understandings from their fields of media. These have included assessments such as these:

- Media (for example journalism, advertising, the arts, etc.) are not – nor should they be – engaged in social benefit.
- We just describe what is happening in society.
- Media are businesses and their goal is to make revenue for the shareholders. The degree to which they do that is the degree to which they can be a force in the world.

- Audiences (viewers, readers, etc) are most engaged by stories of violence, conflict, and injustice.
- Our primary job is to attract audiences.

In the course of a series of dialogues, such as the Miami Images and Voices of Hope dialogue, or a Summit, such as the World Summit of Images and Voices of Hope, dialogue participants create new spaces of meaning:

- Those of us who work in media are not neutrally describing a world; our history and experiences have made us certain kinds of observers. When we experience changes in our awareness, we become different observers and describe a different world to others.
- Businesses can be profitable and also bring benefit to society.
- Audiences might be equally engaged by images and stories that create positive emotions, such as joy or elevation, as they are by images and stories of fear and despair.
- We are not alone in our desire to use our work as means of bringing benefit; there are many others who feel the same, including those in this room.
- The actions we can take to produce a new kind of impact may be as subtle as showing up in a regularly scheduled meeting with a different awareness.

In public dialogues we have the opportunity to bring people together around old issues in new and generative ways, and when we do, we may find that we are in new relationships, with ideas and with one another, and that

> Hopefulness replaces cynicism
> Expectation replaces resignation
> Personal empowerment replaces helplessness
> Civic and social engagement replace detachment
> Community replaces strangers

We may find that in the course of public dialogue, we have become a community that is generating a new story of the world.

REFERENCES

Cooperrider, D. (1990). Positive image positive action: The affirmative basis of organizing. In: S. S. Srivastva & D. L. Cooperrider (Eds), *Appreciative Management and Leadership: The Power of Positive Thought in Organizing* (pp. 99–125). San Francisco: Jossey-Bass.

Cooperrider, D. (2000). The surprise of friendship. *Journal of Organizational Development Practitioner, 32*(2), 46–49.

Cooperrider, D., & Srivastva, S. (1987). Appreciative inquiry into organizational life. In: R. Woodman & W. Pasmore (Eds), *Research in Organizational Change and Development* (Vol. 1).

De la Cruz, R. (2002). Looking for the good in bad news. *South Florida Sun Sentinel* (February 10).

Fowler, A., Gamble, N., Hogan, F., Kogut, M., McComish, M., & Thorp, B. (2001). Talking with the enemy. *Boston Globe* (January 28).

Fredrickson, B. L. (1998). What good are positive emotions? *Review of General Psychology*, 300–319.

Gergen, K., Gergen, M., & Barrett, F. (2003). Dialogue: Life and death in the organization. In: D. Grant, C. Hardy, C. Oswick, N. Phillips & L. Putnam (Eds), *Draft Copy for Handbook for Organizational Discourse*. Thousand Oaks, CA: Sage.

Haidt, J. (2000). The positive emotion of elevation. *Prevention & Treatment*, *3*(3).

Smith, A. (2000). *Talk to me: Travels in media and politics*. New York: Anchor Books.